AF473793

THE ART OF
Naval Portraiture

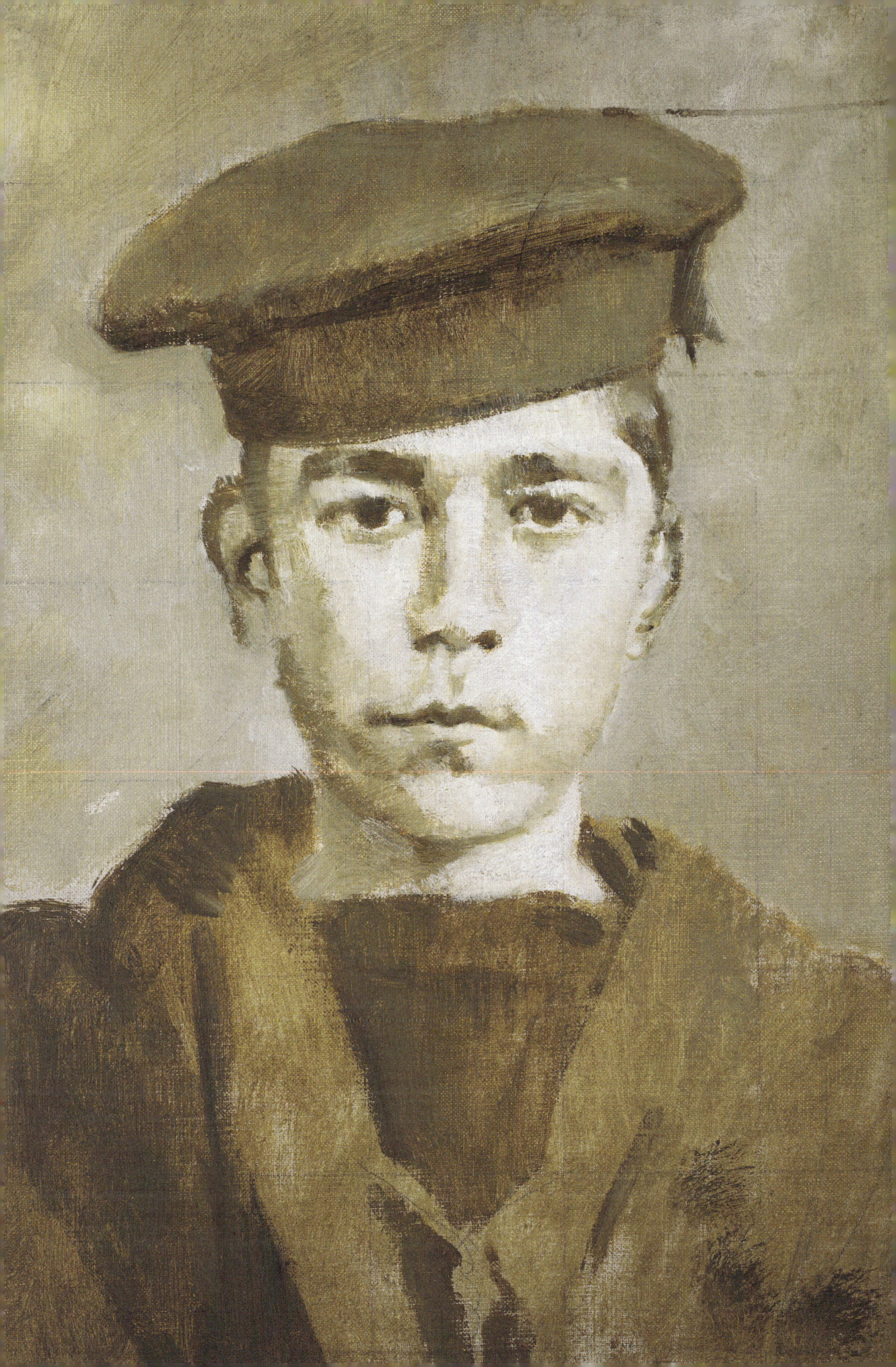

THE ART OF
Naval Portraiture

Katherine Gazzard

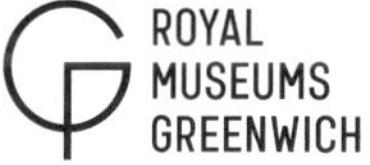

To my grandparents:
Joyce and Stan, who met in the navy,
Bernard and Eileen, who lived by the sea.

First published in 2024 by
Royal Museums Greenwich, Park Row, Greenwich,
London, SE10 9NF

ISBN: 978-1-739154-20-2

At the heart of the UNESCO World Heritage Site of Maritime Greenwich are the four world-class attractions of Royal Museums Greenwich — the National Maritime Museum, the Royal Observatory, the Queen's House and *Cutty Sark*.

rmg.co.uk

A CIP catalogue record for this book is available from the British Library.

Design by lizzie b design

Printed and bound in Latvia

Contents

A Sea of Faces

Thomas Davidson painted the patriotically titled *England's Pride and Glory* in 1894 (fig. 1). The picture represents a mother and son visiting an art gallery. Gilded frames butt up against one another on the crowded walls. A large painting on the left shows a dramatic scene from a naval battle. The wooden sailing ships within it come from an earlier era than the art gallery visitors, who are attired in late-nineteenth-century costume: the battleships of their time were made from iron and powered by steam. The painting illustrates an incident from the previous century, the destruction of the French warship the *Orient* in an explosion of fire and smoke at the Battle of the Nile in 1798. However, it is not this spectacular blaze that captures the boy's attention. Under the watchful gaze and guiding hand of his mother, he stares intently at the portrait of a naval officer, which hangs beside the battle painting.

The officer's uniform belongs to the same historical period as the ships in the adjacent picture. He wears a large naval hat and the front of his coat is bestrewn with medals and decorations. He has lost his right arm, the empty sleeve hanging from a button on his chest. Most viewers in Davidson's time would have immediately recognised this one-armed vice-admiral as Horatio Nelson, perhaps the most famous naval officer in British history. Nelson gained a legendary reputation through a series of triumphs in the Napoleonic Wars, culminating in the Battle of Trafalgar in 1805, where he was killed and his fleet secured victory. The portrait shown in Davidson's picture is one of several iconic depictions of Nelson that Lemuel Francis Abbott painted in the late 1790s. *England's Pride and Glory* implies that the boy, who is dressed as a naval cadet, will be roused to emulate Nelson's heroic example through his contemplation of Abbott's 100-year-old portrait.

Davidson's image highlights the Victorian attitude towards portraiture as an artistic genre with a serious moral purpose, capable of transmitting the supposed virtues of historical figures to their successors in the present. This view was manifest in the proliferation of printed portraits in illustrated history books, biographies, periodicals and newspapers of the period. Many naval commanders (past and present) were among the eminent individuals whose portraits circulated in this way, feeding a widespread cultural perception of the Royal Navy as a source of national pride. As Davidson's painting suggests, naval images were imagined to serve an exemplary function, inspiring future generations with idealised visions of masculine leadership and heroism.

This nostalgic and patriotic view of naval portraiture peaked in the nineteenth century. Today, naval portraits are often regarded as, at best, dull depictions of dead white men and, at worst, offensive glorifications of an imperial system that allowed privileged individuals to profit from the suffering of others. None of these attitudes are unjustified. Naval portraits can be both boring and problematic. At the same time, they remain for some people a source of inspiration. What all of these responses fail to acknowledge is the complexity and variety of the genre. There is much more to naval portraiture than is first perceived. From elite officers to ordinary sailors, the representation of naval personnel has been a significant branch of British art for over 500 years. Britain began seriously developing its naval strength in the sixteenth century, in tandem with a nascent programme of colonial expansion, which laid the foundations for the establishment of a vast maritime empire. In the centuries that followed, naval and imperial propaganda yoked Britain's national identity to its sovereignty of the seas. The Royal Navy became a central force in the nation's social, political and cultural affairs. Naval portraits have much to tell us about this context. They reveal how British naval power was understood at different moments in history. They also grant us access to individual stories and perspectives, conveying the concerns and aspirations of officers and sailors caught up within the naval machine. Naval portraits forged, reinforced and challenged ideas of masculinity, heroism and loyalty. They functioned as icons of empire, demonstrations of professionalism and personal mementos for loved ones. The history of naval portraiture is also one of creativity and innovation, which can be linked to major developments in art.

This book explores the artistic and historical significance of naval portraits focusing on paintings and pastels. Importantly, it also examines the prejudices and biases that have shaped the genre. Who got to have their portrait painted, and who did not? Whose interests were served by these artworks, and whose were not? Asking these questions opens up a diverse array of stories, leading to recognition of difficult historical truths and acknowledgement of the enduring impacts of past events on people and communities today.

With a small number of important exceptions, the sitters featured in naval portraiture are male, white and middle- or upper-class. This reflects the limited range of individuals who have historically held power within the Royal Navy. Few portraits in the book represent women, who were not permitted to engage in naval service until the twentieth century. Meanwhile, many draw upon the outdated ideologies of race upon which the British Empire was built, sometimes even representing colonial violence in heroic terms. The labour of common sailors is seldom recognised. A portrait was an expensive status symbol; to commission one required either a significant personal fortune or wealthy friends who were willing to cover the cost. In practice, this meant that senior officers had their portraits painted far more often than their lower-ranking colleagues. The emergence of photography in the second half of the nineteenth century enabled a broader variety of naval personnel to have their likenesses recorded, but photographic portraits rarely held the same prestige as painted ones.

As well as considering who is absent and excluded from naval portraiture, it is also important to recognise how the genre engages with stereotypes and, in certain cases, challenges them. For example, while some portraits directly associate naval warfare with masculine virility via the phallic symbolism of swords and cannons, others offer more complex and multifaceted portrayals of male identity, highlighting creativity, ingenuity and emotional intelligence.

Class insecurities are present in many naval portraits, particularly those from the eighteenth century. During this period, the naval profession offered greater social mobility than most other career paths. As a result, the majority of officers came from middle-class backgrounds: they were the sons of merchants, shopkeepers, clergymen, lawyers and physicians, hoping to make their names and their fortunes at sea. Progressing through the ranks enabled these individuals to amass status and wealth, thanks in part to the prize money system, through which officers received shares of the monetary value of captured enemy ships and cargo. However, high society did not always welcome naval incomers. Low-born officers faced snobbery and condescension. Jane Austen (herself the sister of two naval officers) satirised such behaviour in her novel *Persuasion* through the character of 'foolish, spendthrift baronet' Sir Walter Eliot, who declares: 'a man is in greater danger in the navy of being insulted by the rise of one whose father,

(fig. 1) *England's Pride and Glory*
Thomas Davidson
1894, oil on canvas
918 x 711 mm
BHC1811

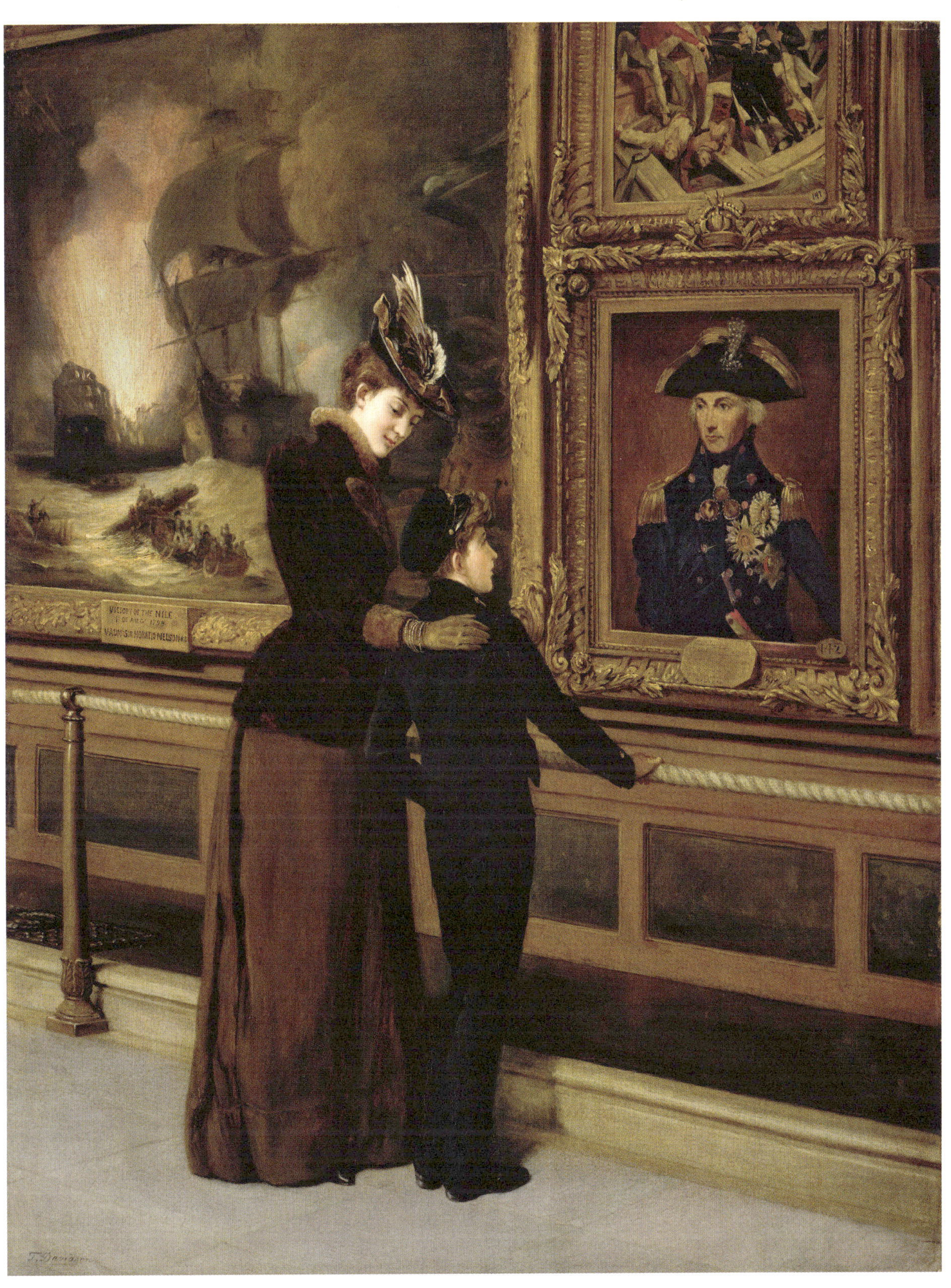

his father might have disdained to speak to'. Confronted with attitudes like Sir Walter's, some officers experienced anxiety about their social status. These feelings often found expression in portraiture, with some officers attempting to assimilate into the elite while others defiantly celebrated their middle-class origins. Only in the Victorian era, when prolonged peace denied naval officers the opportunity to earn prize money and prove their professional credentials in battle, did the relatively meritocratic profession of the eighteenth century harden into something more elitist and socially selective.

Portraits were often commissioned to commemorate a change in the sitter's personal or financial circumstances, such as inheritance, marriage or the purchase of property. A naval officer's career provided additional professional milestones that could also be marked with a portrait, including promotion to a higher rank or victory in an important battle. Such events were often expressed via visible changes in the officer's uniform, including additional bands of gold lace, new epaulettes or campaign medals.

Portraits were also painted in anticipation of lengthy and dangerous voyages. There has long been an association between portraiture and the mediation of absence, as expressed by Jonathan Richardson in his influential *An Essay on the Theory of Painting* (1715): 'the picture of an absent relation, or friend, helps to keep up those sentiments which frequently languish by absence, and may be instrumental to maintain, and sometimes to augment friendship, and paternal, filial, and conjugal love, and duty.' This function of portraiture was particularly advantageous to naval personnel, who spent protracted periods away at sea with no guarantee of safe return. Officers sometimes commissioned portraits so that their families would remember them while they were away and if they never came back.

The artists who produced naval portraits were usually society portraitists catering to a varied clientele, including noblemen, landowners, military officials, performers and society wives, as well as naval officers. Naval officers' likenesses therefore share common conventions with other types of portraiture and need to be understood as part of a broader continuum of imagery. However, certain symbols are particular to naval portraiture. Their use has developed over time, evolving in tandem with historical shifts in both maritime affairs and artistic practice. By the early eighteenth century, it was conventional to include ornaments appropriate to a sitter's character within his or her portrait, as the French artist Gerard de Lairesse explained in his influential treatise, *The Art of Painting*, first published in 1707 and translated into English in 1738: 'A Figure too lonesome may be embellished with a Pillar, Pedestal, Flower-pot, Table and such Things as are proper to it; which serve not only for Ornament and Grandeur, but also to express the Sitter's Lustre and Virtue.' For an 'admiral or commander at sea', Lairesse recommended including 'a Sea-Fight' in the distance. Naval battles did indeed often feature in officers' portraits during this period and would continue to do so for at least another century. The ubiquity of this convention makes it easy to overlook its complexity. In most cases, the depicted battle was not a generic image of naval combat but rather a specific incident from the sitter's past. The sitter therefore technically appears twice within a single image: once posing in the foreground and again as a participant in the distant action, a visual conceit that turns the portrait into a kind of painted biography.

Other details often included in naval portraiture are anchors, cannons, globes, telescopes and swords, referencing the equipment associated with a seafaring career. All of these motifs started appearing in naval portraits during the sixteenth and seventeenth centuries. However, it was in the mid-eighteenth century that the most significant development in naval imagery occurred. The introduction of naval uniform in April 1748 enabled artists to show a sitter's affiliation with the Royal Navy without the need for additional props. Initially, uniform was only granted to officers in order to reinforce class distinctions in a ship. The authority and superiority of the officers was manifested through their gold-laced coats, which set them apart from the ordinary sailors in their loose-fitting slops (naval slang for working clothes). Uniforms were not introduced for the lower ranks until 1857. Through its badges, insignia and decorations, uniform provided a visual system for logging distinctions of rank, specialism and experience. However, uniform regulations could be adapted or subverted to suit the individual circumstances of a particular sitter or patron. Portraitists often faced the challenge of needing to express the sitter's identity as an individual, while also demonstrating his or her conformity to institutional rules. It is therefore also important to remain attentive to subtleties and nuances within the genre.

Naval portraits were displayed in a variety of private and public settings, from middle-class homes and grand country houses to town halls and pleasure gardens. The audience for a naval portrait could be very small, consisting only of the sitter's closest relations. However, many portraits enjoyed more widespread visibility, either through their inclusion in public exhibitions or through their reproduction as prints and book illustrations. Exhibition reviews from historic newspapers provide a flavour of the different ways in which audiences in the past responded to naval portraiture. As well as fawning tributes extolling creative genius and heroic service, reviewers also gave playful, satirical and critical responses, commenting on everything from the artist's technical ability to the romantic affairs of the sitter and current political debates. In this way, portraiture helped to foster a cult of naval celebrity, through which officers became public figures.

Founded in 1824, the National Gallery of Naval Art in Greenwich – also known as the Naval Gallery – provided another public arena for the display of naval portraiture. For over a century, it remained a popular attraction. Consisting of portraiture, marine painting and sculpture, the gallery's displays were designed to deliver a visual history of British naval supremacy, founded upon a perceived synergy between art, navy and nation. Importantly, the Naval Gallery was the institutional predecessor of the National Maritime Museum. At its closure in 1936, the Naval Gallery's collection, including around 150 portraits, was transferred on long-term loan to the Museum, which had recently been established in a neighbouring set of buildings. Works from the Naval Gallery collection still form the core of the Museum's collection of naval portraits today, alongside hundreds of later acquisitions. No other collection of naval portraiture has such significant provenance or pedigree. For this reason, the National Maritime Museum collection is the perfect gateway to understanding naval portraiture as a genre.

CHAPTER 1

Uncertain Beginnings

1547–1660

The first stirrings of English naval power could be traced back to the ad-hoc fleets of the medieval period, which were brought together for particular campaigns and then disbanded. However, the development of a standing navy – that is, a fleet maintained on a permanent basis – belongs firmly to the Tudor dynasty, beginning with Henry VII, who took the throne in 1485 and invested in ships and dockyards. His son Henry VIII, who ruled from 1509 until 1547, continued and expanded this programme of shipbuilding. He also oversaw the construction of coastal defences and established an administrative infrastructure for naval affairs. Although his immediate successors, Edward VI and Mary I, did not build upon this legacy, Elizabeth I returned maritime matters to a position of high importance during her 45-year reign from 1558 until 1603.

The Elizabethan period witnessed the iconic victory of the English fleet over a Spanish invasion force, known as the Armada, in 1588. This event prompted widespread public commemorations, laying the foundations for a national mythology built around naval supremacy. England began to imagine itself as a rival to the great maritime powers of Spain and Portugal. English merchants and privateers attacked Spain's global trade routes and colonial ports, which funnelled treasure and goods from the Far East, Central and South America, and the West Indies towards European shores. The first English voyages transporting enslaved people from Africa to the Caribbean took place in the 1560s. Two decades later, Humphrey Gilbert claimed Newfoundland on behalf of Elizabeth I, establishing England's colonial presence in North America. These ventures were tentative and chaotic but paved the way for the more systematic slave-trading and large-scale colonial enterprises of the seventeenth and eighteenth centuries. The Elizabethan era marked the emergence of an imperial consciousness.

One consequence of this flourishing maritime activity was that seafaring became a desirable career option for individuals looking to garner prestige, influence and personal wealth. It was especially attractive because no qualifications were required and continuous service was neither expected nor demanded. An individual could therefore combine the occasional naval voyage with other interests, from court politics to intellectual study. This meant that naval officers of the time lacked a coherent identity, comprising an assortment of noble courtiers, like Charles Howard, 1st Earl of Nottingham, and professional sailors, like Sir Francis Drake.

Portraits demonstrate the disparate identities of naval commanders in this period. Some allude to the seafaring exploits of their sitters, while others do not, preferring instead to showcase political allegiance or scholarly interests. Moreover, there were no consistent conventions for signifying naval experience within portraiture. It was only under the Stuart dynasty in the seventeenth century that a formula for naval portraiture began to emerge, combining anchors and other nautical props with coastal settings and distant views of warships in action.

Thomas Seymour, 1st Baron Seymour of Sudeley

possibly Nicholas Denizot

1547–49, oil on panel
560 x 510 mm
BHC3021

Today, the term 'Renaissance man' is used to describe an individual with wide-ranging talents and interests. It evokes the cultural and artistic flourishing that took place in the fifteenth and sixteenth centuries, a period now known as the Renaissance. The stereotypical Renaissance man is a learned figure, whose activities encompass literary, creative and scientific pursuits. However, an expanded definition of the term might also encompass the varied careers of Renaissance courtiers, who advanced their political manoeuvrings and personal intrigues through intellectual projects, diplomatic missions, commercial speculation, military service and seafaring adventures.

Seen in this light, both the subject of this painting, Thomas Seymour, and its supposed artist, Nicolas Denizot, could be called 'Renaissance men'. Seymour was the fourth son of Wiltshire landowner Sir John Seymour. The family's influence rose significantly in 1536, when Jane Seymour, Thomas's sister, married King Henry VIII and gave birth to a son, Edward, Prince of Wales (later Edward VI). As uncle to the future monarch, Thomas Seymour went as a diplomat to the court of the French king François I and served as a marshal in the English army in the Low Countries in 1543. After Edward VI's accession to the throne in 1547, Seymour was ennobled as Baron Seymour of Sudeley and appointed Lord High Admiral, but his success was short-lived. Having secretly married Henry VIII's widow Katherine Parr and suspected of plotting against his elder brother, the Duke of Somerset, he was arrested and executed for treason in early 1549.

Denizot, meanwhile, was a French poet, translator, scholar and amateur artist. He visited England between 1547 and 1549, gaining a position as tutor to the Duke of Somerset's three daughters, Anne, Margaret and Jane. He was therefore connected to the Seymour family and may have had the opportunity to paint Thomas's portrait, although there was growing tension between the Seymour brothers throughout this period. Denizot's contemporaries wrote enthusiastically about his skills as a portrait painter. His portrait of the learned French princess Marguerite de Navarre is known through a woodcut illustration, but no confirmed examples of his paintings survive. It was suggested in the 1950s that he had painted this portrait of Thomas Seymour, which entered the collection at the National Maritime Museum in January 1933 as the work of an unidentified artist. The painting came from the estate of the Reverend George Berens-Dowdeswell, whose family had owned it since at least the 1810s. The attribution to Denizot remains speculative.

The work appears at first glance to be a straightforward image, lacking the complex symbolic and heraldic devices often found in Tudor portraiture. Seymour sits against a plain green background, turning slightly to his right. He is soberly dressed in black with a long, reddish-brown beard and a feathered cap, but small details demonstrate his wealth and refinement. The lining of his cape is patterned with small black-on-black dots and his cap is ornamented with a jewelled badge. Careful inspection of the badge reveals that the Norman-French phrase 'HONI SOIT [QUI MAL Y PEN] SE' ('shame on anyone who thinks evil of it') is written around the edge (fig. 1). This maxim is the motto of the Order of the Garter and appears

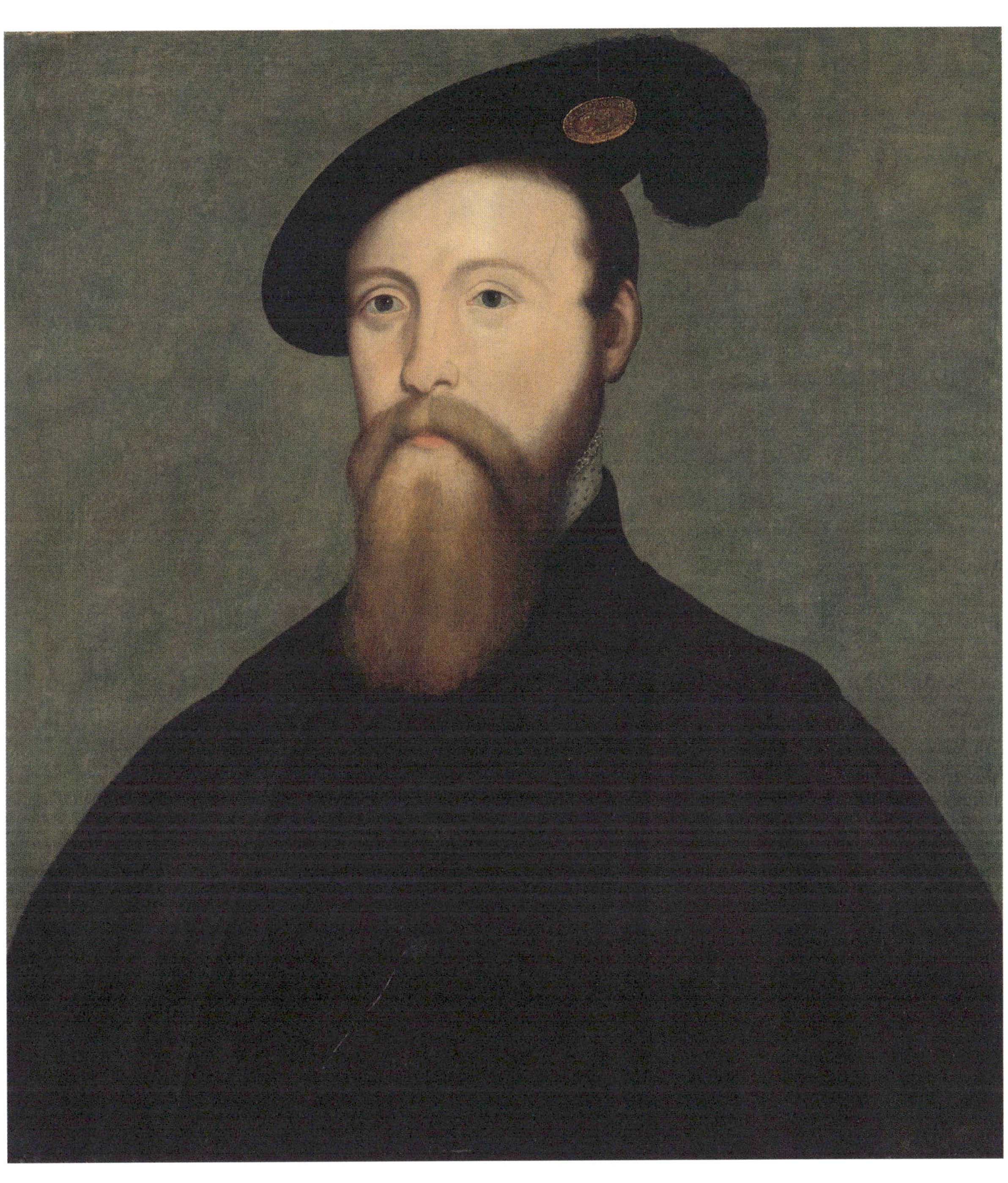

on its insignia. Seymour became a Knight of the Garter in 1547, which is therefore the earliest possible date for the painting.

The painting is significant because it has claim to be the oldest naval portrait in the National Maritime Museum's collection, although this depends how the words 'naval' and 'portrait' are defined. The portrait may be considered naval insofar as the sitter held a major naval office, having been Lord High Admiral in the 1540s. It was for this reason that the Museum acquired the picture. Yet the painting makes no reference to the sitter's naval responsibilities, presenting him instead as a wealthy courtier. Moreover, Seymour did not have a lengthy naval career and never served afloat. The English navy was in its infancy as an institution during this period. While Henry VIII and his father, Henry VII, had invested in the construction of warships and dockyards, there was no formal system for the appointment of naval commanders. Many courtiers dabbled in naval affairs, despite having little prior knowledge of seafaring, because they thought it would bring them wealth or prestige. In this way, Seymour's portrait represents a time before the emergence of a defined sense of naval identity.

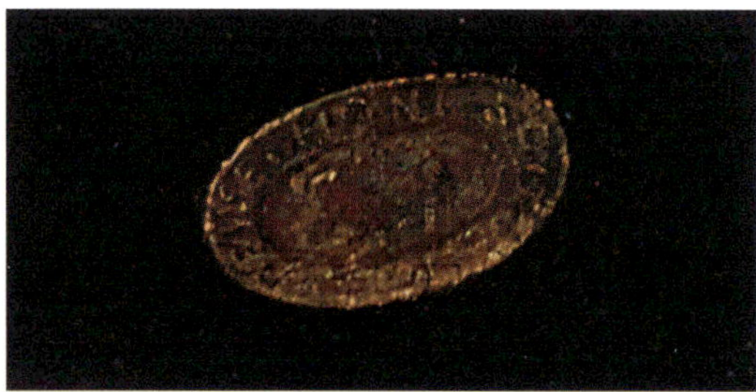

(fig. 1) Detail of hat badge in *Thomas Seymour, 1st Baron Seymour of Sudeley* attributed to Nicholas Denizot, 1547–49

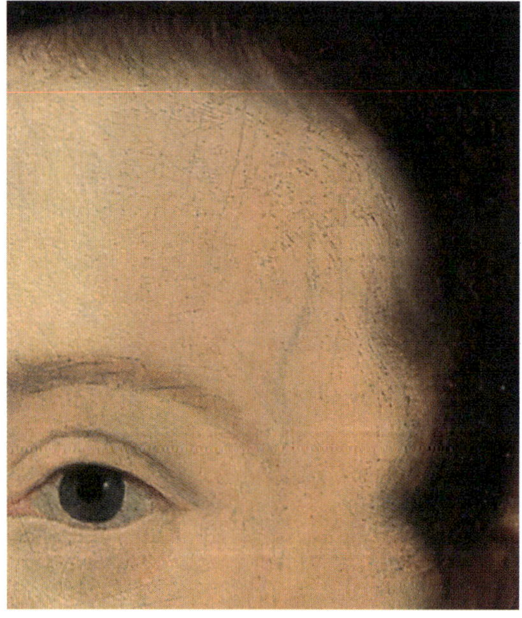

(fig. 3) Detail of veins in *Thomas Seymour, 1st Baron Seymour of Sudeley* attributed to Nicholas Denizot, 1547–49

The picture's claim to be the oldest naval portrait in the collection is also only true if one is looking at oil paintings exclusively. There are earlier representations of naval sitters in other media. Some key examples are portrait miniatures. A portrait miniature is a small-scale portrait painting usually executed in watercolour or enamel on vellum, card or, in later periods, ivory, and framed in a gold or bejewelled case. For the Tudors, miniatures were an important social tool, at least within courtly circles. Showing or giving one's own miniature portrait to someone else demonstrated trust or intimacy, the distillation of the sitter's image onto a small surface via a series of precise brushstrokes being seen to offer a uniquely direct expression of character.

Miniatures are especially important to understanding Seymour's portrait because the painting itself appears to have been based on a miniature, which is also now in the collection of the National Maritime Museum (fig. 2). Currently attributed to a follower of the Flemish artist Lucas Horenbout, this miniature has lost its original case and is instead mounted in a nineteenth-century frame with a scroll nameplate at the bottom. Seymour is depicted in the miniature against a blue background. His pose and costume correspond with the larger painting: he wears a black outfit with a feathered cap.

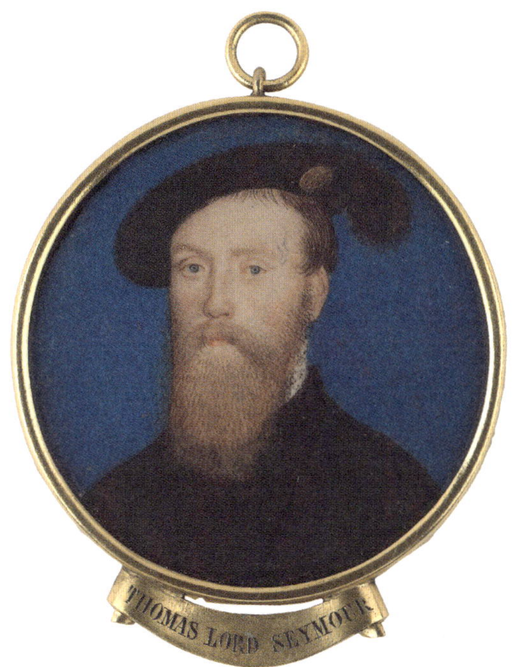

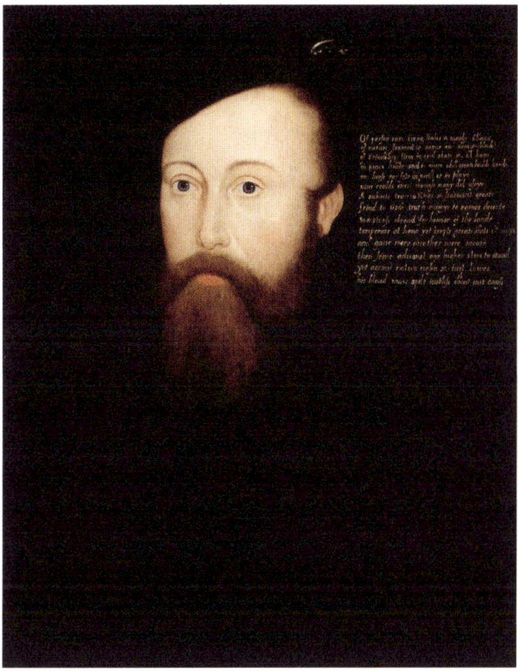

(fig. 2) *Thomas Seymour, Baron Seymour of Sudeley*
Unknown artist in the style of Lucas Horenbout
about 1545, bodycolour on vellum
42 x 42 mm
MNT0137

(fig. 4) *Thomas Seymour, Baron Seymour*
Unknown artist
second half of 16th century, oil on panel
533 x 419 mm
National Portrait Gallery (NPG 4571)

In the miniature, two blue veins are visible on Seymour's temple. This kind of heightened bodily detail was often included in miniatures to make the viewer feel closer to the sitter. Looking closely, it is possible to see a faint echo of these veins in the larger painted portrait (fig. 3). This suggests that Denizot (if he was the artist) was copying from the miniature, which is believed to be earlier in date. Other painted copies of the portrait exist. A version at the National Portrait Gallery bears an inscription declaring that Seymour's blood was split 'without just cause', which indicates that the picture was made after Seymour's execution (fig. 4). It is not clear whether the portrait attributed to Denizot was made before or after the sitter's death. However, through the veins on the temple, this sensitive copy retains a trace of the miniature's intimacy.

Admiral Sir John Hawkins (possibly)

The Master of the Countess of Warwick

about 1565, oil on panel
595 x 395 mm
BHC4185

Until recently, this portrait was believed to depict Admiral Sir Richard Hawkins and to have been painted in the early 1590s, sometime after his participation in the defeat of the Spanish Armada in 1588 and before his capture in South America in 1594. The identity of the artist was not known. All of this changed, however, when the portrait featured in an exhibition at Compton Verney Art Gallery in Warwickshire in spring 2023.

The exhibition was dedicated to a talented but largely forgotten Tudor portrait painter, the so-called Master of the Countess of Warwick. Distinctive features of this artist's style include heads that appear enlarged in proportion to the body with sharply outlined facial features, protruding eyes and a delicate flush of colour on the cheeks. The sitter's clothing and jewellery is often delineated in immense detail. These features are exemplified in a portrait of Anne Russell, Countess of Warwick (now at Woburn Abbey), from which this painter's epithet is derived.

Based on a close study of contemporary documents, the Compton Verney exhibition claimed to reveal the master's true identity, suggesting that he may have been Arnold Derickson, a pupil of the Flemish painter Hans Eworth. This theory offers a tantalising solution to a longstanding mystery of Tudor art, but many questions remain unanswered, not least in connection with the Hawkins portrait.

The exhibition's curators presented a strong case for attributing this painting to the Master of the Countess of Warwick, citing both technical and stylistic evidence, such as the age of the wooden panel, the angle of the sitter's head and the rendering of the eyes. Yet, in answering the question of the portrait's authorship, this research threw both the date of the portrait and the identity of the sitter into doubt. The Master of the Countess of Warwick was active in the 1560s and dendrochronology (tree-ring analysis) confirms that the panel is made from an oak tree felled around this time. This challenges the traditional dating of the portrait to the 1590s. It also rules out Richard Hawkins as the sitter, given that he was only a child in the 1560s. Who, then, does the portrait depict?

One possibility is that it represents Richard's father, Admiral Sir John Hawkins. Evidence for this theory comes from the earliest record of the painting, which relates to its sale in 1802. At that time, the painting was described as depicting Sir John Hawkins. In 1824, the picture came into the hands of a Mr Bryant, whose brother sold it to Mr R.S. Hawkins of Oxford in 1866. It was only after this date that the identification of the sitter was changed from father (John) to son (Richard).

During the sixteenth century, the Hawkins (or Hawkyns, as it was spelt at the time) family was a major force in shipbuilding and seafaring, operating out of Plymouth on the south-west coast of England. A successful merchant, naval commander and administrator, Sir John Hawkins was the most famous member of the family. Around the time that this portrait was made, he captained three voyages transporting enslaved African people across the Atlantic for sale to the Spanish settlers in the Caribbean. These voyages represented the first English involvement in the Transatlantic Slave Trade, which the Spanish and Portuguese had previously monopolised. Although it would be more than a century before English merchants became involved in slave-trading on a larger scale, Hawkins's voyages presaged what was

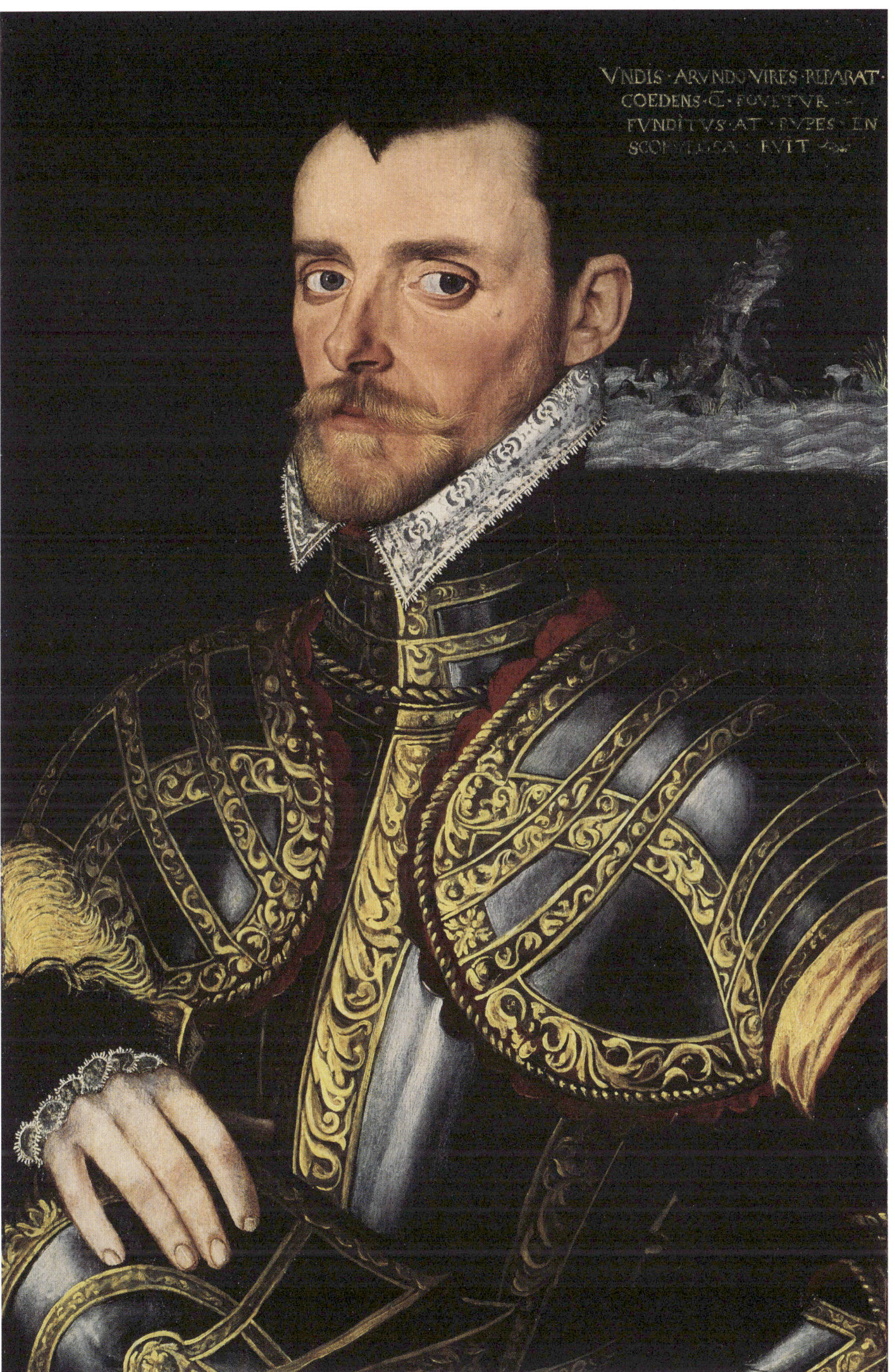
VNDIS·ARVNDO·VIRES·REPARAT·
COEDENS·Œ·FOVETVR
FVNDITVS·AT·RVPES·IN

(fig. 1) *Sir John Hawkins*
Unknown artist
1581, oil on panel
620 x 520 mm
BHC2755

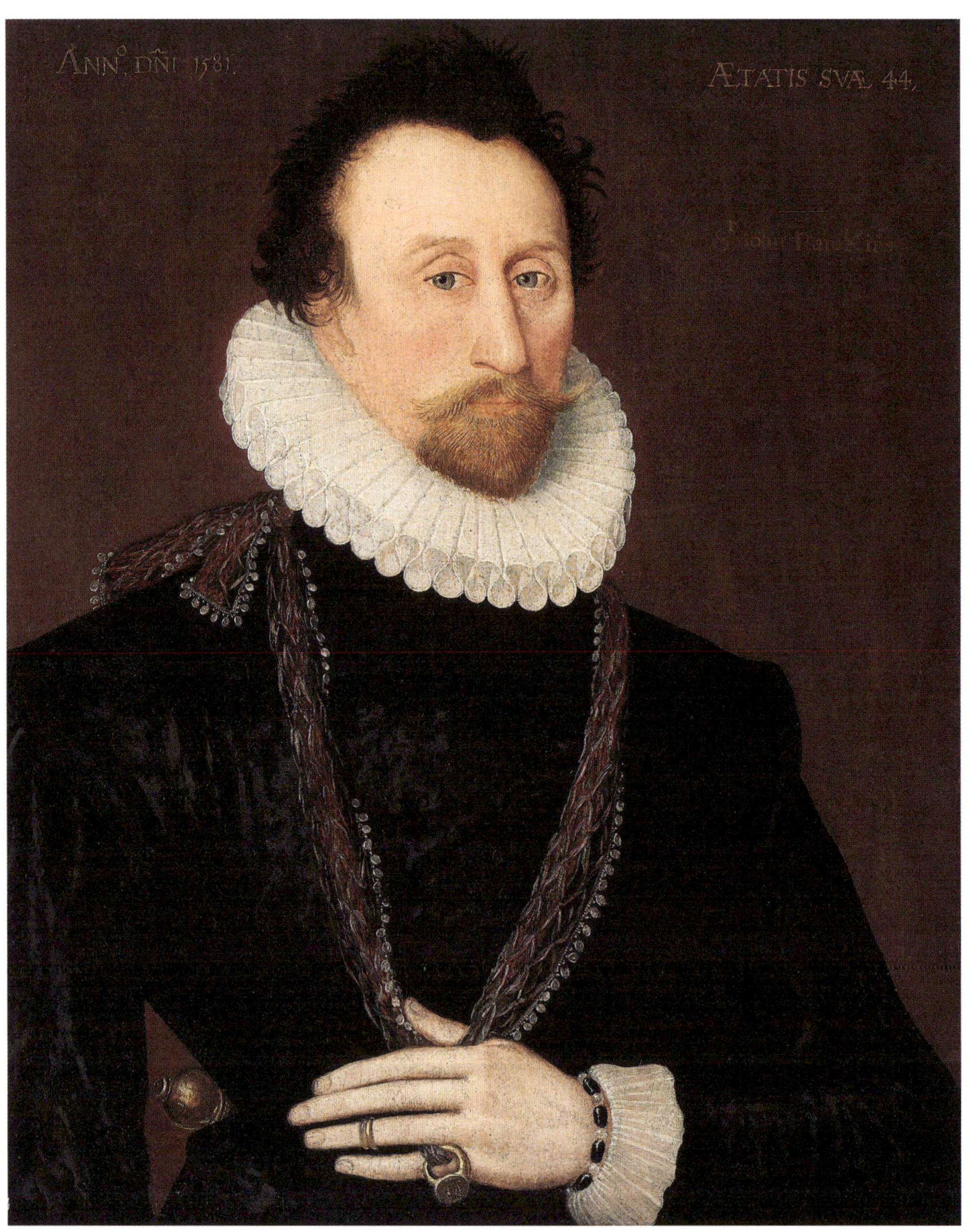

to come. They were an example of the colonial and commercial speculation that characterised the Elizabethan age.

There is a likeness between the man depicted here and Sir John Hawkins, whose appearance is known through a portrait dated 1581 (fig. 1). Shared features in the two images include the sitters' dark hair, ginger beards, curling moustaches and blue eyes. Nevertheless, the association of this portrait with Sir John Hawkins remains somewhat speculative.

It is not even possible to say for certain that this individual was a naval officer. There are no maritime motifs in the painting, although this was not unusual for portraits of naval men at this time, most of which were indistinguishable from portraits of non-seafaring courtiers and gentlemen. The sitter in this portrait is dressed in ornate armour, the blued steel plates decorated with patterned bands of gold. His right arm rests on the plumed helmet. Armour of this sort, the best examples of which were made at the Royal Armouries in Greenwich, was designed for court jousts, tournaments and entertainments, rather than for battle. In wearing this armour, the sitter is presenting himself as a refined courtier.

Perched atop the high-necked armour, the sitter's pointed face is rendered in exquisite detail, from the bristly hairs of his ginger moustache to the pale wrinkles around his wide eyes. The effect is extraordinarily lifelike. Yet this startling realism does not extend to the portrait's background. No attempt is made to evoke a convincing sense of space around the sitter. Instead, there is a plain black backdrop, upon which is superimposed a small landscape scene and an accompanying Latin inscription, floating in the empty space above the sitter's shoulder. In the landscape scene, waves crash into jagged rocks and flow around clumps of reeds. The inscription reads 'UNDIS. ARUNDO VIRES. REPARAT. / COEDENS. Q. FOUETUR / FUNDITUS. AT. RUPES. E / SCOPULOSA. RUIT', which translates as 'the reed recovers strength amid the waves and by yielding grows strong, but the rugged cliff perishes utterly'.

Similar devices were commonplace in portraiture of this period. Known as *imprese*, they used a combination of word and image to express an idea or philosophy that held significance for the portrait's sitter. They could appear floating ambiguously in the background, as occurs in this instance, or they could be shown more naturalistically, for example as an object in the sitter's hand. An *impresa* was like a riddle for the viewer to solve, its meaning conveyed through symbolism and metaphor. The idea that hidden meanings and obscure truths lurked beneath visible appearances was a familiar one for Elizabethan viewers, who were living in an intellectual culture that did not distinguish between astronomy and astrology, chemistry and alchemy or mathematics and magic. In this context, far from being a strange or secretive addition as it might seem today, an *impresa* actually increased the extent to which a portrait was seen as informative and revealing. Complementing the likeness, which recorded the sitter's appearance, the *impresa* offered an insight into their thoughts and outlook.

Imprese were often drawn from proverbs and fables, as well as from emblem books. These were published collections of allegorical illustrations with written explanations. The example in this portrait appears to be an unusual variant of an emblem involving reeds and an oak tree, which derived from one

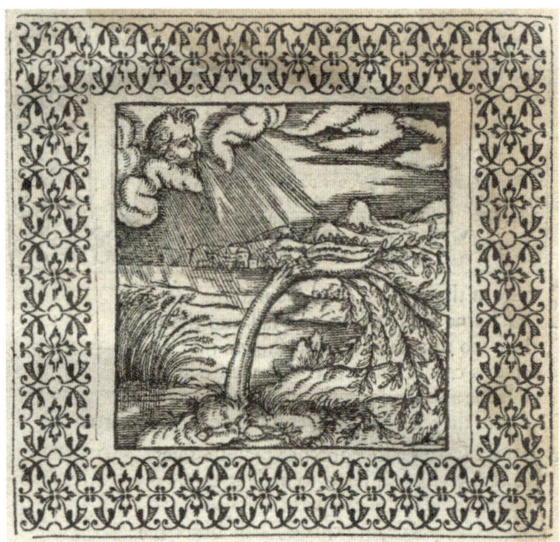

(fig. 2) Geffrey Whitney, *A Choice of Emblemes, and other devises* (Leyden: Christopher Plantyn, 1586), pl. 220.

of Aesop's lesser-known fables and appeared in several sixteenth-century emblem books, including Hadrianus Junius's *Emblemata* (1565) and Geffrey Whitney's *A Choice of Emblemes* (1586). Whitney's illustration shows an oak tree breaking in a gale, while the surrounding reeds bend and bow, their elasticity ensuring that they remain intact (fig. 2). The accompanying poem reminded readers to endure life's challenges with patience and forbearance, represented by the flexible reed, rather than reacting with stubbornness and force, symbolised by the unyielding oak. Though its specific source is unclear, the cliff variant of this proverb would be appropriate for John Hawkins, if he is indeed the sitter, since the maritime setting alludes to his seafaring activities, anticipating the coastal backgrounds that would later become a hallmark of naval portraiture.

However, there is a further twist in the tale of this painting. X-rays of the portrait reveal that, although it looks like the devices found on other Elizabethan portraits, the *impresa* is a later addition, painted over the picture's original background. It is not known exactly when the *impresa* was added, but analysis of the paint layers suggests that it could have been as late as the nineteenth century. The original background is revealed in x-ray photographs. Ignoring the black speckles that indicate areas of paint loss, the ghostly forms of round tents with striped canopies can be discerned (fig. 3). Together with the sitter's ornate armour, these tents were presumably intended as a reference to a tournament or military campaign, associating the depicted individual with courtly virtue and martial prowess.

The portrait thus remains something of a mystery. New technical evidence or archival discoveries might one day shed further light on the sitter's identity and explain the changes in the background. Many sixteenth-century portraits pose similar challenges and identifying sitters is sometimes a game of educated guesses. For naval portraits, this period poses even greater issues, since a mariner was often painted as a courtier without any reference to his seafaring profession.

(fig. 3) X-radiograph image of *Admiral Sir John Hawkins* by the Master of the Countess of Warwick.

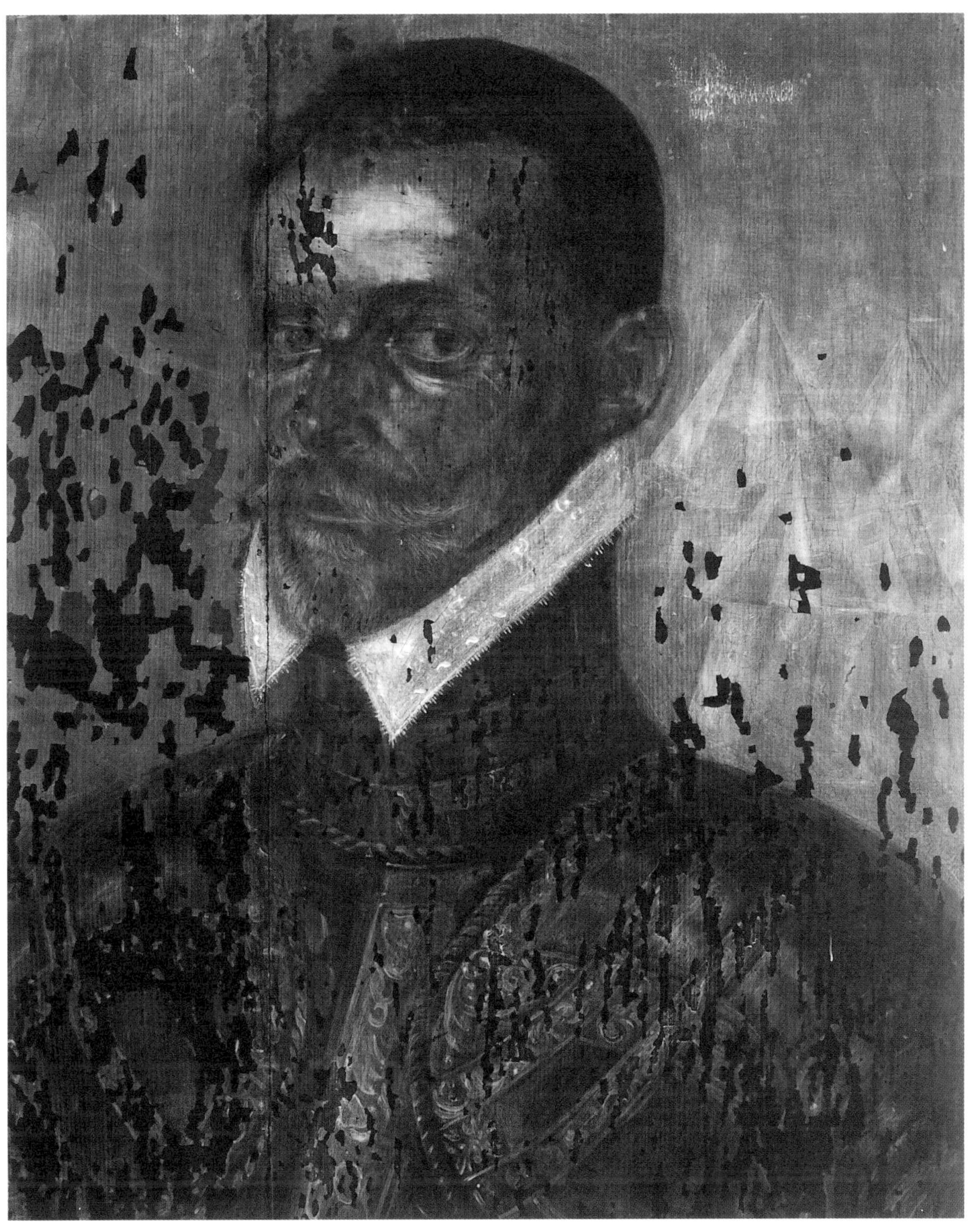

Sir Francis Drake

Marcus Gheeraerts the Younger

1591, oil on panel
1168 x 914 mm
BHC2662

According to art historian Sir Roy Strong, 'the name of Marcus Gheeraerts the Younger is one which is liable to be attached to almost any painting produced in England between the years 1590 and 1630'. Born in about 1561, Gheeraerts moved as a child from his native Bruges to England, travelling with his father, Marcus the Elder, from whom he learnt the painter's craft. In London, the Gheeraertses joined a flourishing community of Dutch and Flemish artists at a time when foreign émigrés dominated painting in England. Marcus the Younger is first recorded working as a portrait painter in the 1590s and appears to have practiced until his death in 1636. Today, only a handful of surviving paintings bear his signature or are reliably documented as his work. His name has been associated with many more pictures from the period, but these attributions are often disputed.

Depicting Sir Francis Drake, one of the most famous seafarers of the Elizabethan era, this portrait is currently attributed to Gheeraerts. The year '1591' is inscribed in dark numbers in the top right corner, apparently referring to the picture's date of production. However, an alternative theory suggests that the painting is a copy of an earlier picture and that the '1591' date is erroneous. Another version of the portrait survives at Buckland Abbey with minor differences in the sitter's pose and the date '1594' in the upper right.

The National Maritime Museum purchased the '1591' version in the early 1930s from the actress Lily Grundy, who had reportedly acquired the painting from 'a descendent of Drake', suggesting that, whatever questions surround the picture's date and attribution, it was linked in some way to the sitter's family.

The son of a humble farming family in Devon, Drake pursued a successful career as a privateer, which enabled his rise to a position of significant wealth, social status and political influence. He participated in and benefitted from the transatlantic slave-trading voyages of his cousin John Hawkins in the 1560s, before undertaking a series of lucrative raids on Spanish colonial ports in the Americas. Between 1577 and 1580, he circumnavigated the globe, becoming the first English commander to do so. Elizabeth I underwrote the voyage, which involved numerous attacks on Spanish ships and ports, netting £160,000 for the Treasury and a sizeable profit for Drake himself. He was knighted on his return. Later, he was a vice-admiral of the English fleet that defeated the Spanish Armada in 1588.

The painting commemorates his achievements. Drake's wealth and status are signalled through his fashionable black doublet and through the superimposition in the upper left of his coat of arms, which he was granted along with his knighthood in 1581. Sheathed in a fine embroidered leather glove, his left hand holds his hat at his side. This frames the portrait as a polite encounter, for which Drake has respectfully removed his headgear. Beside his hand is the hilt of his sword, a symbol of his service to the crown. In this way, the painting is consistent with other portraits of royal favourites, emphasising formal honours, personal wealth and the performance of courtly manners.

Another detail of the portrait alludes specifically to Drake's seafaring adventures. Resting on a cloth-covered table at his side is a globe, referring to his circumnavigation. Earlier portraits of naval sitters often lacked such explicit

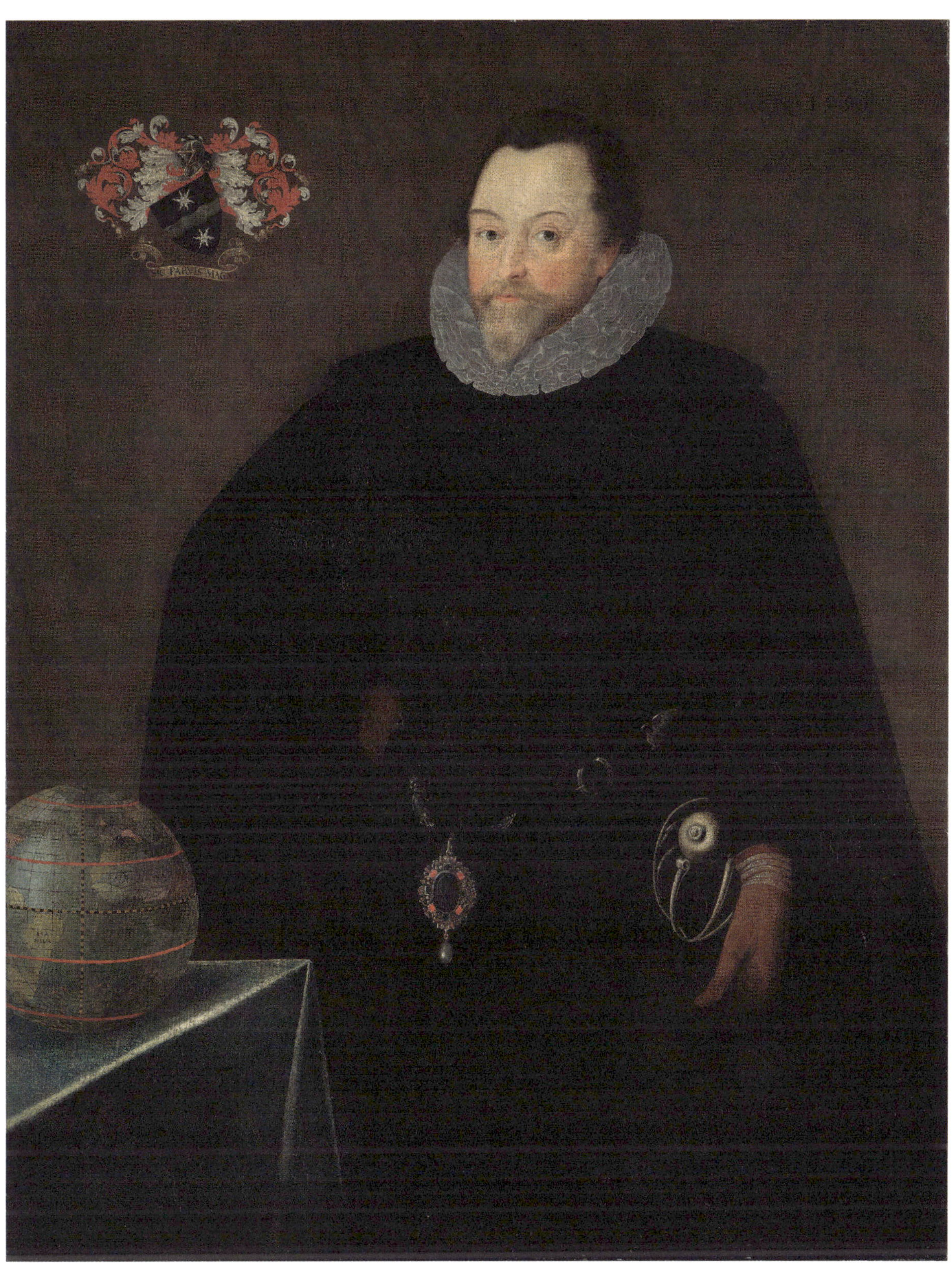

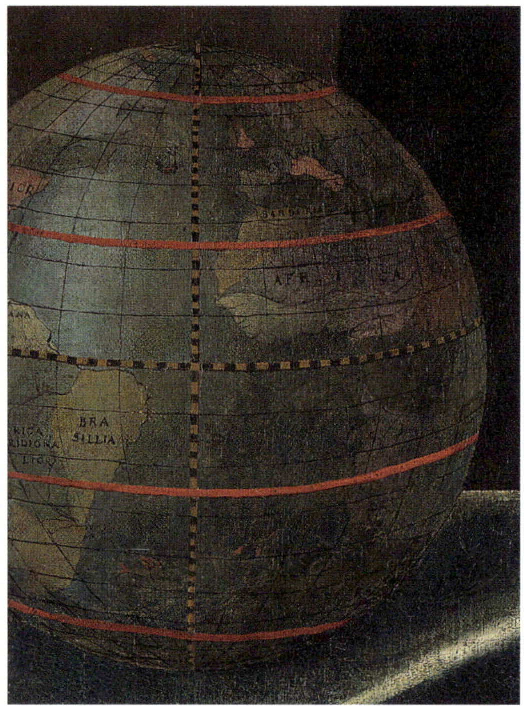

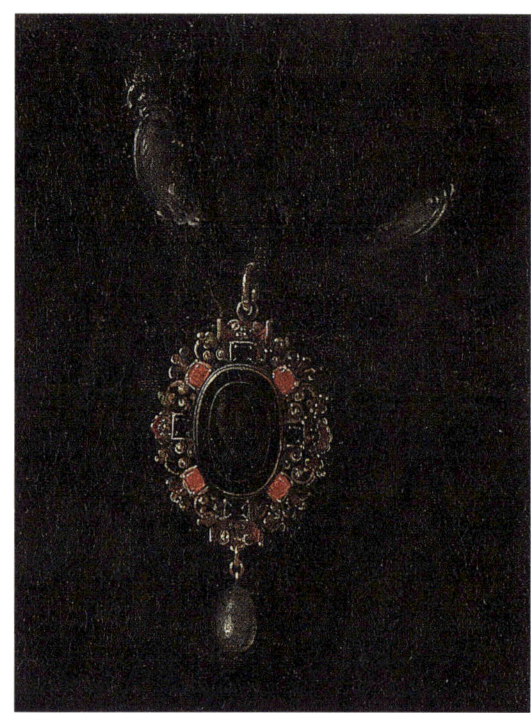

Left: (fig. 1) Detail of *Sir Francis Drake* by Marcus Gheeraerts, 1591

Right: (fig. 3) Detail of *Sir Francis Drake* by Marcus Gheeraerts, 1591

acknowledgement of seafaring. In this sense, Drake's portrait marked an important shift in the visualisation of maritime identity.

The globe is turned to show the Atlantic, framed by the African and South American coasts. A small ship flying English colours crosses the ocean, not only tracing the path of Drake's various transatlantic adventures but also manifesting England's burgeoning colonial aspirations in the so-called 'New World' (fig. 1). In 1577, the mathematician John Dee had published *General and Rare Memorials Pertayning to the Perfect Arte of Navigation*, which called for the creation of an English 'Empire' through the establishment of colonies in the Americas. Six years later, Humphrey Gilbert claimed Newfoundland on behalf of Elizabeth I, taking a step towards realising Dee's vision. The inclusion of the globe in Drake's portrait alludes to this context of maritime ambition, expansion and exploitation, echoing the representation of the Queen herself, in the famous Armada Portrait, which was painted to commemorate the defeat of the Spanish fleet in 1588 and of which Drake himself appears to have owned a version (fig. 2).

Consisting of a central cameo in a gold surround set with rubies, diamonds and a suspended teardrop pearl, the jewel hanging at Drake's waist creates a further link to Elizabeth I, having been a gift from the Queen (fig. 3). Known as the 'Drake Jewel', this precious item survives in a private collection. The cameo features the profiles of an African man and a European woman, making ingenious use of the brown and white layers within the sardonyx (a variety of quartz) from which it is carved. The male figure is dressed in the clothes of a Roman emperor. One interpretation of the jewel's complex symbolism suggests that the black emperor represents Saturn, the king of the gods in Roman mythology, while the white woman is Astraea, the virgin goddess. Their combination alludes to the legendary 'Age of Gold', in which Saturn oversaw a period of peace and prosperity, while Astraea distributed blessings. The implication is that Elizabeth, whose miniature portrait was revealed when the jewel was opened, would reign over a renewed 'Age of Gold' and become an imperial ruler like Saturn himself. The level of detail in the portrait is not sufficient for viewers to see the intricacies of the jewel's design, but the portrait's intended audience included Drake's fellow courtiers, friends and rivals, who would have been familiar with its complex symbolism.

For those viewers without detailed knowledge of the jewel, it functioned as a more general indication of royal favour. The date on the miniature inside the jewel is 1586, but it is possible that it was not presented to Drake until several years later, the gift commemorating his role in the defeat of the Spanish Armada. Elizabeth often bestowed jewels as a reward for services to the crown. They were designed to reflect glory back onto the Queen herself. Their imagery exalted Elizabeth's virtue, rather than the achievements of the recipients, who wore them to confirm their devotion to the Queen and to proclaim their standing in her eyes.

In deciding to wear the jewel in this portrait, Drake was thus identifying himself as a royal favourite. Yet this was not necessarily the case at the time of the painting's creation. Although feted in the aftermath of the Armada campaign, he fell out of favour in 1589, following his command of a disastrous expedition to attack Spanish and Portuguese targets. He was not trusted with another naval command for almost six years. If the year inscribed on the painting (1591) is correct, then it was created at the height of Drake's disgrace. In this case, his wearing of the jewel can be seen as an attempt to rescue his reputation by highlighting the regard that he previously enjoyed.

Whatever its precise date, this painting demonstrates how portraits could serve to advertise and consolidate a sitter's reputation. In Drake's case, his naval career was central to his wealth and social prominence, hence his portrait acknowledges his seafaring exploits. As a nod towards his circumnavigation, the globe anticipates the plethora of nautical symbols that would come to define naval portraiture in the centuries that followed. With portraits like this one, we begin to see the emergence of the naval officer as a distinct public persona, no longer subsumed within other identities, such as that of the courtier or the politician.

Overleaf: (fig. 2) *Elizabeth I (The Armada Portrait)*
Unknown English artist
about 1588, oil on panel
1,125 x 1,270 mm
ZBA7719

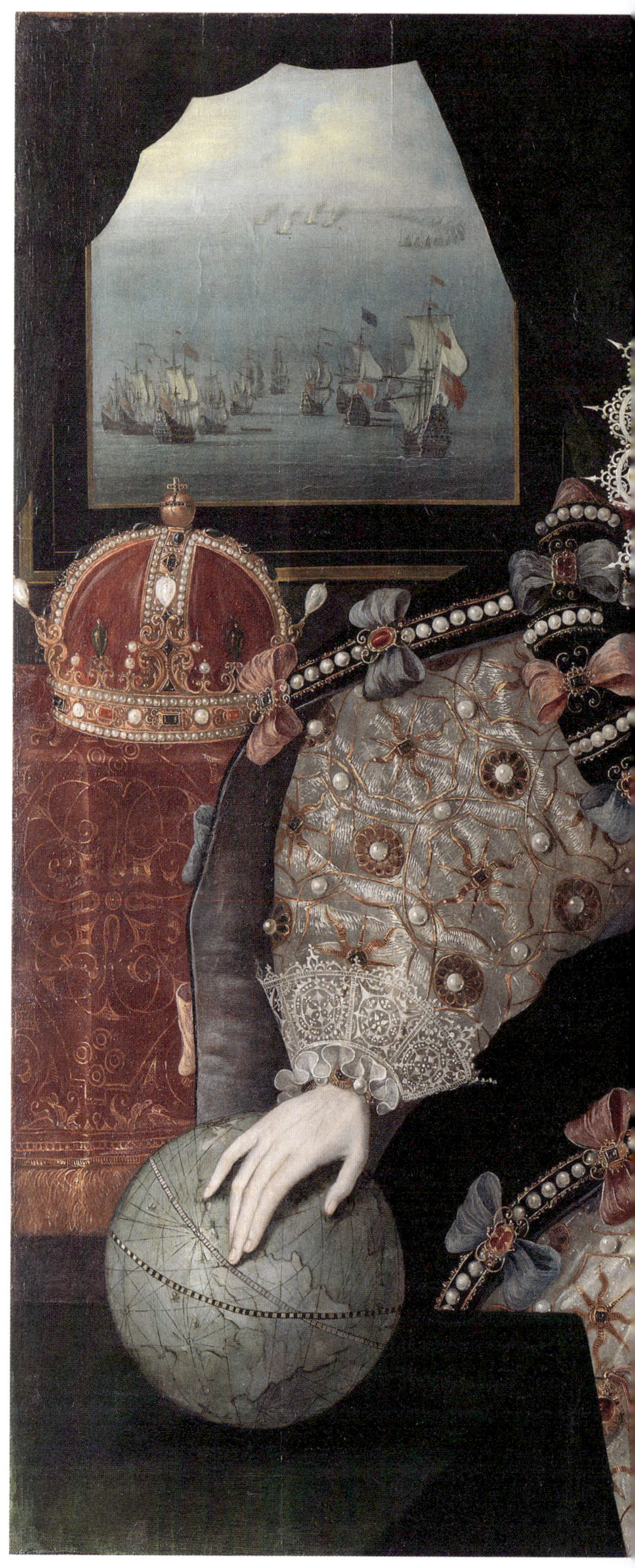

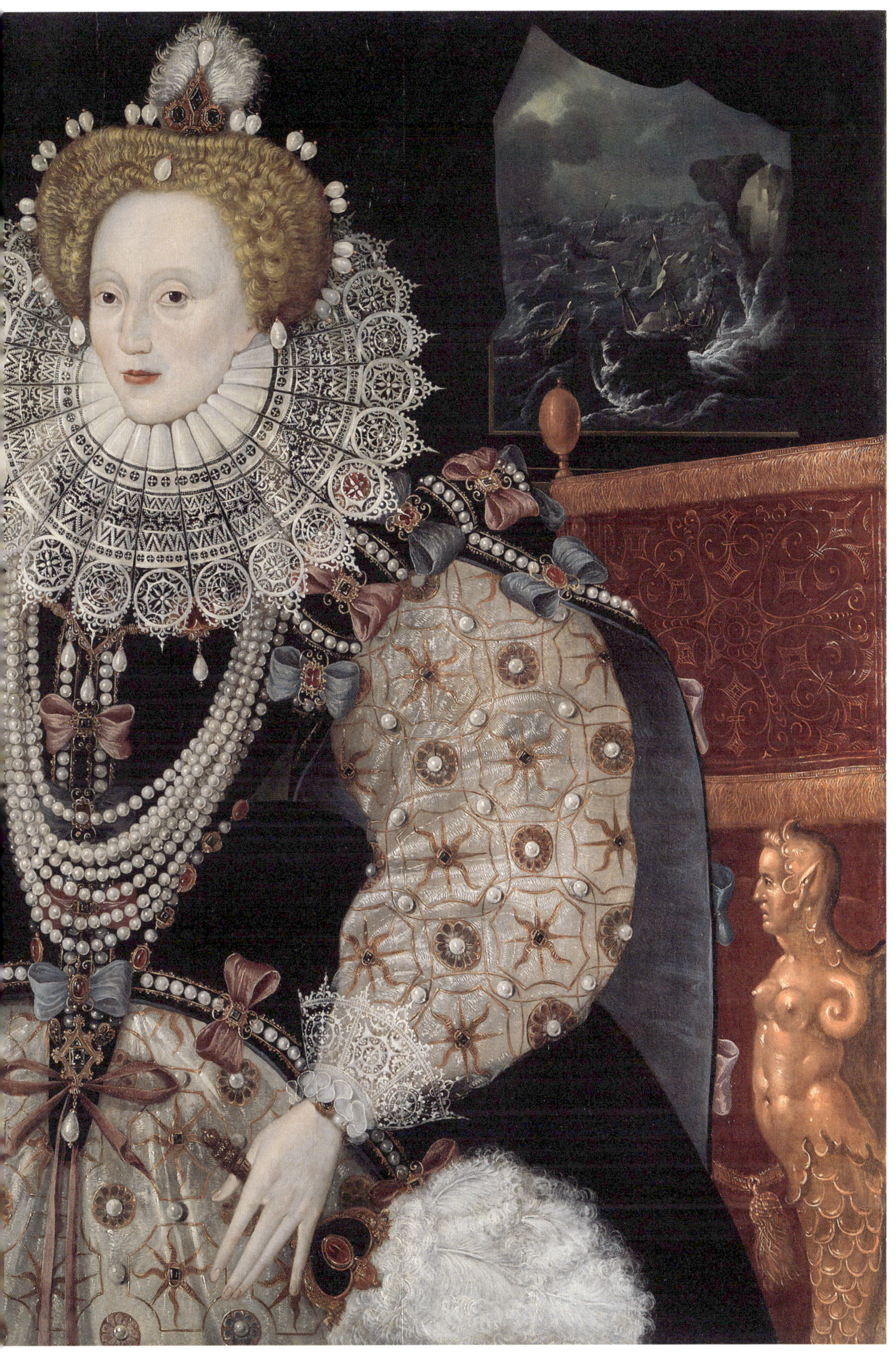

Charles Howard, 1st Earl of Nottingham

Studio of Daniel Mytens the Elder

about 1620, oil on canvas
2,085 x 1,395 mm
BHC2786

In the early seventeenth century, English portraiture underwent a stylistic transformation. Where earlier portraits had featured flat surfaces, stiff poses and even light, newer paintings seemed more three-dimensional with varied light and shadow. The Dutch artist Daniel Mytens was one of the painters responsible for this transformation. He was born into a family of artists in Delft and trained as a painter in The Hague, where he learnt to paint in a naturalistic style, before moving to London in the mid-1610s. He quickly found patrons at the English court, eventually gaining the patronage of King James I and VI and his son and successor, King Charles I. Mytens had a large studio and many of his pictures were predominately the work of his studio assistants.

Depicting Charles Howard, 1st Earl of Nottingham, not long after his retirement from the office of Lord High Admiral, this portrait is Mytens's earliest documented commission from James I and VI. Royal accounts from the time include an order dated 25 May 1620 authorising a payment to be made to Mytens 'for making the picture of the Earl of Nottingham by His Majesty's Commandment, with a gilded frame for the same'. The painting remained part of the royal collection until the 1820s, when George IV presented the picture to the National Gallery of Naval Art at Greenwich Hospital, from where it passed to the National Maritime Museum in 1936.

Howard belonged to an influential noble family and became a central figure at the court of Elizabeth I, rising through various positions until his eventual appointment as Lord High Admiral in 1585. In that role, he served as commander-in-chief of the English fleet that defeated the Spanish Armada in 1588. Though Howard's leadership attracted criticism from the Queen herself, he demonstrated significant concern for the welfare of his men and used his own money to pay for their food and clothing when the inadequate official provisions ran out. He reaped greater personal reward for his part in the English raid on Cadiz in 1596, after which he was created 1st Earl of Nottingham, but it was the Armada campaign that would ultimately define his legacy. The famous victory prompted widespread public commemorations at the time and in the decades that followed came to be seen as a defining moment in a golden age of military, naval and imperial triumph. After ascending to the English throne following Elizabeth's death in 1603, James I embraced the imagery of protestant militarism and maritime triumph that had flourished during her reign, though his own foreign policy focused on diplomacy rather than conflict. The new King retained Howard in the role of Lord High Admiral and his respect for the naval commander is suggested through the commissioning of this portrait after Howard's retirement in 1618.

The painting follows an established formula for court portraiture at this time. Accessories such as the green curtain in the background and the patterned carpet draped over the table on the right were commonplace in paintings of nobles and courtiers. With its Kufic borders and keyhole-like 're-entrant' motif, the carpet is of Turkish origin, exemplifying the extensive trade between Europe and the Ottoman Empire throughout this period. Carpets of this type were often included in portraits to represent opulence, luxury, wealth and status.

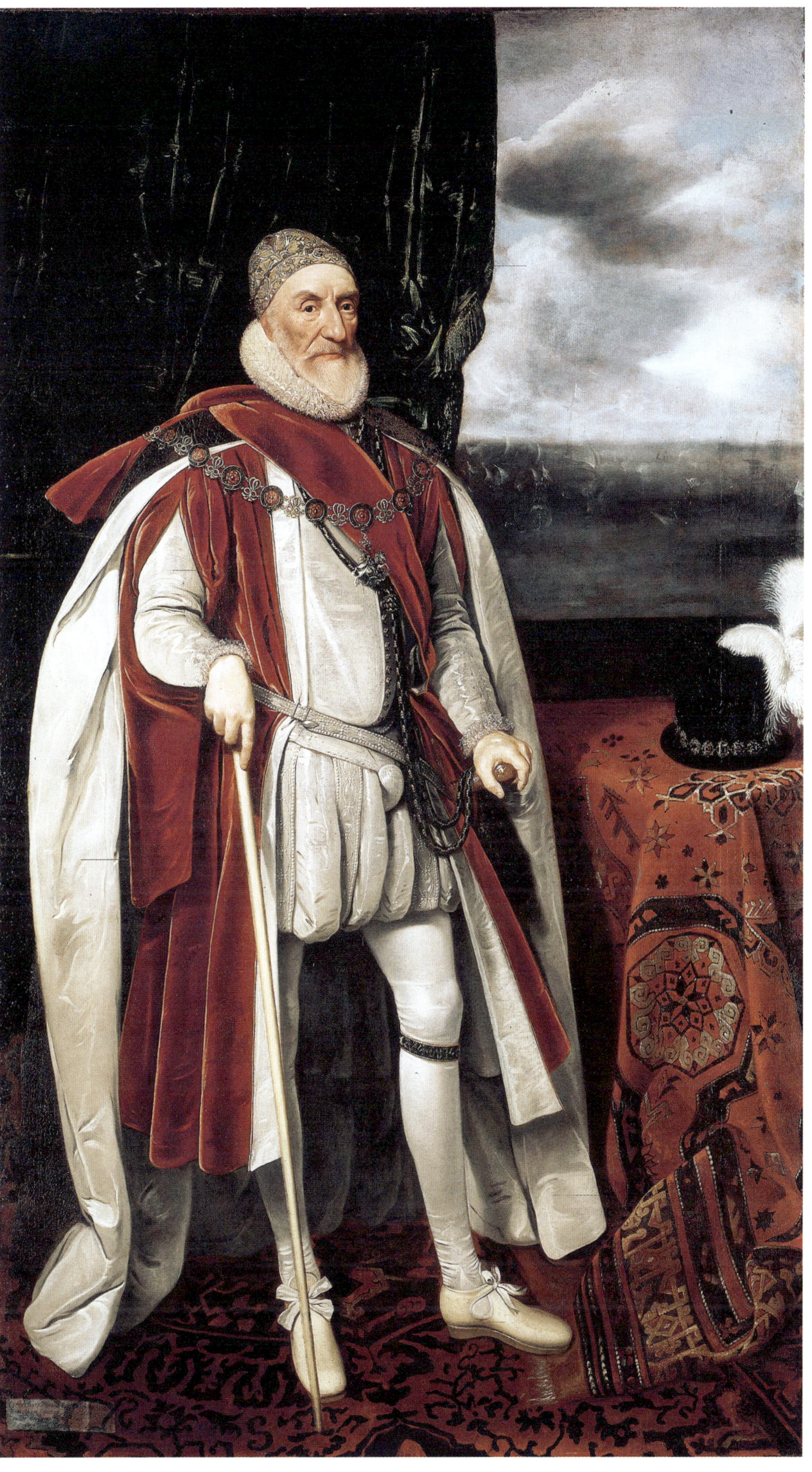

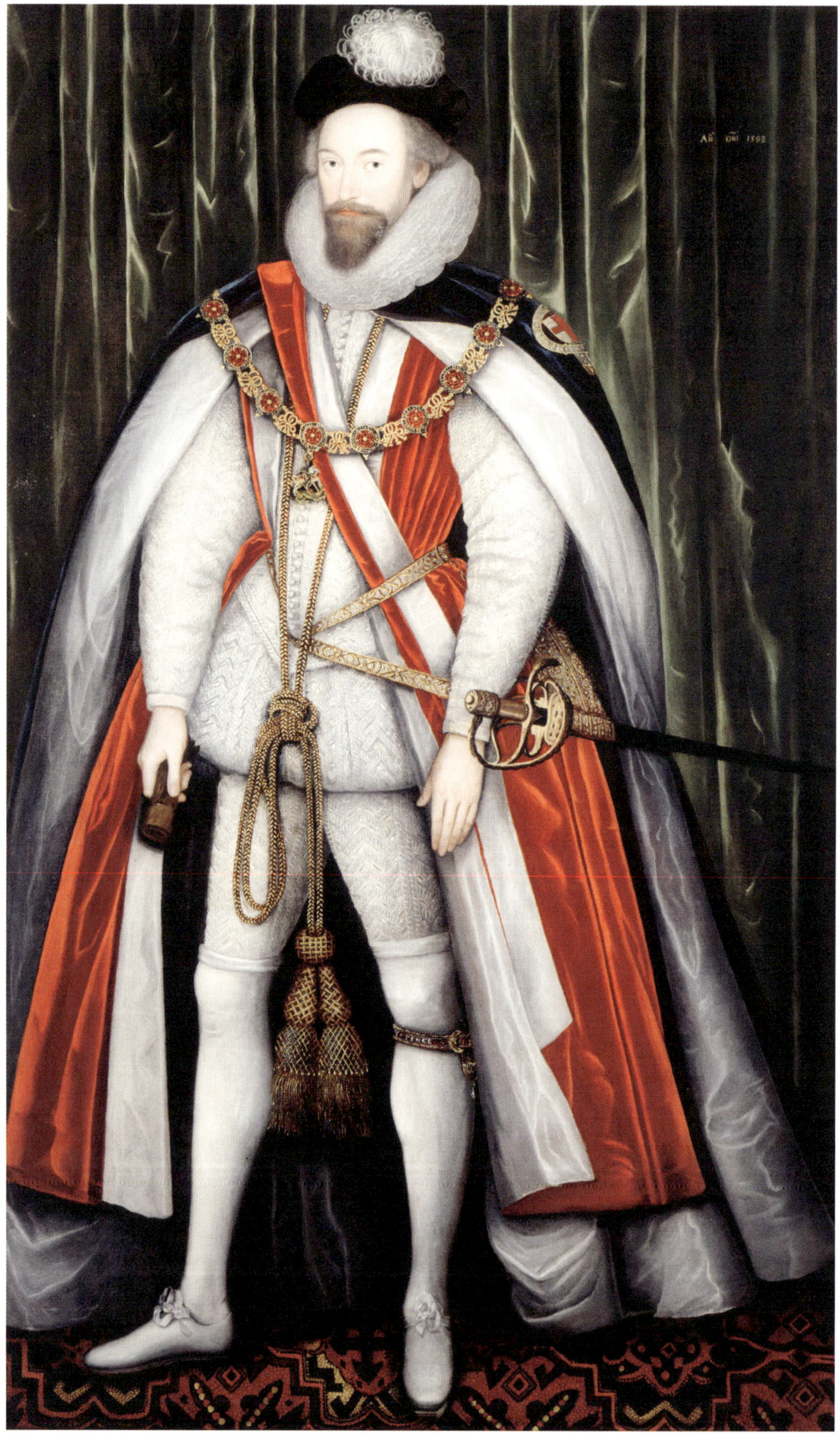

Howard himself is dressed in the elaborate ceremonial vestments of the Order of the Garter, consisting of a white doublet and hose, a red velvet coat and sash, a dark blue cloak and a gold collar. Completing this regalia are a black hat adorned with white ostrich feathers, which rests on the table beside him, and the order's titular garter, a blue velvet strap that he wears buckled around his left calf. The Order of the Garter is the most senior order of knighthood in England. Taking inspiration from the Knights of the Round Table in Arthurian legend, Edward III founded the order in 1348 as a society for fighting men, who were to be united in their pursuit of martial valour and their loyalty to the sovereign. The order took on renewed significance during Elizabeth's reign, as she used garter appointments in a strategic way to elevate selected male courtiers into a privileged circle of trust and intimacy. Furthermore, the order's martial and chivalric associations amplified her efforts to present herself as a protestant heroine with a record of military and naval success. As a consequence of the order's heightened prominence, many courtiers opted to be painted in their robes, giving rise to a tradition of garter portraiture which continued long after Elizabeth's death and to which Howard's picture belongs. An earlier example of this tradition is a portrait of Lord Thomas Howard de Walden at Kenwood House (fig. 1), which includes a similar combination of garter regalia, green curtain and Turkish carpet.

Howard's portrait was thus conventional in much of its imagery. Yet one aspect of the portrait was more innovative. In the background, the curtain is pulled aside to reveal a view of the sea. According to the painting's entry in a catalogue of the royal collection made at Charles I's accession in 1625, this area originally depicted '[the defeat of] the Spanish Armado [sic] of [15]88'. The scene has suffered damaged over time, leaving the paint thin, discoloured and abraded. Now only ghostly traces of sails, masts and rigging remain visible. Nevertheless, the inclusion of a maritime background within the portrait is highly significant, even if the details are no longer legible.

Depictions of contemporary naval battles, as opposed to historical, biblical or classical ones, are rare in European art before the late sixteenth century. At this point, two significant events – the Battle of Lepanto in 1571 (a conflict between a coalition of Catholic states and the Ottoman Empire) and the defeat of the Spanish Armada in 1588 – combined with increased overseas trade and colonial expansion to create demand for artworks commemorating and promoting maritime themes. The result was the development of a distinct and specialist artistic genre, usually referred to as marine painting. However, some of the earliest and most important examples of this genre in England were woven, rather than painted, and Howard himself was responsible for their creation. In the 1590s, he commissioned a series of ten large-scale tapestries depicting battle scenes from the Armada campaign. Hendrick Cornelisz Vroom,

(fig. 1) *Lord Thomas Howard de Walden*
English School
1598, oil on canvas
2,110 x 1,255 mm
English Heritage, Kenwood (88019326)

Below: (fig. 2) *The Spanish Fleet coming up the Channel, opposite to the Lizard (From the Tapestry Hangings in the House of Lords)*
John Pine after a drawing by Clement Lemprière from a tapestry woven by Francis Spierincks based on a design by Hendrick Cornelisz Vroom
1739, engraving on paper
418 x 638 mm
PAI6230

Opposite, left and detail (pp, 36-37): (fig. 3) *Robert Rich, 2nd Earl of Warwick*
Studio of Daniel Mytens the Elder
about 1632, oil on canvas
2,210 x 1,395 mm
BHC3080

Opposite, right: (fig. 4) *George Villiers, 1st Duke of Buckingham*
Studio of Daniel Mytens the Elder
early to mid-17th century, oil on canvas
2,085 x 1,395 mm
BHC2582

an artist from Haarlem who is often described as the 'father of marine painting', drew the designs, which were woven at the Spiering manufactory in Delft. Howard displayed the finished tapestries in his London residence, Arundel House, but it was rumoured at the time that he intended to present them to the Queen herself. They did eventually enter the royal collection, James I purchasing them in 1616, four years before commissioning Howard's portrait.

Although the tapestries were destroyed in a fire at the House of Lords in 1834, their designs are recorded in a series of eighteenth-century engravings, beginning with the first tapestry in the series, a depiction of the Spanish Fleet coming up the Channel (fig. 2). As these prints show, the tapestries incorporated portrait medallions of English officers in their borders, creating a precedent for the depiction of naval commanders alongside their seafaring triumphs. Mytens developed this precedent in his portrait of Howard, blending court portraiture with the emergent taste for marine painting. The artist's studio used the same format in several other

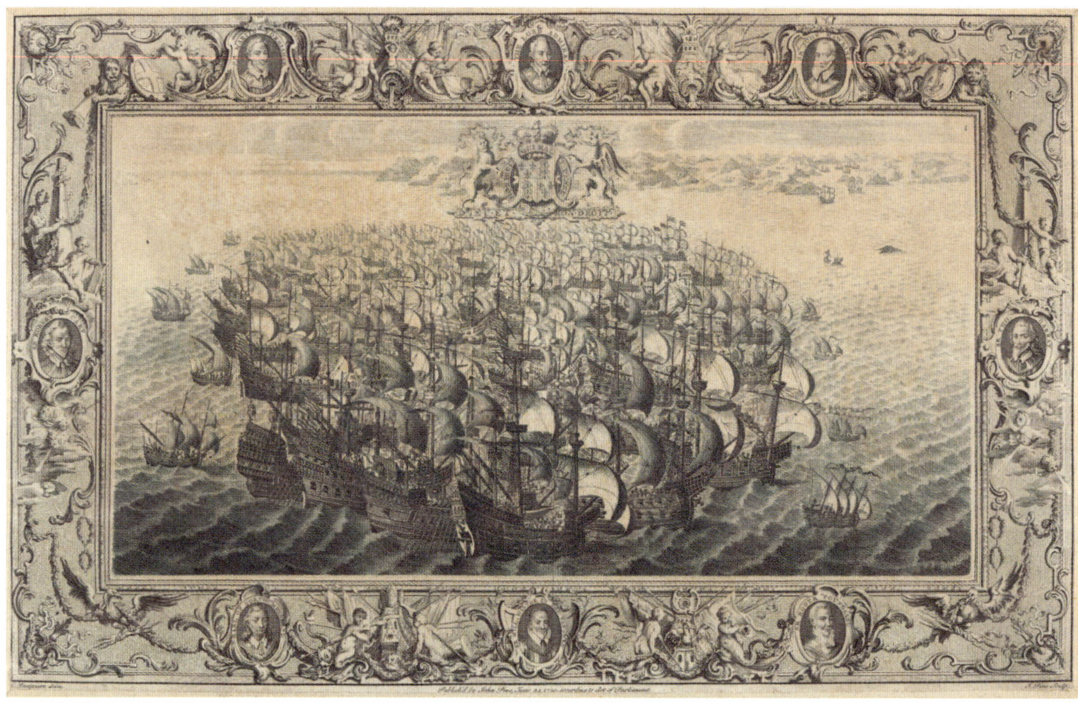

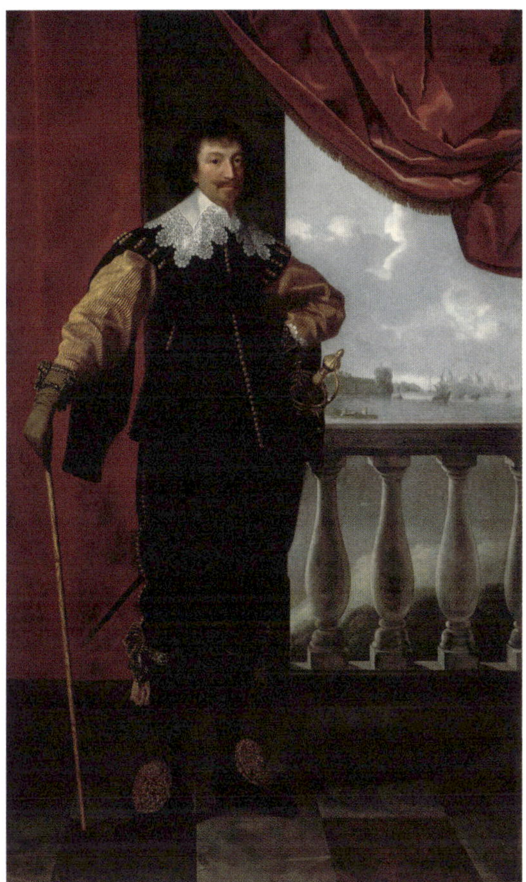

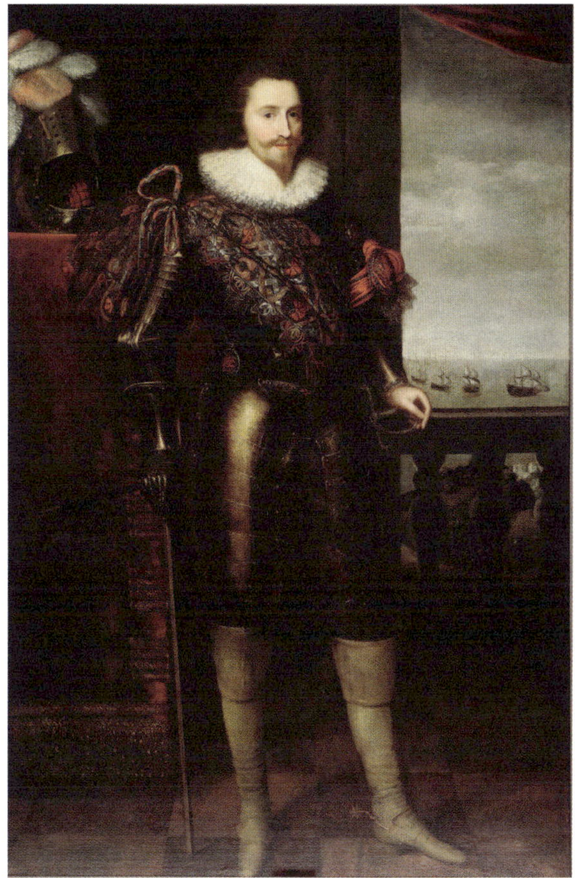

portraits of the naval sitters from this era, including Robert Rich, 2nd Earl of Warwick (fig. 3), and George Villiers, 1st Duke of Buckingham (fig. 4).

These works mark an important watershed in the development of naval portraiture. Previously, maritime heroes had been represented as noble courtiers with little reference to their naval careers. Beginning in this period, however, naval sitters were increasingly depicted alongside maritime imagery, drawing attention to their seafaring identities. The advent of marine painting was an important factor in this shift, since it created a maritime visual tradition that could be incorporated into portraiture. On a deeper level, the evolution of naval portraiture and the growth of marine painting shared a common cause. Both were products of the emerging cultural, political and economic significance of maritime trade, naval warfare and colonialism for England and its European rivals. The defeat of the Spanish Armada – the most famous incident of Howard's career and the incident in the background of his portrait – was an important symbol of this new maritime consciousness.

Robert Erle of warwicke

Sir Kenelm Digby

Studio of Anthony van Dyck

1630s, oil on canvas
915 x 710 mm
BHC2658

'When Van-Dyck came Hither,' wrote the London-based portraitist Jonathan Richardson in 1715, 'he brought Face-Painting to Us; ever since which time ... England has excell'd all the World in that great Branch of the Art.' These comments referred to the Flemish painter Sir Anthony van Dyck, who arrived at the court of Charles I in 1632. A former pupil of the celebrated master Peter Paul Rubens, Van Dyck came to England with a formidable reputation for producing portraits and paintings of religious and mythological subjects. He had patrons and admirers across Europe, especially in his native Antwerp and in Italy. His decision to relocate across the English Channel in the 1630s followed a well-established pattern. There were many other Flemish artists working in London at that time.

Yet Van Dyck was in a different league, both in terms of his profile and his impact. His court portraits had an immense influence over subsequent generations of artists, many of whom idolised Van Dyck as the 'founding father' of English portraiture. Richardson's comments exemplify this attitude, crediting Van Dyck with inspiring a tradition of portraiture that 'excell'd all the World'. The claims for Van Dyck's significance were often exaggerated – reading Richardson's account, one might think that England had no portraitists whatsoever before the great master's arrival – but he is nevertheless a pivotal figure.

This portrait depicts Van Dyck's friend and patron, Sir Kenelm Digby, who was equally remarkable in his own way. Digby's legacy is hard to define because his interests and activities were so wide-ranging. He was a courtier, diplomat and intellectual. His work in the fields of alchemy and natural philosophy led to his election as a founding fellow of the Royal Society. At the same time, he also authored literary criticism and theological treatises.

His career was profoundly influenced by his religious background and the memory of his father, Sir Everard Digby, a Catholic insurgent who was executed in 1606 as a traitor for his involvement in the Gunpowder Plot. This failed conspiracy was intended to destabilise Protestant rule in England through the assassination of King James I. Kenelm was just two years old at the time of his father's death. He grew up in the Catholic faith but became an Anglican in the 1620s to qualify for government office, only to convert back to Catholicism some years later. His personal notoriety increased further in 1625 after his marriage to his childhood sweetheart Venetia Stanley, a woman of celebrated beauty but considered to be of questionable reputation after scandalous rumours about her alleged affairs with other men.

Amid all this public activity and private intrigue, Digby undertook a privateering voyage in the late 1620s, capturing Spanish, Flemish, French, Dutch and Venetian ships, and afterwards became a naval administrator. It was because of this naval connection that the National Maritime Museum purchased his portrait in the 1940s, though it is impossible to separate Digby-the-seafarer from Digby-the-academic. Even when at sea, he wrote romantic prose. Perhaps more than anyone else, Digby embodies the kind of hybrid career that was possible in the seventeenth century, before naval command became a distinct profession.

The portrait dates from the late 1630s, a dark period in Digby's life that saw him step back from

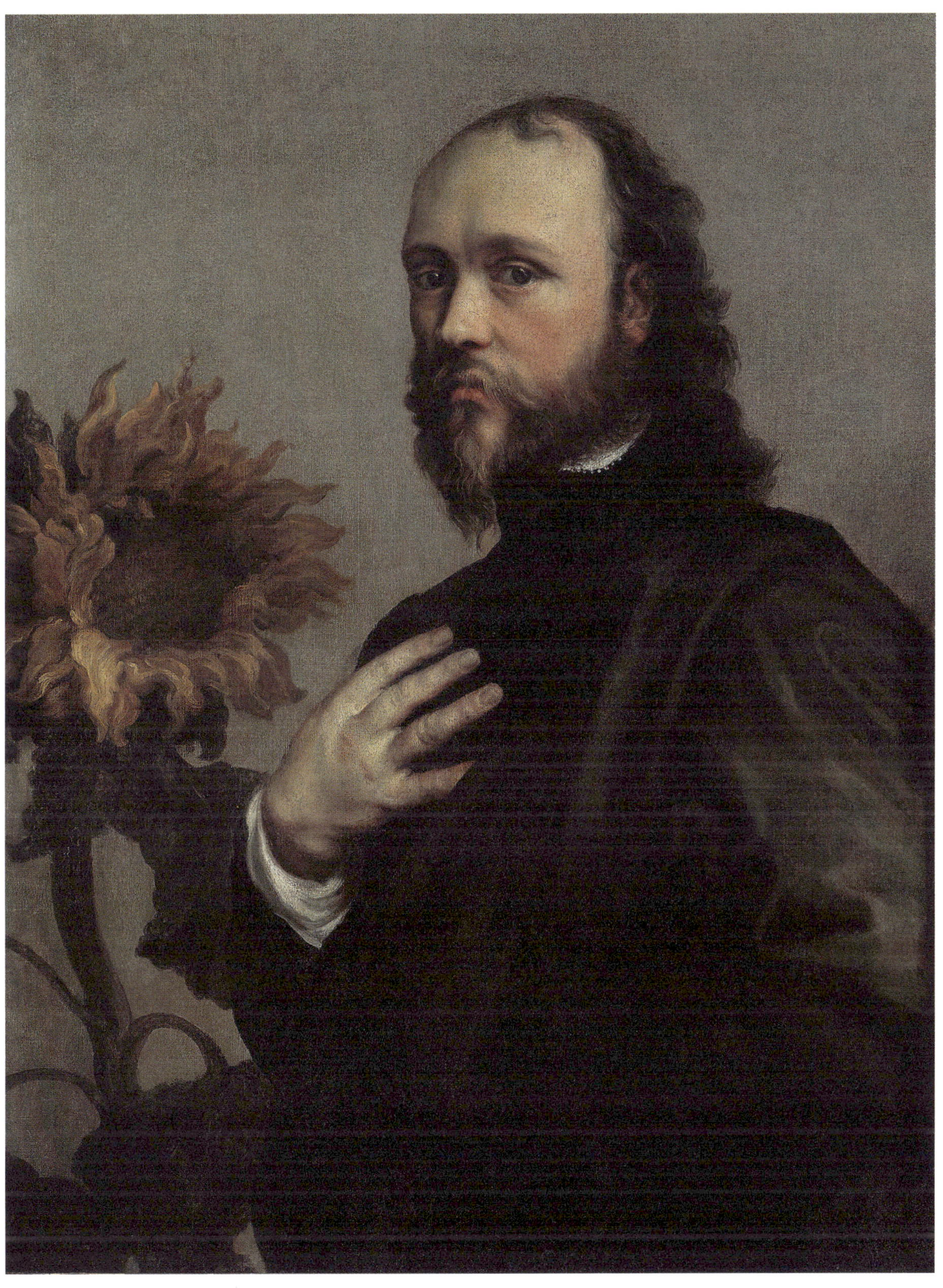

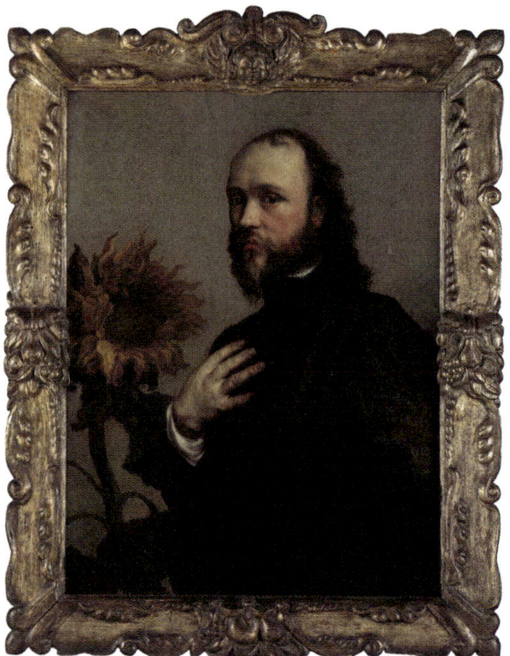

(fig. 1) Silvered auricular frame associated with *Sir Kenelm Digby*, BHC2658

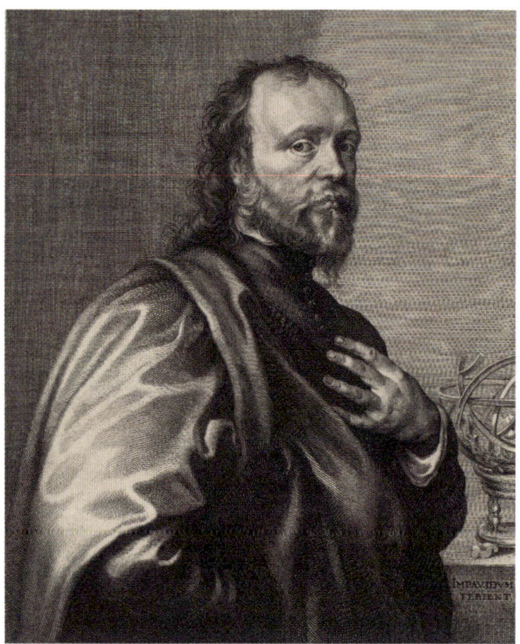

(fig. 2) *D. Kenelmus Digbi Eques*
Robert van Voerst, after Anthony van Dyck
1641, etching on paper
268 x 197 mm
PAF3225

public affairs following the death of Venetia, who passed away suddenly and unexpectedly in her sleep. Retreating into mournful seclusion, Digby wrote philosophical letters to his friends and renewed his Catholic faith. He also called upon the services of Van Dyck, whom he counted as a friend. They shared, according to Van Dyck's biographer, Gian Pietro Bellori, 'a mutual relationship of sympathy and goodwill'. The artist had previously painted Digby and his family. He now produced, at Digby's request, a haunting portrait of Venetia's body as it was found on the morning of her death, together with a number of portraits of Digby himself.

Several versions of this portrait exist. Some are attributed to Van Dyck himself, while others, this one included, are thought to be copies produced within his studio. This version has an exceptional period frame with an elaborate pattern of lobed decoration, known as an auricular design (fig. 1). Such frames were the height of fashion in the seventeenth century but surviving examples are rare.

In all versions of the portrait, Digby is dressed in black clothing, including a loose-fitting cloak. While this outfit suggests mourning, Bellori described it in his biography of the artist as being 'the dress of a philosopher', implying that it was also intended to represent Digby's intellectual activities. The first version of the portrait included a broken armillary sphere, an astronomical model that used metal rings to illustrate lines of celestial longitude and latitude. The portrait with the armillary sphere is now lost but its appearance is preserved in an etching (fig. 2). A similar but unbroken sphere had featured in Van Dyck's earlier portrait showing Digby with his wife and their two sons, painted before Venetia's death. In that portrait, the sphere symbolised Digby's study of natural science and philosophy. Its reappearance in the later portrait suggested his continued interest in these subjects, while also providing a poignant reminder of the family portrait – the sphere's damaged condition evoking the shattering of his domestic happiness after Venetia's loss.

Subsequent versions of the portrait, including the National Maritime Museum's copy, did not feature the armillary sphere, substituting a sunflower in its place. This motif echoed a self-portrait that Van Dyck had painted a few years previously, in which he depicted himself posing with a sunflower (fig. 3). The friendship between Digby and the artist might explain this correspondence in the imagery of their portraits.

The meaning of the sunflower in both paintings is a subject of debate among art historians. In Van Dyck's self-portrait, the sunflower is most often interpreted as a symbol of the painter's devotion to his royal patron, King Charles I. Sunflowers were often associated with loyalty or devotion in emblem books and allegorical texts of the time. This meaning derived from the fact that sunflowers are heliotropic: their blooms track the movement of the Sun. One interpretation of the self-portrait is that, therefore, the sunflower represents Van Dyck himself, with King Charles as the Sun that he follows. Supporters of this interpretation note that the painter is wearing a gold chain in the painting. This is assumed to represent the medal and chain that he received as a token of appreciation from the King, suggesting that the portrait may be about their relationship.

However, some historians argue that Van Dyck was too proud to depict himself as a royal servant. Furthermore, the use of the sunflower in Digby's portrait would not fit this interpretation, as, unlike Van Dyck, Digby was not in the pay of the crown. It may be that the sunflower is meant to imply general sympathy for the royalist cause, rather than a specific patronage relationship. Such an explanation is plausible, given that Digby was a supporter of the King. He had assisted Charles's marriage negotiations in the early 1620s and he had gone to sea as a privateer in the King's service. Later, when tensions between Charles and Parliament erupted into conflict in the 1640s, pitting Catholic-leaning royalists against Protestant militants, Digby acted as chancellor to the exiled Queen, Henrietta Maria, and travelled to Italy seek papal assistance for her husband. During the war, Van Dyck's *Self-portrait with a Sunflower* was used as propaganda for the royalists, reinforcing the idea that the sunflower had political meaning.

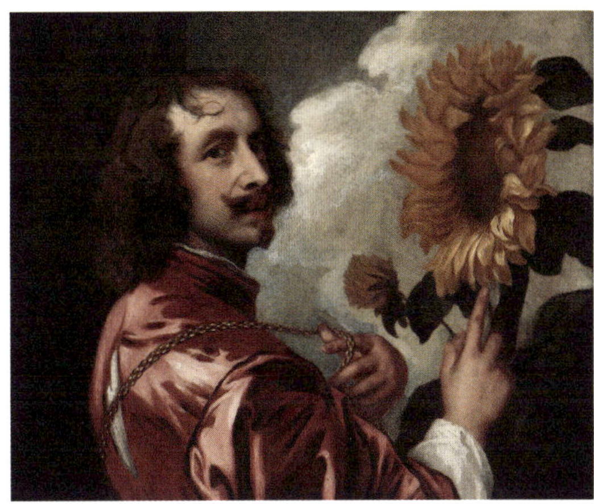

(fig. 3) *Self-portrait with a Sunflower*
Anthony van Dyck
1632, oil on canvas
730 x 600 mm
Private collection

On the other hand, other readings of the flower are possible. Digby's writings frequently used the Sun as a metaphor for intellectual and spiritual enlightenment, while some versions of the portrait included the Latin motto 'omnis in hoc sum' ('in this I am wholly absorbed'), referencing an epistle in which the Roman poet Horace discusses the study of truth. Seen in this context, the sunflower becomes a representation of philosophical and theological enquiry, the pursuit of which occupied Digby throughout his life and particularly in the aftermath of his wife's death. A reference may also be intended to Digby's academic pseudonym, 'Il Fiorito' (Italian for 'the flowery one'), which he adopted in order to join the Accademia dei filomati in Siena in 1620. This nickname alluded to the flowering of knowledge and understanding. Van Dyck seems to have shared his friend Digby's interest in philosophy and the sunflower may have similarly been intended to connote a quest for enlightenment. This does not invalidate the interpretation of the flower as a royalist symbol. Its meaning may have been multifaceted. Such complexity would be appropriate for a figure like Digby, whose career and interests were so varied.

Richard Deane, General at Sea

Robert Walker

about 1653, oil on canvas
940 x 1,270 mm
BHC2646

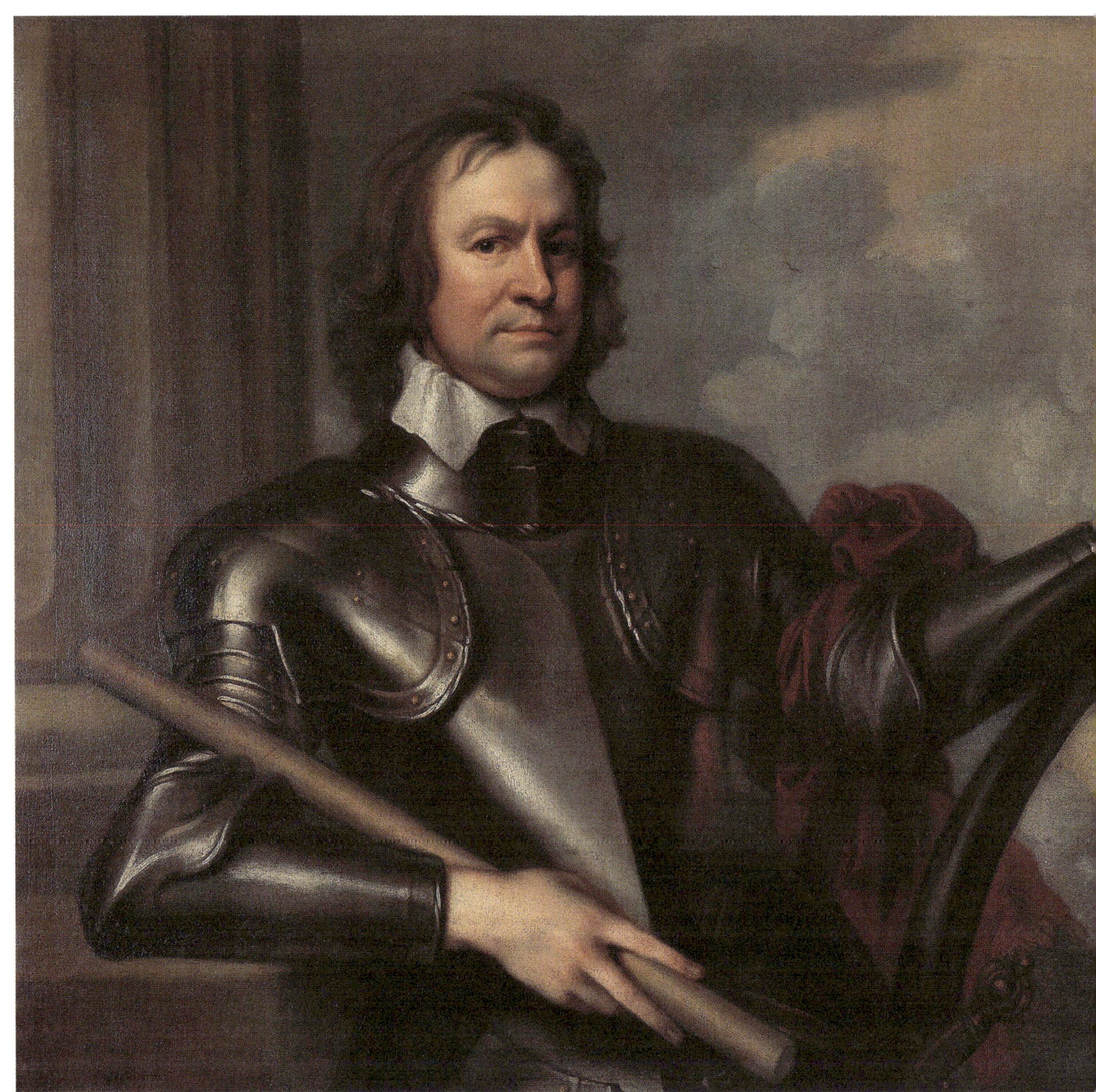

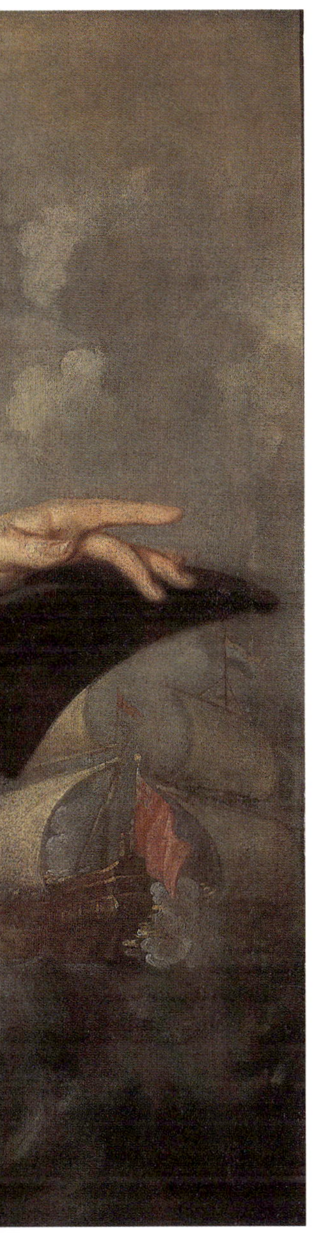

In August 1642, the fraught relationship between Charles I and Parliament dissolved into armed conflict, launching a decade of fighting and factionalism known as the Wars of the Three Kingdoms. The causes of the conflict were complex, but key factors included the King's efforts to evade parliamentary scrutiny and his introduction of controversial religious reforms within the Church of England. It was against this backdrop of civil conflict that Robert Walker made his name as a portraitist. He found favour with leading Parliamentarians, while his rival William Dobson painted their royalist opponents. The fact that each side had their own preferred portraitist might suggest that the divide between the two groups was all-encompassing, extending to art and culture as well as politics and religion. In fact, Walker's paintings reveal a more complicated reality. He borrowed extensively from Anthony van Dyck, drawing upon a shared visual culture that cut across partisan lines.

This portrait is one of Walker's most famous works. The sitter, Richard Deane, was a military and naval leader. Not much is known of his life before he joined the Parliamentarian army as a volunteer in the artillery in the early 1640s. Rising to a position of command, Deane became closely associated with Oliver Cromwell, a central figure in Parliamentarian circles who was also his distant relative. With the Parliamentary forces in the ascendancy, Deane and Cromwell were among the 59 commissioners who signed Charles I's death warrant in January 1649, having been active in instigating the King's trial for high treason.

After the regicide, Cromwell took charge of the government, assuming the title of Lord Protector. He appointed several senior figures from the army, Deane included, to serve as naval commanders or 'generals-at-sea', as they were called at the time. These appointments reflect a time when military qualifications often took precedence over seafaring experience in the promotion of naval officers, though Deane might have had some prior knowledge of shipping through an earlier career as a merchant. He served during several battles of the First Anglo-Dutch War, a conflict over trade routes, before suffering fatal injuries at the Battle of the Gabbard on 1 June 1653.

This portrait dates from around the time of Deane's death. Deane wears a suit of armour, an outfit which, though not necessarily intended for seafaring conflict, identifies him as a battle-hardened figure. In the crook of his right elbow rests a baton, which was, at the time, understood as an emblem of command. He leans against a fluted column, an architectural motif often used

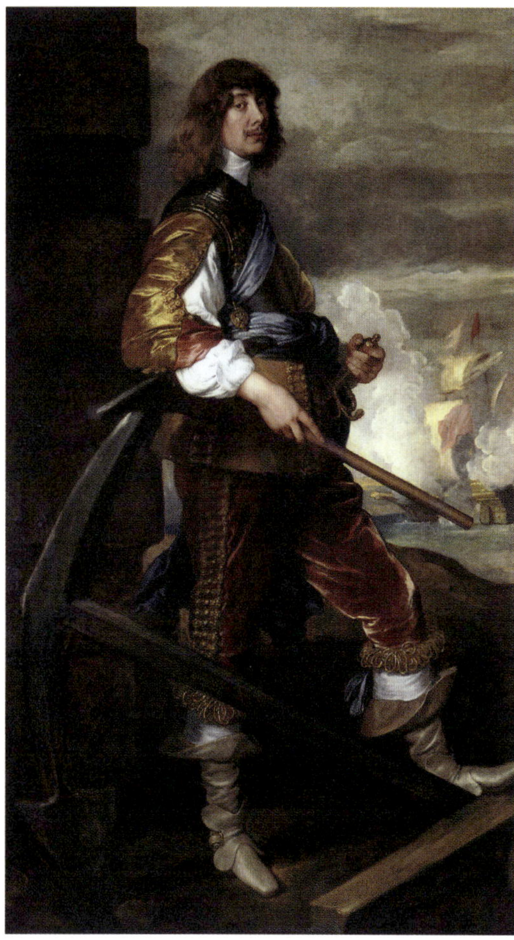

(fig. 1) *Algernon Percy, 10th Earl of Northumberland*
Anthony van Dyck
about 1636–38, oil on canvas
2,219 x 1,302 mm
Alnwick Castle, Northumberland

Opposite: (fig. 2) *Algernon Percy, 10th Earl of Northumberland*
Anthony van Dyck
about 1638, oil on canvas
725 x 1,345 mm
Alnwick Castle, Northumberland

in portraits of important persons to connote strength, stability and grandeur, while also acting as a framing device.

On Deane's other side, maritime and naval details are introduced. His hand rests on the fluke of an anchor. The flukes are the barbed tips on the end of the curved arms at the base of an anchor, designed to dig into the seabed. Used to prevent vessels from drifting, anchors were a fundamental piece of ship technology. They were also an important symbol of naval activity, appearing as an official mark on Admiralty papers from around 1600 and associating the sea service with the moral virtues of steadfastness and resolution. In portraiture, seventeenth-century painters began including anchors as props in their portraits of naval subjects, inaugurating an artistic tradition that would endure for centuries.

Behind the anchor in Walker's portrait is a view of a naval engagement between English and Dutch ships, identifiable through their national flags. This may allude to the Battle of Portland in February 1653, during which Deane was one of the commanders of the English fleet. Although the viewer is encouraged to accept this composition without much thought, the representation of an incident from the sitter's naval career in the background is in fact an artificial artistic contrivance. Deane is represented in two places at once: he is both standing in the foreground and participating in the distant battle.

For the next two centuries, this conceit remained a common formula for naval portraiture, its appeal intertwined with the development of marine painting and the growing taste for the genre. Clients were, in effect, getting two artworks in one: a portrait and a marine painting. On an emblematic level, the inclusion of a battle from an individual's career served to authenticate his credentials as a successful naval officer. Moreover, the representation of the sitter as a separate figure, standing apart from an action in which he had fought, served as a visual metaphor for the qualities of detachment and oversight associated with command, manifesting the officer's ability to step back and see the bigger picture.

Walker's painting thus exemplifies several details that would feature in later naval portraits,

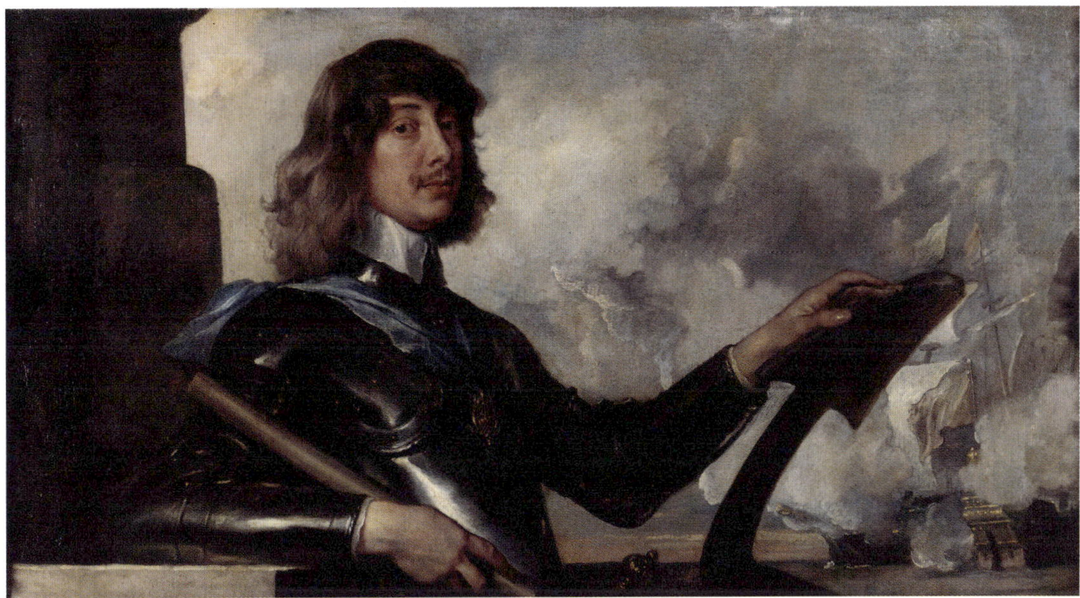

including the anchor and the distant sea battle. Yet Walker was not the originator of these motifs. Although several earlier painters had depicted admirals with naval actions in the background, it was Van Dyck who provided the immediate model for Deane's portrait with one of his portraits of Algernon Percy, 10th Earl of Northumberland.

Van Dyck was the former court artist to whom Walker often looked for inspiration, despite their clients coming from the opposite ends of the political spectrum. He painted Percy, an aristocratic naval commander, in the 1630s. The first version of the portrait was a full length (fig. 1). It showed the sitter standing astride an anchor, his elbow resting on the fluke and his foot propped on the stock, in a rocky coastal landscape. He is framed on the left with a fragment of architecture and a naval battle is visible on the right. This portrait exercised a profound influence over later naval imagery, inspiring many subsequent paintings.

Van Dyck also painted a revised version of the portrait, compressing the same motifs into a smaller format. This second version showed Percy from the waist upwards on an unusually wide canvas, possibly intended to hang over a doorway (fig. 2). The sitter wears a suit of armour, leans against a rusticated pillar, cradles a baton of command in his elbow and rests his hand on the fluke of an anchor behind which is a naval engagement. This is the exact composition that Walker reused for Deane in the 1650s, the only notable change being the substitution of a column for Van Dyck's pillar. Despite having sought royal favour in the past, Percy had sided with the Parliamentarian cause, but later distanced himself due to his opposition to the regicide. Yet his portrait served as a model for the representation of Deane, who signed the king's death warrant.

Art historians often cite this example as an important demonstration of the blurred boundaries between royalist and Parliamentarian culture. However, it also testifies to the emergence of an appealing new formula for naval representation, combining coastal settings, architectural elements, swaggering poses, distant battles, anchors and other nautical paraphernalia. This imagery would continue to dominate naval portraiture for centuries.

CHAPTER 2

Catholic Tastes

1660–1748

In 1660, Charles II returned from exile in Europe to reclaim the throne of his father, Charles I, who had been executed 11 years previously. The new King embraced art as a means to reassert the power and splendour of the monarchy after the upheaval of the Wars of the Three Kingdoms (1639–53). Artists from abroad continued to dominate English painting during his reign, as they had done under his predecessors. In part, this reflected the cosmopolitan and Catholic tastes that Charles developed during his exile on the Continent and transmitted to his court. However, it was also a result of the chronic lack of artistic training and opportunities in England, which prevailed for decades after Charles II's death.

An experienced yachtsman with a keen knowledge of navigation and ship design, the King took a deep interest in the Navy, appointing his brother, James, Duke of York (later James II), to the position of Lord High Admiral. A process of reform and professionalisation followed, spearheaded by the naval administrator, and famous diarist, Samuel Pepys. Developments such as the introduction of a qualifying examination for all lieutenants created the basic framework of training, payment and promotion that structured naval officers' lives and careers throughout the next century and beyond. The maritime strategy of the Stuart royals also included a campaign of colonial expansion and exploitative trading ventures.

As the naval officer's profession began to take shape, so did specific conventions for naval portraiture. Royal patronage played an important role in this process. In his position as Lord High Admiral, James, Duke of York, commissioned a series of influential naval portraits from court artist Sir Peter Lely in 1665, known as the Flagmen of Lowestoft. These paintings later inspired Prince George of Denmark, husband of James's daughter, Queen Anne, to commission a similar set of officers' portraits from painters Sir Godfrey Kneller and Michael Dahl in the early eighteenth century. Other naval portraits began to employ the same conventions that these two royal series had established. Officers were shown in coastal settings, framed on one side by rocks or architecture and on the other by a distant view of a naval battle. Attributes of their profession, including telescopes, anchors, cannons and globes, were also frequently incorporated. This formula would dominate officers' portraits until well into the nineteenth century, but there were always some artists willing to break the mould.

George Monck, 1st Duke of Albemarle

Peter Lely

1665–66, oil on canvas
1,270 x 1,015 mm
BHC2508

A native of the Low Countries, Peter Lely trained as an artist in the Netherlands, before emigrating to England around 1643. Sir Anthony Van Dyck had died a few years before, creating an opening for a new artist to dominate English portraiture. Lely aspired to succeed Van Dyck, though to do so he had to negotiate the political turmoil of the Wars of the Three Kingdoms, which pitted Royalists against Parliamentarians and culminated in Charles I's execution. Lely managed to build a flourishing practice catering to sitters of all political persuasions. When the monarchy was restored in 1660, he was sworn in as court painter to Charles II. The new King understood that art could be used to re-establish royal authority after the Restoration, although it was his brother James, Duke of York, who provided Lely with the most commissions.

This portrait comes from a series of 13 paintings (the others are figs 1–12) that Lely painted for the Duke of York to commemorate the victory of the English fleet over the Dutch at the Battle of Lowestoft on 13 June 1665. All 13 pictures depicted naval officers who had fought in the battle. Most of these men were flag officers (that is, senior commanders whose presence on board a ship was signalled with a flag), hence Lely's portraits became known as the 'Flagmen of Lowestoft'. As Lord High Admiral, the Duke of York had been commander-in-chief at the battle, though his portrait was not part of the set. George Monck, the officer depicted in this portrait, was Deputy Lord High Admiral. He had played a decisive role in bringing Charles II to the throne after switching allegiance from the Parliamentarian cause.

Lely's 'Flagmen' are mentioned in Samuel Pepys's diary, one of the most important primary sources for life in Restoration London. In April 1666, Pepys wrote that he had visited Lely's studio and 'there saw the heads, some finished, and all begun, of the Flaggmen [sic] in the late great fight with the Duke of Yorke against the Dutch. The Duke of Yorke hath them done to hang in his chamber, and very finely they are done indeed.' These comments reveal that Lely and his studio worked on the 13 paintings concurrently, rather than completing them one at a time. As was his established practice, Lely painted the heads himself and left his assistants to fill in the bodies and backgrounds.

The Battle of Lowestoft was one of the opening engagements in the Second Anglo-Dutch War. Underpinning this conflict was the commercial rivalry between the English and the Dutch, with the former seeking to break the latter's stranglehold on lucrative global trade routes. After the English enjoyed early success, the Dutch regrouped and ultimately won the war. But the 'Flagmen of Lowestoft' were never really about the war effort. Lely's portraits need to be understood as part of the political theatre of the royal court.

Most of the set hung together in the Great Chamber at Culford Hall, the Duke of York's country residence. As the Hall's main state room, this space was where the Duke entertained his court. The 'Flagmen' dominated the chamber's decorative scheme, which also included silk damask hangings, gilt sconces, calico window curtains and what was described at the time as a 'Jemaicawood table'. This was presumably a table made from an exotic hardwood from Jamaica or elsewhere in the Caribbean. As Governor of the

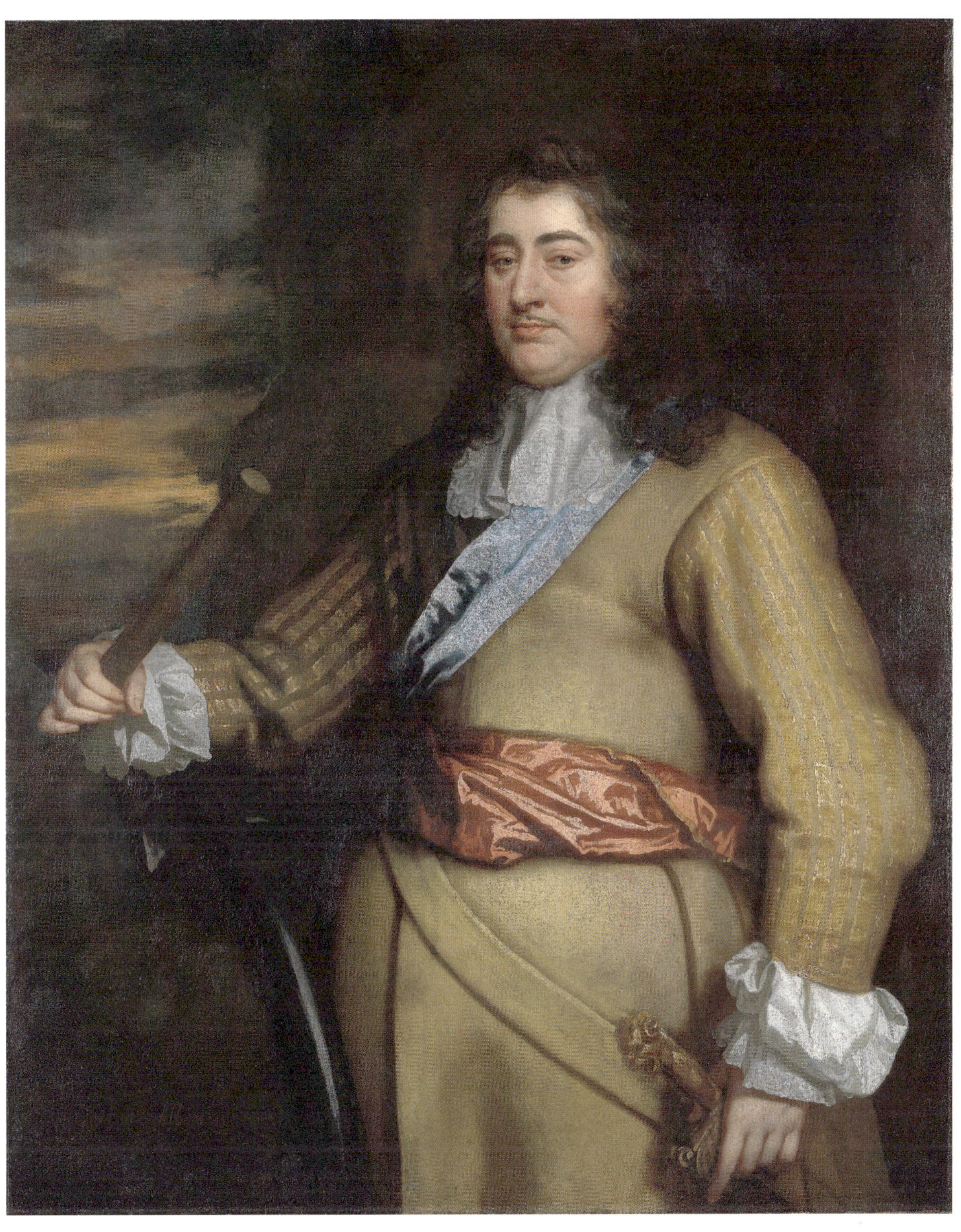

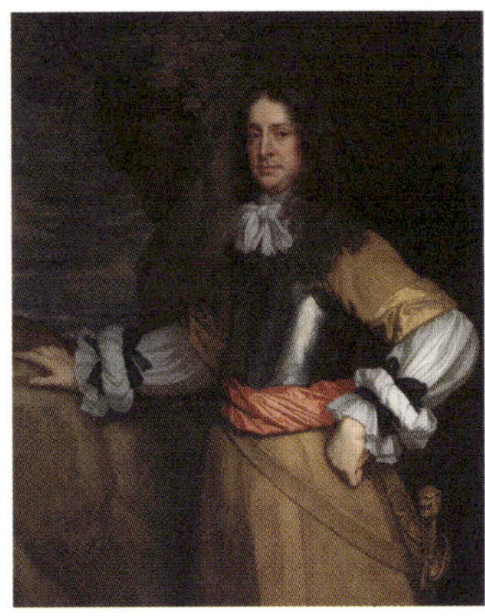

Vice-Admiral Sir William Berkeley
1,270 x 1,015 mm
BHC2553

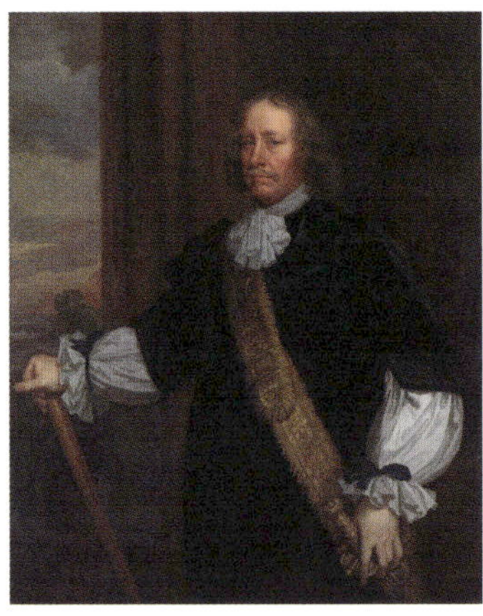

Vice-Admiral Sir Joseph Jordan
1,270 x 1015 mm
BHC2812

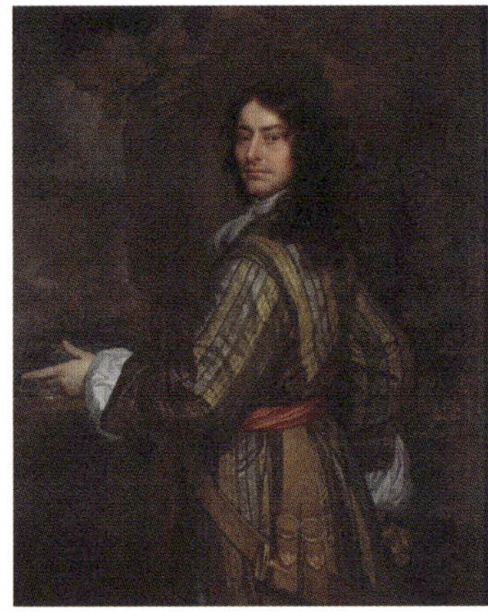

Admiral Sir John Harman
1,270 x 1015 mm
BHC2750

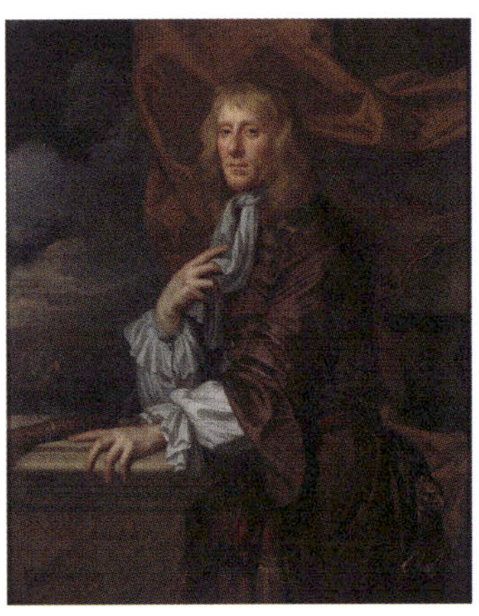

Sir Jeremiah Smith
1,270 x 1,015 mm
BHC3031

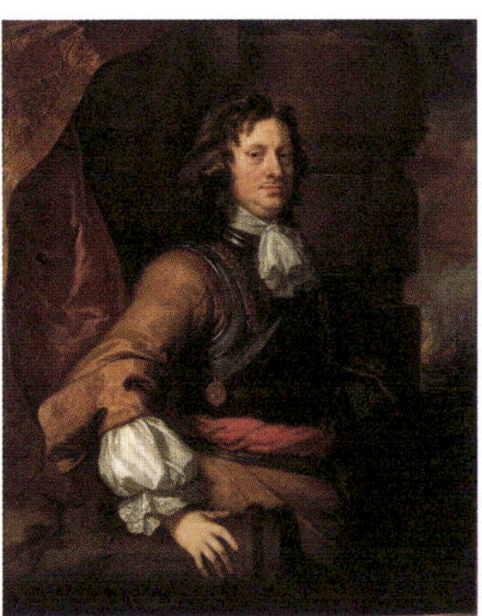

Edward Montagu, 1st Earl of Sandwich
1,270 x 1,015 mm
BHC3007

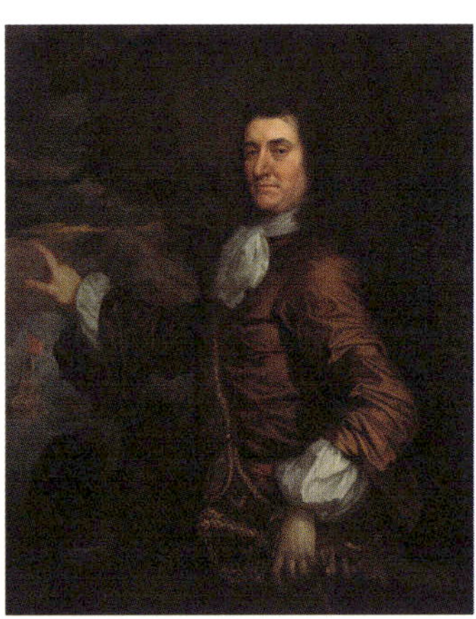

Admiral Sir Thomas Allin
1,270 x 1,015 mm
BHC2512

(figs. 1–12) 'The Flagmen of Lowestoft'
Peter Lely
1665–66, oil on canvas

Royal African Company, the Duke was central to the establishment of English plantations in the Caribbean and to the enslavement and forced transportation of African people to provide plantation labour. Through its portraits and its furnishings, then, the Great Chamber advertised the Duke's involvement in English sea power, both as a naval commander and a transatlantic trader.

Lely's 'Flagmen' balanced warrior-like machismo against courtly refinement, echoing the Duke's desire to be admired as both a naval commander and a royal prince. Monck's portrait provides a potent example. With one arm on the fluke of an anchor and a baton of command

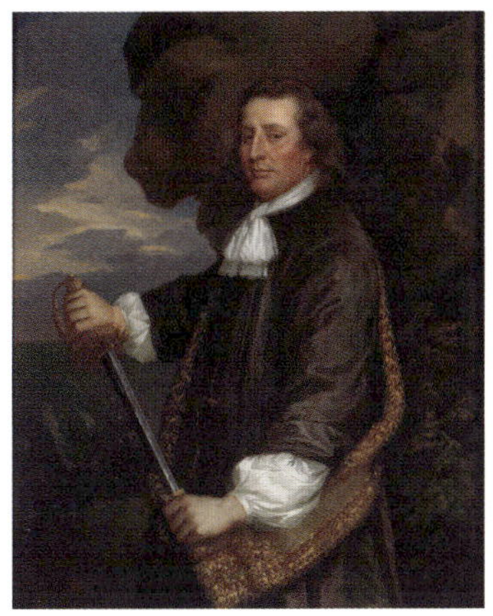

Vice-Admiral Sir Christopher Myngs
1,240 x 1,017 mm
BHC2874

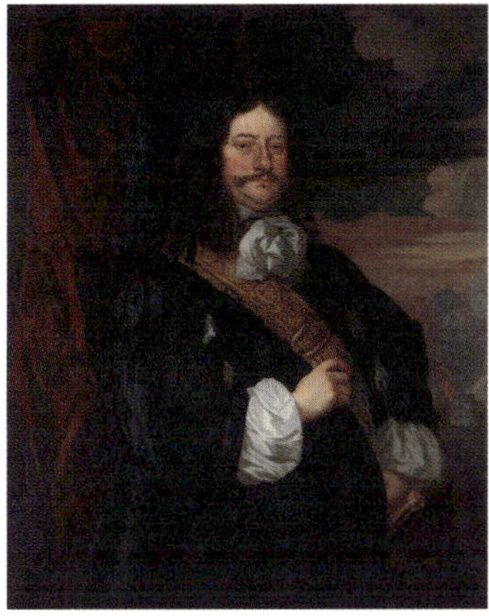

Vice-Admiral Sir Thomas Teddeman
1,270 x 1,015 mm
BHC3167

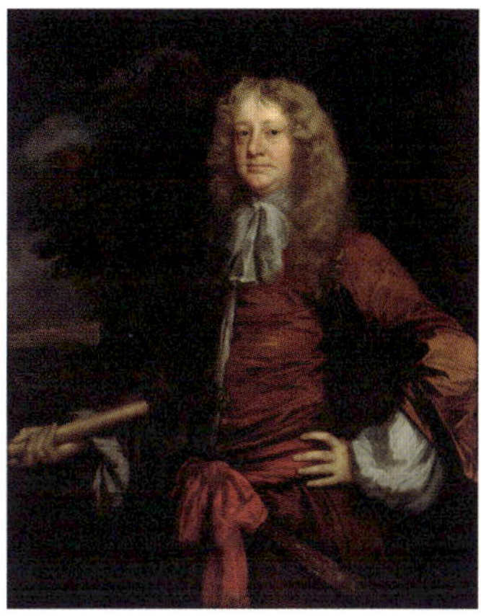

Admiral Sir George Ayscue
1,270 x 1,015 mm
BHC2522

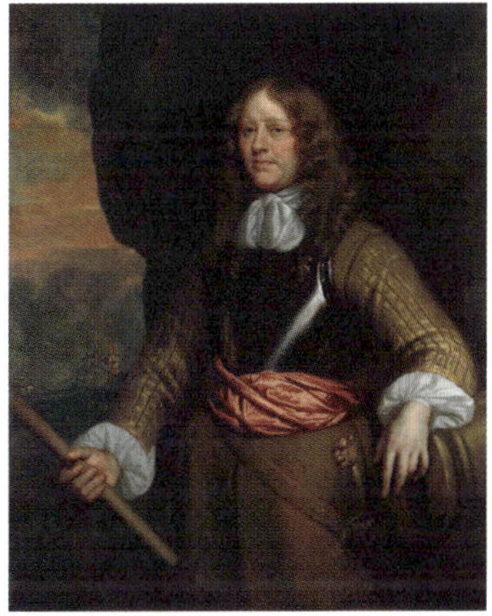

Admiral Sir John Lawson
1,230 x 1,010 mm
BHC2833

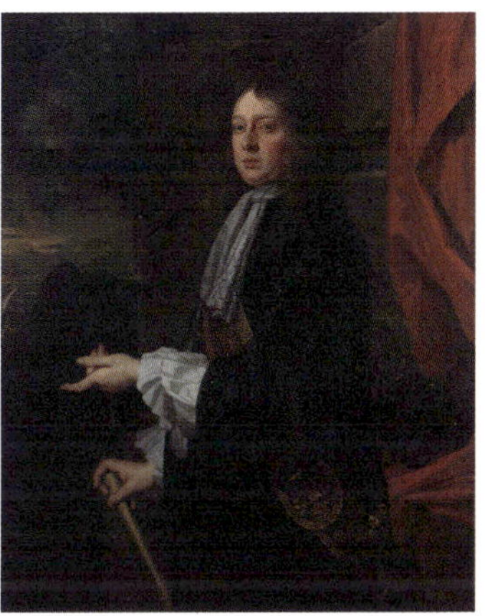

Admiral Sir William Penn
1,270 x 1,015 mm
BHC2946

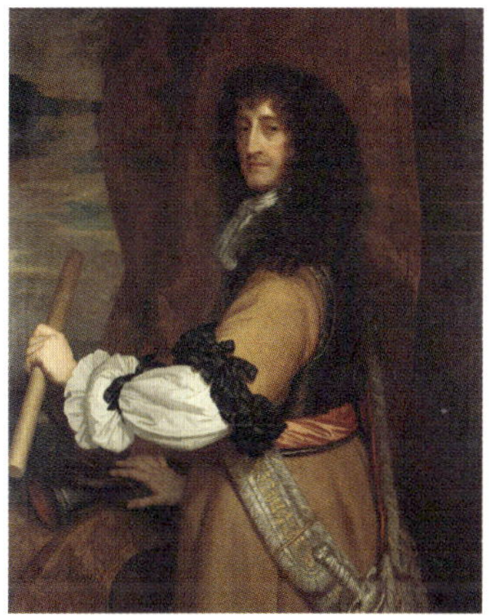

Prince Rupert
1,230 x 1,008 mm
Royal Collection, RCIN 405883

in his hand, he returns the viewer's gaze with a confident and steadfast look of his own. He is dressed in a buff coat, a padded leather garment used in this period as a flexible and comparatively lightweight alternative to a suit of armour. In this coat, Monck appears as a practical modern officer, the physical embodiment of an efficient and battle-ready navy. At the same time, the buff coat's plain and hardwearing leather provides a foil for more luxurious fabrics, including an ornate lace neckcloth, a red satin belt and the blue sash of the Order of the Garter. Gold stripes have even been worked into coat's sleeves, imbuing the leather with a subtle shimmer. Thanks to these decorative touches, the painting would not have looked out of place in the opulent interiors of the Duke's royal apartments.

A similar combination of robustness and elegance can be seen in the other 'Flagmen', though no two portraits in the series are exactly alike. The sitters are depicted in rugged coastal settings alongside attributes of naval command, which vary from painting to painting. Examples include cannons, globes, swords or – in Monck's case – anchors. In the background, rocks or architecture frame views of the sea and, in most cases, distant naval battles. This imagery followed an established formula for representing

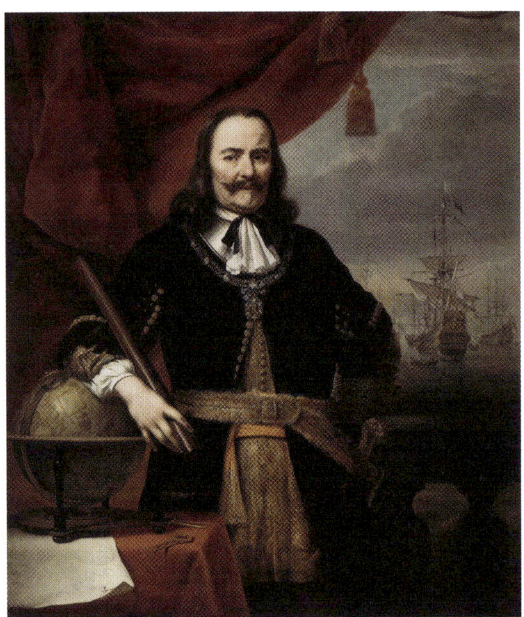

(fig. 13) *Lieutenant-Admiral Michiel de Ruyter*
Ferdinand Bol
1667, oil on canvas
1,500 x 1270 mm
BHC2997

naval officers, which Van Dyck had popularised in England with his portrait of the Earl of Northumberland (p. 42). Lely may have also taken inspiration from contemporary portraits of Dutch admirals, which followed a similar formula, as exemplified by Ferdinand Bol's portrait of Lieutenant-Admiral Michiel de Ruyter leaning on a globe and holding a baton of command (fig. 13). As well as seeking to usurp the dominance of the Dutch navy at sea, the English court was also keen to appropriate the Netherlands' flourishing traditions of maritime art. Having trained in Haarlem, Lely was ideally placed to capitalise upon this desire for Dutch-style portraiture. Other artists, such as father-and-son marine painters Willem van de Velde the Elder and Younger, enjoyed similar success when they moved to England from the Dutch provinces.

There is, however, more to the 'Flagmen of Lowestoft' than Anglo-Dutch naval and artistic rivalry. The series also responded to gender dynamics within the Restoration court. In furnishing his Great Chamber with a series of portraits, James was emulating the example of his wife, Anne Hyde, Duchess of York, who had filled the White Room in St James's Palace (her main residence) with paintings of leading female courtiers. These paintings, now known as the 'Windsor Beauties', were also Lely's work. Unlike the 'Flagmen', which were all painted at the same time, the 'Beauties' were painted in a piecemeal fashion between 1662 and 1664. They promoted a languid and eroticised vision of femininity, which has since become synonymous with the Restoration court. A typical example is the portrait of Mary Bagot, Countess of Falmouth and Dorset, in which the sitter wears a flowing length of blue fabric over one shoulder, revealing her linen shift and pale bosom (fig. 14). Bagot's ostentatiously informal outfit could not be further from Monck's practical and protective buff coat. This contrast is deliberate, Lely having crafted the vigorous masculinity of the 'Flagmen of Lowestoft' as a counterpoint to the soft, sleepy-eyed femininity of the 'Windsor Beauties'. Together, the two series demonstrate the role that portraiture played in defining gender norms and ideals for royal courtiers at this time.

(fig. 14) *Mary Bagot, Countess of Falmouth and Dorset*
Peter Lely
about 1664–65, oil on canvas
1,243 x 1,013 mm
Royal Collection (RCIN 404958)

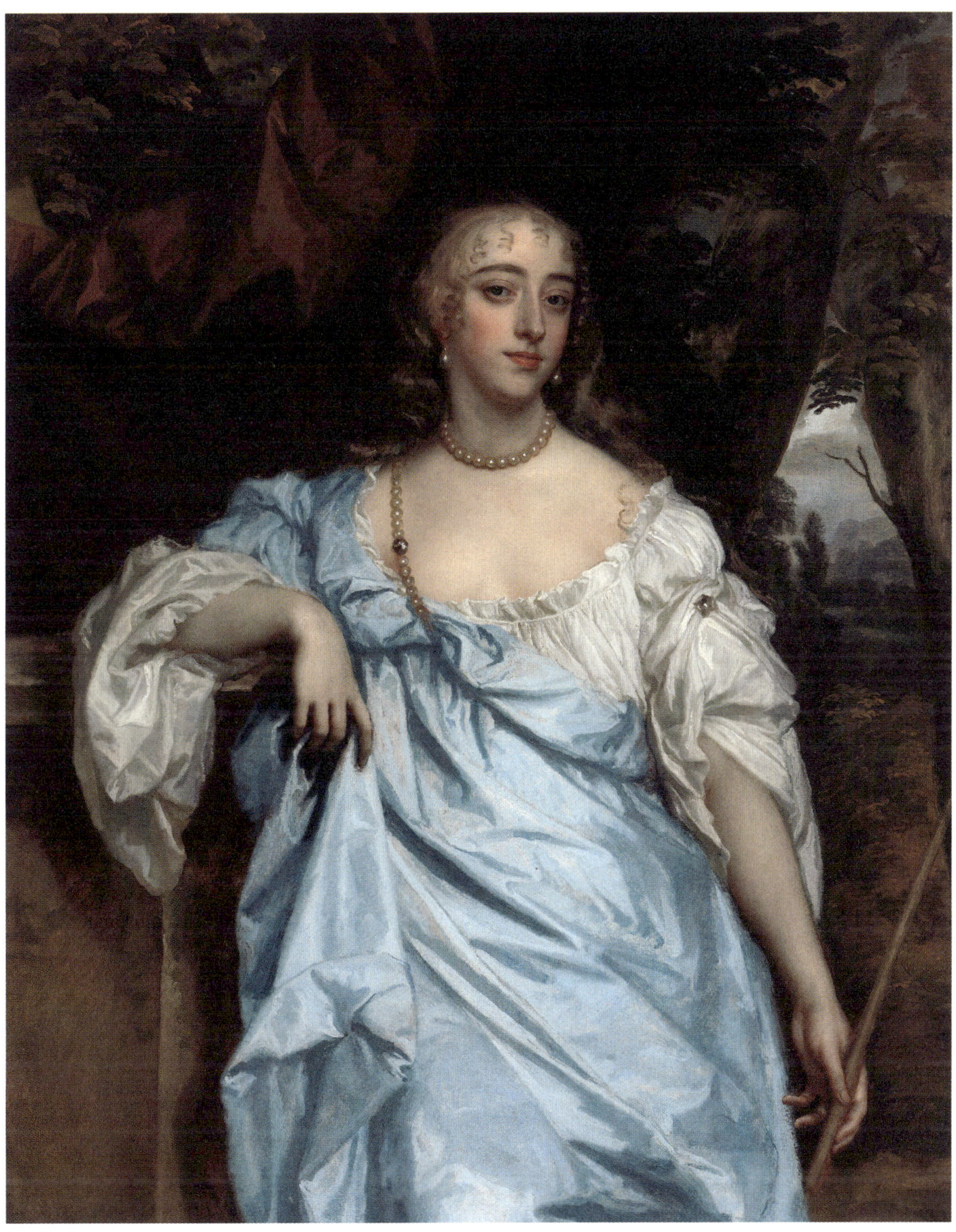

James, Duke of York

Henri Gascar

1672–73, oil on canvas
2,286 x 1,625 mm
BHC2797

French artist Henri Gascar trained in Paris and Rome before leaving to work in England around 1672, reputedly at the invitation of Charles II's mistress, Louise de Kéroualle, Duchess of Portsmouth. He quickly built up a large base of clients in Charles's court, usurping Peter Lely as the royal family's preferred portrait painter. His success can be ascribed to the Francophile tastes of the court, which encompassed art, culture and – more controversially – religion and politics. The court's apparent approval of the French monarchy's Catholic faith and absolutist rule raised concerns among Protestant parliamentarians, who retaliated with a programme of anti-French and anti-Catholic legislation. It may have been this rise in Francophobic sentiment that prompted Gascar's decision to return to his native Paris in 1678, putting an end to his short-lived English career.

Painted shortly after Gascar's arrival in England, this portrait depicts Charles II's brother and heir, James, Duke of York, in his role as Lord High Admiral. James was both a successful fleet commander and a skilled naval administrator, who worked closely with Samuel Pepys to modernise the English navy technologically, tactically and structurally. He was also the first director of the Royal African Company, which, between its foundation in 1660 and its dissolution in 1752, transported more enslaved African people to the Americas than any other company. This painting may have been produced to commemorate the Battle of Solebay in 1672, on which occasion James commanded the victorious English fleet.

The portrait combines allegorical, historical and contemporary details. This admixture of imagery reveals the conflicting cultural influences and political ideologies swirling around the royal court at this time. James is flamboyantly dressed in a colourful costume modelled after ancient Roman armour. He wears a gold breastplate with a fringed skirt over a mauve tunic striped with gold. A blue tasselled sash is tied around his waist and a red cape embellished with silver and gold lace is fastened around his shoulders. He also wears green hose and jewelled sandals, which are cross-gartered with gold-edged blue ribbons, terminating in lion-head ornaments. This vivid outfit exemplifies the excessive decorative detail that characterised Gascar's style, ensuring his success within a court culture that valued extravagance and theatricality. James is not presented as a modern naval commander in the mode of the 'Flagmen of Lowestoft', the series of portraits which he had commissioned from Lely in the mid-1660s (p. 50). Instead, James's classical costume casts him as Mars, the Roman god of war. This role-playing makes manifest the presumption of royal divinity associated with absolutist monarchies.

On the ground beside James's right foot is a garniture of gold-embellished steel armour, and a young attendant presents him with a matching plumed helmet. Like James, the attendant is dressed in an approximation of ancient Roman dress, though his tunic and sandals are less decorated than his master's. The armour on the floor, however, belongs to a different historical era, being reminiscent of the suits that belonged to James's father, Charles I, and uncle, Henry, Prince of Wales, in the early seventeenth century. By 1660, these royal heirlooms were held in the Tower of London, where Gascar might have seen them.

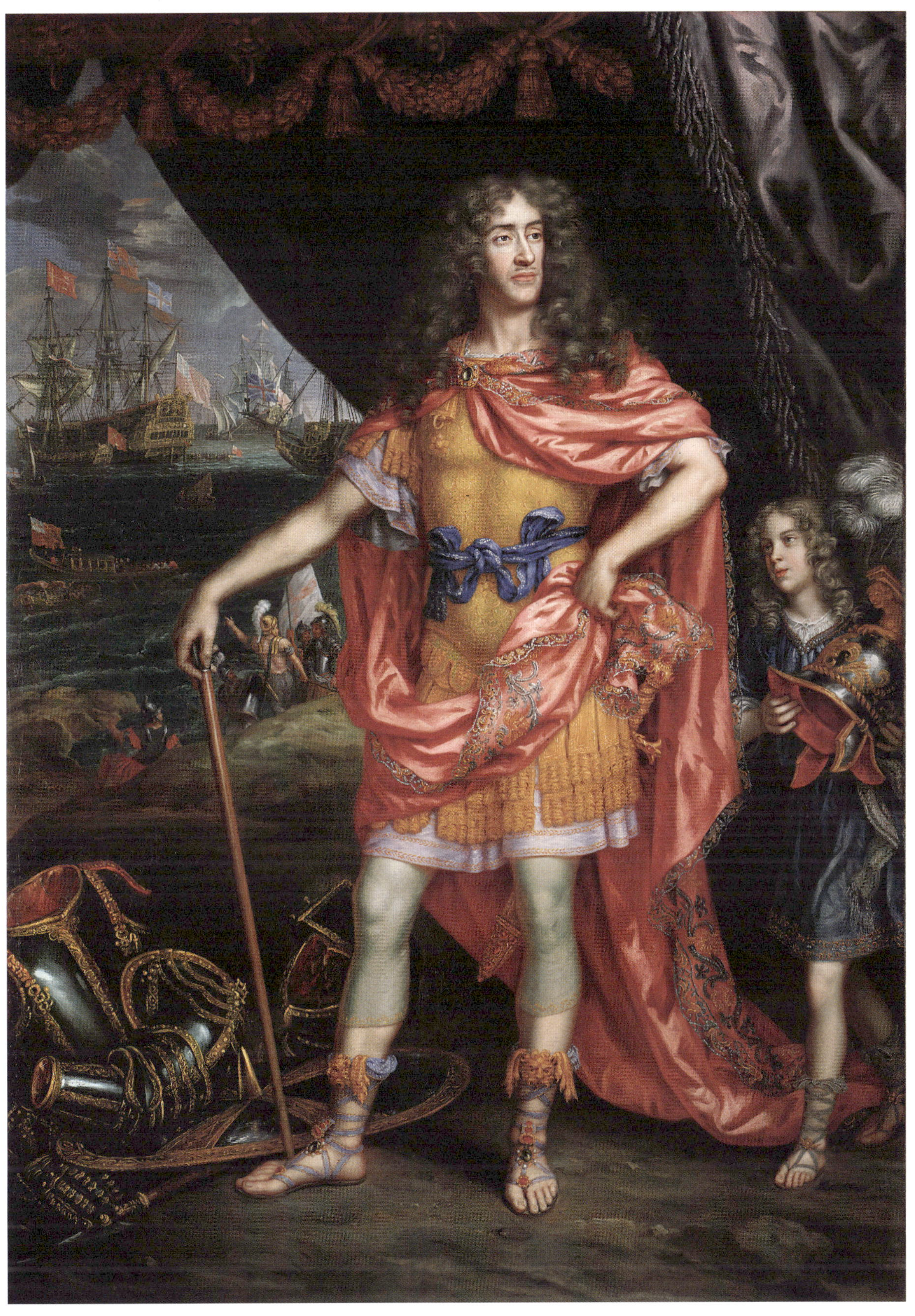

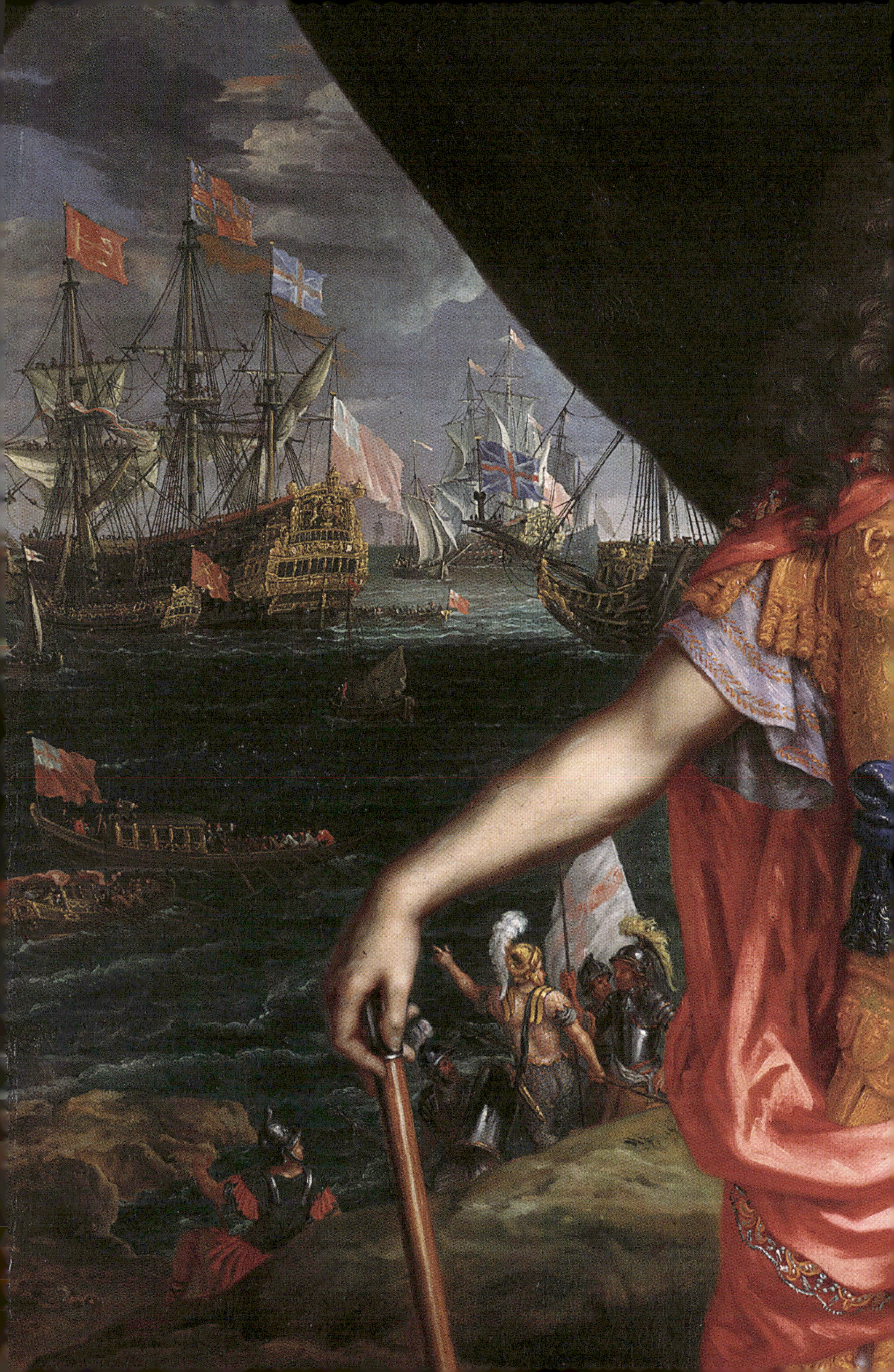

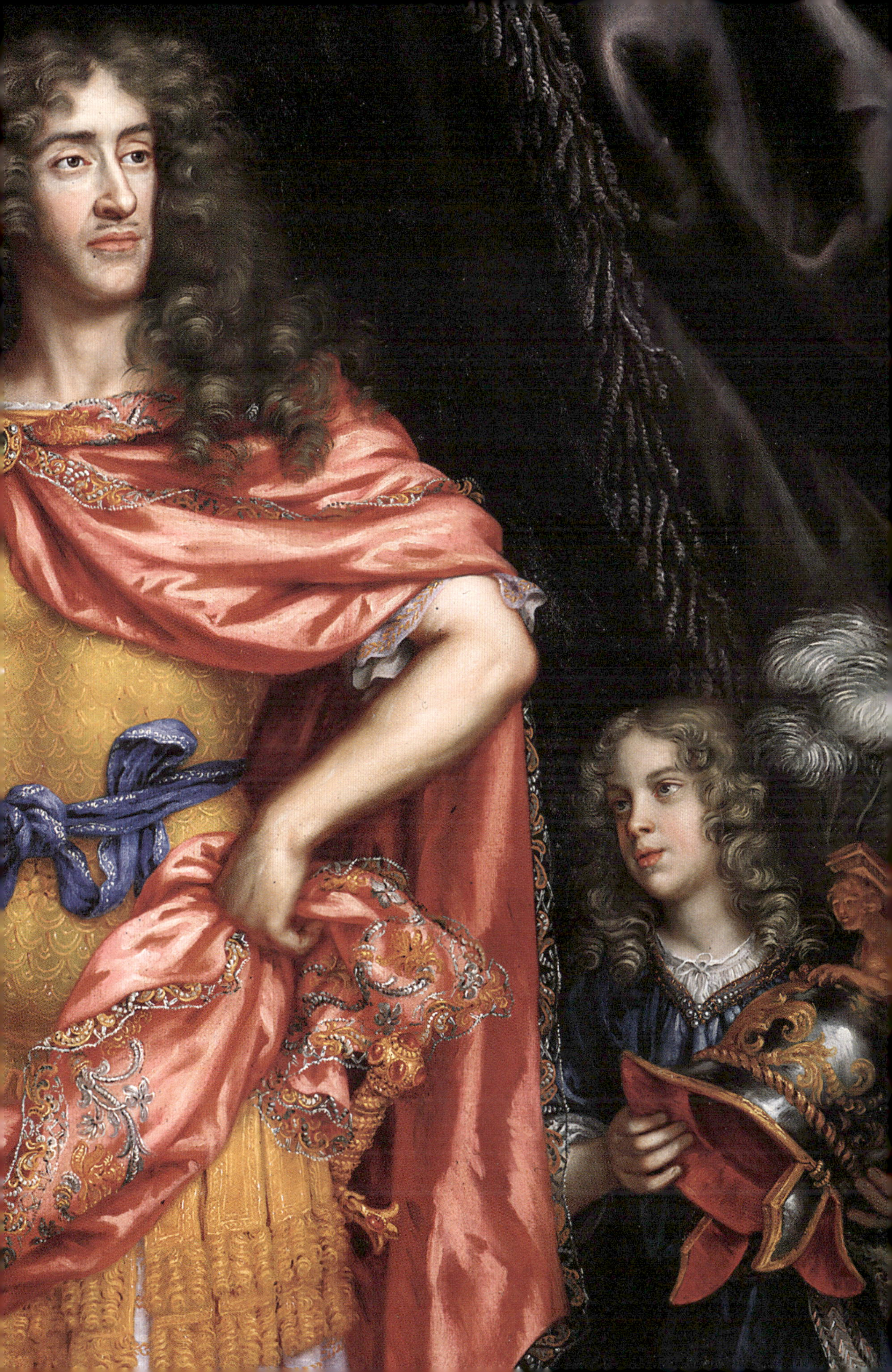

The inclusion of this armour in the painting created continuity, linking James to an earlier generation of Stuart princes and rewriting recent royal history as a narrative of survival and endurance, as if the regicide of Charles I had never happened. Moreover, the armour itself evoked an even older historical tradition. At the Tudor and Stuart courts, highly decorated armour served ceremonial, rather than practical, functions. Worn at tournaments and processions, it allowed princes and courtiers to appear like figures from Arthurian legend, binding the monarchy to a far-distant past of chivalrous knights and virtuous kings. Standing over a spectacular garniture, James staked his own claim to this mythic inheritance.

Behind him, the presence of a large curtain adds to the theatrical air of the portrait. This curtain has been swept aside to reveal a view of the *Royal Prince*, the Duke's flagship, together with barges, small craft and a royal yacht. The combination of flags flying from the *Royal Prince*'s masts (Admiralty flag at the fore, Royal Standard at the main and Union flag at the mizzen) indicate that the King, Charles II, is on board for a royal visit. This naval scene is represented according to the conventions of Dutch marine painting, a distinctive artistic genre that developed in the Netherlands during the late sixteenth and early seventeenth centuries.

As a genre, Dutch marine painting was grounded in realism. Artists strove to produce convincing representations of ships and fleets. Yet, under the pretence of accuracy, this imagery of hulls, masts, yards, sails, rigging and flags conveyed symbolic meanings, which were all the more powerful for their subtlety, from glorifying the technological sophistication of modern shipping to emphasising the grandeur of a naval fleet. At a time when England was seeking to become a maritime power capable of rivalling the Dutch Republic, the propagandistic effects of this visual tradition were apparent to Charles II. He therefore hired as court artists the celebrated Dutch marine painters Willem van de Velde and his son of the same name (known as the Elder and the Younger) after they emigrated from Amsterdam to London in late 1672. The scene in the background of Gascar's portrait was probably based on one of Van de Velde the Younger's paintings. No surviving paintings by the Dutch artist match the portrait exactly, but the composition is very similar to a large painting of a royal visit to the fleet now held at the National Maritime Museum (fig. 1).

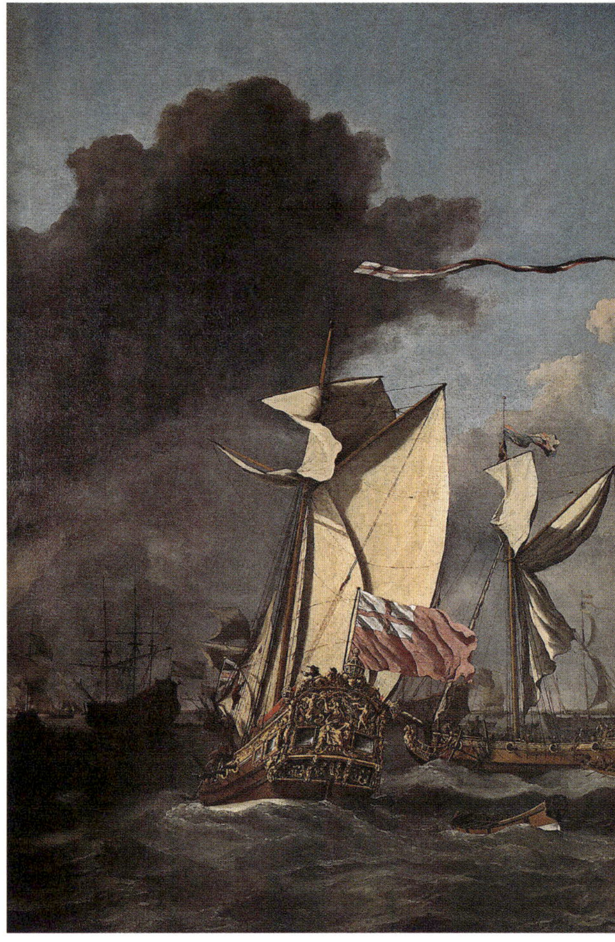

There is, however, something incongruous about the combination of this realistic depiction of naval activity, which had its roots in the Protestant artistic traditions of the Dutch Republic, with the theatrical representation of the Duke as a Roman god, which owed more to the Baroque excesses of Catholic France. In bringing together these divergent sources, Gascar's portrait encapsulated the cosmopolitan culture of the royal court at this time, as well as its inherent political and religious tensions. Moreover, the

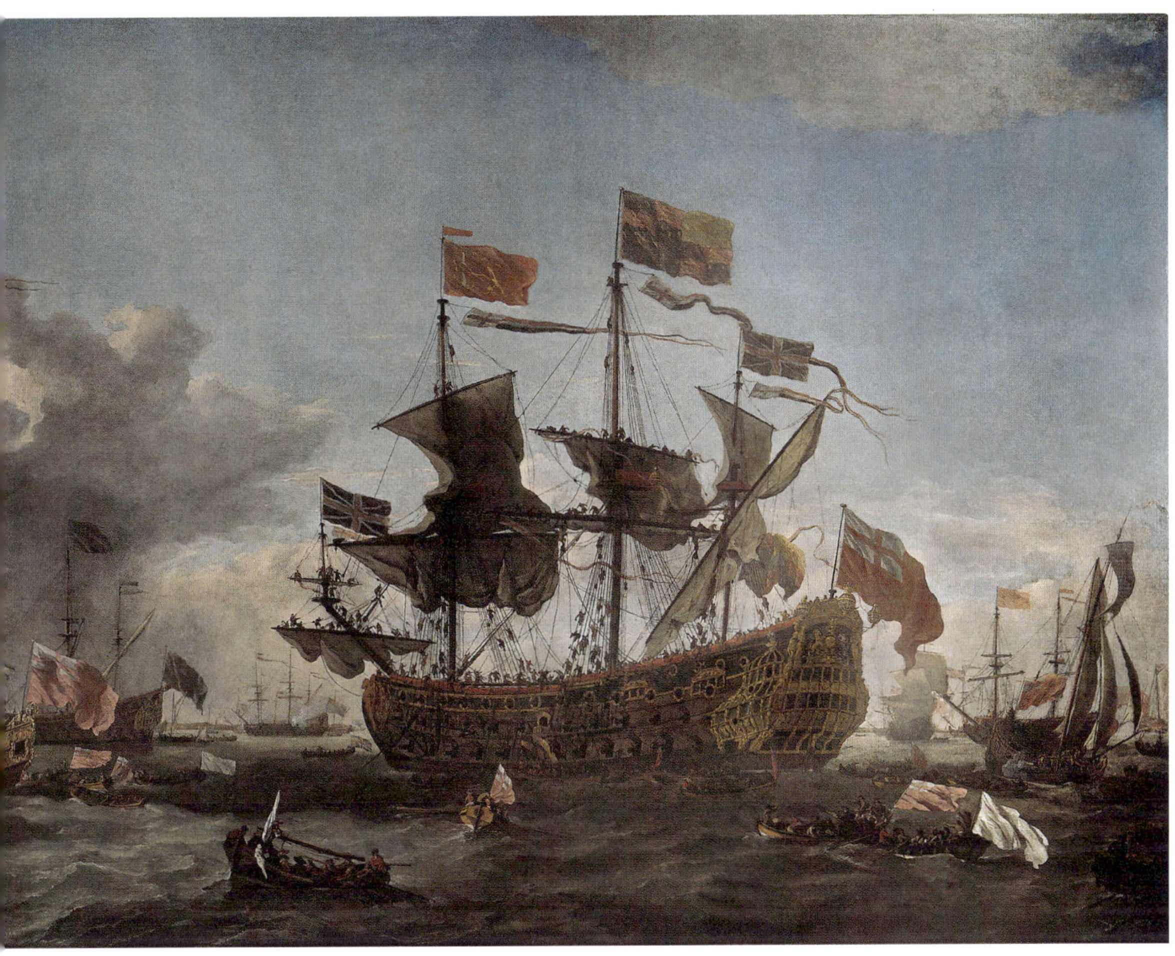

(fig. 1) *A Royal Visit to the Fleet in the Thames Estuary, 6 June 1672*
Willem van de Velde the Younger
1672–96, oil on canvas
1,651 x 3,300 mm
BHC0299

painting highlighted the importance of maritime affairs in this context through its presentation of James as both prince and naval commander. Yet his tenure as Lord High Admiral ended soon after the painting was completed, when the Test Act forced him to resign his office in 1673. This Act required all civil, military and religious officials to swear an oath disavowing key tenets of Catholicism. James refused, outing himself as a practising Catholic and making himself a target for Protestant anger. He survived several attempts to remove him from the line of succession and took the throne following his brother's death in 1685. However, his reign was short-lived, ending when he was overthrown in 1688 and replaced with his Protestant daughter Mary and her Dutch husband, William of Orange (who also had a claim to the throne through his mother).

Admiral George Byng, 1st Viscount Torrington

Godfrey Kneller

1707–09, oil on canvas
1,275 x 1,030 mm
BHC2589

German-born painter Godfrey Kneller trained with some of Europe's leading artists, including Rembrandt in Amsterdam and Bernini in Rome, before arriving in London in 1676. His first paintings after emigrating emulated the vibrant, decorative works of Henri Gascar, the French artist who at that time enjoyed favour among Charles II's courtiers. However, Kneller soon began using more subdued colours and less precise brushstrokes, aligning himself with the artistic tradition of Anthony van Dyck and Peter Lely, painters who – like him – hailed from Continental Europe. After Lely's death in 1680, Kneller succeeded him as principal painter at the royal court. He continued in this role during the joint reign of William III and Mary II and also under the next monarch, Queen Anne.

George Byng, the officer depicted in this portrait, first came to prominence when, as a naval lieutenant, he supported the replacement of James II with William and Mary in 1688. Under Anne, he served with distinction in the Mediterranean. Anne's husband, Prince George of Denmark, commissioned this portrait and 15 others in a series representing the leading naval commanders of the day (figs 1–15). These portraits became known simply as the 'Admirals'. The painting of the series was divided between two artists, Kneller and his Swedish-born rival Michael Dahl. Byng's portrait was one of Kneller's contributions to the series.

England was at war for 11 out of the 12 years of Anne's reign, after she allied with the Austrian Habsburg dynasty against the French Bourbons in the War of the Spanish Succession (1702–13). She was therefore keen to associate her authority with martial prowess. However, as a female monarch, she could not assume military command herself. Instead, she appointed her husband to the position of Lord High Admiral, allowing him to take on command responsibilities on her behalf. This appointment was almost entirely honorary because George's ill-health prevented him from engaging in active service. Nevertheless, in fulfilling the ceremonial aspects of the Lord High Admiral's position, the Prince acted as a royal figurehead for the armed forces. George's decision to commission and display portraits of leading naval commanders further reinforced his persona as a warrior-prince.

The 'Admirals' functioned as a kind of sequel to the 'Flagmen of Lowestoft' (p. 50). There were differences between the two series. Lely's portraits were all painted at the same time and commemorated a specific naval victory in which all the sitters had fought. By contrast, the 'Admirals' series grew in a piecemeal fashion over several years. Its sitters were selected on the merit of their individual achievements, rather than their shared experience. Yet, although the context of its production was not exactly the same, the 'Flagmen' provided an important source of creative inspiration for Dahl and especially for Kneller.

The paintings of the 'Admirals' series follow the basic format of the 'Flagmen'. Shown from the thigh upwards (a view known as three-quarter-length), the sitters stand in coastal settings alongside attributes of their profession, such as batons, swords, telescopes, globes, anchors and cannon. A view of a naval battle appears in the distance, typically framed on one side by rocks or fragments of architecture. Byng, for example, leans against a stone plinth beside a rocky

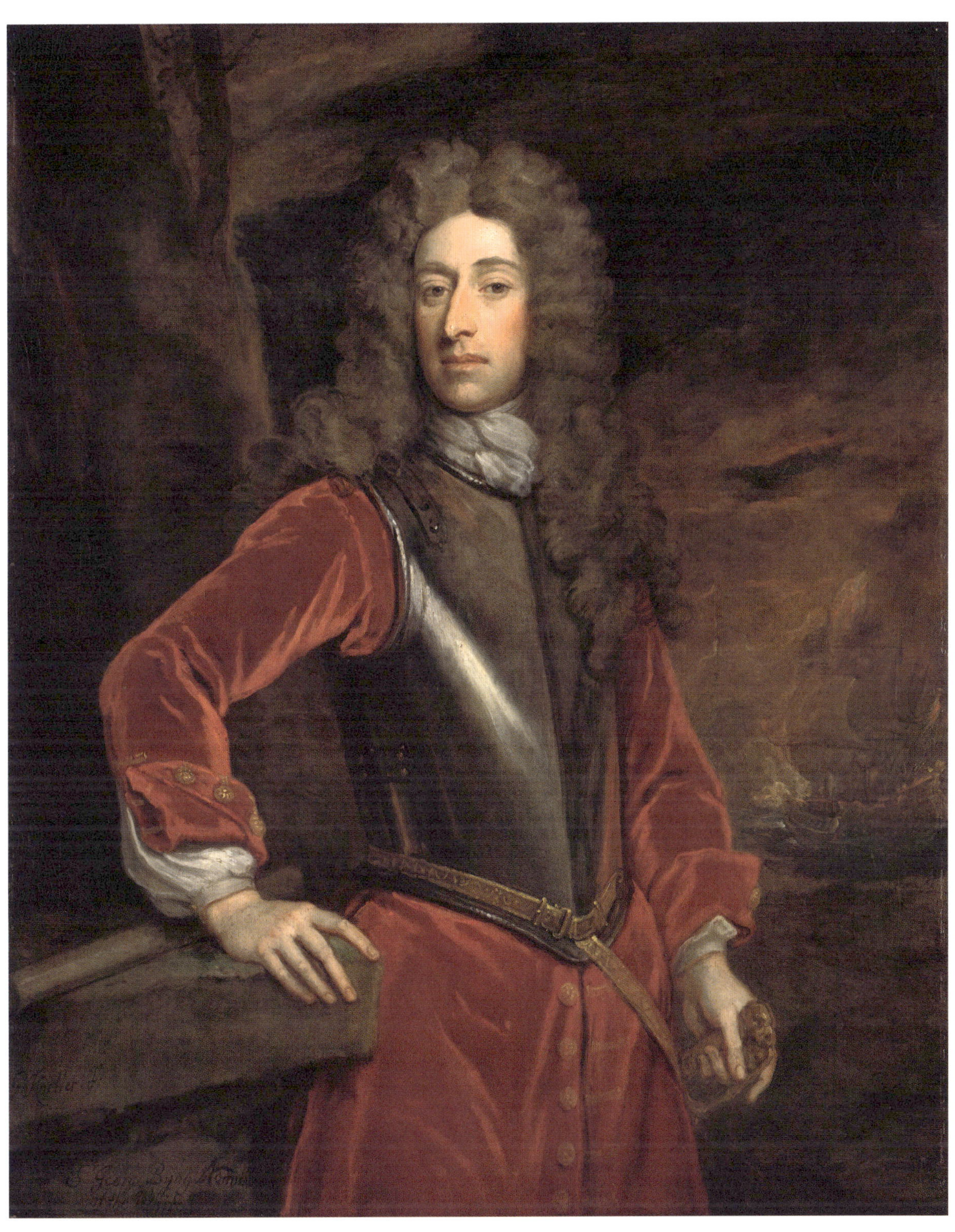

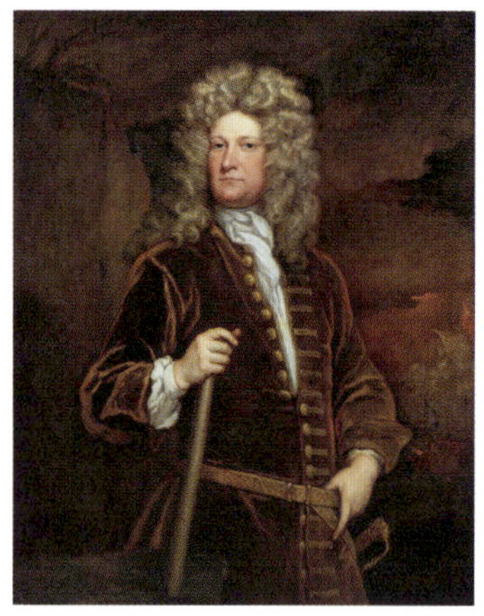

Sir Thomas Dilkes
Godfrey Kneller
1,273 x 1,016 mm
BHC2659

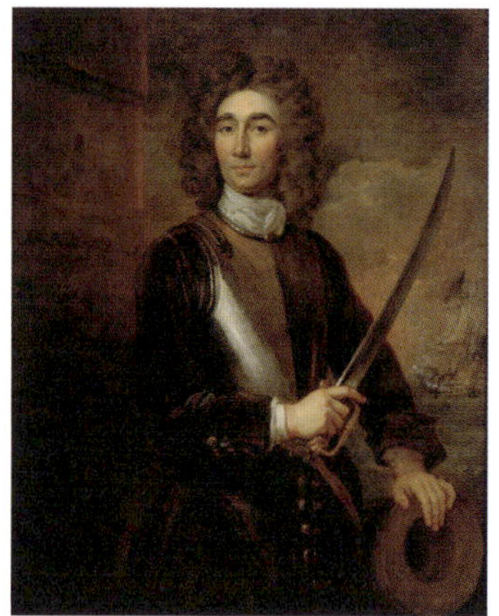

Vice-Admiral John Benbow
Godfrey Kneller
1,270 x 1,015 mm
BHC2546

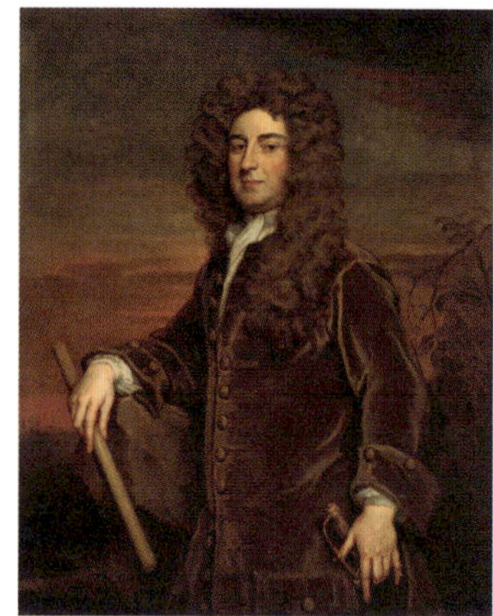

Vice-Admiral John Graydon
Godfrey Kneller
1,265 x 1,016 mm
BHC2723

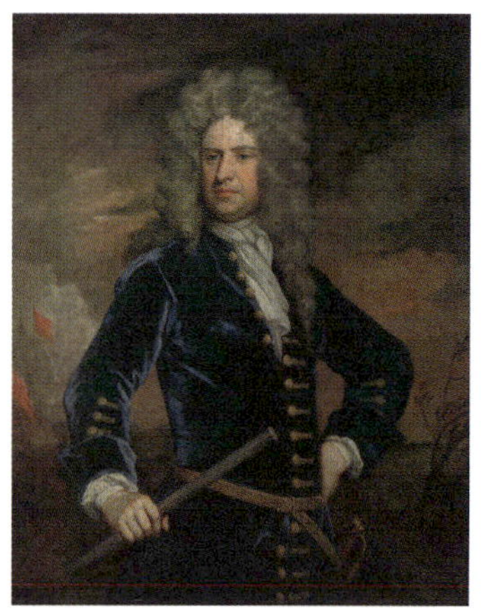

Vice-Admiral Sir Stafford Fairborne
Godfrey Kneller
1,275 x 1,020 mm
BHC2686

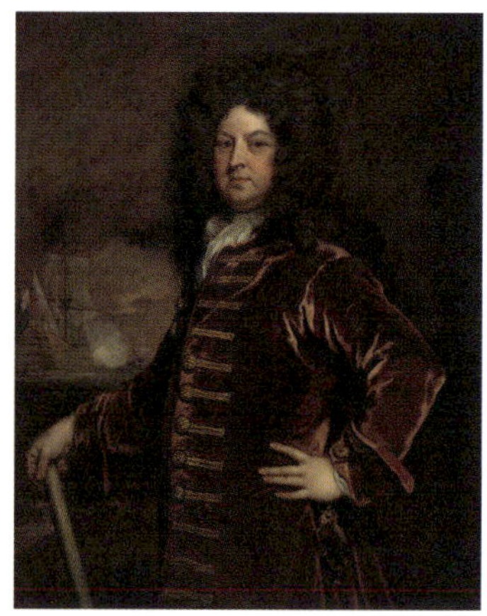

Admiral George Churchill
Godfrey Kneller
1,267 x 1,025 mm
BHC2611

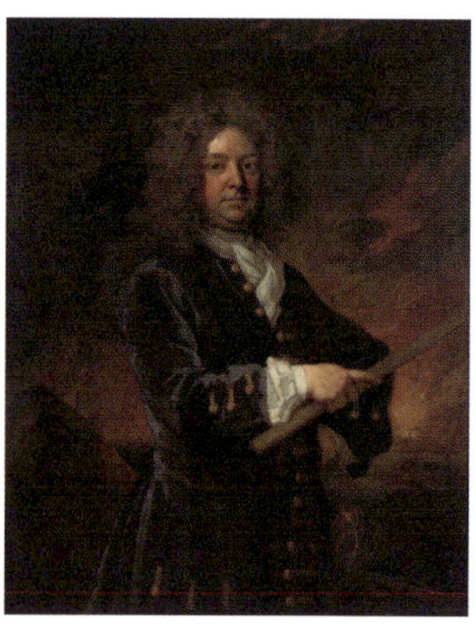

Vice-Admiral Sir John Leake
Godfrey Kneller
1,270 x 1,016 mm
BHC2835

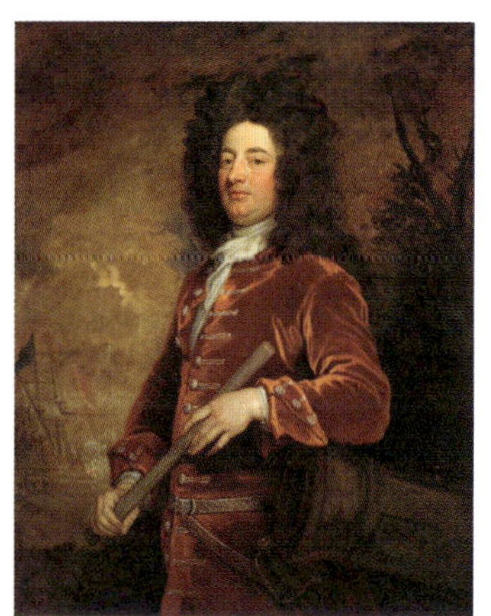

Admiral Sir John Jennings
Godfrey Kneller
1,265 x 1,020 mm
BHC2805

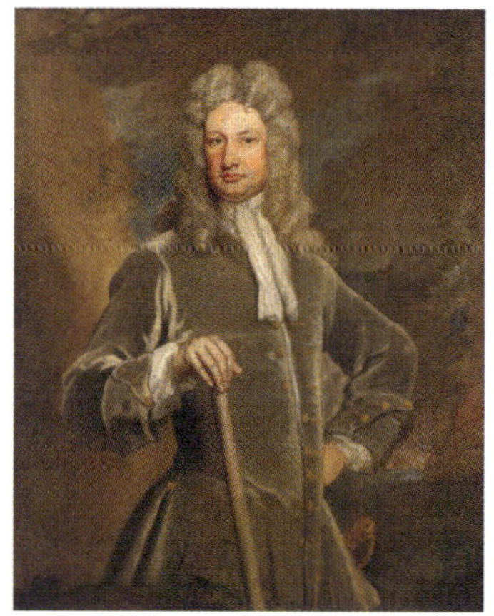

Sir Charles Wager
Godfrey Kneller
1,255 x 1,016 mm
BHC3074

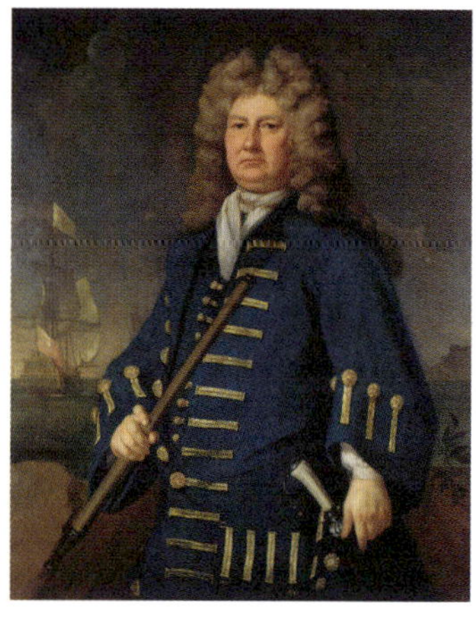

Sir Cloudesley Shovell
Michael Dahl
1,270 x 1,015 mm
BHC3025

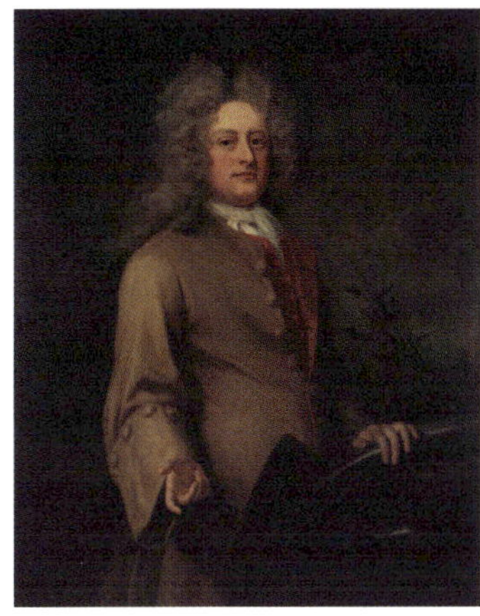

Rear-Admiral Basil Beaumont
Michael Dahl
1,270 x 1,015 mm
BHC2542

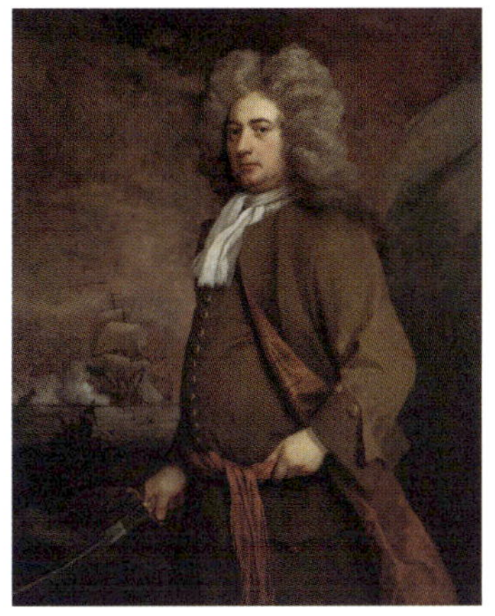

Sir James Wishart
Michael Dahl
1,270 x 1,015 mm
BHC3101

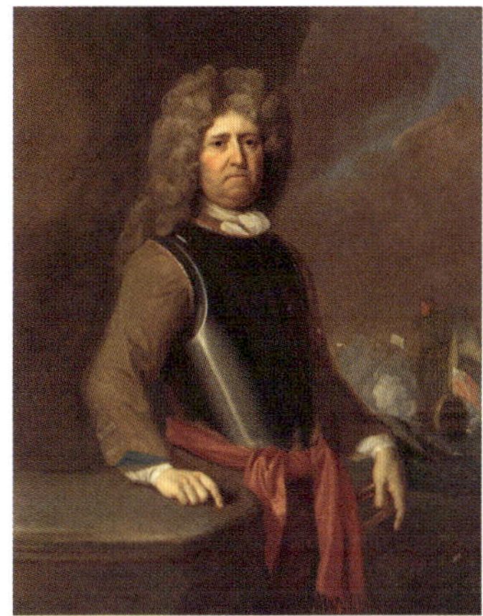

Rear-Admiral Sir John Munden
Michael Dahl
1,270 x 1,015 mm
BHC2873

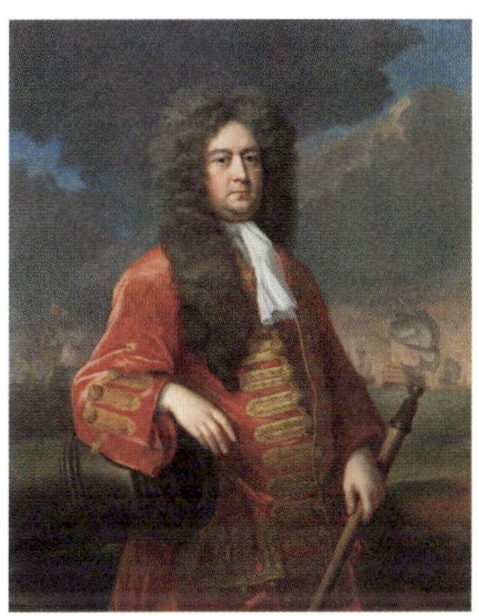

Admiral Sir George Rooke
Michael Dahl
1,245 x 1,016 mm
BHC2978

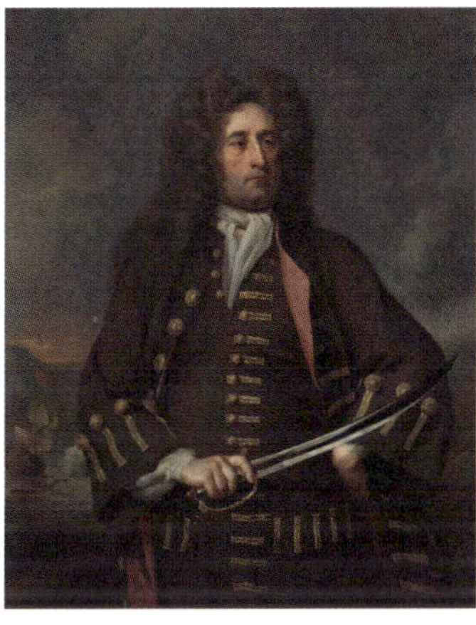

Sir Thomas Hopsonn
Michael Dahl
1,270 x 1,015 mm
BHC2782

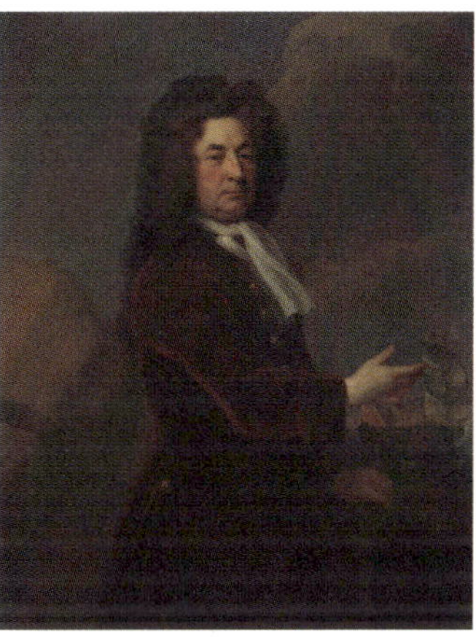

Rear-Admiral Sir William Whetstone
Michael Dahl
1,270 x 1,015 mm
BHC3088

(figs 1–15)
'The Admirals'
Godfrey Kneller and Michael Dahl
1701–10, oil on canvas

outcrop, one hand resting on the hilt of his sword. On the plinth beside him is a baton of command and in the background is a warship and billowing gunsmoke.

It is only in their clothing that the admirals of Anne's reign are distinct from their predecessors. They wear single-breasted, full-skirted velvet coats with wide turned-back cuffs or slit sleeves, a style fashionable in the early eighteenth century. Decorative flourishes are introduced in the form of coloured linings, sashes and, as in Byng's case, patterned buttons and elongated, gold-edged

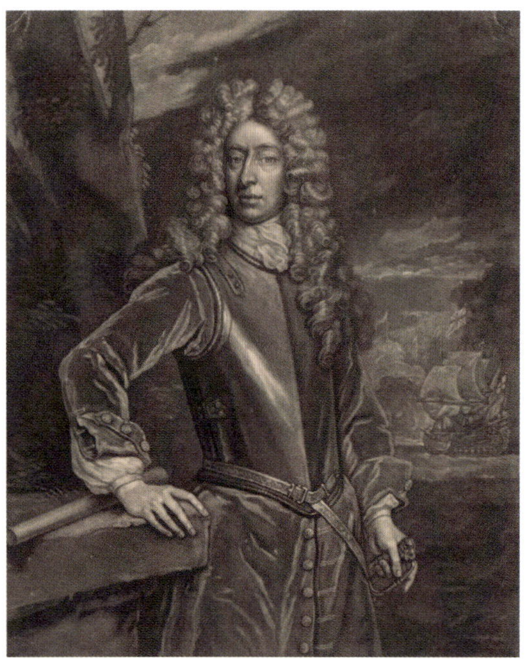

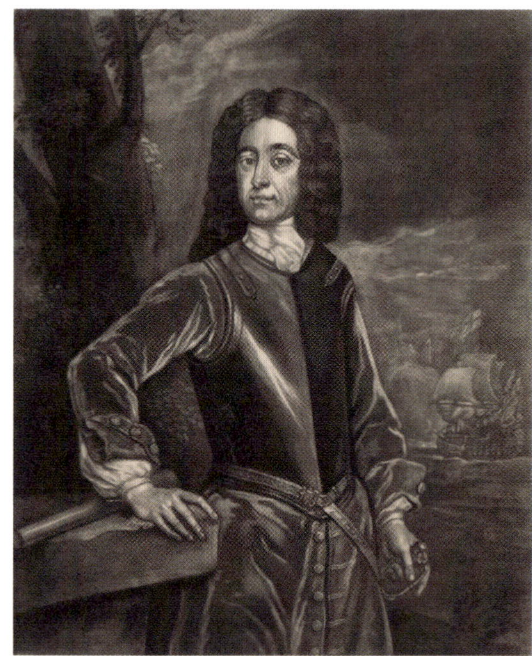

(fig. 16) *The Right Honourable George Byng*
John Faber the Elder after Godfrey Kneller
1718, mezzotint on paper
367 x 263 mm
PAD4610

(fig. 17) *The Honourable Edward Vernon*
John Faber the Elder after Godfrey Kneller with alterations by an unknown artist
about 1740, mezzotint on paper
347 x 252 mm
PAF3396

buttonholes. Byng does, however, wear a metal breastplate, like some of the 'Flagmen' before him, adding to the sense of continuity between the two series of portraits.

The 'Admirals' helped to entrench the conventions of the 'Flagmen of Lowestoft' as a dominant pattern for naval portraiture. This effect is testament to the high profile that the series enjoyed. The portraits were, for example, often mentioned in palace guidebooks and art publications, encouraging artists to follow their example when producing new naval portraits.

Reproductive prints – prints that reproduce other works of art – played a major role in spreading the influence of the 'Admirals'. In the early eighteenth century, there was a growing market for fine art prints, fuelled by economic developments, including the emergence of an affluent middle class, and technological advancements, such as the invention of mezzotint (a new technique that could emulate the subtle shading of an oil painting). A mezzotint was made by roughening a copper plate, then selectively polishing certain areas. The rougher parts would hold more ink and print as dark tones, while the more polished areas would hold less ink and print as light tones.

Portrait prints of well-known public figures were especially successful because they catered to an emerging culture of celebrity. The public wanted to collect images of individuals about whom they had read in the newspapers. This included naval officers, whose achievements frequently featured in the press. A number of the 'Admirals' were therefore translated into print. However, once in the public domain, the portraits took on lives of their own. Byng's portrait provides a case in point. The celebrated printmaker John Faber the Elder published a mezzotint of the painting in 1718 (fig. 16). Twenty-two years later, an anonymous publisher issued an amended version of the print (fig. 17). Byng's body, his clothing, the plinth at his side and the ship in the distance are all unchanged, but his head is entirely new with larger eyes, darker eyebrows and a mid-eighteenth-century bag wig, in place of Byng's old-fashioned full-bottomed one. The pale halo around the head indicates where the copper plate was burnished smooth and re-engraved with this new head. The inscription beneath the image has also been erased and rewritten. According to the new text, the portrait is now intended to represent Vice-Admiral Edward Vernon, not George Byng.

Vernon became a popular hero after his capture of Porto Bello (now in Panama) from the Spanish in November 1739 with a force of only six ships. Porto Bello was the first major action in a conflict between the British and the Spanish over trade in the Americas. The victory prompted mass celebrations in Britain. Poems, ballads, plays, pamphlets, ceramics and prints were produced to commemorate Vernon's achievements, and bonfires, processions and other public festivities were held in his honour. For publishers eager to profit from Vernon's sudden popularity, creating a portrait mezzotint of the Vice-Admiral from a pre-existing plate had obvious advantages, saving valuable time, money and energy. Yet the enterprise would only be worth pursuing if Kneller's 30-year-old portrait could be expected to pass as an image of a contemporary naval officer. The fact that this was felt to be the case demonstrates the extent to which certain conventions for representing the naval profession had become entrenched, thanks in no small part to the 'Admirals' series.

Commodore the Honourable William Kerr

Michael Dahl

about 1706, oil on canvas
1,250 x 1,020 mm
BHC4146

Michael Dahl arrived in England from his native Sweden in 1682. Although he had trained in drawing and painting in his homeland, it was in Godfrey Kneller's studio in London that he learnt the business of professional portraiture. He then finessed his skills with a five-year tour around Continental Europe, taking in Paris, Venice and Rome, before rejoining London's cosmopolitan art scene in 1689. He received commissions from various wealthy patrons and found favour with Queen Anne and her husband, Prince George of Denmark, who – perhaps feeling solidarity with Dahl as a fellow Scandinavian – hired the artist to collaborate with Kneller on the series known as the 'Admirals' (p. 62).

Depicting Scottish naval officer William Kerr, this portrait shares certain features with those in the 'Admirals' series, including a rocky coastal setting and a distant view of a warship. However, it is not one of the grand works that Dahl produced for Prince George. Designed to hang alongside a portrait of the sitter's wife, Catherine (fig. 1), the painting was a private commission intended for domestic rather than courtly display. This may explain the relative informality of Kerr's clothing, compared to the buttoned-up and bewigged decorum that prevails in the 'Admirals'. Kerr eschews a neckcloth, his unbuttoned shirt revealing a sliver of bare skin. Instead of a formal wig, he wears his own brown hair in tumbling waves around his shoulders. This accords with a late seventeenth- and early eighteenth-century fashion for having one's portrait painted in relaxed attire, known as 'undress', especially when the painting was intended to suggest familiarity, friendship or affection.

The ship in the portrait's background has been identified as the *Rupert*, which Kerr commanded on a two-year posting in the West Indies between 1706 and 1708. The palm tree beside Kerr's right elbow may have been included as a specific allusion to his service in the Caribbean. This suggests that the portrait was produced either in anticipation of his departure or in celebration of his return. The former is perhaps more likely, given that his time in the West Indies produced little cause for celebration, the chief incidents having been unsuccessful attacks on Spanish-held Cartagena and Hispaniola (modern-day Cuba). Moreover, it was commonplace for naval officers to have their portraits painted prior to departing for overseas service because this helped their families to remember them in their absence.

Paired portraits, like those of William and Catherine Kerr, were known as pendants. They often depicted married couples. In such cases, artists created distinct identities for husband and wife, which reflected and reinforced the different social expectations placed upon men and women. The Kerrs' portraits exemplify this phenomenon. Dahl emphasised William's naval career in order to associate him with the stereotypically masculine qualities of heroism, duty and public service. As well as the distant ship and coastal backdrop, other clues to William's seafaring profession include the telescope and ring dial (a type of sundial used in navigation) on the rock beside him.

In contrast to the imagery of professional expertise in her husband's portrait, Catherine Kerr is depicted in an attitude of decorous repose, as befits a wealthy wife. She rests one elbow on a carved plinth, which creates an impression of classical elegance. Dahl evoked traditional ideas

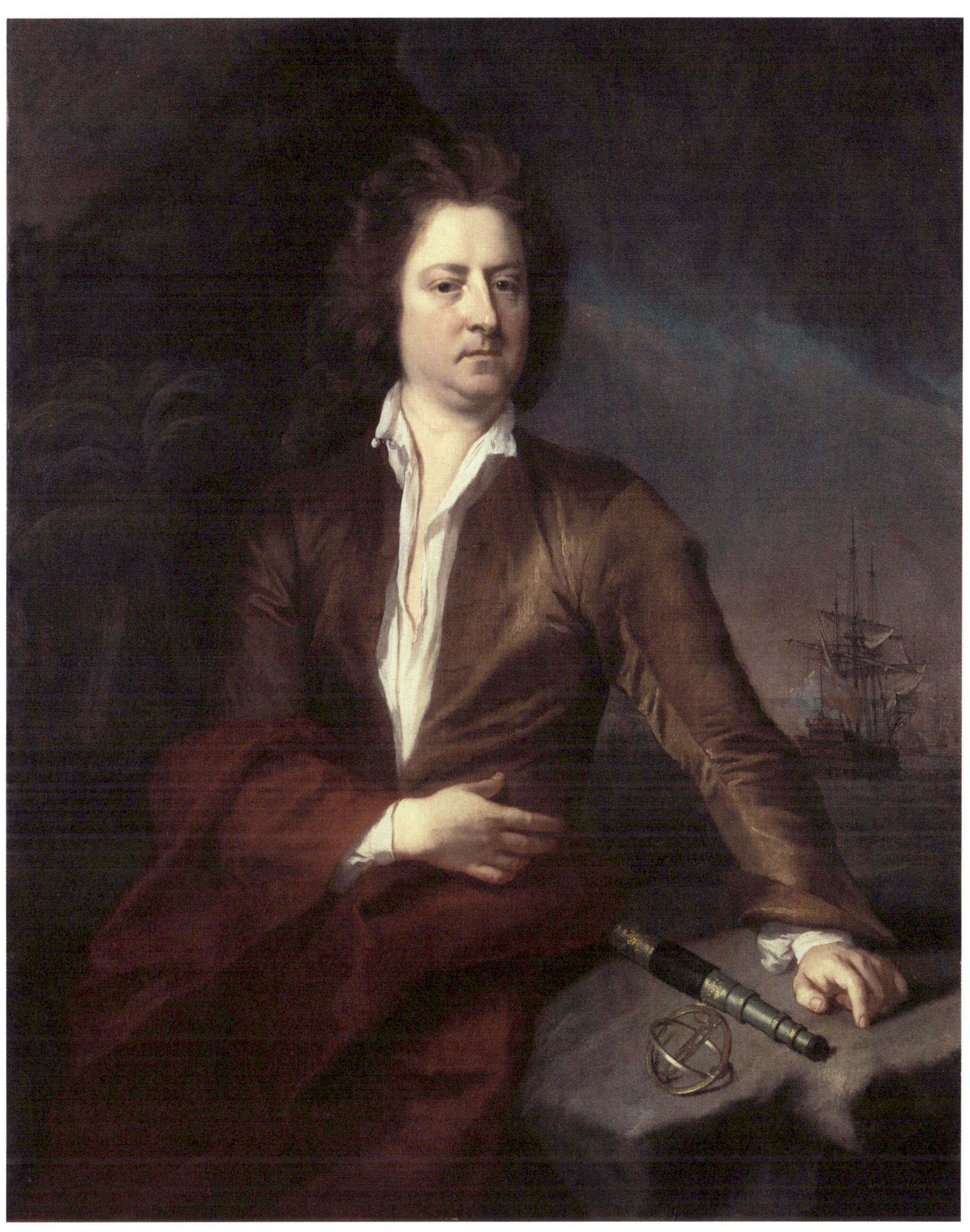

of feminine beauty in the depiction of her low-cut, loose-fitting dress. Long slits in the fabric reveal her white linen shift and pale skin.

Catherine's partial undress mirrored her husband's informal attire, creating continuity between the two portraits. Other details also ensure that the paintings look like a matching pair, in spite of their traditionally gendered differences. Both sitters wear shades of brown and red, for example, and turn their heads in opposite directions such that, when William's portrait is hung on the left and Catherine's on the right, they appear to be leaning towards each other. It was traditional for marital pendants to be displayed in this configuration, since it placed the woman on the man's sinister side (his left, the viewer's right), conforming to patriarchal assumptions about masculine superiority at a time when theological and social formulas characterised the left-hand position as inferior to the right.

However, the conventional representation of gender in the Kerrs' portraits belies the unconventional nature of their relationship. William Kerr and Catherine Dod married in London at Christ Church, Newgate Street, on 5 February 1694. Neither appears to have been married before, which is surprising given that Catherine was 38 years old at the time of the wedding. By the standards of the day, this was unusually late in life for a woman to be entering into her first marriage. The daughter of a wealthy landowning family, she was baptised on 26 June 1656 at the Church of St Peter and Paul, Aston, Warwickshire. William's date of birth is uncertain, but he was probably around a decade younger than his wife. They may have met through Catherine's younger sister, Mary, whose husband David Mitchell was also a naval officer.

As mentioned, William Kerr's portrait can be dated to around 1706 because the ship and the palm tree allude to his departure for the West Indies that year. Catherine would have been 50 years old at this time, but she appears much younger in her portrait. This suggests two possibilities. The first and most probable is that Dahl painted both portraits at the same time and made Catherine look younger than she was, reflecting the importance of youthfulness within female beauty standards of the day and ensuring that there could be no ambiguity about the power dynamics within the Kerrs' relationship: whatever the reality may have been, Dahl's portraits present a conventional image of a younger wife deferring to her middle-aged husband. The other possibility is that Dahl painted Catherine at an earlier date before being rehired to paint a matching portrait of her husband in 1706. This seems less likely because the close correspondence between the two paintings suggests they were conceived as a pair.

The Kerrs' marriage brought no children but considerable wealth. Less than six months after their wedding, the couple inherited a fortune when Catherine's brother was murdered at the White Horse pub on Fetter Lane in London on 27 July 1694. Her husband died in 1724 but she lived for another 27 years as a wealthy widow, before her death aged 92. Her story provides a useful example of how portraiture can skew our perceptions of history. If we took Dahl's paintings at face value, we would think of Catherine Kerr only as the beautiful young wife of a naval officer. Overall, she spent less than a third of her long life as a wife, but Dahl's pendant portraits invite us to see her only through the lens of her marriage.

A postscript on the fates of the two portraits is relevant here. After hanging together for more than 250 years, the paintings appeared in a country house sale in 1982. At this sale, the National Maritime Museum purchased William's portrait, declaring that the painting 'could be hung in the Navigation Gallery where it could be seen to link an officer and his instruments'. The Museum did not, however, bid on Catherine's portrait. This was not because of any specific prohibition against collecting women's images but rather because their stories were seen as less relevant to the technical, and implicitly masculine, version of naval history that the Museum had traditionally prioritised.

Different attitudes now prevail. New acquisitions and displays highlight the roles that women played in naval communities and explore the personal as well as the professional lives of naval men. In this light, William Kerr's portrait is recognised as representing him not only as a naval officer but also as a husband. Furthermore,

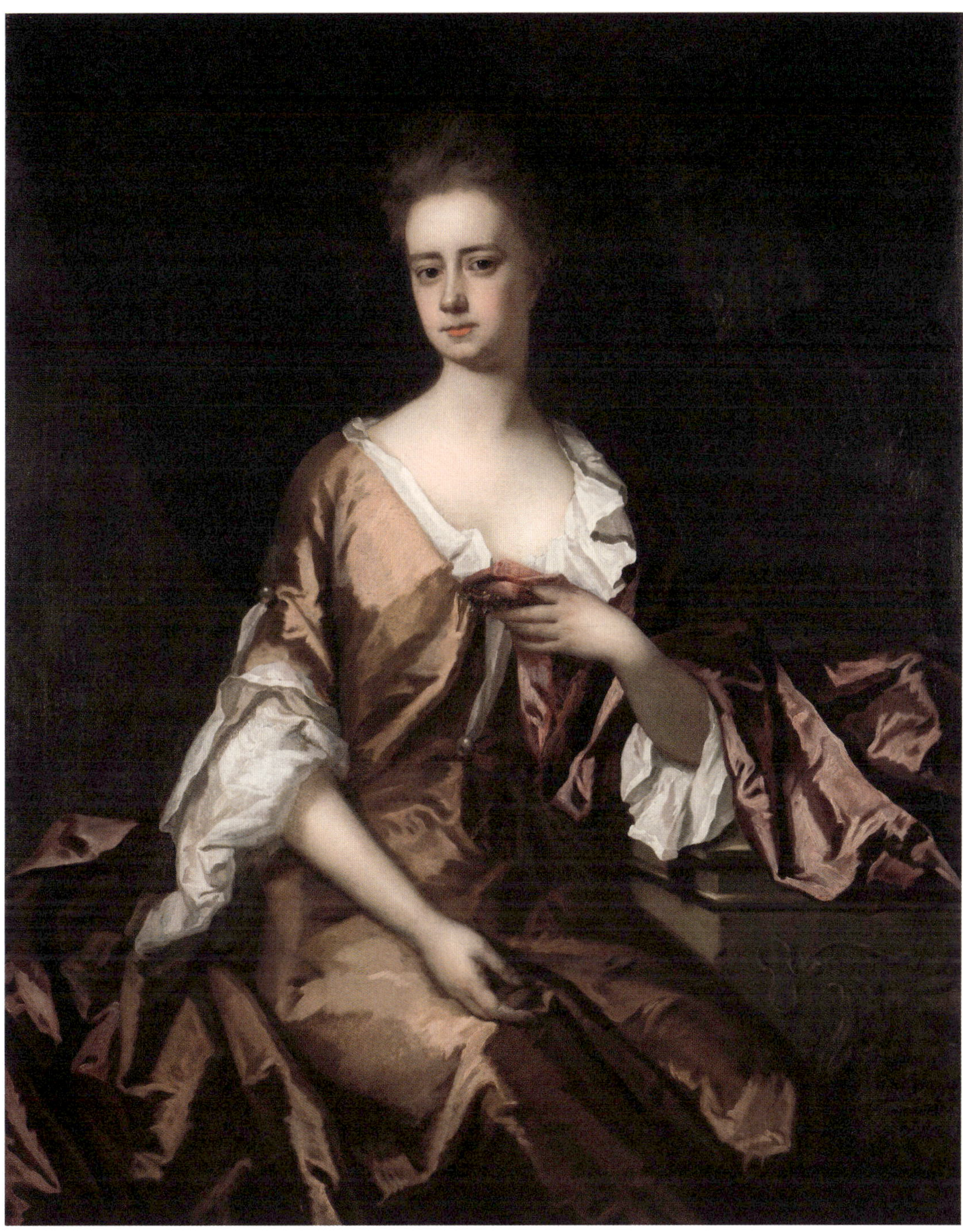

(fig. 1) *Catherine Kerr (née Dod)*
Michael Dahl
about 1706, oil on canvas
1,250 x 1,020 mm
ZBA9230

the Museum was able to acquire Catherine Kerr's portrait at a private sale in October 2019, allowing the two paintings to be seen together once again – as the artist originally intended.

Admiral Thomas Mathews

Claude Arnulphy

1743, oil on canvas
1,270 x 1,015 mm
BHC2855

The French painter Claude Arnulphy was born and raised in Paris, trained in Rome and spent his career working in Aix-en-Provence in the south of France. He never visited Britain but did paint the portraits of several British naval officers in the early 1740s. These portraits provide a fascinating example of artistic production across enemy lines at a time of conflict. The officers in question were serving in the Royal Navy's Mediterranean fleet, which was then blockading French and Spanish warships at the port of Toulon, not far from Aix. Britain and Spain had been at war since 1739 and, though the French did not officially enter the conflict until October 1743, they were offering protection to the Spanish navy for several years before that date.

This portrait depicts Admiral Thomas Mathews, the commander-in-chief of the British fleet. From his arrival in the Mediterranean in June 1742 until the Franco-Spanish fleet left port in February 1744, his squadron moved very little, anchoring for months on end in Hyeres Bay. This monotonous service proved exhausting for the British officers and their crews. Mathews himself wrote to the Admiralty complaining of ill-health and begging for leave, which was not granted. His relationship with his second-in-command, Richard Lestock, became fractious, ultimately leading to the humiliating defeat of their fleet at the end of the blockade.

Yet, despite the professional strain that he was under, Mathews found time during this period to sit for his portrait. The commission may have arisen as a result of his diplomatic duties. Throughout the blockade, he corresponded with French dignitaries, even entertaining some of them on board his flagship. One of his French correspondents was Honoré Armand de Villars, the Governor of Provence, a keen patron of the arts with whom Arnulphy also had dealings. It may have been the Governor or another local official who put Mathews and Arnulphy in touch.

Given that Mathews was never far from his ship during the blockade, Arnulphy must have travelled to the coast to complete the studies for the Admiral's likeness. Indeed, the sittings probably took place inside Mathews's cabin. The background of the portrait represents the British fleet at anchor in Hyeres Bay with Mathews's flagship on the extreme left, flying a red flag at the fore to indicate his rank, Vice-Admiral of the Red. This flag demonstrates that the portrait was produced before October 1743, when Mathews was promoted to Admiral of the Blue. The level of detail suggests that Arnulphy spent considerable time studying the fleet. While Arnulphy was with the fleet, several other officers availed themselves of his services, including Captains Henry Osborn and Arthur Scott (figs 1 and 2). There is only buff-coloured underpaint where Osborn's left hand should be, suggesting that Arnulphy did not have time to finish the portrait before the blockade ended in February 1744.

Even though their nations were on the brink of war, neither the French artist nor the British officers would have seen these portrait commissions as representing a conflict of interest. For his part, Arnulphy was making the most of a lucrative commercial opportunity, the British fleet providing him with a captive audience of potential patrons, all of them desperate for relief from the boredom of blockade duty. Mathews, meanwhile, may have seen employing Arnulphy as a gesture of goodwill towards the local community, which could bolster his diplomatic efforts.

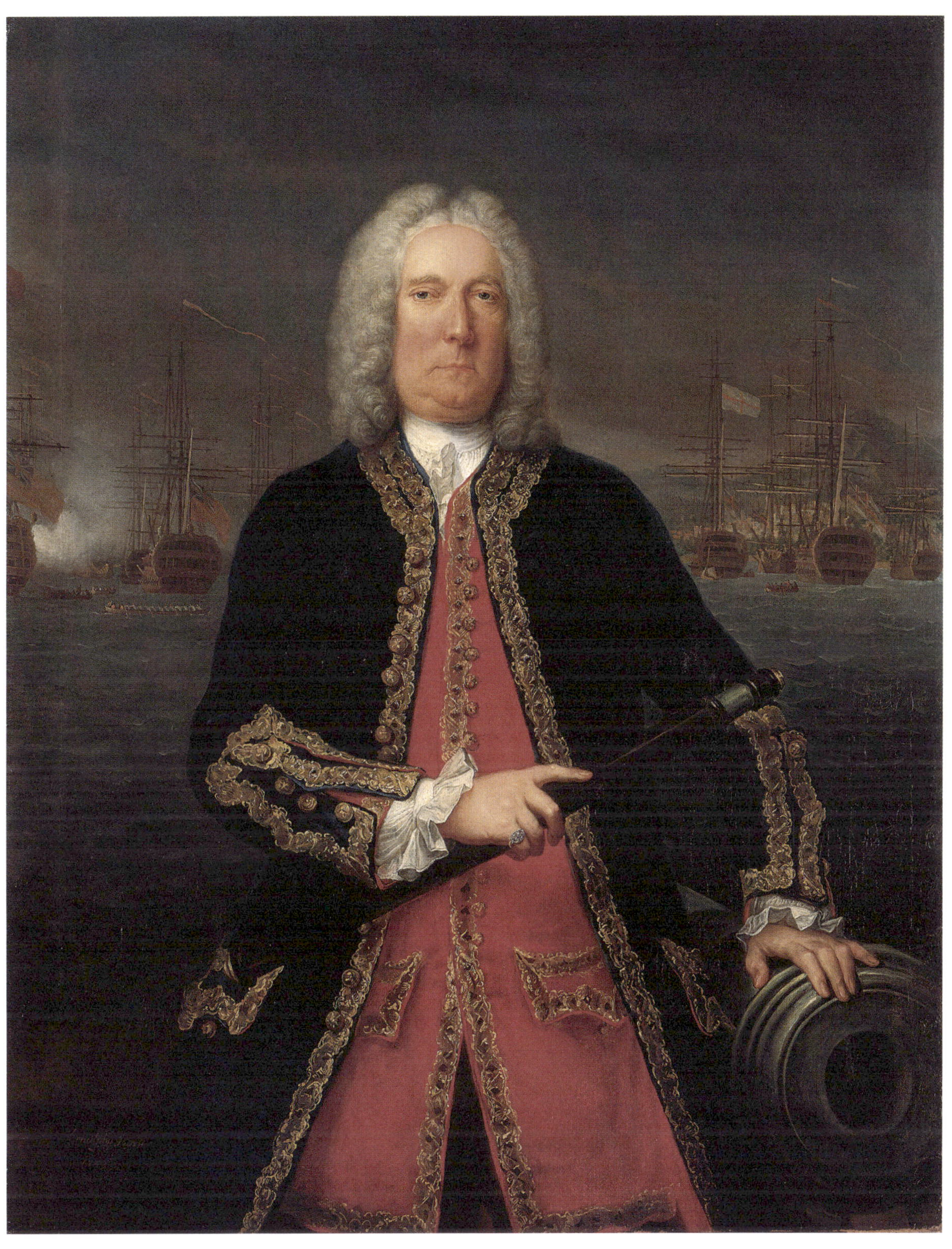

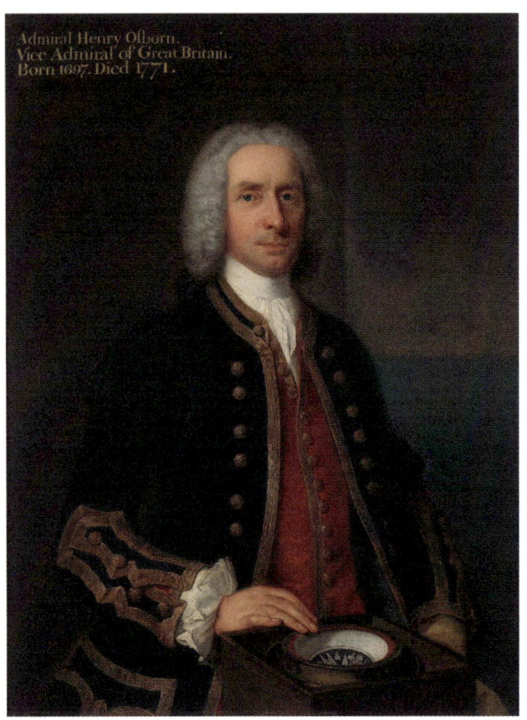

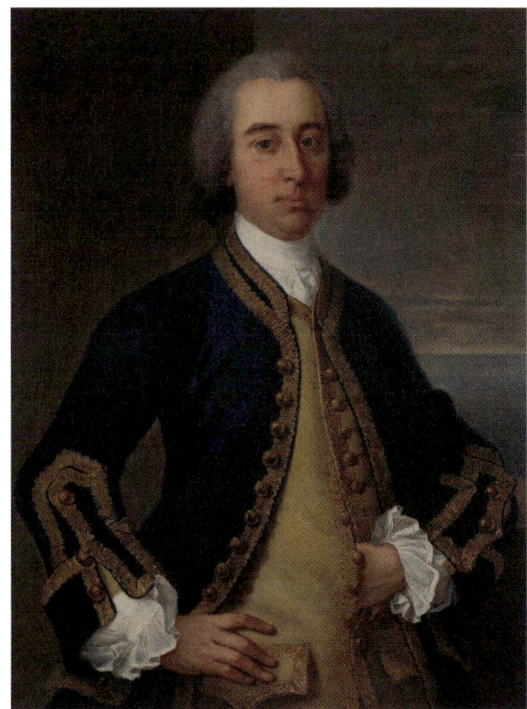

(fig. 1) *Captain Henry Osborn*
Claude Arnulphy
1743–44, oil on canvas
915 x 710 mm
BHC2925

Right: (fig. 2) *Captain Arthur Scott*
Claude Arnulphy
1744, oil on canvas
915 x 710 mm
BHC3017

At the same time, the Admiral and his officers were acting in their own self-interest and acquiring fashionable artworks for their personal collections. With foreign artists still dominating the London art world, as they had done for centuries, French painting exercised a profound influence over British tastes in the early 1740s. Arnulphy himself never visited Britain, one of his closest rivals, Jean-Baptiste van Loo, had been the most sought-after portraitist in London between 1739 and 1742. Prior to this, Van Loo and Arnulphy had been the two dominant painters in the south of France having previously trained with the same artist in Rome, Benedetto Luti. Van Loo retired from painting due to ill-health in 1742 but Arnulphy represented the next best thing for Mathews's officers: in Britain, his portraits would epitomise the height of good taste.

Mathews's portrait is larger than those of Osborn and Scott. The relative grandeur of the Admiral's portrait signals his superior rank (and perhaps also his greater financial resources), relative to his juniors. Arnulphy shows Mathews leaning against a cannon and holding a telescope, drawing from a standard repertoire of nautical props which had become part of the common visual language of European portraiture at this date.

While Mathews's attributes reflect transnational artistic conventions, other aspects of the portrait reveal its French origins. The precise brushwork and the wealth of decorative detail exhibit the fussiness that, at this time, differentiated French art from that of Northern Europe, where plainer, less polished styles were favoured. Mathews's clothing is the chief source of decoration in the painting. His blue coat and long-sleeved red waistcoat are edged with frilly gold lace and peppered with patterned gold buttons, while a diamond ring winks on his little finger. The portrait predates the introduction of official British naval uniform in April 1748, but Mathews's elegant attire communicates his status as a refined gentleman. More intriguingly, his clothing also resembles French naval uniform of the time, the core components of which were a blue coat and red waistcoat, both adorned with gold lace. This similarity cannot be accidental. Arnulphy may have defaulted to the costume that he, as a Frenchman, associated with naval service, but Mathews must have approved this creative decision. He was not alone in doing so: Osborn also wears a blue coat and red waistcoat in his portrait.

Mathews and Osborn would not be the only naval officers of their generation to envy the smart uniforms of their French counterparts. In 1746, the Navy Club – an association of officers who met at Will's Coffee-House in Scotland Yard – presented an address to the Admiralty asserting that 'it is the opinion of 30 Captains who are in Town [London] ... that an Uniform Dress is useful and necessary for the Commissioned Officers, agreeable to the practice of other Nations'. The reference here to 'other Nations' alluded primarily to Britain's age-old rival, France. The Admiralty's decision to introduce British naval uniform responded to this demand from officers for official clothing that signalled their membership of an international officer class and aligned the practices of the Royal Navy with those of the French.

Arnulphy's portraits reveal the complexity of Anglo-French relations in the 1740s. On the one hand, the paintings were themselves products of the escalating political tensions between the two nations, which brought Mathews's fleet to the south of France on blockade. At the same time, the fact that the Admiral and his officers commissioned portraits from a French artist and even appeared in clothing that approximated French naval uniform reveals the influence of Francophile sensibilities on British culture and fashion at this time. However, tastes in Britain were beginning to change as a new generation of home-grown artistic talent came to prominence, headed by William Hogarth.

Captain Lord George Graham in his Cabin

William Hogarth

1742–44, oil on canvas
685 x 889 mm
BHC2720

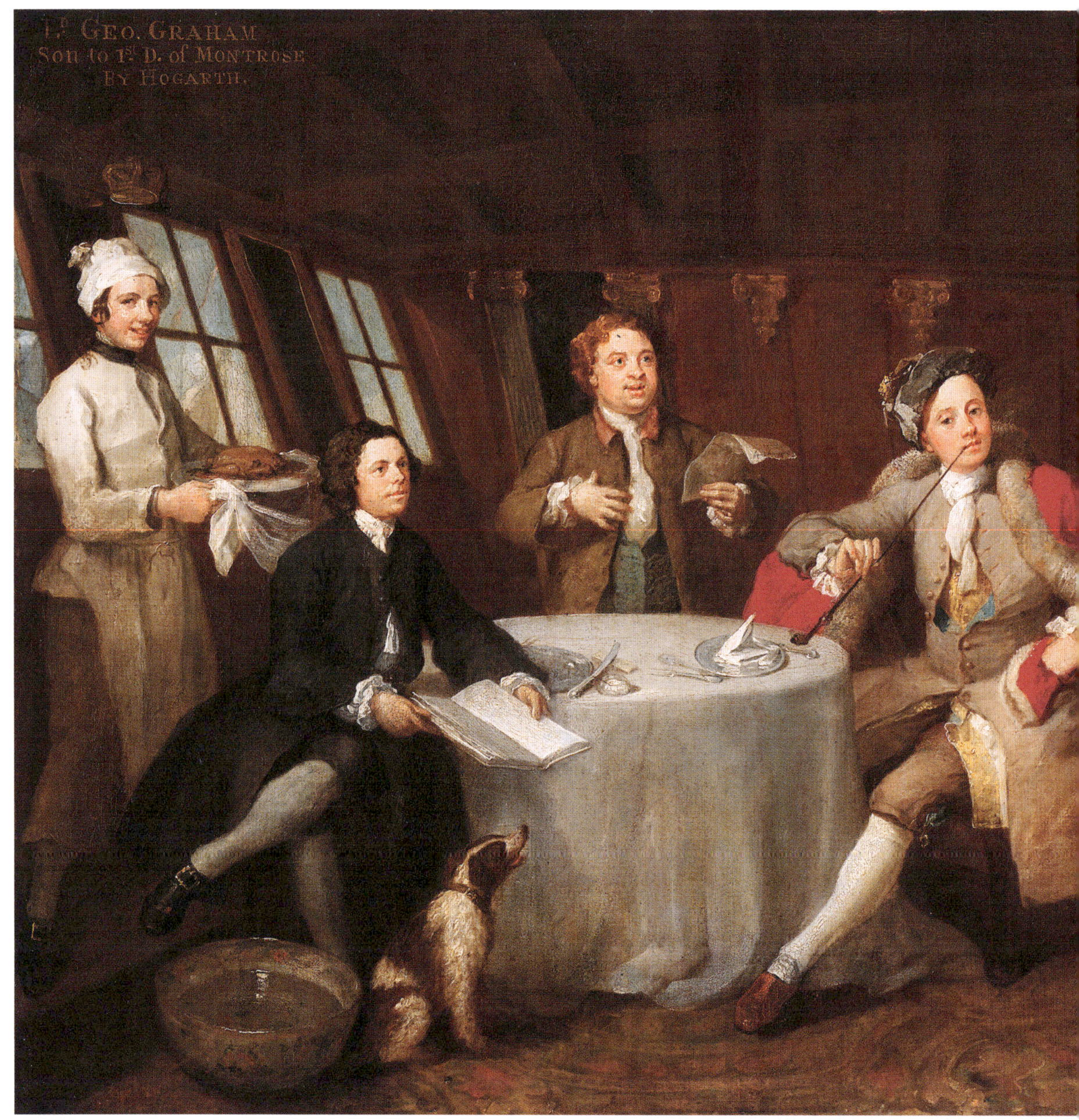

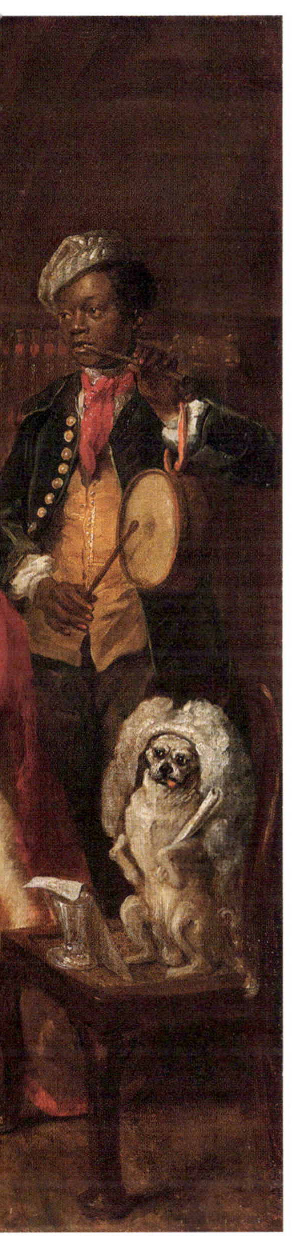

William Hogarth is often regarded as one of the founding fathers of British painting. Not only did the London-born artist enjoy success at a time when foreign painters dominated the British market, he also established the influential St Martin's Lane Academy in 1735, providing artists and designers with an opportunity to attend life-drawing classes in London. This compensated for the lack of academic art education available in Britain during this period and acted as a precursor to the Royal Academy of Arts, which was established 33 years later.

Back in the 1710s, Hogarth's own training had consisted of an apprenticeship with a silversmith, after which he began engraving satirical prints. He gained a reputation as an irreverent observer of vice and corruption in London life, from the drawing rooms of high society to lowly drinking dens. Unlikely as it may seem, these bawdy graphic satires were his launchpad for a career as a polite portrait painter. In the 1730s, he became a leading producer of group portraits in which the wealthy sitters – typically families or gatherings of male friends – were shown engaging in convivial activity. Known as conversation pieces, these paintings enjoyed a vogue during the second quarter of the eighteenth century, their imagery of good-mannered and affable interaction providing the perfect visual outlet for a culture in which polished social skills were regarded as a marker of status. Numerous artists produced conversation pieces, but Hogarth's were the most sophisticated, incorporating humour, narrative and moral messages. The playfulness of his portraits recalled his satirical work, only now he was flattering, rather than critiquing, his subjects.

Painted in the early 1740s, this is one of Hogarth's most complex conversation pieces. Its precise meaning has long mystified art historians. Set in the cabin of a warship, the portrait shows Captain Lord George Graham, an aristocratic naval officer, sitting at a table with a long pipe in his hand. Graham appears to have commissioned the portrait and he later left it to his brother in his will. The Captain had once been something of a man-about-town and was arrested at a brothel in July 1742. However, when this portrait was painted, he was courting Lady Mary Forbes, daughter of Admiral John Forbes, to whom he was subsequently betrothed. It was perhaps intended to emphasise his suitability as a wealthy and respectable marriage prospect.

In the portrait, his attire is luxurious but informal, a fur-lined robe hangs around his shoulders and a velvet cap covers his wigless pate. The table is set for two with plates, cutlery, napkins and a small pot of salt. A porcelain punchbowl rests on the floor at the feet of Graham's dining companion, who holds open a large volume, perhaps a naval logbook. Soberly dressed in a black suit, this figure has been identified as the Scottish poet David Mallet, who had tutored Graham and his elder brother during their adolescence and remained a trusted adviser of the Captain in later life.

An apron-wearing cook stands behind Mallet with a roast fowl, gravy spilling over the edge of the dish. It looks at first glance as if the hot liquid is about to drip down the unsuspecting poet's back, but closer inspection reveals that the cook has a napkin in place to catch the drips. Typifying the gentle humour for which Hogarth's conversation pieces were famed, this detail teases the viewer with the illusion of imminent disaster in order to emphasise the refinement and decorum of the scene.

The touch of humour complements other light-hearted elements within the painting, including the two performers who provide musical entertainment. Behind the table, a singer is giving a hearty rendition of a song called 'Arragh my Judy', the title being written on the sheet music in his hand. The Irish singer Michael Stoppelaer performed a song of this name at Covent Garden in May 1741 and again at Masonic lodges in May and June the following year. Since both Hogarth and Graham were Masons, a reference to Stoppelaer's performances may be intended. Accompanying the singer is a Black drummer playing the pipe and tabor. The identity of this figure is not recorded but he has more individuality and dignity than was often accorded to Black people in eighteenth-century British artworks. Against the background of the Transatlantic Slave Trade, racialised stereotypes were commonplace in European art and culture at this time. Hogarth's own satirical engravings sometimes included heavily caricatured depictions of Black servants and enslaved people, making his decision to depict the humanity of the drummer in this portrait all the more striking.

Two dogs also participate in the scene. A spaniel, perhaps belonging to Graham, sits on the floor, its mouth opened as if to add its own howls and barks to the singing. Meanwhile, at the drummer's feet is a pug dressed in Graham's discarded wig. Standing on his hind legs atop a chair, he pretends to conduct the human performers and his fellow hound. A drinking glass serves as his music stand and a rolled paper is tucked beneath his foreleg in lieu of a baton. Hogarth kept pet pugs throughout his life, the most famous being one called Trump, whom the artist often included in his work as a proxy for himself. Trump may well have been the model for the bewigged pug depicted here, whose pantomime conducting symbolises both Hogarth's role as the orchestrator of the painting and also his refusal to take the business of portraiture too seriously.

On one level, this complex painting is, like most conversation pieces, about wealth and status. The depiction of social occasions, such as tea parties, card games and convivial dinners, provided artists with a pretext for showing off their sitters' exquisite homes and possessions under the guise of celebrating their politeness and sociability. In Graham's cabin, the patterned carpet, the Chinese porcelain punchbowl, the gilt-framed mirrors between the windows and the shelves of leather-bound books in the background all testify to his wealth. These features were not standard fixtures in an officer's cabin, but anecdotal records show that prosperous captains did sometimes furnish their shipboard accommodation in lavish style. Captain Richard Tiddeman, for instance, filled his cabin in the *Eltham* with mahogany furniture, two tea chests, four chests of clothes and china, a large quantity of silverware, a looking glass in a gilt frame and six prints of the royal family in 1750. In this portrait, however, the elegant environs may be the artist's invention, rather than an accurate representation of the Captain's cabin, because Hogarth needed to create a refined setting that befitted his sitter's elevated social rank.

The choice of a cabin as the portrait's setting referred on an obvious level to Graham's profession as a naval officer. However, it appears that Hogarth also took inspiration from an earlier painting, Bartolomeo Nazari's *Gustavus Hamilton, 2nd Viscount Boyne, and Friends in a Ship's Cabin*. Painted in the early 1730s, the painting was reputedly so popular that over 30

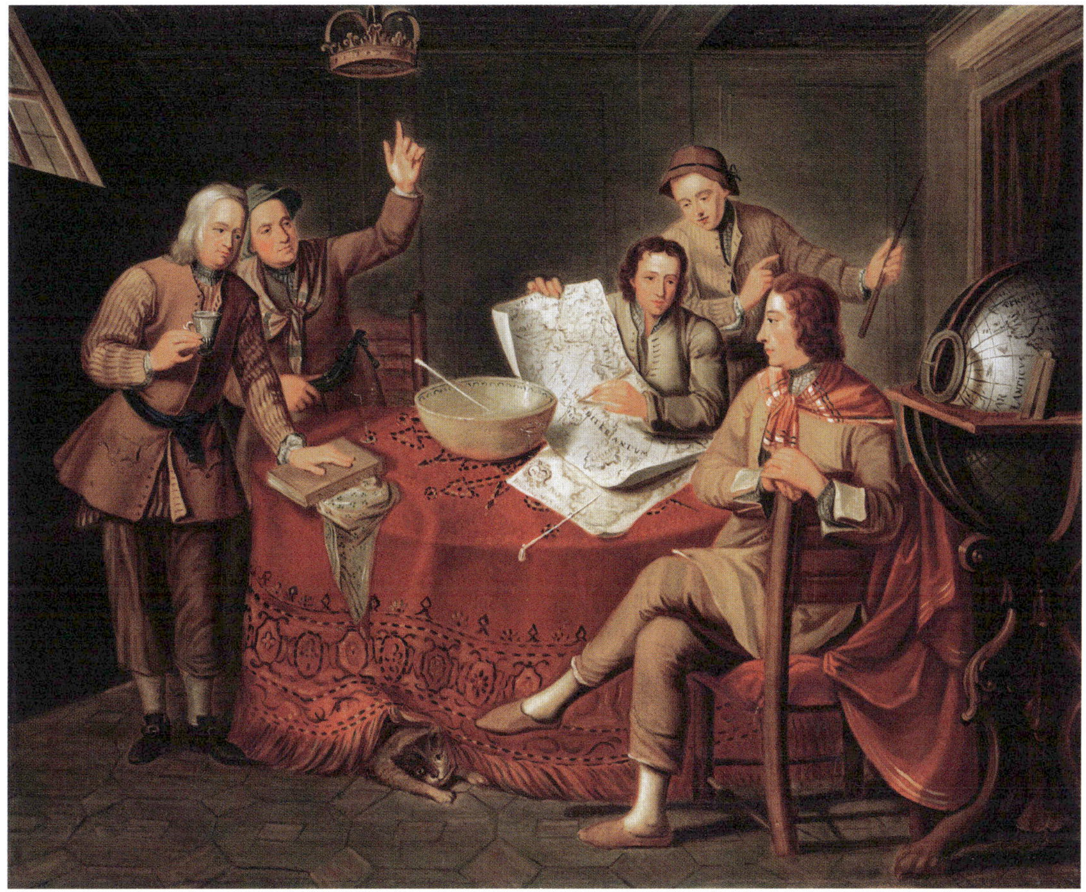

(fig. 1) *Gustavus Hamilton, 2nd Viscount Boyne, and Friends in a Ship's Cabin*
Unknown artist after Bartolomeo Nazari
1731–32, oil on canvas
660 x 815 mm
BHC2567

copies were made, one of which now features in the National Maritime Museum collection (fig. 1). Like Hogarth's painting, Nazari's shows a young aristocrat (Viscount Boyne) seated at a table in a ship's cabin, a red cloak around his shoulders. He is surrounded with male companions and attendants. The scene includes a porcelain punchbowl, a long pipe and a crown compass hanging from the ceiling, details which would later appear in *Captain Lord George Graham in his Cabin*. There is even an animal interloper, the cat peeping out from under the tablecloth, anticipating Hogarth's playful canines. These correspondences seem too many to be coincidental, suggesting that Hogarth designed his picture in homage to Nazari's well-known work.

In the earlier painting, though, the shipboard setting alluded to leisure travel, rather than naval service. Produced in Venice, it commemorated the grand tour that Viscount Boyne undertook between 1731 and 1732. The term 'grand tour' described an extended journey around Europe, which combined educational activities, such as the study of classical texts and ancient ruins, with more pleasurable pursuits, like drinking and carousing. Such journeys served as a rite of passage for young noblemen in the eighteenth century, giving rise to a powerful association between travel and privilege. Prior to embarking on his naval career, Lord George Graham had completed his own grand tour together with his older brother, to whom he later bequeathed Hogarth's painting, and his tutor, David Mallet, who features in the portrait. Seen in this light, it seems possible that the picture was intended to evoke memories of the trio's European travels.

According to art historian Elizabeth Einberg, Hogarth's painting may have also carried further personal significance for Graham and his friends. Einberg has theorised that the portrait is about the captain's health as much as his wealth. In June 1741, Graham had returned exhausted and unwell after convoying merchant ships to Turkey and back. He was immediately redeployed to the Kent coast. This new posting exacerbated his illness, which he described as scurvy. At the same time, he was also under considerable emotional strain owing to both professional difficulties with the Admiralty and also the illness and death of his father. Graham ultimately resigned his command and spent three years ashore recovering his physical and mental health before resuming his naval career in 1745. Hogarth's painting appears to have been made towards the end of his extended leave of absence.

(fig. 2) *A Midnight Modern Conversation*
William Hogarth
1733, etching and engraving on paper
383 x 521 mm
The Metropolitan Museum of Art, New York, Gift of Sarah Lazarus, 1891 (91.1.77)

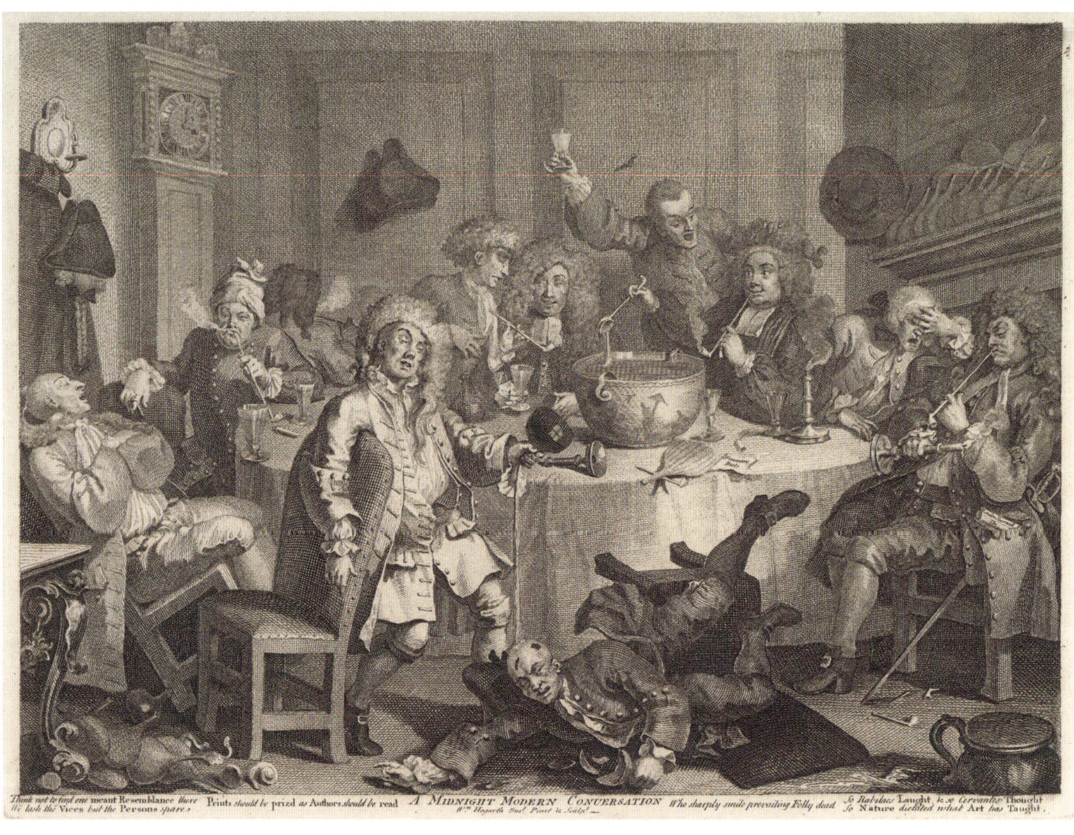

When Graham went ashore, he declared his intention to 'take the waters' at the fashionable spa in Cheltenham. Although it is not recorded whether he acted on this intention, his interest in healing waters offers a tantalising explanation for the prominent inclusion of a salt cellar in Hogarth's painting. Positioned on the table between the aristocratic captain and his lower-ranking tutor, the cellar has been interpreted as a visual pun on the phrase 'to sit above/below the salt', which distinguished the social elite (those 'above') from their acolytes and attendants (those 'below'). However, Einberg suggests it could also allude to the mineral salts that spas like Cheltenham sold to visitors who wanted to enjoy the curative effects of their waters at home.

Other details in the painting might also refer to health and recovery. This includes the roast bird on the cook's platter, white meat being seen as healthier than red meat at this time. Furthermore, eighteenth-century authors often recommended cheerful music as a remedy for melancholy, which might explain the presence of the singer and the drummer. Einberg also notes that Graham's long pipe could be used for smoking medicinal substances, such as opium or cannabis, and that the punchbowl on the floor is filled with clear liquid, suggesting that the Captain is drinking water instead of alcohol in adherence to the advice of certain eighteenth-century medical treaties, which warned their readers to avoid alcoholic beverages. Taking all of these elements into account, Einberg concludes that the painting, through its representation of restorative remedies, commemorated the recovery of the Graham's health and celebrated the role of his friends, Mallet chief among them, in supporting his recuperation.

This is a compelling interpretation, but it is not an obvious one, the symbolism of health emerging only when one starts looking for it. Apart from Graham's friends, who knew the details of his illness, most viewers seeing the painting for the first time might have initially associated the scene with boisterous revelry, rather than virtuous self-care. After all, the portrait shares certain elements with one of Hogarth's most famous satirical prints, *A Midnight Modern Conversation*, first published in 1733 (fig. 2). As the title suggests, this print mocks the polite conventions of conversation-piece portraiture. It depicts a punch party which has degenerated from decorous conviviality into drunken disarray. Within the image, there is a prominent punchbowl, as in *Captain Lord George Graham in his Cabin*, and several members of the dissolute group go without wigs and puff on long pipes, just like Graham does. Thus, when looking at the captain's portrait, eighteenth-century viewers might have been reminded of the well-known print, the memory of its debauched imagery emphasising, through contrast, the healthier and more restrained behaviour of Graham and his fellows.

Defined by the author Jonathan Swift as 'something that at first appears a Reproach but by some turn of Wit ends in a compliment, and to the Advantage of the Person it was addressed to', raillery was key component of eighteenth-century conversational humour. Flirting with accident, silliness and even disrepute to emphasise his sitters' respectability, Hogarth's group portraits provided his patrons with a visual equivalent to this verbal art. With its clowning canines and its multi-layered imagery of wealth, health, geniality and gentility, *Captain Lord George Graham in his Cabin* provides an example par excellence of this playful irony. Through its wit and complexity, it emphasises the many different facets of the Captain's identity: naval captain, nobleman, grand tourist, convalescent, former rake and now potential husband. No wonder, then, that James Caird, who purchased the portrait for the National Maritime Museum in April 1932, confidently declared it would make the Museum 'the shrine of all Hogarth worshippers'.

CHAPTER 3

The Triumph of Britannia

1748–1775

During the mid-eighteenth century, British art underwent rapid transformation. In the 1740s, many of the most fashionable portrait painters working in London were European émigrés, as had been the case for centuries, and young artists had few opportunities to receive instruction or to show their work. By the 1770s, everything had changed. A new generation of British-born painters was in the ascendency and art was more prominent in British public life than it had ever been before, thanks to the advent of annual exhibitions, as well as a booming print market. Founded in December 1768, the Royal Academy of Arts not only provided formal artistic training to talented students but also created an official body to represent the artistic community on the national stage.

It is not a coincidence that the same period also witnessed intense military and naval activity, which resulted in a dramatic expansion of Britain's colonial holdings and maritime empire. Victory in the Seven Years' War (1756–63) enabled Britain to make extensive territorial gains in India and North America, while James Cook's three voyages to the Pacific in the late 1760s and 1770s endeavoured to advance scientific understanding of the geography, people, flora and fauna of the region. Carried out with little regard was given to the Indigenous populations, these developments ultimately laid the foundations for the future expansion of the British Empire.

Artists took advantage of the growing sense of national confidence and imperial purpose that these events inspired, arguing that Britain needed to join the hard power of military and naval triumph with the soft power of cultural and artistic achievement. For many painters, this meant turning their talents to the representation of the nation's latest victories and its most successful commanders. Although often painted for private reasons, such as to celebrate friendship, naval portraits were increasingly displayed in public settings, such as exhibitions, print shops or even pleasure gardens, where they were seen by large public audiences. Rather than fixating on conflict and conquest, some artists celebrated their naval sitters' achievements in other fields, such as navigation, administration and innovation. Such imagery emphasised the Royal Navy's status as a modern, well-organised and technologically advanced institution, disguising colonial expansion as an enlightened and civilised process, rather than a violent one.

Meanwhile, the introduction of naval uniform in April 1748 helped officers to maintain a professional appearance, as well as reinforcing social distinctions within the Navy's ranks. Excluding warrant officers and common sailors, the new clothing regulations applied only to commissioned officers and midshipmen. This would create, the Admiralty declared, 'the Appearance which is necessary to distinguish their Class to be in the Rank of Gentlemen'. As a visual manifestation of an individual's naval rank and social status, uniform immediately became a key component of naval portraiture.

Captain the Honourable George Edgcumbe

Joshua Reynolds

1748, oil on canvas
1,270 x 1,015 mm
BHC2677

Sir Joshua Reynolds was a key figure in the history of British art. The leading portrait painter of his day, he became the inaugural President of the Royal Academy of Arts in 1768, a role he held until his death in 1792. He also enjoyed a prolonged and creatively stimulating relationship with the Royal Navy, which began during his childhood and early career in Plymouth, the location of one of the busiest naval dockyards in eighteenth-century Britain.

Painted in 1749, this portrait is one of the last works that Reynolds created in Plymouth before leaving to undertake a tour of Europe, after which he relocated his artistic practice to London. Captain George Edgcumbe stands in a pose evocative of polite authority with his sword clasped in his left hand. Visible in the distance is the *Salisbury*, the ship he commanded between January 1746 and November 1748. In this vessel, Edgcumbe captured several wealthy prizes, including a large French East Indiaman laden with eight cases of silver. The inclusion of a distant ship was a longstanding convention of naval portraiture. Here it is combined with a newer symbol of naval authority in the form of Edgcumbe's blue-and-gold full-dress uniform. Naval uniform was introduced for commissioned officers less than a year before this portrait was painted, but it would quickly become a mainstay of naval imagery. At first glance, then, this painting appears to be a typical naval portrait. However, closer inspection reveals more complex layers of meaning.

Edgcumbe stands before two classical columns with an ivy-covered wall on his left. These architectural elements suggest a grand and venerable property, indicating that the young officer belongs to a noble family with a large estate. Edgcumbe was the second son of Richard, 1st Baron Edgcumbe, whose estate at Mount Edgcumbe overlooked Plymouth Sound. The three cannons in the bottom left-hand corner of the portrait allude to the gun battery that Captain Edgcumbe installed at Mount Edgcumbe for the purpose of saluting ships in the Sound below. He may have created this battery in his role as the landowner's son but, as a naval officer, he often found himself on the receiving end of its salutes. Like the battery, Reynolds's portrait knits together Edgcumbe's naval and aristocratic identities. The painting can be split into two zones: the maritime zone on the left, containing the sea and the *Salisbury*; and the architectural zone on the right, evoking an aristocratic country estate. Edgcumbe's body straddles the divide, symbolising his ability to move between naval service and patrician authority.

Joining Edgcumbe in the portrait is an unusual animal companion – a black bird with a rust-coloured neck and a long tail, which perches on the ivy above the Captain's left shoulder. This avian interloper is a long-tailed paradise whydah (specifically a male in his breeding plumage), a species native to Eastern and Central Africa. In the eighteenth century, there was an extensive trade in African wildlife, fuelled by a fashion in Europe for exotic pets, which served as conspicuous displays of their owners' wealth and social status. Parrots and canaries were the most widely traded African birds, while whydahs were rarer and thus more prized. It is unclear how Edgcumbe came to possess one. Perhaps he seized the bird as booty from a captured merchant ship, or maybe he purchased the whydah with his

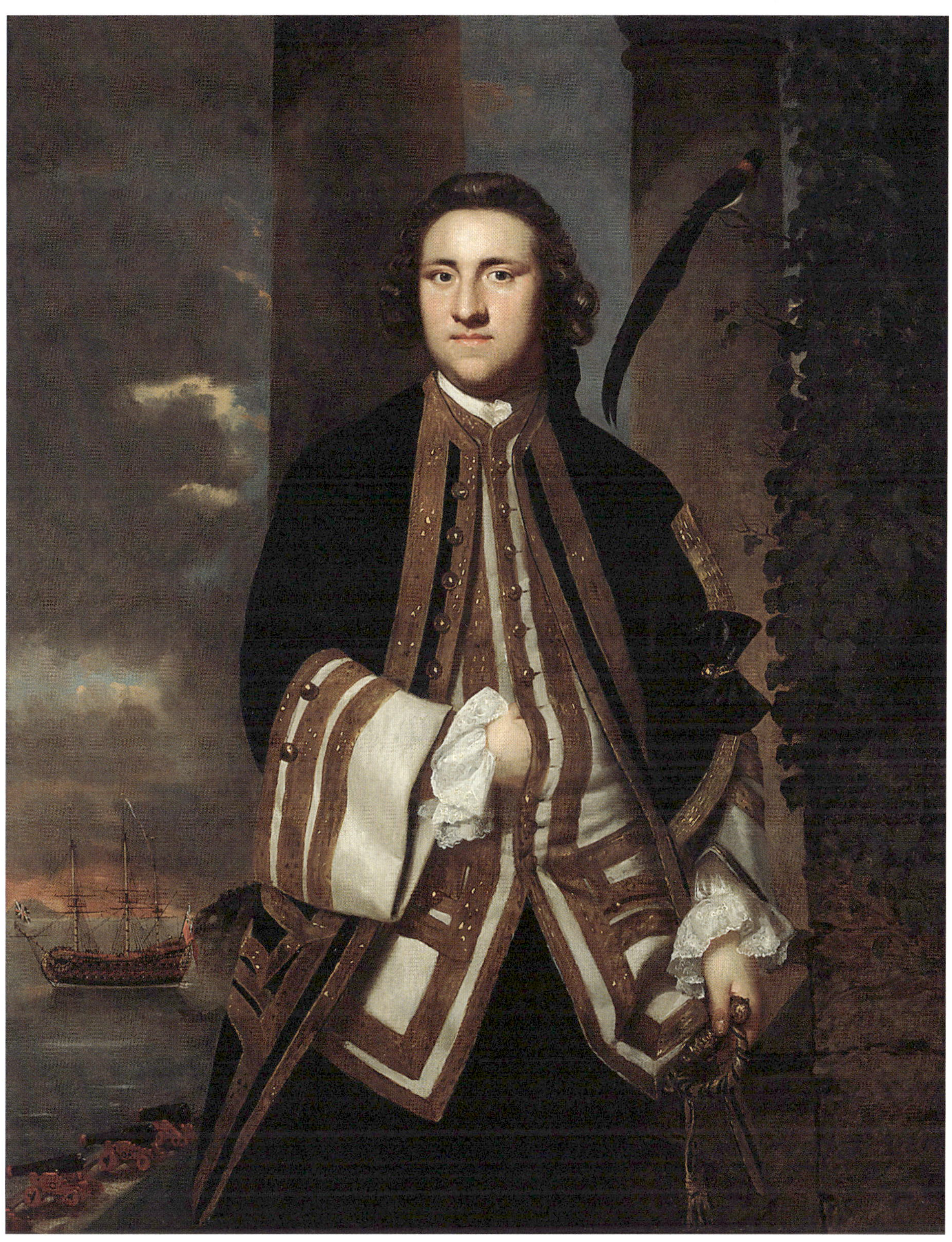

(fig. 1) *Lieutenant Paul Henry Ourry with 'Jersey'*
Joshua Reynolds
1748, oil on canvas
1,270 x 1,016 mm
National Trust (Saltram, NT 872160)

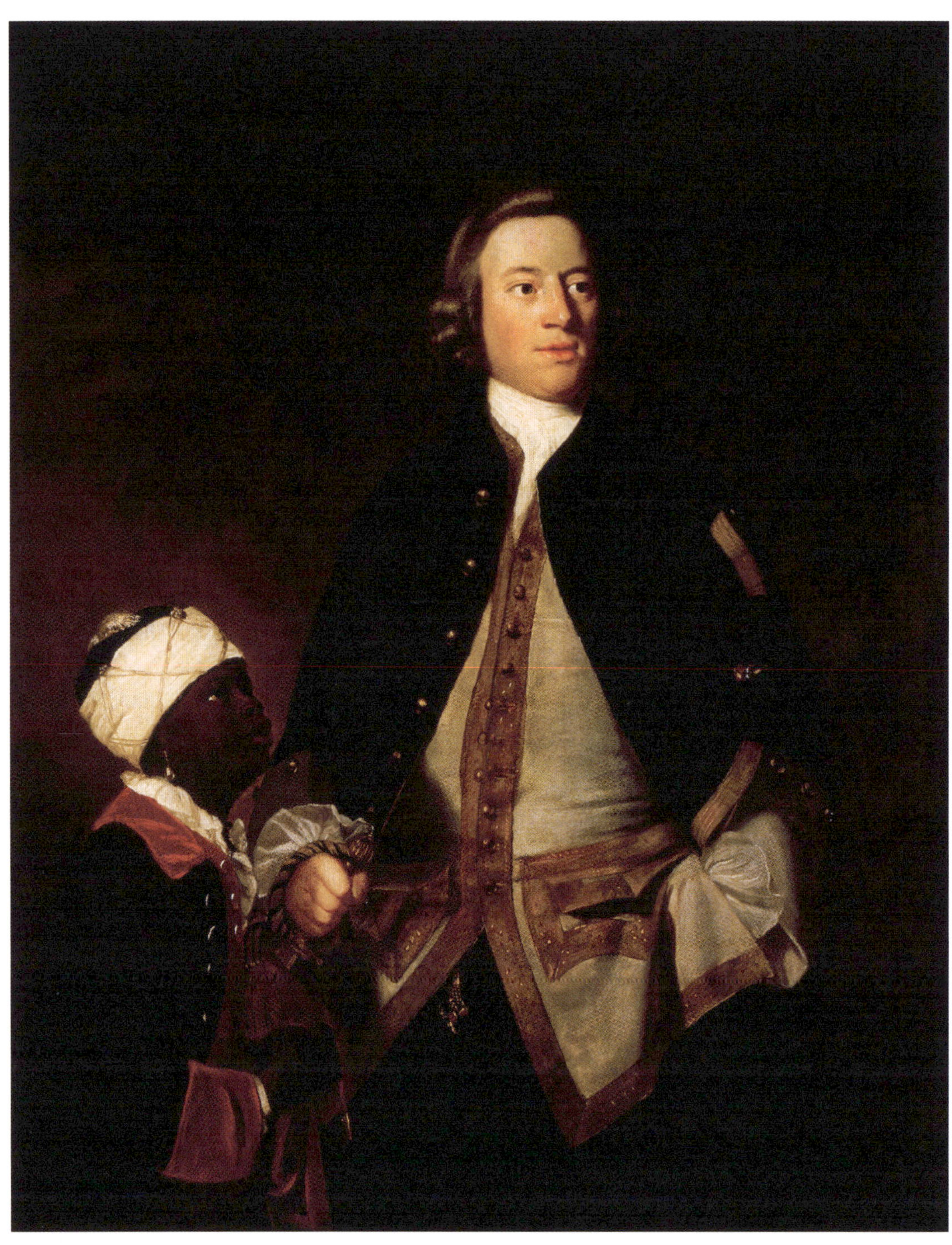

personal wealth. Whichever the case, his feathered friend is a potent symbol of overseas trade and exploitation, signalling Edgcumbe's involvement in growing and maintaining Britain's maritime empire.

The maritime themes in this painting are echoed in Reynolds's portrait of Edgcumbe's second-in-command, Lieutenant Paul Henry Ourry (fig. 1). Painted at the same time, the two pictures were designed to be displayed as a pair, although they have since been separated. Ourry's portrait is now part of the National Trust collection at Saltram, near Plymouth. The son of an army officer, Ourry joined Plymouth's social elite in the year this portrait was painted, when he married Charity Treby, the daughter of an important family of local landowners.

Like Edgcumbe, Ourry is shown wearing naval uniform, although his coat is devoid of gold lace, signalling his subordinate rank as a lieutenant. He is attended by a young Black servant, who – like Edgcumbe's whydah – would have been understood at the time as a symbol of maritime commerce. The boy, who was given the name 'Jersey' after Ourry's Channel Island birthplace, is a reminder of how humans were treated as cargo and brought to European shores via Atlantic trade routes in this period. Although most of the enslaved African people were taken to plantations in the West Indies, a small number, predominantly children, were brought to Europe to become domestic servants. The motif of a Black attendant staring up at a white master has a long history in seventeenth- and eighteenth-century portraiture. The young boy in Ourry's portrait is dressed in a smart livery, a sign of ownership which marks him as belonging to a particular household. He is also characterised as an exotic curiosity through his white turban and gold jewellery. Various social and racial power dynamics are at play, placing the British lieutenant in a position of dominance: servant is played off against master, child against adult and black against white. When the portraits of Edgcumbe and Ourry were seen together, as originally intended, the whydah and the boy emphasised Plymouth's status as a gateway to Atlantic trade routes. Today, these details are haunting reminders of the exploitative practices that underpinned eighteenth-century maritime trade.

The two paintings were commissioned by the Corporation of Plympton to hang in the town's Mayoralty House. Plympton was situated just a few miles from Plymouth Dockyard, and the Corporation formed the electorate for the local parliamentary borough of Plympton Erle. In practice, this meant voting in the preferred candidates of the most powerful local landowners – the Edgcumbes and the Trebys. Given that Captain Edgcumbe and Lieutenant Ourry were connected to these families, the Corporation's decision to display the officers' portraits was a demonstration of political loyalty. At the same time, Reynolds's paintings also celebrated the Navy's pervasive influence within Plymouth's social affairs. Together, the two portraits reveal the intimate connections between politics, empire and polite society in mid-eighteenth-century Britain.

Captain the Honourable Augustus Keppel

Joshua Reynolds

1752–53, oil on canvas
2,390 x 1,475 mm
BHC2823

One of the defining moments in Joshua Reynolds's artistic career came in early May 1749 when he set sail on a voyage to Italy. Prior to this, Reynolds had been running a small portraiture studio in his home city of Plymouth. Taking in Rome, Florence and Venice, his Italian sojourn provided an opportunity to study Renaissance masterpieces and classical ruins. The experience transformed his creative practice. Arriving back in England in autumn 1752, he set up a new studio in London and quickly became one of the capital's most celebrated portrait painters.

(fig. 1) *Apollo*
after Pierre Le Gros the Younger
early 18th century, bronze
height 660 mm
Royal Castle, Warsaw (ZKW/577)

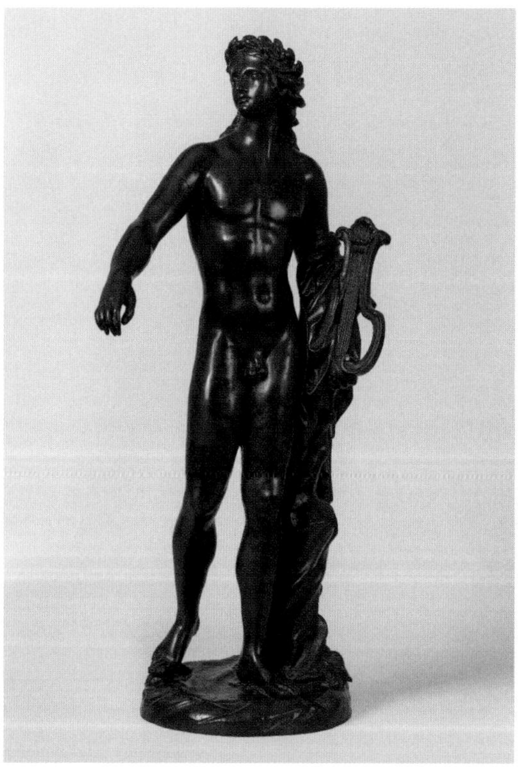

This portrait was among the first that Reynolds produced following his travels. By all accounts, it was immensely successful in helping the young painter break into London's competitive market for fashionable portraiture. To this day, it is regarded as one of the great masterpieces of eighteenth-century British art.

The sitter, Captain the Honourable Augustus Keppel, was the second son of the Earl of Albemarle. When this portrait was painted, he was already one of the Navy's most highly regarded officers at the age of only 27 – two years younger than Reynolds. Having travelled to Italy on board Keppel's ship, the *Centurion*, the artist had the aristocratic Captain to thank for his European adventure. The two men formed a strong bond during the journey, as Reynolds explained in a grateful letter to Lord Edgcumbe, the Plymouth landowner who had originally introduced them: 'I had the use of [Keppel's] cabin, and his study of books, as if they had been my own; and when he went ashore he generally took me with him; so that I not only had the opportunity of seeing a great deal, but I saw it with all the advantages as if I had travelled as his equal.' As well as a friend, Keppel also became an important source of creative inspiration for the artist. Over almost five decades of friendship, he sat for Reynolds for seven portraits, including this one.

Since Keppel is not recorded as having paid for this portrait, it is thought that Reynolds

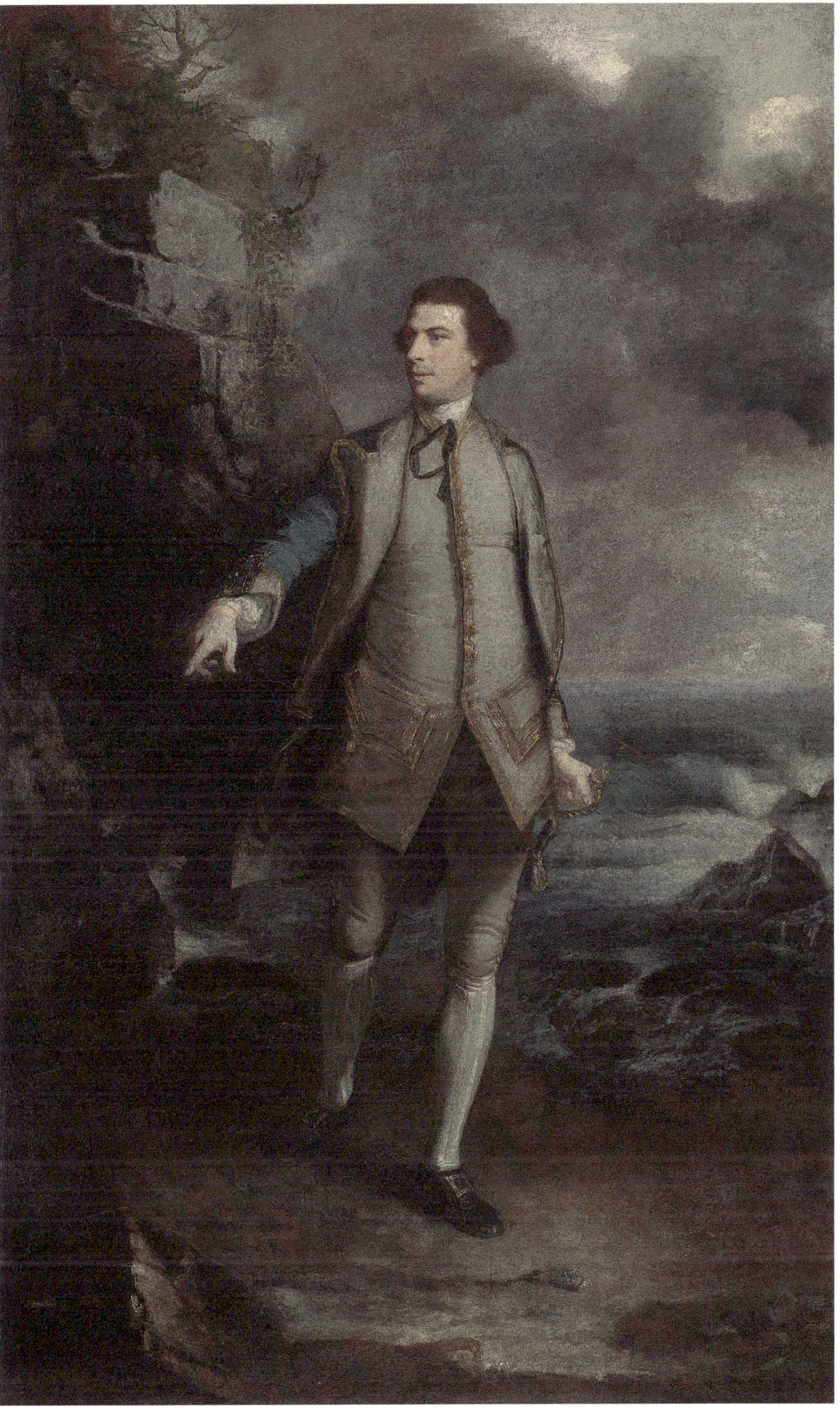

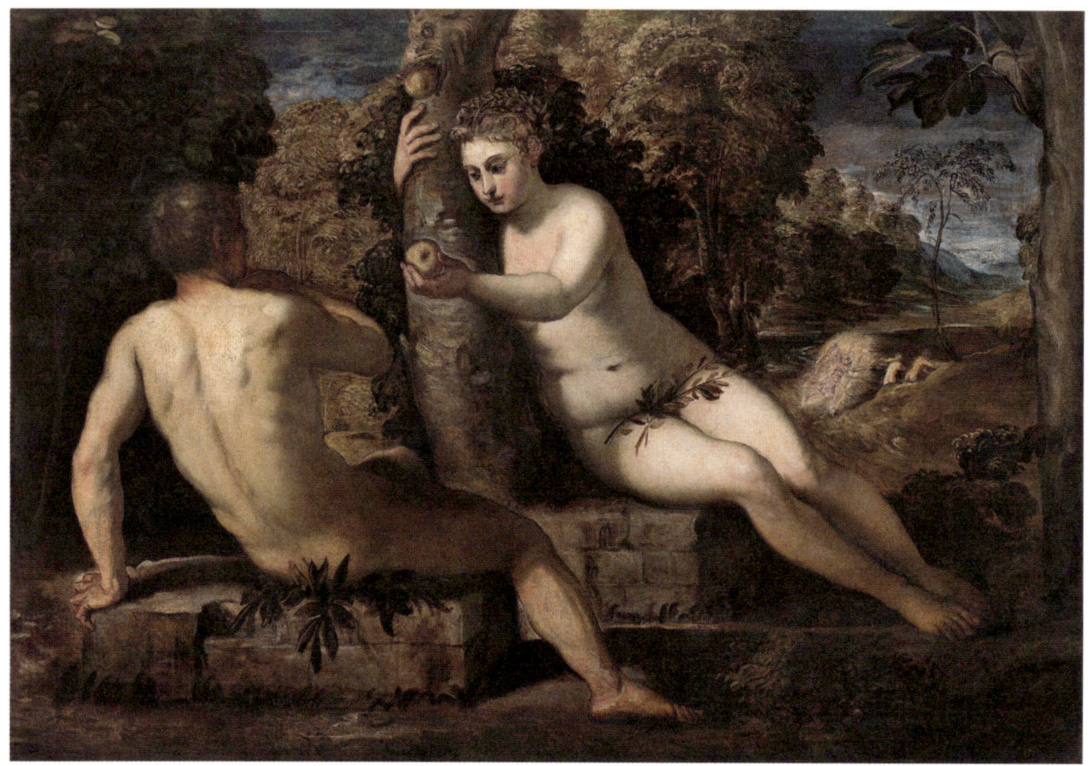

(fig. 2) *The Temptation of Adam*
Jacopo Tintoretto
1550, oil on canvas
1,500 x 2,200 mm
Gallerie dell'Accademia, Venice (43)

created the painting partly as a celebration of their friendship. At the same time, it also functioned as an advertisement for Reynolds's artistic talents. The painting is believed to have been displayed for several years in his studio, where it provided potential clients with a demonstration of the skills that he had developed in Italy.

The work is threaded through with references to the kinds of classical and Renaissance art that Reynolds had encountered on the Continent. Keppel's striding attitude and pointing gesture owe a profound debt to ancient sculpture. The figure is often likened to the *Apollo Belvedere*, but more recent research has demonstrated that Reynolds in fact borrowed the pose from a seventeenth-century statue of Apollo – itself based upon the *Apollo Belvedere* – by the French sculptor Pierre Le Gros, a cast of which the young painter had sketched sometime before 1753 (fig. 1). Reynolds combined this sculptural reference with painterly effects drawn from the works of sixteenth-century Venetian masters.

The sombre blue-grey tonality of the painting and the atmospheric use of light and shade are reminiscent of Tintoretto in particular. Cloaked in the same dark shadows that dominate the portrait's rocky coastal setting, Keppel is visually integrated within the landscape that surrounds him. Reynolds had admired this quality in Tintoretto's *The Temptation of Adam* (fig. 2), which he saw in Venice, writing in his notebook: '[Adam's] back forms a mass of light, his thigh lost in the ground, the shadows, in general, full.'

It was not, however, Reynolds's familiarity with Old Masters like Jacopo Tintoretto that most impressed his contemporaries. Instead, Keppel's portrait won acclaim for its 'display of animated character', as the painter Joseph Farington later wrote. Seemingly oblivious to the viewer's presence, Keppel strides determinedly across a storm-battered beach. The foaming sea in the background is peppered with thin strokes of brown paint, representing debris from a shipwreck (fig. 3). This detail is believed to allude to a specific incident from Keppel's career: the wreck of his ship, the *Maidstone*, on the Brittany coast on 27 June 1747. The viewer is thus invited to imagine that the portrait shows Keppel taking command in the aftermath of this disaster, although he is anachronistically dressed in the new naval captain's undress uniform, which was not introduced until nine months after the wreck of the *Maidstone*. Intriguingly, the breeches, waistcoat and facings of Keppel's uniform are coloured grey, rather than regulation white. Officers in this period did sometimes modify their uniforms to suit their own tastes, but artistic licence may be a more likely explanation here, since the grey accents seem designed to complement the portrait's stormy blue colour palette.

Reynolds's animated portrayal of his naval sitter represented a significant departure from the prevailing conventions that had characterised British portraiture since Sir Godfrey Kneller in early eighteenth century. Whereas Kneller and his followers depicted their male sitters holding polite poses in front of distant backdrops (for example, p. 60), Reynolds presented Keppel as a mobile figure amid an unfolding situation. In doing so,

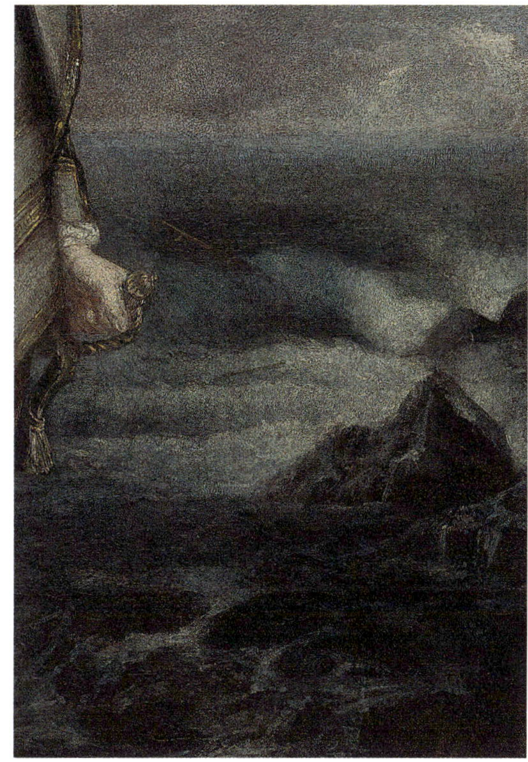

(fig. 3) Detail of shipwreck debris in *Captain the Honourable Augustus Keppel* by Joshua Reynolds, 1752–53

the artist blurred the boundaries between two artistic genres, portraiture and history painting. A history painting is one that represents a moment in a narrative, usually a biblical, mythological or historical scene chosen for its moral or didactic significance. Such paintings were viewed in the eighteenth century as the most prestigious form of artistic production. Reynolds's emulation of this prestigious genre in Keppel's portrait represented an important shift in British art, inaugurating a new style of so-called 'grand manner' portraiture, which took inspiration from history painting.

While the allusion to the wreck of the *Maidstone* imbued the painting with drama and urgency, it did not necessarily flatter Keppel's professional abilities. The young captain had taken command of the *Maidstone* in November 1745. Over the next 18 months, the (fig. 4) X-ray showing the central section of *Captain the Honourable Augustus Keppel* by Joshua Reynolds (1752–53). The outline of a column is visible behind the sitter's left shoulder and the position of his head has been altered.

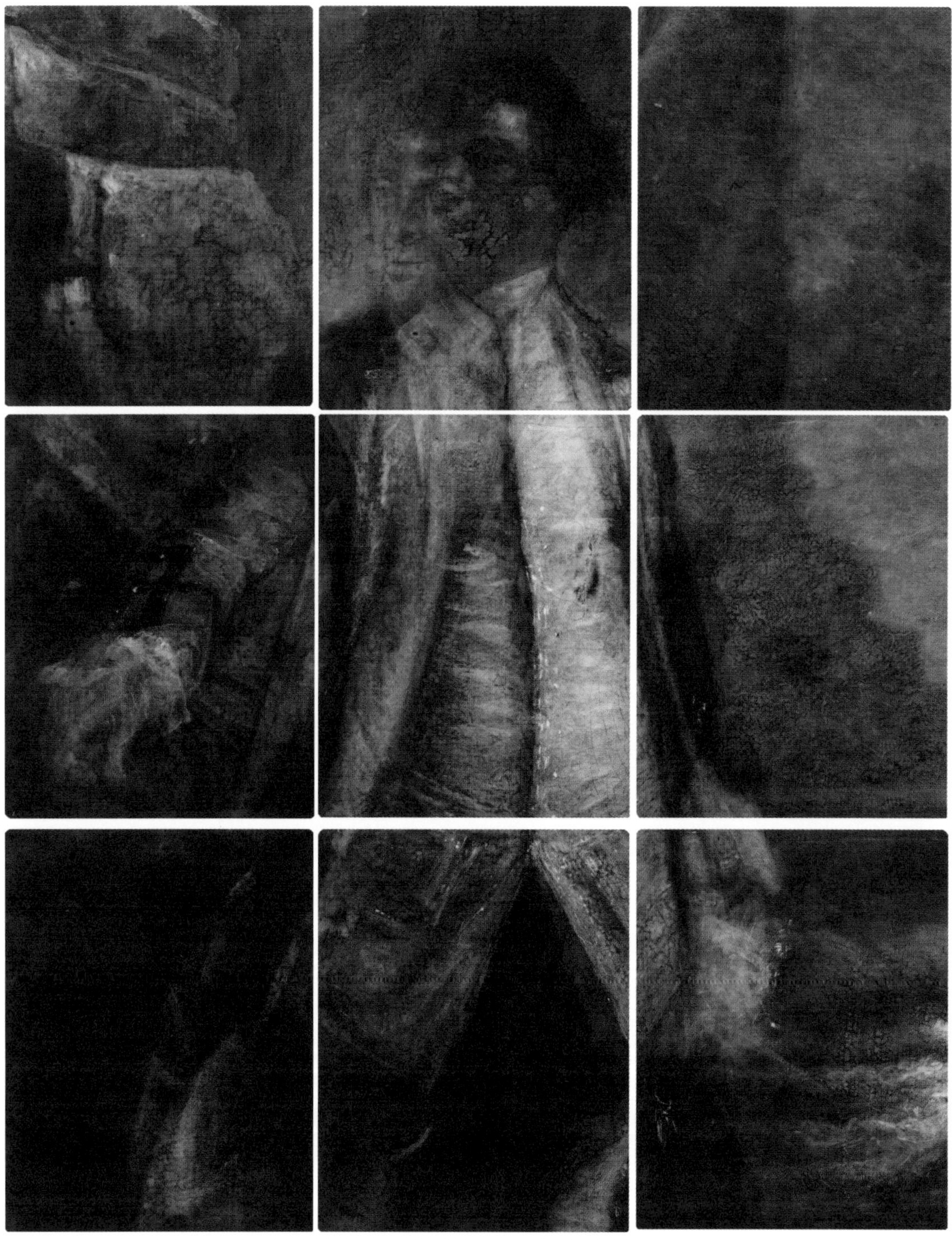

ship successfully captured numerous enemy vessels. However, one stormy day in June 1747, Keppel's determined pursuit of a French merchant took the *Maidstone* into dangerously shallow waters on the Brittany coast, where it foundered on the rocks. Writing to the Admiralty several days later, Keppel estimated that he had lost 27 men in the disaster. The survivors were taken prisoner by the French, but Keppel soon returned to England on parole, where he was cleared of negligence at an Admiralty court martial. Senior naval officers put a positive spin on Keppel's recklessness, Admiral Sir Peter Warren writing that he liked Keppel's 'eagerness to come at the enemy'. Reynolds may have assumed his viewers would share Warren's optimistic interpretation of the *Maidstone* incident, taking the wreck as evidence of Keppel's willingness to risk disaster in pursuit of victory. However, the floating debris could also be read as a warning against hubris or as a reminder of the fine line between life and death at sea. This multivalent symbolism distinguished Reynolds's painting from the more straightforward glorifications of naval heroism found in most other naval portraits and recalled instead the sophisticated moralising associated with the genre of history painting.

Technical investigation of the painting reveals that Reynolds made a deliberate decision to depart from the traditional imagery of British portraiture. X-rays show that the stormy sea and shipwreck debris were painted over an earlier composition, in which Keppel was stood beside a classical column – a more typical backdrop for a naval portrait at this time (fig. 4). The artist's drastic revision of his original design emphasises his desire to produce a work that was bold and innovative, which transcended the traditional functions of portraiture. Yet Reynolds's innovation would not have been possible without the Royal Navy. As a naval officer, Keppel had facilitated Reynolds's journey to Italy, where he found so much creative inspiration; in the *Maidstone* disaster, his seafaring career provided the impetus for the portrait's drama.

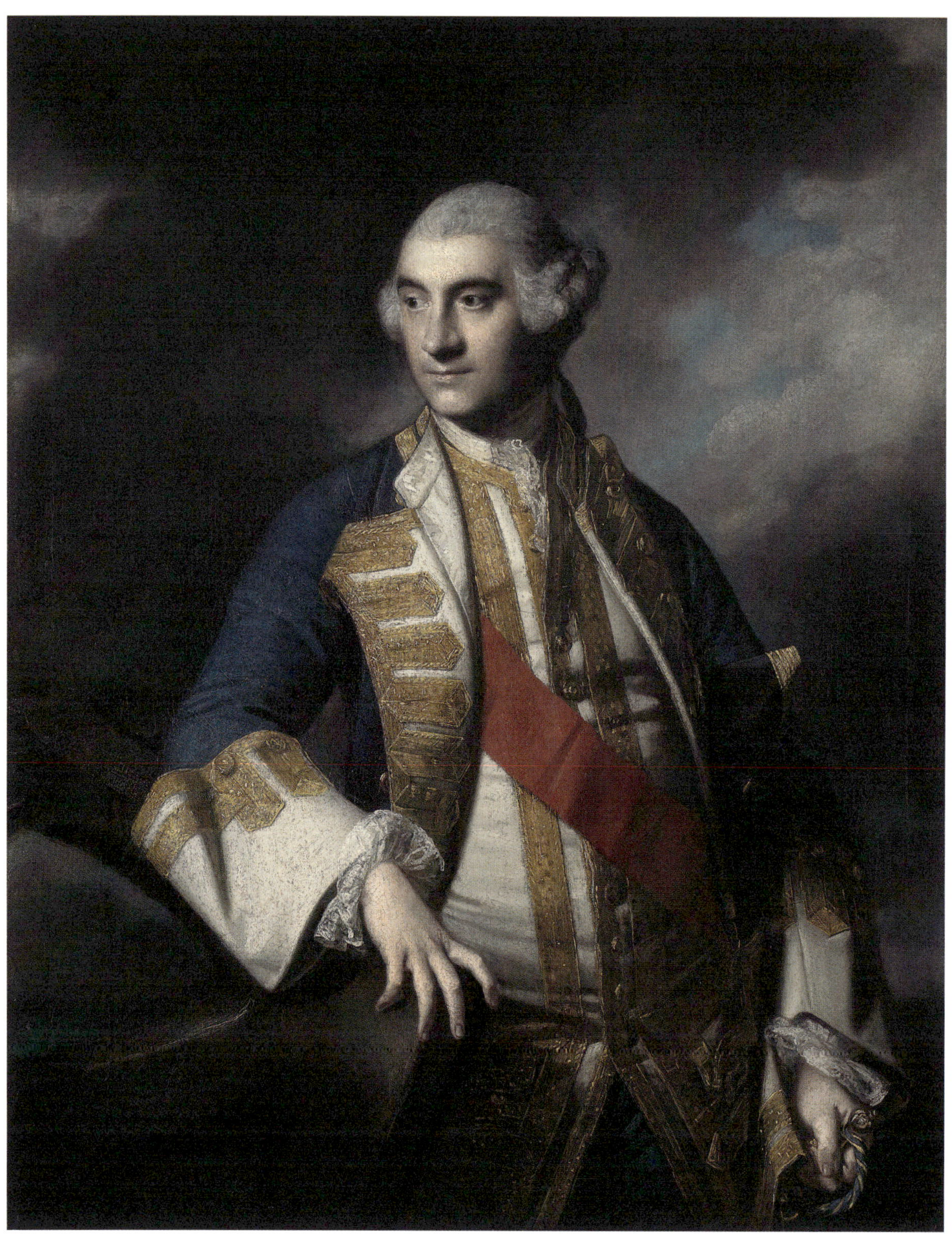

Vice-Admiral Sir Charles Saunders

Joshua Reynolds

about 1760, oil on canvas
1,270 x 1,015 mm
BHC3012

In the early 1750s, Joshua Reynolds exploded onto the London art scene with a dynamic depiction of his friend, Captain Augustus Keppel (p. 86). He soon attracted commissions from all manner of wealthy and influential clients, including aristocrats, politicians and actors. At the same time, naval officers remained an important segment of his business. Word-of-mouth was central to the artist's success as a naval portraitist and many of his sitters knew each other through the intertwined networks of patronage and friendship that structured the Navy's officer corps. Within these networks, Reynolds's paintings were exchanged as tokens of respect and camaraderie. Meanwhile, printed reproductions of the portraits spread the fame of their sitters among the wider public.

Depicting Vice-Admiral Sir Charles Saunders, this portrait typifies Reynolds's approach to representing naval personnel in this period. The sittings for the portrait took place in March and early April 1760, when Saunders was briefly in London between overseas postings in North America and the Mediterranean. The Seven Years War (1756–63) was then at its height, pitting Britain against France in a fierce struggle for control of colonial holdings around the world. The conflict had begun with several humiliating defeats for Britain, but a sequence of decisive victories in the so-called 'annus mirabilis' of 1759 placed the nation firmly in the ascendency. Saunders had been a central actor in one of these victories. He posed for this portrait shortly after commanding the British fleet in the St Lawrence River, where he co-operated with Major-General James Wolfe in the amphibious assault that led to the capture of Quebec.

However, the portrait does not directly refer to Saunders's recent glory, featuring instead an atmospheric backdrop of agitated storm clouds, which transcends specificity of time and place. What the painting lacks in narrative, it makes up for in the visual drama of texture, pattern and colour within the Vice-Admiral's uniform: the glitter of gold lace, the sharp contrasts of blue and white and the delicate flourishes of lace cuffs and shirt ruffles. The red sash is a later addition, commemorating Saunders's installation as a Knight of the Bath in May 1761. Stark contrasts of light and dark accentuate the movement of his twisting body: appearing almost like a coiled spring, tensed and primed for action, Saunders's left side is turned away from the light, while his head faces in the opposite direction. The splayed fingers of his right hand clench the crown of an anchor, while his dark, arching eyebrows emphasise the intensity of his gaze, which is fixed on some unseen point in the distance. He appears thoughtful yet vigilant, animated yet composed. The portrait reads as a study of character, more than a celebration of achievement.

Saunders had served with Reynolds's friend Keppel under Admiral George Anson during his famous voyage around the world in the early 1740s. Anson's family owned this portrait in the nineteenth century, suggesting that the Admiral was the work's original patron, while another version of the painting is associated with Keppel's family. Saunders himself paid Reynolds for a portrait of Anson in the 1750s. These provenances suggest how Reynolds's friendship with Keppel led to commissions from the latter's naval associates. By displaying each other's portraits in their own homes, Saunders, Keppel and Anson

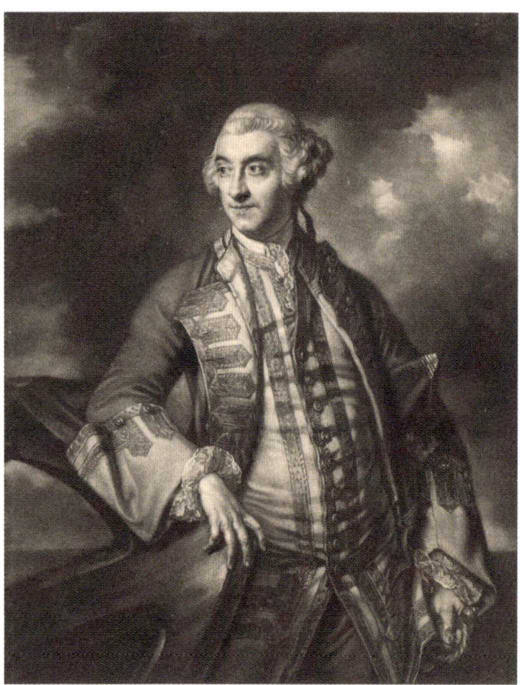

(fig. 1) *Charles Saunders Esq.*
James Macardell after Joshua Reynolds
1760, mezzotint on paper
393 x 278 mm
PAF3691

celebrated their shared personal and professional bonds. Since they were already familiar with each other's achievements, they did not need to be reminded of specific battles or victories. In this context, Saunders's subdued but characterful portrait may have been more appealing than a bombastic glorification of his triumph in Quebec.

However, the Vice-Admiral's naval colleagues were not the only audience for his portrait. Soon after the painting's completion, printed reproductions of the work began appearing for public sale. The earliest of these prints was James Macardell's high-quality mezzotint (fig. 1). This was an authorised print, produced with Reynolds's permission and perhaps even at his request. It is inscribed beneath the image with Saunders's name, rank and coat of arms. Unlike the linear art of engraving, mezzotint was a tonal medium and therefore well-suited to the reproduction of oil paintings, especially those with rich *chiaroscuro* – an Italian term used to describe the contrast of light and shadow. Saunders's portrait makes extensive use of *chiaroscuro*, raising the possibility that Reynolds designed the painting with a view to its later reproduction in mezzotint. The artist often worked with Macardell, an accomplished engraver whose fine mezzotints commanded high prices at the luxury end of the print market.

Once an image entered the public domain, however, it could be pirated and reproduced by other engravers to make cheap prints, as well as illustrations in popular magazines and histories – a process over which the artist had little control. Naval officers were prominent figures in mid-eighteenth-century Britain and their likenesses were in high demand as a result, as the example of Saunders's portrait shows. In August 1760, an image derived from Reynolds's portrait (almost certainly via Macardell's mezzotint) was published in *The Royal Magazine, or Gentleman's Monthly Companion* (fig. 2), alongside an article entitled 'A succinct Account of the gallant Actions of Charles Saunders, Vice-Admiral of the Blue'. Although the copying of the facial features is crude, the angle of the head, the details of the uniform and the fall of shadow all match up with Reynolds's original. The following year, another version of the image was published in the fourth and final volume of

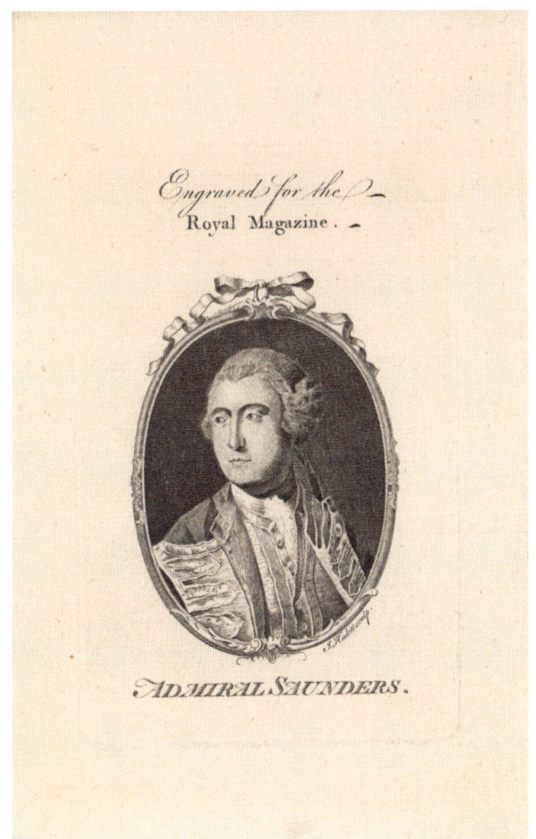

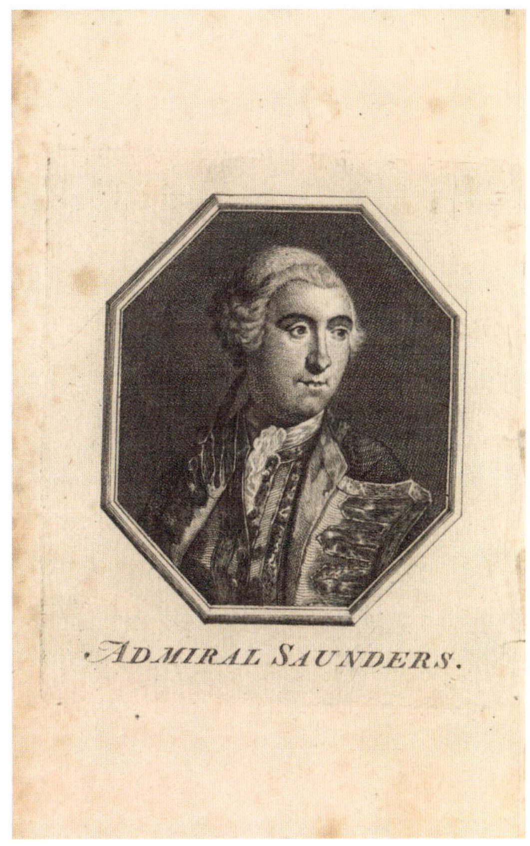

(fig. 2) *Admiral Saunders*
James Hulett after Joshua Reynolds
1760, engraving on paper
206 x 128 mm
PAD2847

(fig. 3) *Admiral Saunders*
Unknown engraver after Joshua Reynolds
1761, engraving on paper
170 x 106 mm
PAD2844

John Barrow's *The Naval History of Great Britain, With the Lives of the most Illustrious Admirals and Commanders* (fig. 3), although in this case the portrait has been reversed – Saunders' faces to the right, rather than the left.

The Vice-Admiral's likeness also made an appearance at Vauxhall Gardens, a leading venue for public entertainment in mid-eighteenth-century London. At Vauxhall, fashionable visitors strolled through tree-lined avenues, enjoying musical performances, masquerades, illuminations, paintings and sculptures. In May 1762, painter Francis Hayman completed a vast new artwork in the gardens. Called *The Triumph of Britannia*, Hayman's canvas measured more than 15 feet across and celebrated British naval supremacy. The original painting no longer survives, but it is known through an engraving (fig. 4). In this print, Neptune escorts Britannia across the sea in a shell-backed chariot while

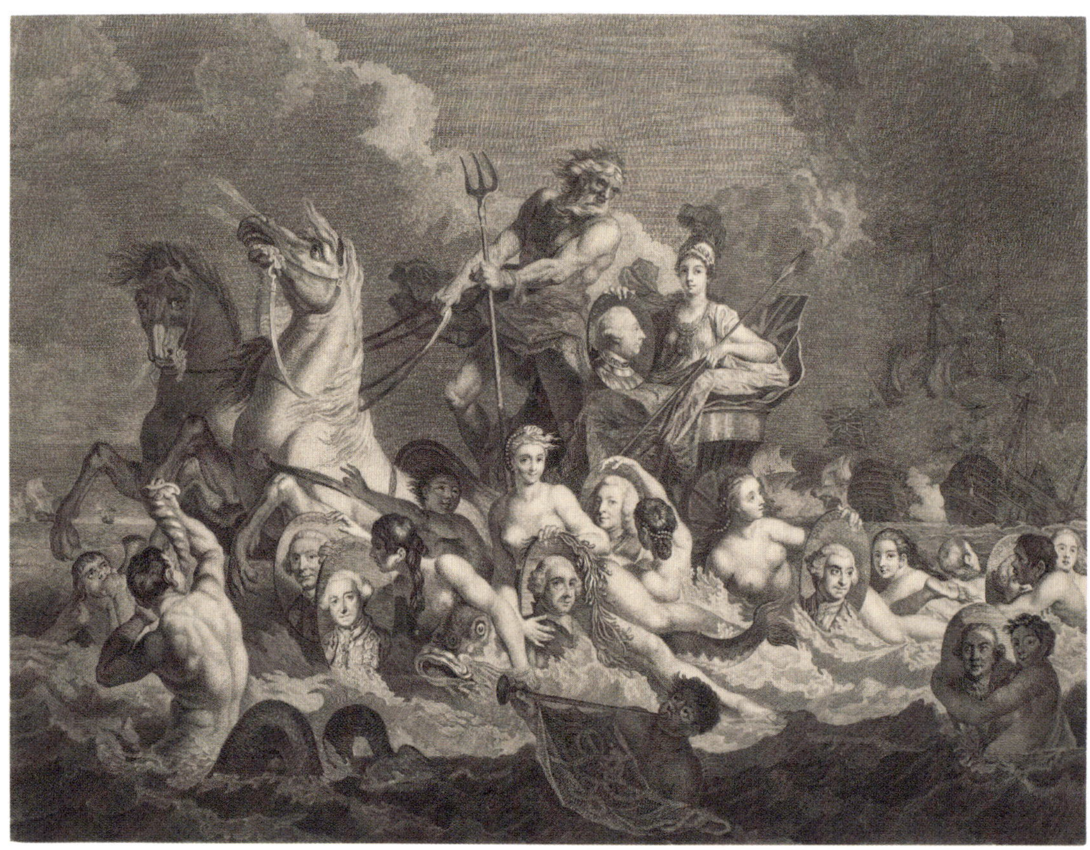

(fig. 4) *The Triumph of Britannia*
Simon François Ravenet after Francis Hayman
1765, etching and engraving on paper
422 x 524 mm
PAH7479

(fig. 5) Detail of *The Triumph of Britannia* by Simon François Ravenet after Francis Hayman, 1765

she holds aloft a portrait of George III – the reigning monarch at the time of the artwork's completion. Sea nymphs, tritons and bug-eyed sea monsters accompany the procession. In an eccentric combination of classical imagery and eighteenth-century portraiture, each nymph cradles the likeness of a celebrated naval officer from the 1760s. These officers would have been instantly recognisable to the Vauxhall crowds because Hayman had copied their images from well-known prints. Saunders appears towards the right-hand side of the composition, where a sea nymph rests his portrait on her naked thigh (fig. 5). Reynolds's portrait is without doubt the source for the Vice-Admiral's likeness, though once again the image appears in reverse. As this example shows, Reynolds's portraits suffused British popular culture in the 1760s, stimulating and sustaining a taste for naval celebrity.

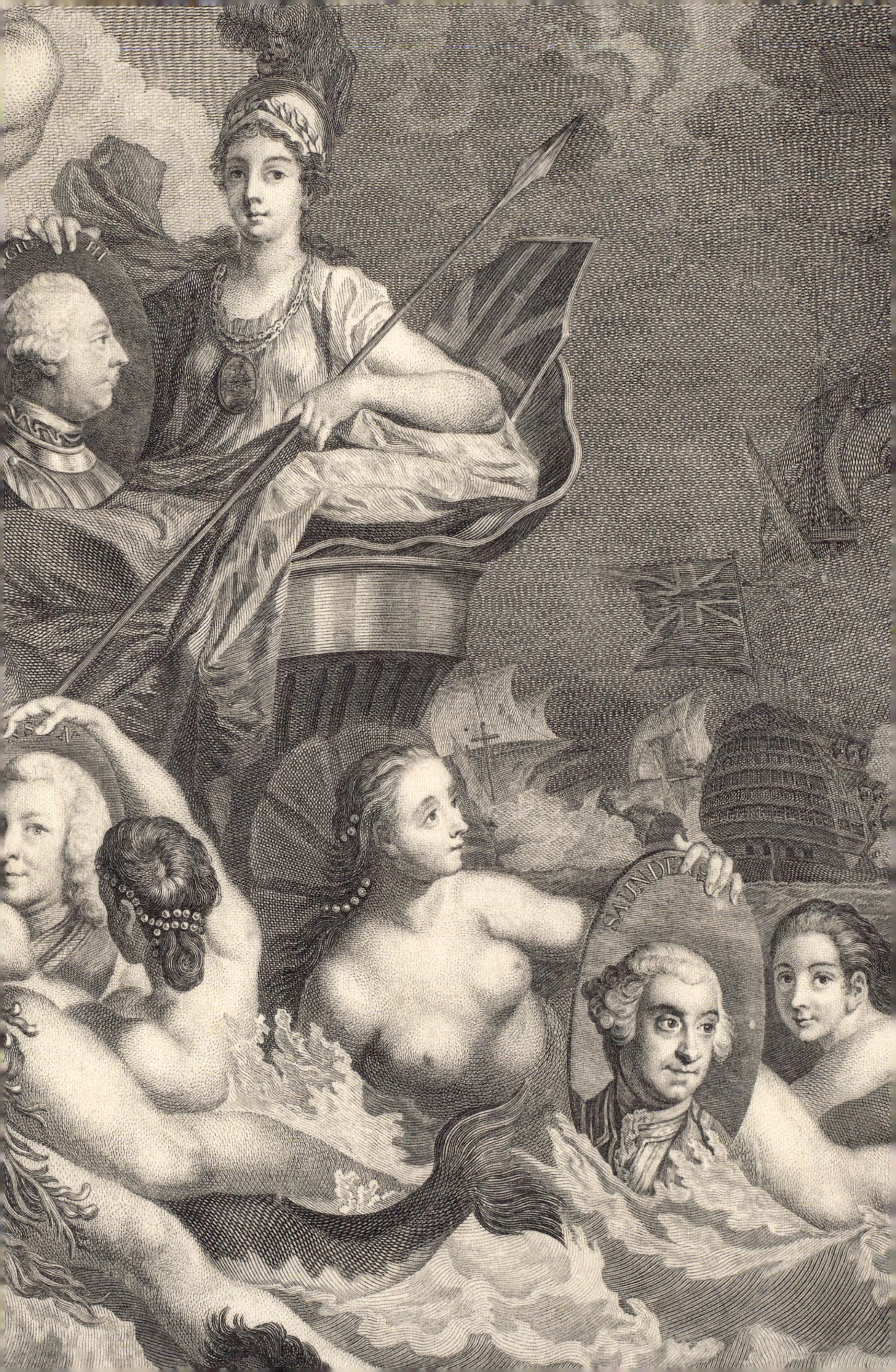

Captain Frederick Cornewall

Thomas Gainsborough

1762, oil on canvas
1,270 x 1,016 mm
BHC2633

'If any little jealousies had subsisted between us, they were forgotten,' declared Joshua Reynolds in a moving account of his final meeting with his long-term rival Thomas Gainsborough, who was dying from cancer. 'He turned towards me,' Reynolds recalled of the deathbed encounter, which took place in summer 1788, 'as one who was engrossed in the same pursuits, and who deserved his good opinion, by being sensible of his excellence.' The two painters had divergent artistic outlooks and had often been critical of one another, but the mutual respect described here seems genuine. Reynolds and Gainsborough dominated British portraiture in the second half of the eighteenth century. Reynolds's art was associated with intellectual pretension, incorporating artistic and literary references, which drew upon his youthful travels in Italy. Meanwhile, Gainsborough never left England. He styled himself as an intuitive virtuoso of visual effects, whose spirited brushwork could bring to life the movement of leaves, the softness of fabric or the glint in someone's eye.

Gainsborough grew up in Suffolk before training as an artist in London under the French painter Hubert-François Gravelot. After getting married in 1746, he returned to Suffolk with his wife, Margaret, to work as a portrait painter to the local gentry. Thirteen years later, the couple and their two daughters moved to Bath, a fashionable spa town which regularly attracted cosmopolitan and aristocratic visitors, providing Gainsborough with a plentiful supply of wealthy clients. Having established himself as the leading artist in Bath, he moved back to London in the 1770s, where he remained for the rest of his career.

This portrait dates from the artist's time in Bath. *Boddley's Bath Journal*, a local newspaper, reported the presence of the sitter, Captain Frederick Cornewall, in the city on 15 March 1762, suggesting the portrait was painted around that time. The picture was perhaps intended to commemorate the 55-year-old captain's retirement from active naval service the previous year.

The painting's quiet dignity would have been appropriate for a retirement portrait. In the previous decade, Reynolds had dazzled the British art world with his dramatic and dynamic naval portraits, including his celebrated full-length depiction of Augustus Keppel. Gainsborough, however, utilised a more sedate aesthetic in this work. Cornewall stands against a plain brown background, holding his hat in his left hand. His torso is angled to one side, while his careworn face turns to fix the viewer with a steady gaze. His respectable appearance signals his comfortable social position. In his retirement, he was enjoying the life of a wealthy country squire, living in the new mansion which he had built at Delbury Hall in Shropshire after purchasing the estate in 1752.

Gainsborough emphasises the neat lines of the captain's bag wig and uniform coat. With another artist, this might result in an appearance of heaviness and inert formality, but the scintillating brilliance of Gainsborough's brushwork lifts and enlivens the portrait. The artist's lightness of touch is especially obvious in the most detailed areas of the picture, such as the lace cuff around Cornewall's left wrist. There is no corresponding cuff at the end of the right sleeve, which hangs empty across the captain's stomach. A loop has been sewn to the edge of the sleeve so that it can be secured to a button on his waistcoat.

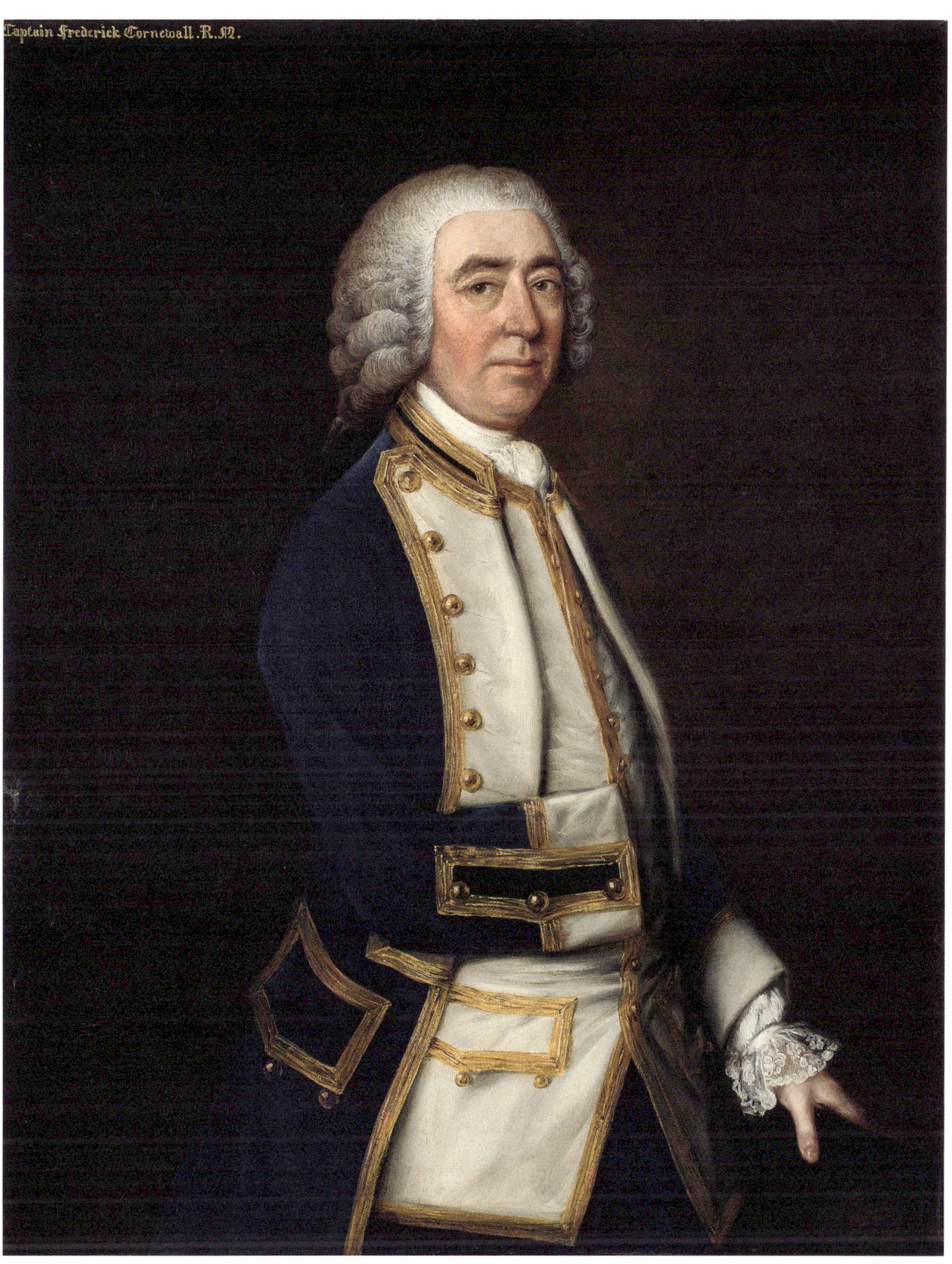
Captain Frederick Cornewall .R.M.

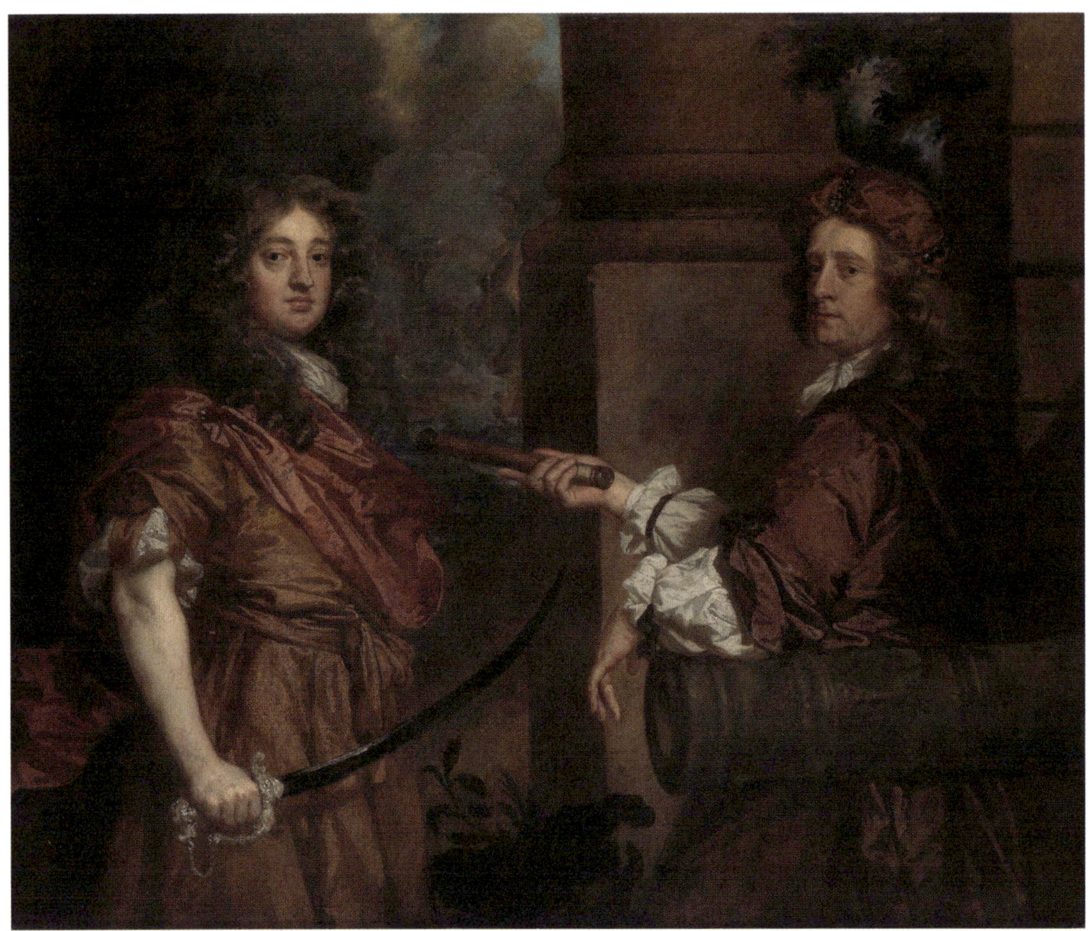

(fig. 1) *Sir Frescheville Holles and Sir Robert Holmes*
Peter Lely
about 1672, oil on canvas
1,320 x 1,625 mm
BHC2770

Cornewall's right arm had been amputated after he was wounded at the Battle of Toulon in February 1744.

The missing limb is an important detail within the portrait, the artist and the sitter having made a deliberate choice to highlight the injury. Gainsborough could have depicted Cornewall with his body facing in the opposite direction, obscuring this from view and placing his remaining arm in the foreground. There was an art-historical precedent for this approach. A century earlier, Peter Lely had painted a double portrait of naval officers Sir Frescheville Holles and Sir Robert Holmes, in which the former (standing on the left) turns his right side towards the viewer in order to conceal the absence of his left arm (fig. 1). His remaining arm appears strong and muscular, the rolled-up sleeve of his Turkish-inspired costume revealing his bare forearm. The prominence of this arm further distracts from the loss of the other. Cornewall, in contrast, hides his surviving limb and draws attention to the missing one.

Today, viewers of Cornewall's portrait might be reminded of a later naval officer, Horatio Nelson, who was celebrated for his role in the Napoleonic Wars. Like Cornewall, Nelson lost his right arm as the result of an injury, and his empty sleeve became a defining feature of his public image. In Cornewall's time, however, the one-armed commander was not yet a naval trope. There are earlier portraits that show officers with amputated limbs, including Allan Ramsay's 1790 portrait of Admiral Charles Stewart resting on a cannon, dated 1740 (fig. 2), but such images were not commonplace.

In Cornewall's case, the arrangement of the empty sleeve echoes a familiar pose from other portraits of the time. Male sitters in the mid-eighteenth century were often painted tucking one hand into their waistcoat. Viewers who did not look closely at the painting might therefore have assumed that Cornewall was hiding his right hand, rather than lacking it. Eighteenth-century comportment manuals, such as François Nivelon's *Rudiments of Genteel Behaviour* (1737), described the hand-in-waistcoat pose as signifying 'manly Boldness ... temper'd with becoming modesty'. This meaning was ultimately derived from the classical art of rhetoric, in which withdrawing one's hand was used in public speaking to demonstrate the exercise of self-restraint. Translated into portraiture, the pose came to symbolise masculine stoicism and reserve. Gainsborough's portrait invites us to associate these qualities with Cornewall's missing limb. The captain's disability is thus presented as proof of his fortitude, humility and willingness to set aside his self-interest for the sake of his duty.

This interpretation makes sense in the context of Cornewall's naval career. When he lost his arm at the Battle of Toulon, Cornewall was serving in the *Marlborough* as a lieutenant under his cousin, Captain James Cornewall. The ship was heavily engaged in the battle, and James was killed. Frederick took over command until he too was wounded. Their efforts were to little avail, however. The battle was a humiliating defeat, the British fleet succumbing to a combined Franco-Spanish force. A public scandal ensued after the fleet's commander, Admiral Thomas Mathews, alleged that his deputy, Vice-Admiral Richard Lestock, had refused to fight. Lestock counterclaimed that Mathews had rushed prematurely into action. Public opinion sided with Mathews but, controversially, the Admiralty courts came to the opposite conclusion. Lestock was cleared of all charges at a court martial in June 1746, then, five months later, Mathews was condemned and discharged from the Royal Navy. Observers were baffled that, in the words of the *Gentleman's Magazine*, 'one great naval officer' had been 'rendered incapable of service for his fighting...while another was acquitted for keeping due distance and looking on'. As a correspondent to the *Old England Journal* remarked, the verdict seemed to prove that 'fighting officers were not in vogue'.

The Cornewalls were among the few officers who escaped from the affair with their reputations intact. The cousins' wounds, fatal and non-fatal, were seen as proof that they, at least, were 'fighting officers'. It helped that James had influential friends in political circles, who persuaded parliament to erect a monument to his honour in Westminster Abbey. The monument's Latin inscription declared that 'he bequeathed as a legacy to his comrades-in-arms his own zeal'.

Memories of this episode may have informed Frederick's behaviour 12 years later, when he was involved in an even more high-profile naval debacle. In spring 1756, Cornewall was captain of the *Revenge* in Vice-Admiral John Byng's Mediterranean fleet. On 20 May, the fleet attempted to assist the British garrison on the island of Minorca, which was under siege from a French naval squadron. The attempt was not successful, and Byng decided to retreat to Gibraltar. The garrison held out for another month, before eventually surrendering the island on 29 June. Various factors contributed to the defeat, including faulty intelligence. However, the official response focused on Byng's withdrawal.

(fig. 2) *Admiral the Honourable Charles Stewart*
Allan Ramsay
1740, oil on canvas
1,040 x 1,120 mm
BHC3037

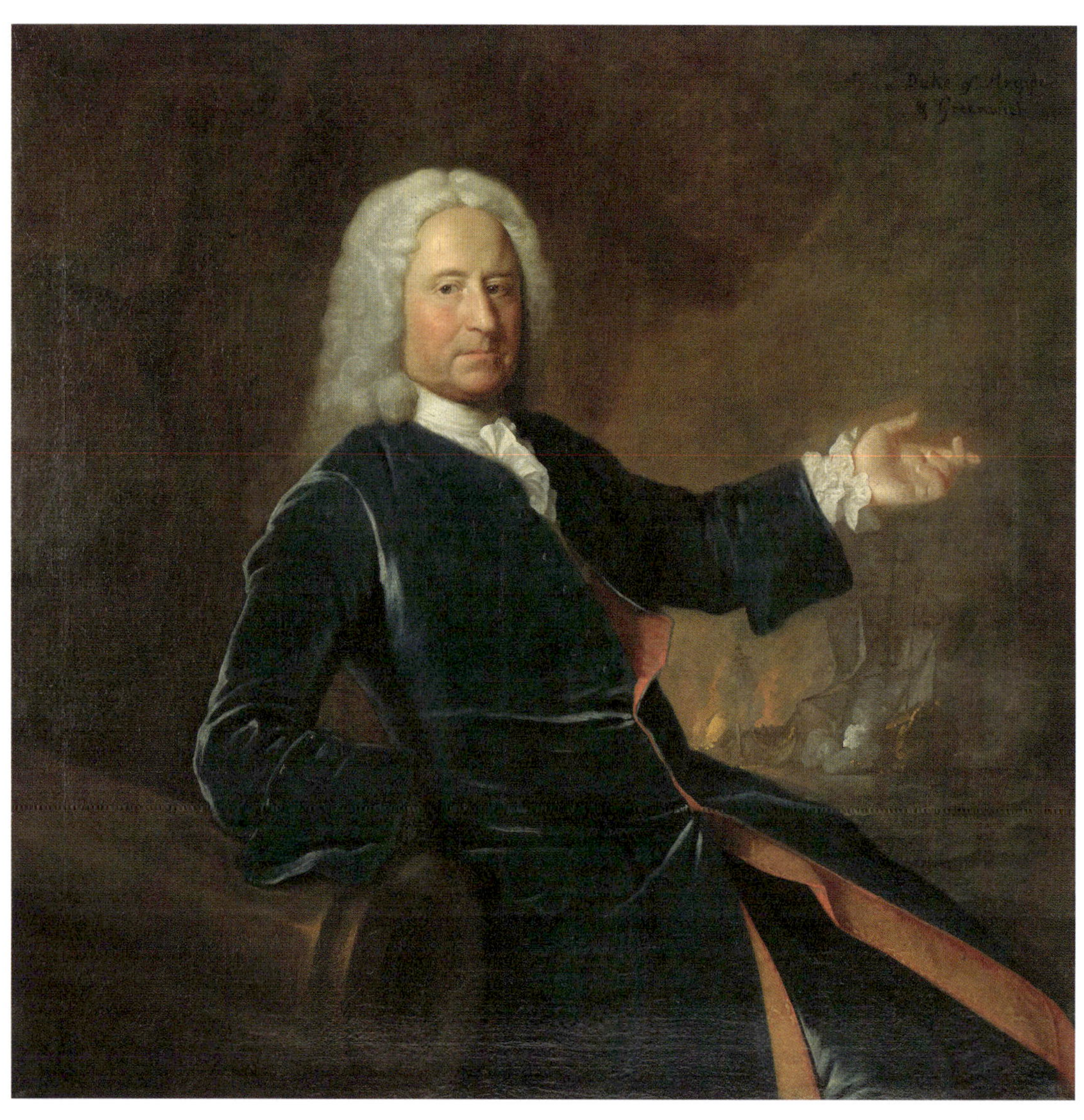

A court martial ruled that the vice-admiral had not done 'his utmost to take, seize and destroy the Ships of the French King', constituting a breach of the 12th Article of War, an offence which carried a mandatory death sentence. The punishment was not usually enforced, and the officers of the court called upon the King to commute the sentence, but their appeals were not heeded. On 14 March 1757, Byng was executed by firing squad, sending shockwaves through the Royal Navy.

Cornewall testified at the Admiral's trial, providing some of the crucial evidence that led to the Vice-Admiral's conviction. He insisted that Byng had remained unnecessarily distant from the French ships. Although he did not record his thoughts or feelings about the trial, it is tempting to speculate that Cornewall's earlier experiences at Toulon influenced his condemnation of Byng's caution.

Cornewall's reputation was inextricably bound up with his cousin's death and his own wounding in the notorious action off Toulon. For his valedictory final service before his retirement in 1761, he was given command of a new warship, the *Cornwall*, named in honour of his late cousin (albeit using an alternative spelling of the family surname). The appropriateness of this appointment was not lost on the press, the *Gentleman's Magazine* noting in its report on the ship's launch that Cornewall had 'lost his arm in the same engagement' in which his cousin had died. Given this affirmation of his missing limb as a badge of honour, it is hardly surprising that the Captain chose to show off his empty sleeve in his retirement portrait, painted the following year.

Gainsborough's simple but eloquent composition thus provides a fitting tribute to an officer whose disability had become central to his professional identity. The painting is one of the best works from this period in the artist's career. However, there was a long period in which Gainsborough was not recognised as the portrait's creator, starting with the acquisition of the work by the National Maritime Museum in 1960.

The painting was bequeathed to the Museum by art collector Edward Peter Jones, who had acquired it at an auction in 1918. The seller was the Red Cross, which had received the painting as a gift from a dealer four years previously. The dealer had purchased the painting in a sale of material belonging to the Cornewall family, the sitter's descendants, in 1905. At every stage in this process, Gainsborough was listed as the portrait's artist but, when it reached the Museum, the Curator of Paintings, E.H.H. Archibald, scrawled on the acquisition record that it was, in his opinion, 'too coarse for that painter'. The work was therefore catalogued as being by an unidentified British artist. It was only in 2022 that the painter's identity was rediscovered through the assistance of art historian Hugh Belsey. Both the quality of the work and its provenance leave no doubt that Gainsborough is indeed the artist.

To some extent, the name of the painter is irrelevant. Regardless of who the artist was, the painting deserves to be celebrated as a subtle and sophisticated example of mid-eighteenth-century naval portraiture. However, recognising Gainsborough as the artist deepens our appreciation of his talent for nuanced characterisation.

Vice-Admiral Sir Samuel Cornish, Captain Richard Kempenfelt and Thomas Parry

Tilly Kettle

1768, oil on canvas
1,752 x 1,447 mm
ZBA9432

In the eighteenth century, the most successful British portrait painters operated grand studios in London and mingled with the great and good of the capital's society. Elected President of the Royal Academy at its foundation in 1768, Joshua Reynolds exemplifies this model of metropolitan success. Yet not every artist ascended to such lofty heights. Many struggled in London's competitive environment and instead sought alternative opportunities in Britain's provinces and, increasingly, its colonies. Tilly Kettle was one such painter. With his career stagnating in London, he relocated his business to India, where he became the first British artist to run a profitable practice. Between 1769 and 1776, he made a small fortune painting colonial officials and Indian princes. His success sparked a trend, inspiring other British painters to undertake their own subcontinental sojourns.

Regarded as Kettle's masterpiece, this triple portrait was painted in 1768, a few months before the artist departed for India. It depicts Vice-Admiral Sir Samuel Cornish, seated on the right, issuing orders to his flag captain Richard Kempenfelt, standing on the left. A flag captain oversaw the day-to-day running of an admiral's flagship, allowing the admiral to concentrate on the management of the wider fleet. Cornish's secretary, Thomas Parry, sits between the two officers, his quill poised over a stack of papers. The setting is the admiral's cabin in the *Norfolk* – the ship in which the three men served in the East Indies in 1762. The painting commemorates their involvement in the capture of Manila, a significant Spanish trading base, in late September and early October that year. Although the Spanish government ultimately refused to pay the vast ransom to which the city's governor had originally agreed, the British forces nevertheless derived immense sums in prize money from the action, thanks in no small part to the capture of two Spanish treasure ships: the *Santissima Trinidad* and the *Filipina*.

As a depiction of the interior of an eighteenth-century British warship, the painting recalls Hogarth's *Captain Lord George Graham in his Cabin*, painted two decades earlier (p. 74). Yet the two works are very different in tone. Whereas Hogarth's small-scale conservation piece presents the cabin as a quasi-domestic space for dining and bonhomie, Kettle's vast canvas exudes grandeur and importance. Here the cabin appears as a place for making life-or-death decisions, where the fates of nations are sealed with the stroke of a pen. Although Cornish is the senior officer in the portrait, it is his secretary, Thomas Parry, who takes centre stage, emphasising the importance of bureaucracy and administration within the Navy. Parry's face is almost in the middle of the canvas, his light-coloured clothing standing out against the dark uniforms of his colleagues. While Cornish and Kempenfelt look at one another, seemingly absorbed in conversation, the Admiral's secretary arrests the viewer's attention with his confident gaze.

Parry's prominence reflects his status as the work's patron. It is remarkable that an admiral's secretary had both the aspirational desire and the financial resources to purchase a portrait on this scale. Typically, it was only senior officers (captains and admirals) who could afford to commission their own likenesses in this period. Parry, however, was a man of considerable ambition. The son of a wigmaker, he was admitted

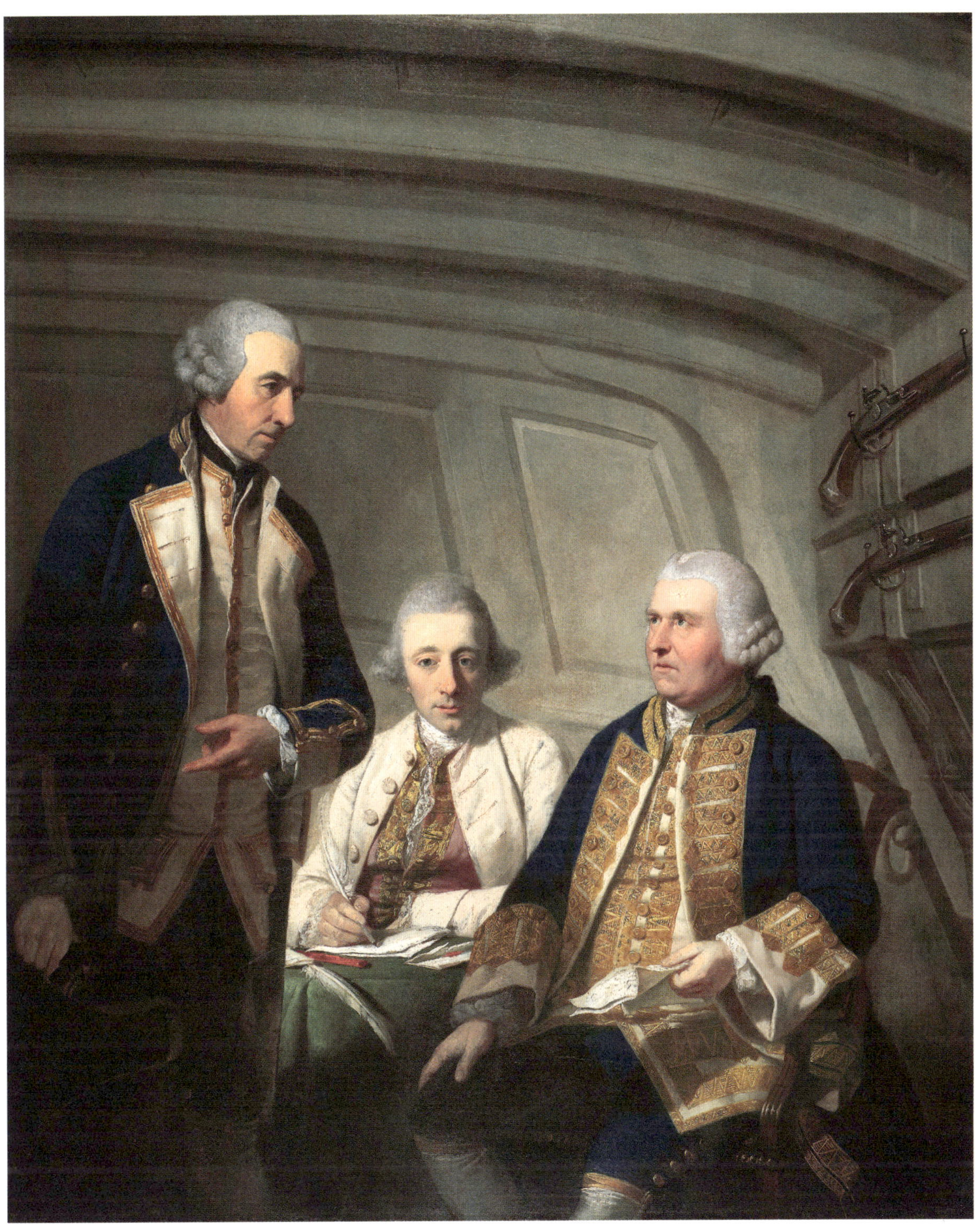

to the Freedom of the City of London in February 1755 through the Girdlers' Company, having completed a seven-year apprenticeship with a girdler, or belt-maker, called Thomas Hall. It was not unusual for young men to embark upon such apprenticeships in order to gain the privileges of City Freemen and the Girdlers' Company may have been no more than a passport to the City as far as Parry was concerned. Three years later, he joined the Navy as a volunteer corporal (an assistant to the Master at Arms) and began steadily climbing the ranks. He advanced first to become a clerk, then obtained a warrant as a ship's purser. As Cornish's secretary, he was a key figure in the financial management of the Manila expedition, from which he derived a sizeable personal profit in prize money. With his newfound wealth, he was able to enter into a respectable marriage with Mary Oakes, the daughter of a senior naval official, and to purchase a newly built townhouse in London's developing West End. Around the same time, he commissioned the triple portrait. Paid for with his growing fortune and providing a grand adornment for his new house, the painting manifested his self-esteem and upwards social mobility.

Parry remained in the Navy until 1781 but never again voyaged away from England, instead combining naval duties in the dockyards of Portsmouth, Woolwich, Deptford and Plymouth, with business interests in London. After leaving the Navy, he became a director of the East India Company, cementing his place in the merchant elite. He also remained close with Cornish's family, a relationship that culminated in the marriage of his son, Richard, to the Admiral's niece, Mary Gambier. The triple portrait remained in the possession of the Gambier-Parry family for many generations, passing through the hands of several important descendants, including the art collector Thomas Gambier-Parry, whose collection of medieval and Renaissance fine and decorative art is now held at the Courtauld Gallery, and the composer Sir Charles Hubert Parry, who is best known for setting William Blake's poetry to music in the choral song 'Jerusalem'. The portrait is thus tied through its provenance to a significant legacy of cultural achievement – a legacy ultimately founded upon Thomas Parry's lucrative career, the beginnings of which are commemorated in the painting.

Underwriting the wealth and privilege that Parry and his descendants enjoyed was the exploitation of people and resources that characterised the British imperial project. Parry's transition from naval secretary to company director demonstrates the interconnectedness of the Royal Navy and the East India Company, which enabled those involved – even administrators – to keep their families in comfort for generations. In Parry's confident gaze, the portrait brings us face-to-face with an individual who, in seeking to improve his own social and financial status, participated in a system of colonial expansion and associated abuses of power.

For the artist, the painting marked an important professional turning point. Kettle had begun working as a professional portraitist in the 1750s, beginning as an itinerant painter in the Midlands and gradually working up to establishing his own London studio. In 1768, the commission for the triple portrait provided the artist with a valuable opportunity to showcase his abilities on the metropolitan stage. As a large-scale group portrait (something Kettle had never previously attempted), it was his most ambitious work to date; its beautifully observed details, such as the glittering lattice-patterned buttons on Parry's waistcoat, provided a bravura demonstration of his painting skill. The portrait enjoyed considerable public visibility, featuring in not one but two major exhibitions at the Society of Artists in London: a special exhibition hosted for the visiting King Christian VII of Denmark in September 1768 and the Society's annual public exhibition the following spring. Public art exhibitions were a novel phenomenon at this time. London's first exhibition of contemporary art had taken place at the Society for the Encouragement of Arts, Manufactures and Commerce in April 1760 and annual displays soon became a fixture of the capital's social calendar.

Exhibitions were fashionable attractions for the urban middle-classes, providing artists with an unprecedented opportunity to indulge in self-promotion on a public stage. However,

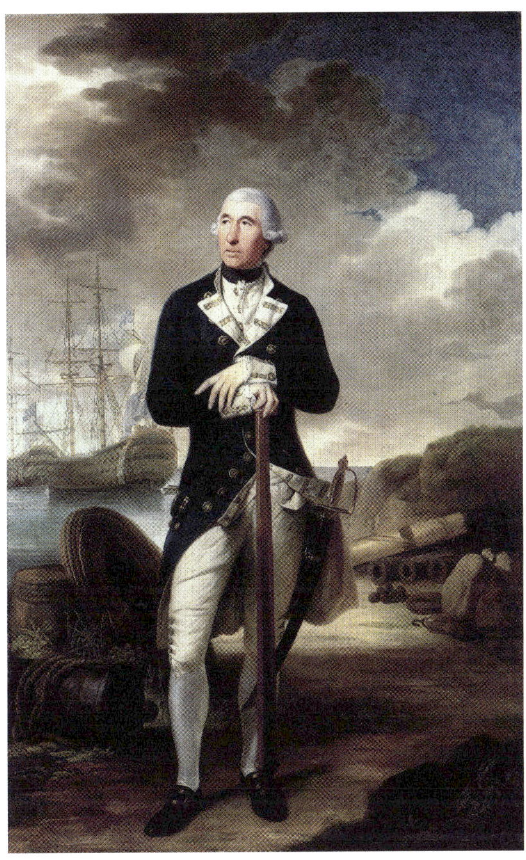

(fig. 1) *Rear-Admiral Richard Kempenfelt*
Tilly Kettle
1782, oil on canvas
2,440 x 1,525 mm
BHC2818

the exhibition of the triple portrait yielded disappointingly few results for Kettle. It did not win him many new clients and he was overlooked for membership of the Royal Academy when it was founded in December 1768. These professional disappointments appear to have prompted his decision to seek his fortune overseas.

Through his work on the triple portrait, Kettle had gained a set of valuable naval connections, who facilitated his voyage to the East Indies. A letter of recommendation from Admiral Cornish helped Kettle secure passage on board an East India Company ship in December 1768. Parry and Kempenfelt may have also helped the artist prepare for his travels and both men supported him when he returned from India in 1776. Parry witnessed the artist's marriage in 1777, while Kempenfelt commissioned him to paint a full-length portrait in 1782 (fig. 1). Their patronage was a boon to the artist, who struggled to find clients in London, his success in the colonies failing to translate into an improved reputation at home. Faced with mounting debts, Kettle set out to return to the East Indies in 1786 but died en route. Encompassing both success and failure, his career exemplifies the interrelation of art, the Navy, migration and trade during a formative phase in Britain's imperial history.

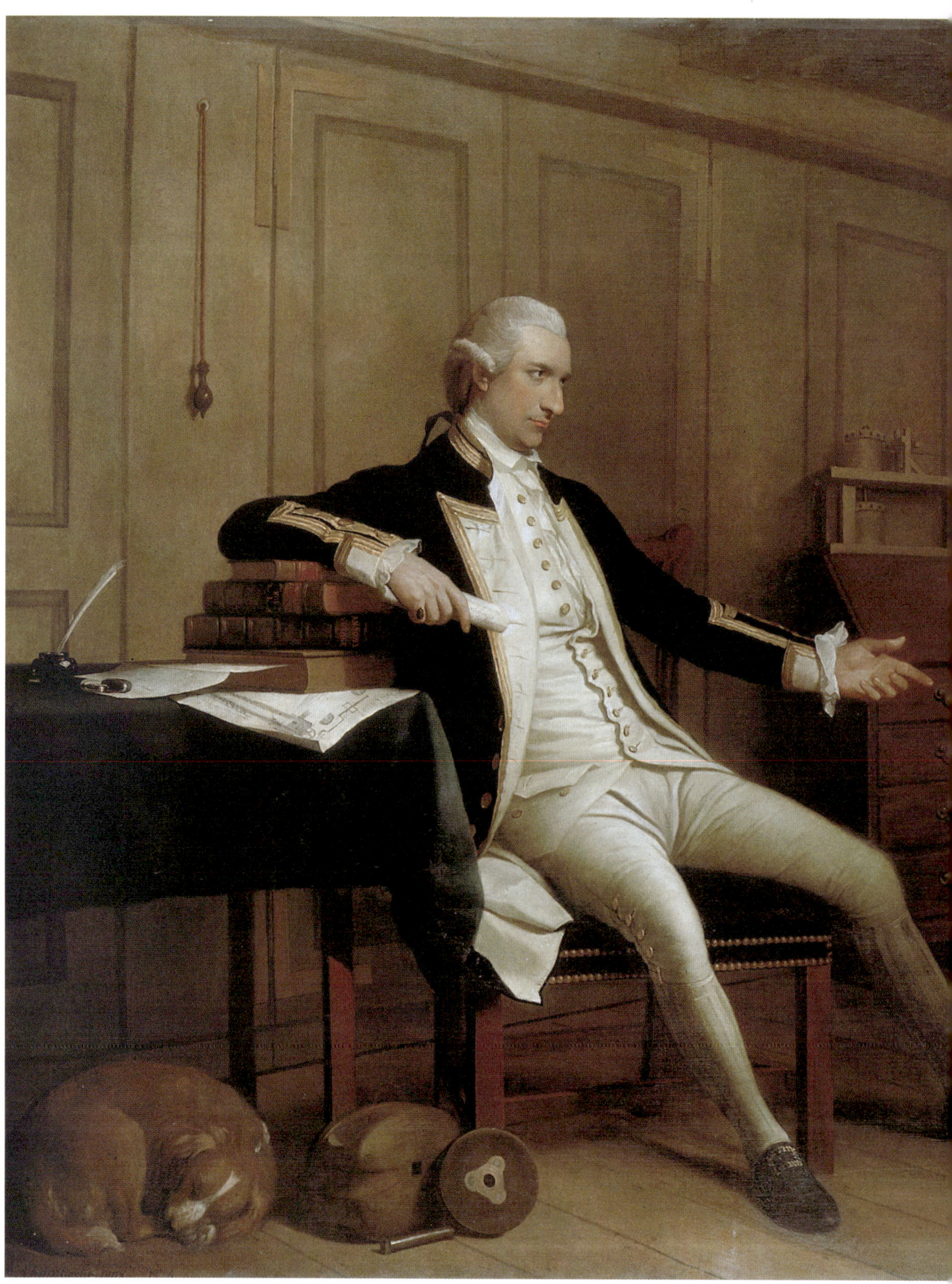

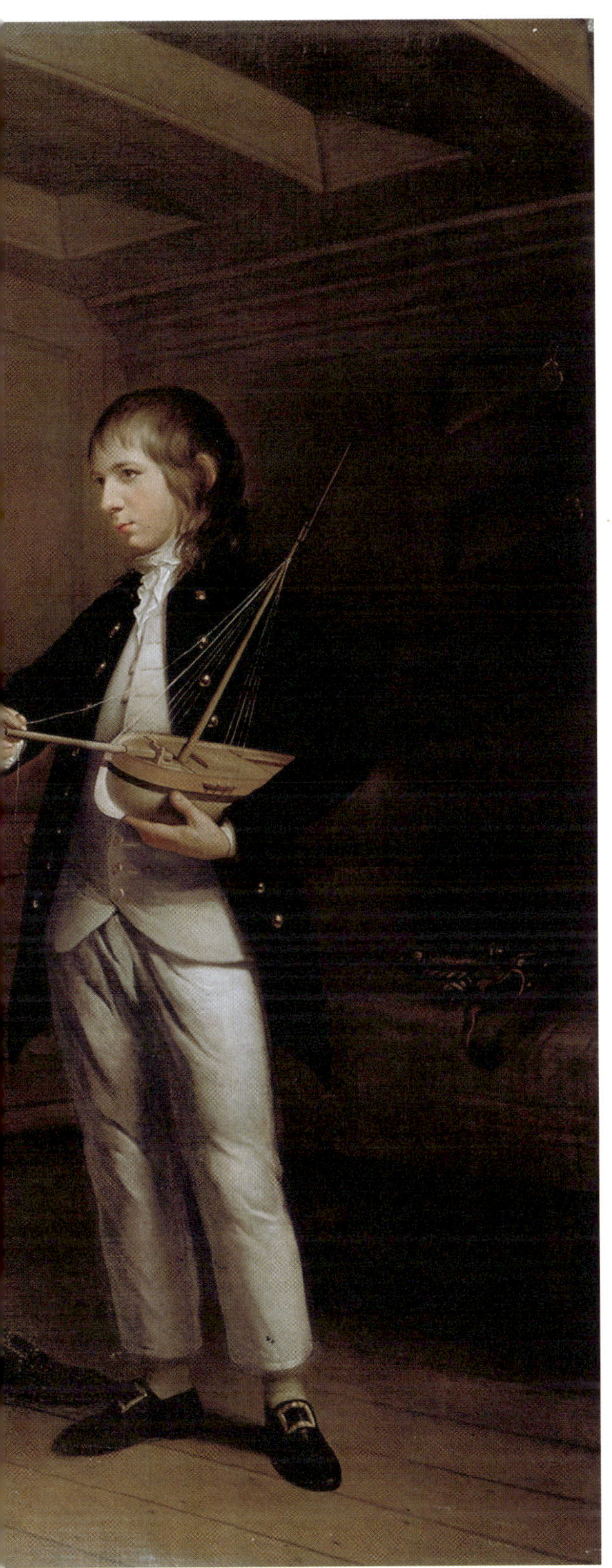

Captain John Bentinck and his Son, William Bentinck

Mason Chamberlin

1775, oil on canvas
1,970 x 2,425 mm
BHC2550

Mason Chamberlin was founding member of the Royal Academy of Arts. While some critics of the time derided his stone-faced and lifeless figures ('Mason Chamberlin's masonry', as one wag put it in the *Morning Post and Daily Advertiser* newspaper on 28 April 1784), his portraits frequently featured in London's annual exhibitions during the 1760s, 70s and 80s. He was particularly successful in attracting commissions from intellectuals, artists and inventors, including the American statesman and polymath Benjamin Franklin, who posed for Chamberlin while visiting London in 1762. The resulting portrait, which referenced Franklin's electrical experiments, complete with a lightning flash in the background, is now Chamberlin's most famous painting (fig. 1).

Painted in 1775, this large double portrait depicts naval officer Captain John Bentinck and his 11-year-old son William. Like Tilly Kettle's image of Cornish, Kempenfelt and Parry (p. 104), the portrait is set in a ship's cabin. Bentinck was between ships when the painting was completed, but the setting may refer to his previous vessel, the *Centaur*, which he commanded between 1770 and 1773. Chamberlin's depiction of a doorway in the bulkhead behind Bentinck's head suggests the possibility of communication between the cabin and the rest of the ship, situating the depicted space within a wider network of working environments. However, the closure of the door underscores the social exclusivity of the captain's cabin, a space reserved for the officer class. Numerous details signal the gentility of this environment, from the bellpull beside the door

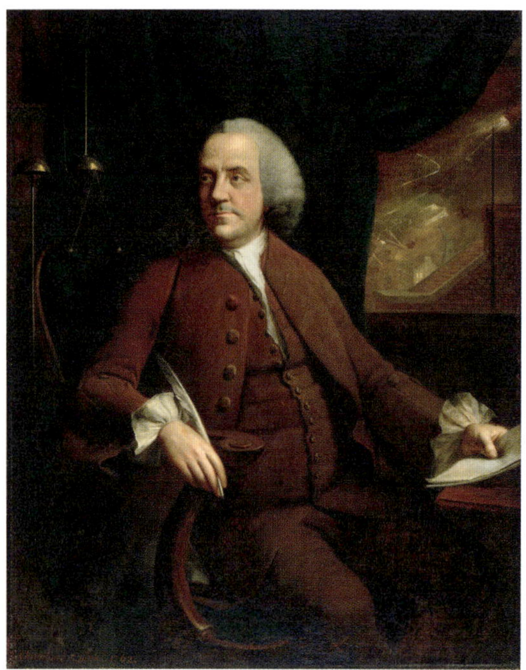

(fig. 1) *Benjamin Franklin*
Mason Chamberlin
1762, oil on canvas
1,280 × 1,035 mm
Philadelphia Museum of Art, Gift of Mr and Mrs Wharton Sinkler, 1956 (1956-88-1)

for summoning servants to the captain's attire, which consists of full-dress naval uniform, a wig and a gold signet ring. More fashion accessory than functional weapon, his dress sword lies on a bench in the background and his pet spaniel snoozes beneath the table.

If not for the wooden decking, curved beams and wall-mounted guns, this portrait could almost represent a gentleman in his study, rather than an officer on board his ship. The furniture, which includes an upholstered chair, a table and a bureau, would not look out of place in a domestic setting. Moreover, with books, papers, models and obscure apparatus scattered about the space, the painting resembles the portraits of scholars and inventors for which Chamberlin was known. Bentinck himself moved in scientific circles and was interested in technological innovation, especially in naval contexts. In fact, he may have been introduced to Chamberlin through the artist's former client Benjamin Franklin, with whom Bentinck worked on a series of scientific experiments in 1773. Using one of the *Centaur*'s longboats, Bentinck and Franklin tested whether pouring oil into the sea could reduce the height or force of waves breaking on the shore. Had their theory proved correct, this technique would have made bringing boats into land safer and easier. In the end, the results were inconclusive but Bentinck's involvement in the experiment demonstrates his commitment to research and innovation.

The portrait emphasises Bentinck's professional expertise and ingenuity. He rests his elbow on books inscribed 'Anson's Voyage' and 'Saunderson's Algebra Vol. 1', referring respectively to the published account of Admiral George Anson's circumnavigation and to a well-known mathematical textbook of the period. Together, these books highlight the specialist knowledge that a career in the Royal Navy required. Meanwhile, several inventions that Bentinck had himself devised are included in the painting. On the floor sits a prototype for his new design of pulley block, while a diagram of his improved chain pump pokes out from under his books. An identical diagram appears in Bentinck's 'Scheme Book', into which he copied his correspondence with the Admiralty concerning his inventions (fig. 2). Inscribed 'Memorandums relative to the Capstan 1770', the rolled paper in Bentinck's right hand also refers to a document in the 'Scheme Book'. This memorandum describes a new design for ships' capstans (revolving cylinders used for winding heavy cables), a model for which is depicted on top of the bureau in the portrait's background. Unsolicited by the Admiralty, Bentinck's inventions were developed on his own initiative, often through trials conducted in his ship, a practice which sometimes brought him into conflict with the navy's official regulations. In May 1772, for example, he received a stern rebuke from the Navy Board for re-rigging his ship according to his own design, which was 'contrary to the Rules of the Navy and the General Printed Instructions'. However, conceding that his new rigging had significant advantages, the Board allowed the offence to pass unpunished. As this incident shows, there was potential for Bentinck to be seen as a rebellious maverick within the Navy's ranks. He instead appears as a responsible, benevolent and paternalistic figure in Chamberlin's portrait, thanks to the inclusion of his young son.

William Bentinck stands before his father in the uniform of the Naval Academy, an Admiralty-run school in Portsmouth Dockyard which provided education for prospective officers. Under his arm, he cradles an incomplete model of a single-masted sailing vessel, from which the boom and sails are missing. William holds a loose rope from the model's rigging in his right hand, the implication being that he is developing his practical understanding of seamanship through the construction of the miniature vessel. Put another way, he is literally learning the ropes from his father, who points at the model in a manner that suggests instruction. Although young officer candidates usually learnt about sailing using full-scale ships, rather than miniaturised models, manual activity was central to a naval education. At the same time, the hands-on lesson depicted in this portrait might also be interpreted as a response to the parenting advice in Jean-Jacques Rousseau's *Emile* (1762), an influential pedagogical treatise which, among other recommendations, suggested that practical work should be used in the education of boys. A friend and correspondent of Rousseau, John Bentinck admired *Emile* and seems to have taken seriously his role as a parent. With its emphasis on the father-son bond, the portrait showcases the 'domestic affections' for which Bentinck was later praised in James Fordyce's *Addresses to Young Men* (1777), a series of moralistic sermons covering subjects such as love, friendship, honour and duty.

Weaving together the themes of gentility, professionalism, creativity and familial affection, Chamberlin's painting highlights the complex mixture of different elements that could constitute naval identity in mid-eighteenth-century portraiture. There is, however, a poignant postscript to the story of this painting. Aged only 37, John Bentinck died from a sudden illness in the same year that the portrait was completed, leaving a widow and seven young children, William included. His bereaved family displayed the painting in their country residence at Indio in Devon.

(fig. 2) *Description of the Improved Chain Pump by John Bentinck, Esq.*
Thomas Powell after John Bentinck
1794, ink and watercolour on paper
SPB/33

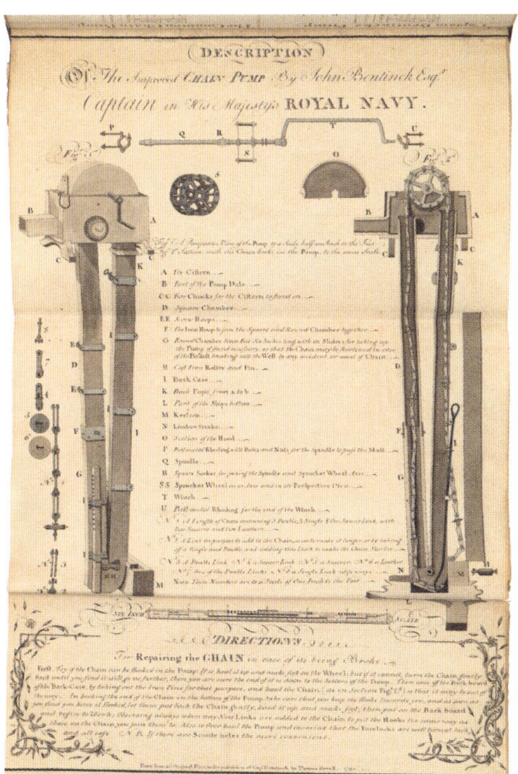

Captain James Cook

Nathaniel Dance

1775–76, oil on canvas
1,270 x 1,016 mm
BHC2628

Nathaniel Dance came from a celebrated artistic family. His father and younger brother, both called Charles, were noted architects, while Nathaniel himself specialised in portrait painting. He spent most of his twenties in Rome, where he studied old masters and worked in partnership with the Italian portraitist Pompeo Batoni. Many of Batoni's clients were young Englishmen on the grand tour, a journey through Europe which served in this period as a rite of passage for the ruling elite. Returning to London in the mid-1760s, Dance used the skills he had developed in Batoni's studio to establish his own business as a fashionable portrait painter.

Captain James Cook posed for this portrait for a few hours before dinner on 25 May 1776, one month before setting sail for the Pacific. This voyage was to be his third – and, as it turned out, final – journey to the South Seas, a part of the world little known to Europeans at this time. Cook's first two voyages (1768–71 and 1772–75) had combined overt scientific objectives, including astronomical experiments and botanical surveys, with covert reconnaissance: the Admiralty had tasked Cook and his men with searching for a theorised great southern continent (*Terra Australis Incognita*) in the hope that its natural resources could be exploited to Britain's advantage. While Cook failed to find evidence of the predicted continent, he did chart the coastlines of New Zealand and eastern Australia (known at that time as 'New Holland'), paving the way for British colonisation of these lands and violence against their Indigenous peoples. The purpose of the third voyage was to search for a north-west passage linking the Atlantic and Pacific Oceans via the Canadian Arctic. Cook never returned from this voyage, losing his life during an altercation with Hawaiian islanders on 14 February 1779. He therefore never saw this portrait completed.

The painting was the result of a commission from the gentleman-naturalist Joseph Banks, who had accompanied Cook on his first voyage to the Pacific. In the public imagination, the wealthy and charismatic Banks was regarded the star of the voyage, while Cook – an experienced but unknown naval officer – was cast in a supporting role. Banks displayed the portrait over the fireplace in the library of his London home, 32 Soho Square. This was consistent with an eighteenth-century tradition of decorating libraries with portraits of friends, associates and 'great men'.

In the portrait, Cook is seated on an upholstered chair, the red brocaded back of which is visible over his shoulder. He points to a large naval chart, which is spread out on a desk in front of him, next to a book and his tricorn hat. Though the inscriptions on the chart are barely legible (it is possible to make out 'A Chart of…' and 'South…'), it without doubt alludes to his famous chart of 'New Holland'. The furniture evokes the idea of a gentleman's study, which is appropriate given that the painting was destined to hang in a library. Seen in this setting, the work of navigation is presented as a refined intellectual pursuit. However, Cook's unidealised features undercut the scholarly ambiance. His hawkish gaze gives an impression of steely authority, while his lined eyes and reddened cheeks testify to a career spent in harsh environments, rather than behind a desk. Furthermore, the blank stone walls behind him do not appear to belong to a domestic building.

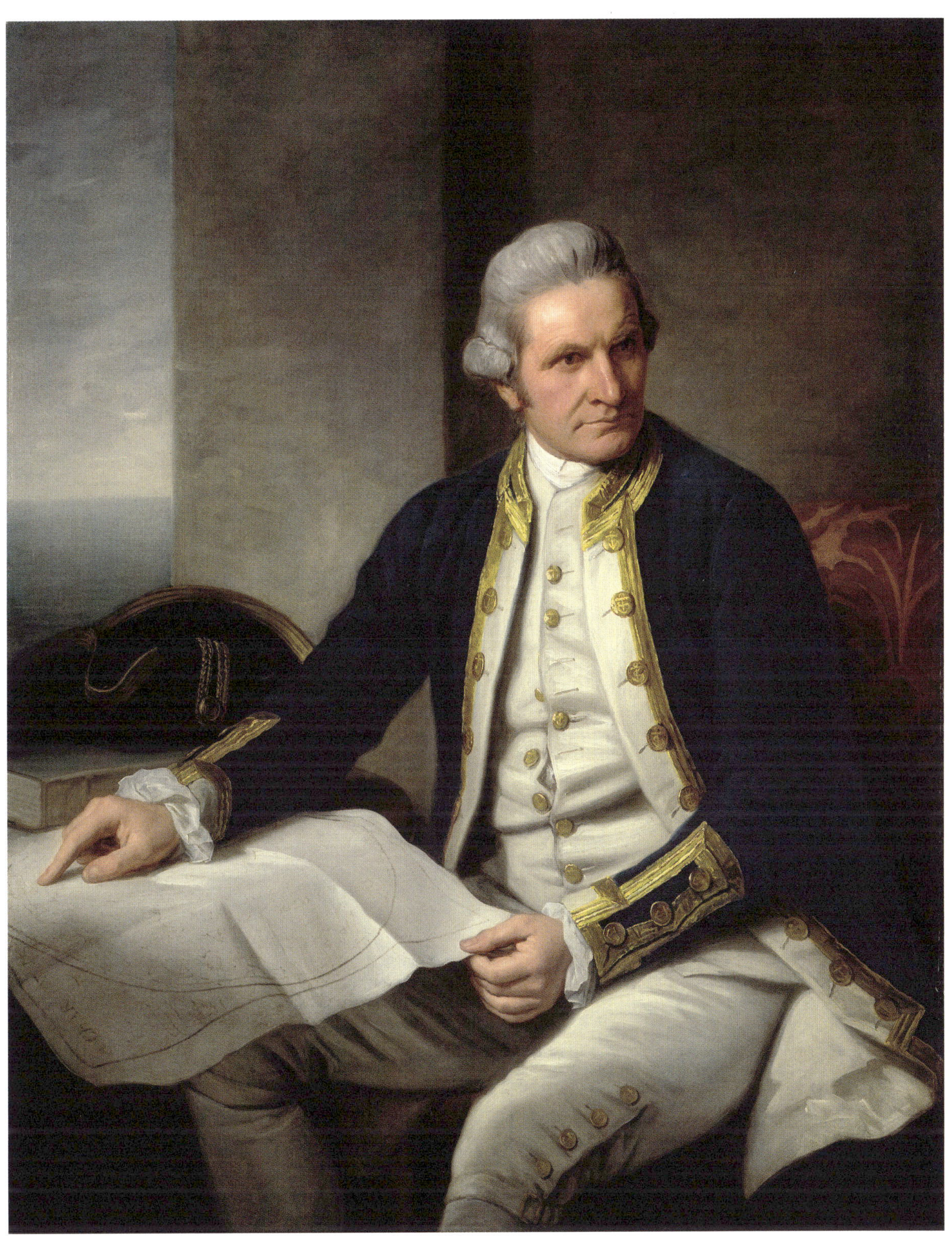

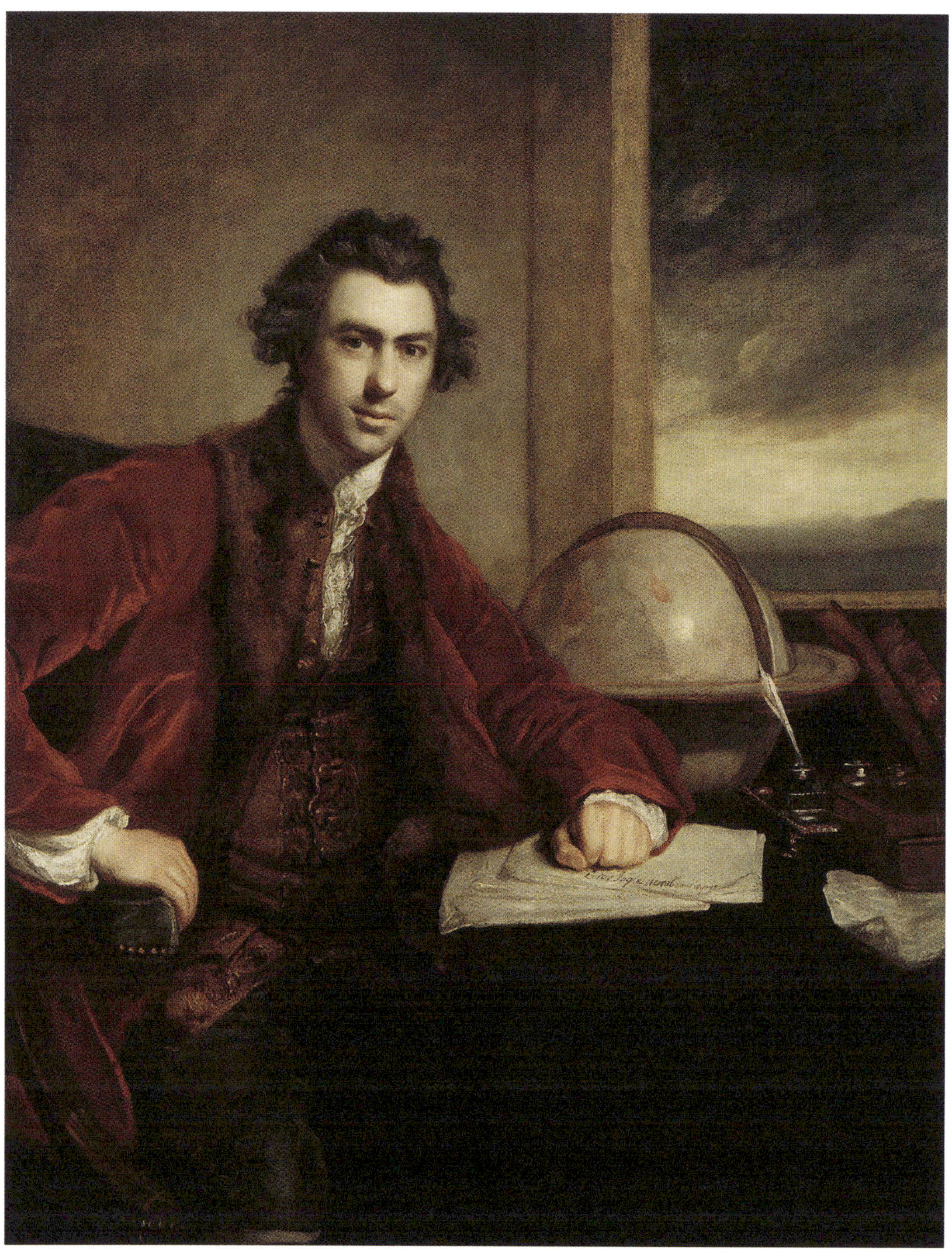

This nondescript space is open on one side to a view of an empty sea, suggesting Cook's status as a traveller to distant and unknown places.

Inspiration for this depiction likely came from a previous portrait that Banks had commissioned from Joshua Reynolds in 1771. The subject of this portrait was Banks himself (fig. 1). With its combination of chair, desk, blank wall and seascape, Reynolds's earlier composition is almost a mirror image of Dance's later one. This resemblance suggests that Dance was responding to Reynolds's portrait. Indeed, Banks may have encouraged Dance to create a similar image to emphasise the professional connection he and Cook shared.

Banks and Cook had become famous as explorers, but the theme of exploration had not been represented in many portraits prior to this time. Reynolds and Dance therefore had to adapt other pictorial traditions to suit their sitters. For both artists, a key influence appears to have been grand tour portraiture – that is, the paintings young aristocrats commissioned in Italy as souvenirs of their European travels. Dance in particular was familiar with this artistic tradition from his time in Rome, where his former business partner Pompeo Batoni dominated the tourist market. Batoni's paintings of visiting Englishmen often showed the subject seated or standing at a table covered in papers, books and maps. Fragments of classical sculpture were sometimes also present, symbolising the accumulation of knowledge and refinement associated with the grand tour (as well as the acquisition of antiques and other luxury goods). In the background, stone architecture framed a view of Italianate scenery. This formula is exemplified in the portrait of Richard Milles, which Batoni painted in around 1759 (fig. 2). Many of the key elements in this painting appear in the portraits of Cook and Banks, including the pointing gesture through which Milles and Cook indicate their respective journeys on a map. The only notable differences are the absence of ancient statues in the explorers' portraits and the substitution of the sea for the Italian countryside in the background.

In adapting the imagery of the grand tour to depict Pacific explorers, Reynolds and Dance extended cultural assumptions about the ennobling effects of European travel and classical learning to encompass their sitters' adventures in the South Seas. Reynolds even included a Latin inscription in Banks's portrait, scrawled on one of the papers on the desk: 'cras ingens iterabimus aequor' ('tomorrow we set out over the vast sea'). This quotation from the ancient Roman poet Horace not only highlighted Banks's status as a traveller but also imbued his travels with an air of classical sophistication. No classical references appear in Dance's portrait of Cook, but the cultural context is implied in the painting's resemblance to a grand tour portrait.

(fig. 1) *Sir Joseph Banks, Bt.*
Joshua Reynolds
1771–73, oil on canvas
1,270 x 1,015 mm
National Portrait Gallery (NPG 5868)

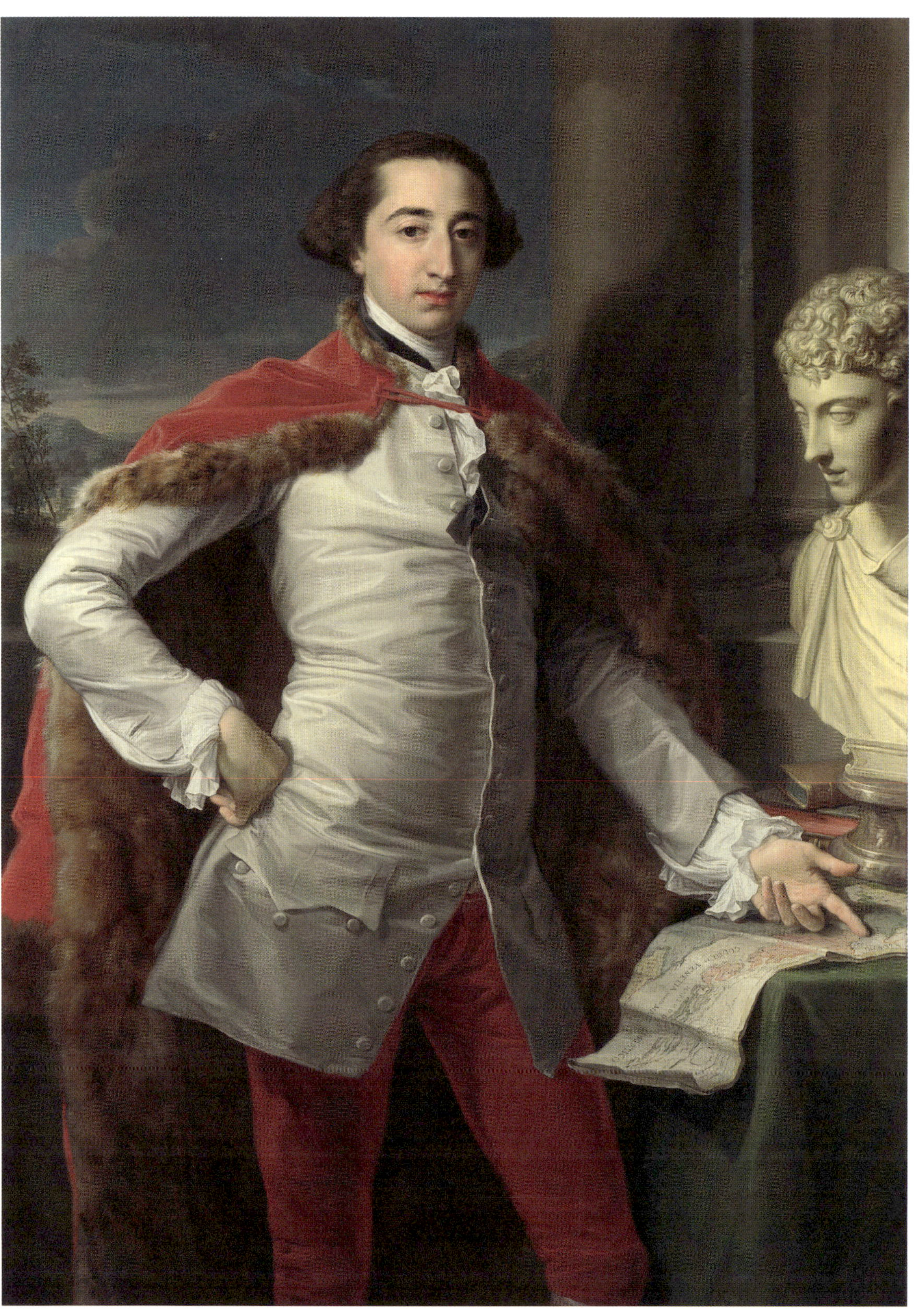

Recognising this implicit classicism, New Zealand-born artist Marian Maguire reinterpreted the painting as part of her lithograph series, 'The Odyssey of Captain Cook', completed in 2005. In the ninth plate of the series, Dance's portrait is extended to encompass a Greek-style vase, similar to the antiquities often featured in grand tour portraits (fig. 3). The decoration on the vase shows the Greek hero Hercules fighting a Māori warrior over a pig. Pitting European mythology against the ancient and sophisticated cultural heritage of the Māori, this imagery challenges the assumptions of cultural superiority over Indigenous peoples that Western explorers and colonisers brought with them to the Pacific. Maguire's reworking of the portrait is a reminder of Cook's controversial legacy.

Opposite: (fig. 2) *Richard Milles*
Pompeo Batoni
about 1759, oil on canvas
1,346 x 963 mm
National Gallery (NG6459)

(fig. 3) *The Odyssey of Captain Cook: Plate IX*,
from the series 'The Odyssey of Captain Cook'
Marian Maguire
2005, lithograph on paper
570 x 700 mm
ZBA7689

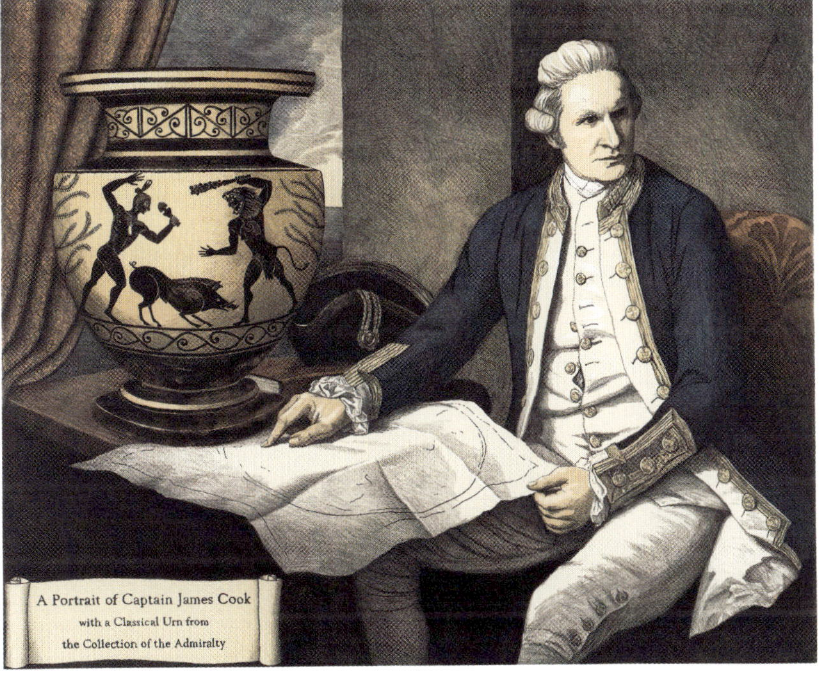

CHAPTER 4

The Age of Revolutions

1775–1815

Historian Eric Hobsbawm popularised the term 'age of revolution' to describe the series of revolutionary political movements that transformed Europe and North America during the late eighteenth and early nineteenth centuries. These movements challenged absolutist monarchies and sought to establish republics and constitutionalist states. Hobsbawm began his book, *The Age of Revolution: Europe 1789–1848* (first published in 1962), with the French Revolution, but many scholars extend his term to encompass the War of American Independence (1775–83). Other events in this tumultuous period include the Irish Rebellion of 1798 and the Haitian Revolution (1791–1804), a successful insurrection of enslaved people against French colonial rule. Major social, economic, technological and cultural shifts also occurred in these years, hence Hobsbawm's famous phrase is now often pluralised to suggest the variety of different revolutions that took place.

Britain did not experience a major political revolution in this period, but it was nevertheless a turbulent time for the nation. Between 1775 and 1783, Britain fought a controversial and unsuccessful war to retain its 13 American colonies. Then, with its declaration of war on the French Republic in 1793, the nation embarked upon a prolonged struggle for military supremacy with its age-old enemy, which lasted until the final defeat of Napoleon at the Battle of Waterloo in 1815. These hostilities inflamed British nationalism and anti-French prejudice. Meanwhile, radical agitation and calls for social change within Britain were met with reactionary conservatism and counter-revolutionary paranoia. The political tension fuelled the production of propaganda and ideologically charged artworks.

For naval officers, the conflict created copious opportunities through which to advance their careers and to achieve celebrity status, although these potential advantages were set against the palpable risk of injury and death. Britain's consistent success at sea during the Napoleonic Wars was seized upon as grist to the mill of national myth-making, constructing a powerful identity for Britain as a 'maritime nation'. It is no coincidence that this period gave rise to the most celebrated naval officer in British history, Horatio Nelson. While Nelson was a charismatic leader, he also had the good fortune to live (and die) at a time when conditions were ripe for turning a successful naval commander into an enduring national hero.

Thanks to the vast number of officers wanting to commemorate their achievements and the intense public demand for their images, naval portraiture proliferated in this period like never before. Painted portraits were often discussed in the press or reproduced as prints and book illustrations, extending their reach to a broader audience. Some portraits of naval officers expressed political ideas, from criticising the government to propagandising the war effort. Others were far more private, helping naval families to cope with the absence or loss of loved ones.

Captain Thomas Baillie

Nathaniel Hone

1779, oil on canvas
914 x 737 mm
BHC2523

Nathaniel Hone was an Irish artist who moved to England as a young man. A founding member of the Royal Academy of Arts, he was a prolific contributor to the Academy's annual exhibitions. He also had a reputation for irreverence and sometimes exhibited works with critical or satirical edge. Painted in 1779, this portrait demonstrates Hone's willingness to support individuals who stood up to those more powerful than themselves.

Whereas most naval portraits celebrate heroic actions at sea, this example highlights Captain Thomas Baillie's work as an administrator. Seated at a writing desk, Baillie holds out his left hand in an explanatory gesture, as if about to speak, and points with his right index finger to an open manuscript, which is inscribed 'Gr[een]wich Hospital'. On the table to the left are two inkwells, a pen and a piece of paper with the inscription 'Lt Gov[e]n[or] Baillie'.

The portrait's inscriptions refer to Baillie's employment at Greenwich Hospital. Housed in a grand architectural complex on the banks of the Thames, Greenwich Hospital (now the Old Royal Naval College), provided support and accommodation for disabled and retired sailors. Its beneficiaries were known as Greenwich Pensioners. Baillie had been appointed as the Hospital's Lieutenant-Governor in 1774. Four years later, he was ousted from the position after challenging the First Lord of the Admiralty – John Montagu, 4th Earl of Sandwich – over corruption in the Hospital's management. Baillie alleged that, while the Pensioners were receiving inadequate food rations of 'bull-beef and sour small-beer mixed with water', Sandwich (the eponymous inventor of the sandwich) was rewarding his political allies with well-paid positions at the Hospital and creating 'elegant apartments' for their use in the Hospital's buildings.

After receiving no response to his official complaints about these issues, Baillie privately circulated a pamphlet detailing the problems in 1778. The manuscript in the portrait may refer to this text. Following the pamphlet's publication, Sandwich immediately dismissed Baillie from his post and brought a case of criminal libel against him. In the resulting court hearing, Baillie was brilliantly defended by the young barrister Thomas Erskine, later an eminent Lord Chancellor. The case is now famous for Erskine's impassioned closing remarks, in which he argued that Baillie had acted according to his 'obligations of duty and conscience' and that, if the corruption in the Royal Navy was not addressed, sailors would refuse to risk their lives in its service.

Erskine's speech was enthusiastically reported in the press, generating public sympathy for the Captain's cause. Baillie was acquitted of the charge of libel, but a motion in the House of Lords to set up an inquiry into the management of Greenwich Hospital was defeated. Furthermore, Sandwich refused to reinstate Baillie to his post at the Hospital or to appoint him to a ship for active service. The Captain therefore had to campaign to save his career, and Hone's portrait was produced to aid this effort.

Echoing Erskine's defence, the portrait highlights Baillie's role as an advocate for the Greenwich Pensioners through the reference to his pamphlet and his rhetorical pose. The painting was engraved in mezzotint by James Watson and published with an inscription that criticised

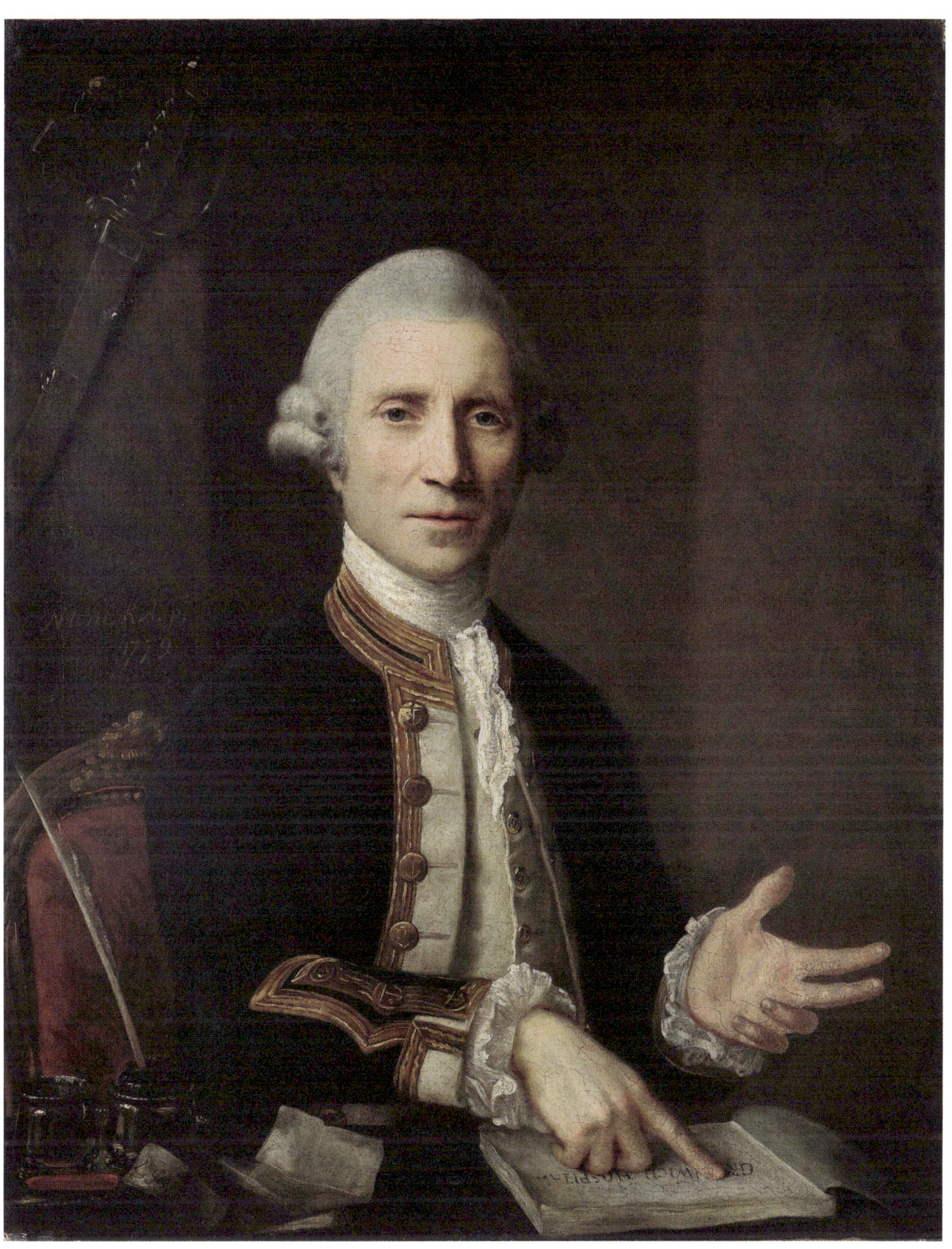

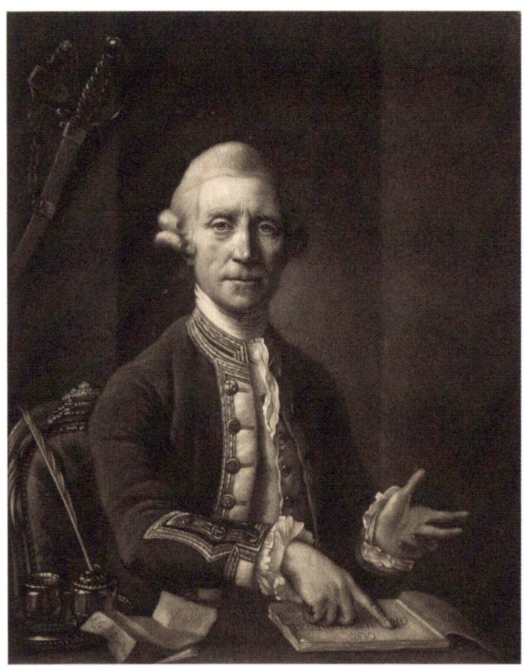

(fig. 1) *Captain Thomas Baillie, Late Lieut. Governor of the Royal Hospital at Greenwich*
James Watson after Nathaniel Hone
1779, mezzotint on paper
346 x 240 mm
PAG6442

Opposite: (fig. 2) *John Montagu, 4th Earl of Sandwich, First Lord of the Admiralty*
Thomas Gainsborough
1783, oil on canvas
2,325 x 1,514 mm
BHC3009

Sandwich and hailed Baillie 'for asserting the rights of British seamen, widows and children' (fig. 1). The print was used as a frontispiece to a pamphlet titled *A Solemn Appeal to the Public, from an Injured Officer, Captain Baillie, late Lieutenant Governor, of the Royal Hospital for Seaman at Greenwich*, published in 1779. The following year, the painting was exhibited at the Royal Academy, where one reviewer commented that Baillie's 'arms appear rather short in proportion, but perhaps the Artist had it in his idea, that a noble Lord has lately taken from his arms' – a satirical barb directed at the Earl of Sandwich, masquerading as an artistic critique.

Despite the controversy, Sandwich remained in office until March 1782. Following his retirement, his career was celebrated in a large portrait, which the Governor of Greenwich Hospital, Admiral Sir Hugh Palliser, commissioned from Thomas Gainsborough – one of most sought-after portraitists of the day (fig. 2). In this painting, Sandwich holds a plan for the new infirmary at Greenwich Hospital, which was erected on his orders in the 1760s, and the buildings of the Hospital are depicted in the background. The Earl is represented as a noble champion of the institution and its Pensioners; Baillie's story reveals the hypocrisy of this depiction.

With Sandwich gone from the Admiralty, Baillie finally found a new position within the Navy, serving as Clerk of the Deliveries in the Board of Ordnance. His fortunes were further revived in 1784 when he received a legacy of £500 from John Barnard, the son of a former lord mayor of London. Barnard's will stated that the money was 'a small token of my approbation of [Baillie's] worthy and disinterested, though ineffectual, endeavours to rescue that noble national charity [Greenwich Hospital] from the rapacious hands of the basest and most wicked of mankind'.

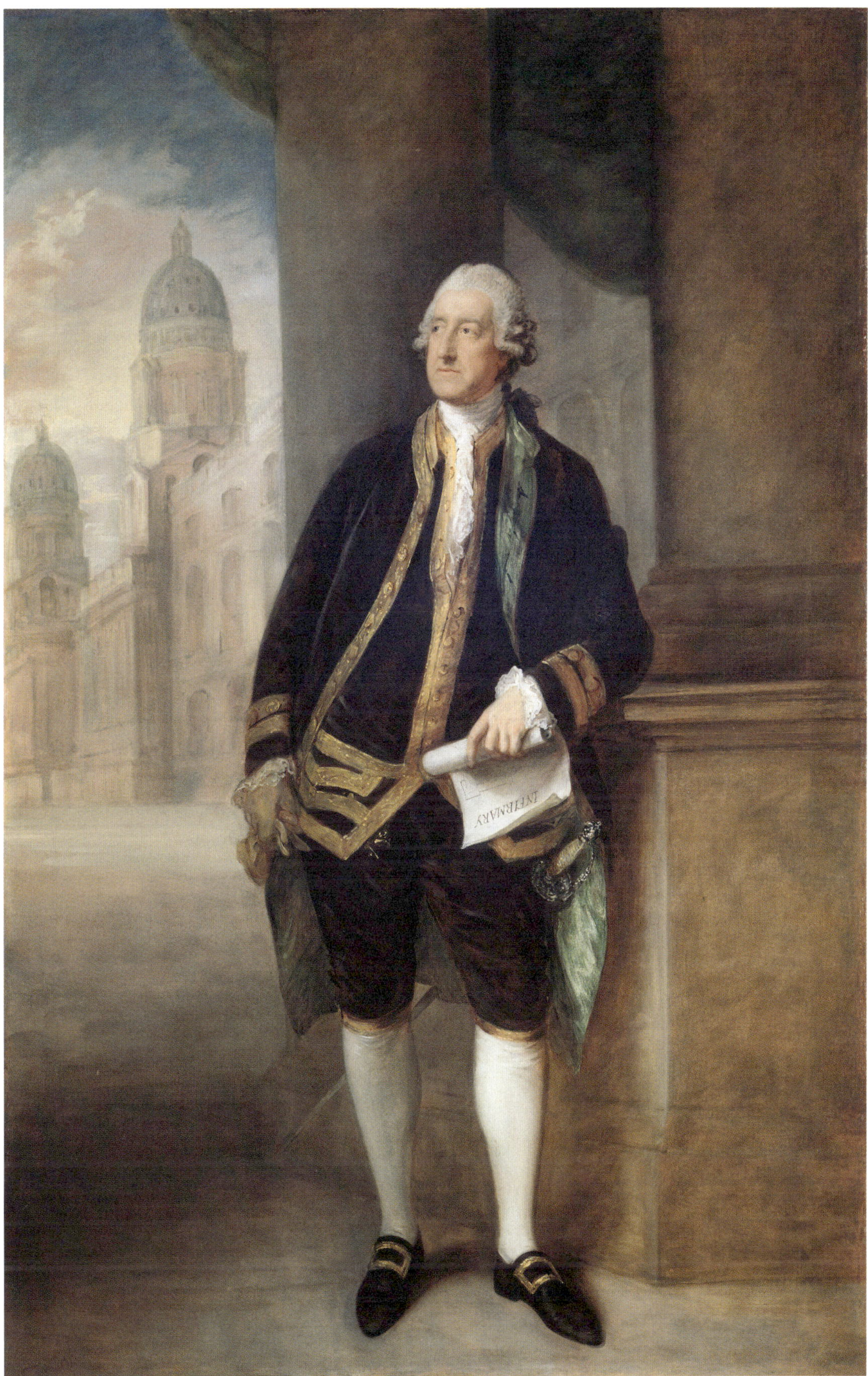
INFIRMARY

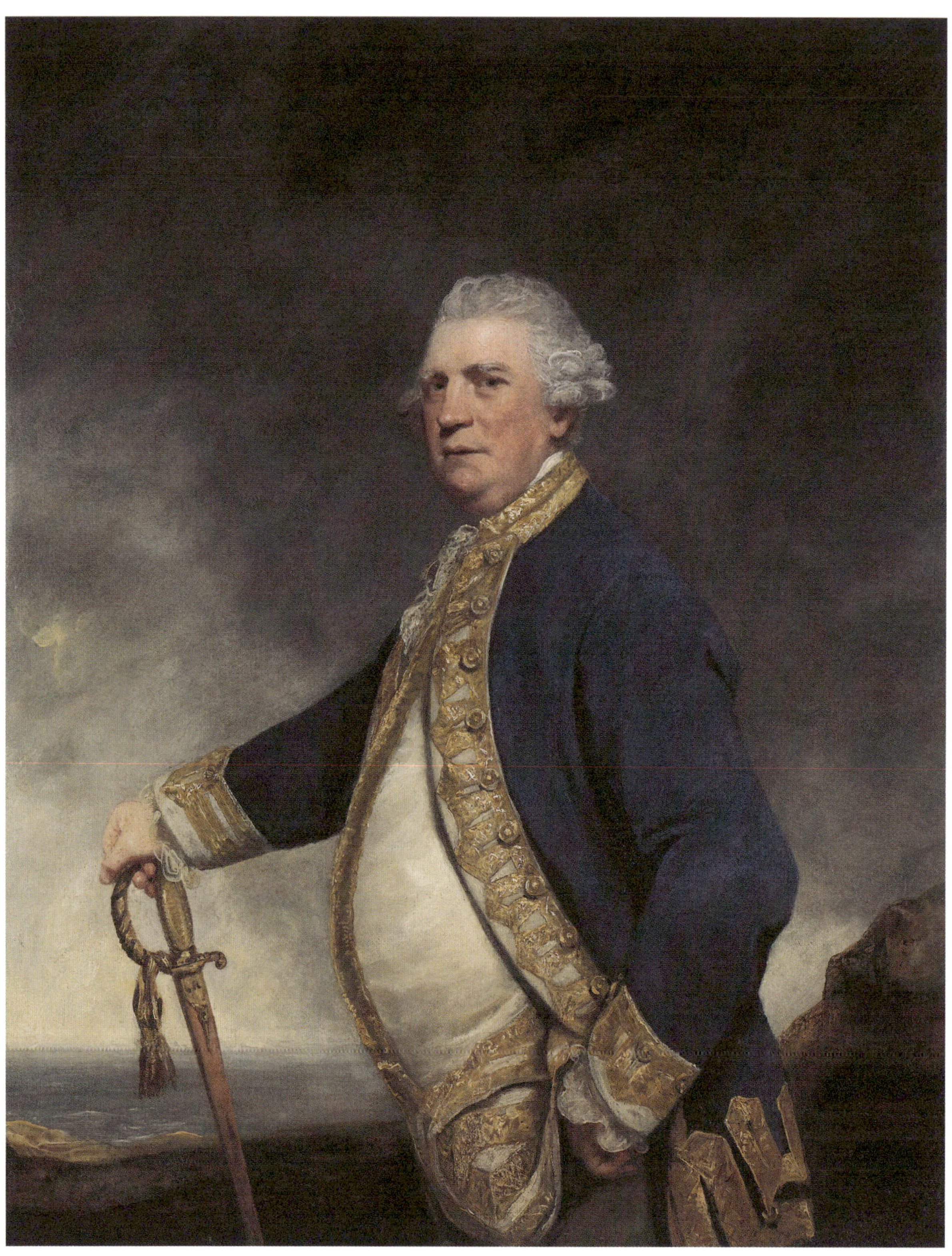

Admiral Augustus Keppel

Joshua Reynolds

1779, oil on canvas
1,270 x 1,015 mm
BHC2822

As President of the Royal Academy of Arts, Reynolds was the public spokesperson for the high-art agenda that had underpinned its foundation. In a series of annual and biennial lectures, known as the Discourses, he encouraged his fellow artists to create edifying paintings of historical scenes. Yet, in his own practice, he remained a society portraitist, flattering the whims and vanities of wealthy clients and exploiting their images for profit. He no longer painted as many naval officers as he had done in his early years in Plymouth, but he was still close friends with Augustus Keppel, the aristocratic officer whose image had launched Reynolds's career in London (p. 86). He painted Keppel on seven different occasions throughout his life, creating a series of paintings that charted the changing identities of both artist and sitter over almost four decades of friendship.

This portrait represents the fifth occasion on which Keppel sat to his friend Reynolds. It was painted in 1779, shortly after Keppel had been acquitted at a high-profile court martial. The charges against him related to his conduct as Commander of the British fleet at the Battle of Ushant in July 1778. At this time, the bulk of Britain's forces were in North America, fighting a losing battle against the American Revolutionaries seeking independence from British colonial rule. Eager to capitalise on Britain's weakness, France allied with the Americans, bringing conflict to European waters. Taking place off the island of Ushant in the Bay of Biscay, the Battle of Ushant was the first major action in this Anglo-French conflict. Its result was inconclusive with no ships lost on either side.

The failure of the British fleet to inflict any meaningful damage prompted a slew of accusations and recriminations from the naval officers involved and their political backers. Keppel blamed his second-in-command Hugh Palliser, who in turn counter-blamed Keppel, demanding that the Admiralty Board charge him with neglect of duty. Facing pressure from the merchant elite, who were worried about the threat that the French fleet posed to their ships and wanted to see someone held accountable for the fiasco at Ushant, the Board allowed Palliser's case against Keppel to proceed.

Political factors exacerbated the dispute between the two men, since Keppel was closely associated with the Whig opposition, while Palliser enjoyed the support of the Tory government. The American War had fractured a long period of political fluidity in Britain, hardening party divides that had once been permeable. Loyal to George III, the Tories supported the fight to retain the American colonies. By contrast, the Whigs opposed the war, condemning the economic and human cost of the conflict and defending the colonists' right to self-determination. Keppel himself refused to fight in North America on the grounds that he disagreed with the war; he would only consent to serve on the European front.

This political dimension ensured that Keppel's court martial, which took place in Portsmouth between 7 January and 11 February 1779, was headline news. The opposition press presented the trial as a cynical attempt on the part of the Admiralty to turn an upstanding senior officer into a scapegoat for the government's failings. Rather than dwelling on the facts of the case,

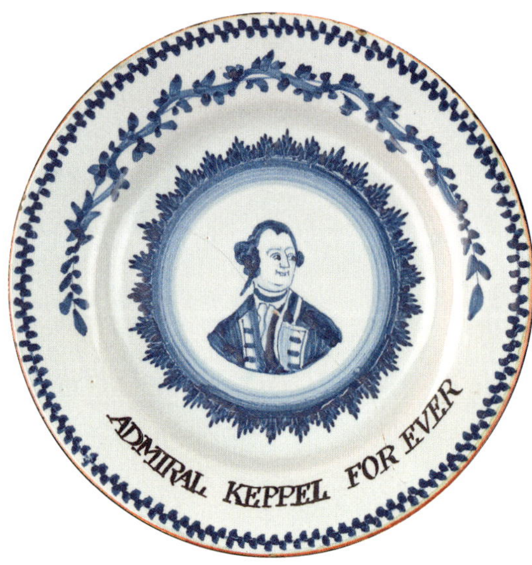

(fig. 1) *Admiral Keppel For Ever*
Unknown English manufacturer
about 1779, delftware plate
30 x 230 mm
AAA4409

Keppel's defence stressed his personal integrity, while accusing the government of corruption, irresponsibility and pettiness. Interpreted as a victory against the government, the Admiral's acquittal at the end of the court martial cemented his status as an opposition hero.

The imagery of Reynolds's portrait complemented this political rhetoric. In his earlier works, the artist had depicted Keppel as a dynamic figure. By contrast, the Admiral appears solid, unmoved and resolute in this painting – an aged hero standing proud in the face of what was, in the eyes of the opposition, scurrilous government persecution. Keppel was a large man and Reynolds emphasises his substantial physical presence, turning the Admiral's body sideways to reveal his bulging belly. The dark clouds in the background allude to the political 'storm' that he has weathered. He stands on a desolate seashore with low rocks in the foreground and an empty sea in the distance, the absence of ships inviting consideration of his character, rather than his actions, much as his defence had done.

The most important detail in the painting is, however, the sword upon which Keppel rests his hand. An officer's sword symbolised his honour as a gentleman. In a naval tradition that continued in Britain until 2004, officers facing court martial were required to surrender their swords. The weapons were then placed on a table in the court room as a reminder that the honour of the accused was in question. If he was condemned, the sword's point would be turned towards him. If acquitted, the hilt would be presented instead, allowing the officer to pick up the weapon, his reputation restored. The return of Keppel's sword had been a key event in his court martial and Reynolds's portrait seems designed to evoke this important moment.

Keppel himself commissioned the painting as a gift for the lawyer John Lee. During the court martial, Lee had acted as one of the Admiral's legal advisers, along with Edmund Burke, John Dunning and Thomas Erskine, the latter fresh from his celebrated defence of Captain Thomas Baillie (p. 120). Following his acquittal, Keppel sent £1,000 to each member of this group, but only Erskine, the least wealthy, accepted the

(fig. 2) *Rear-Admiral Augustus Keppel*
Joshua Reynolds
1765, oil on canvas
760 x 635 mm
BHC2820

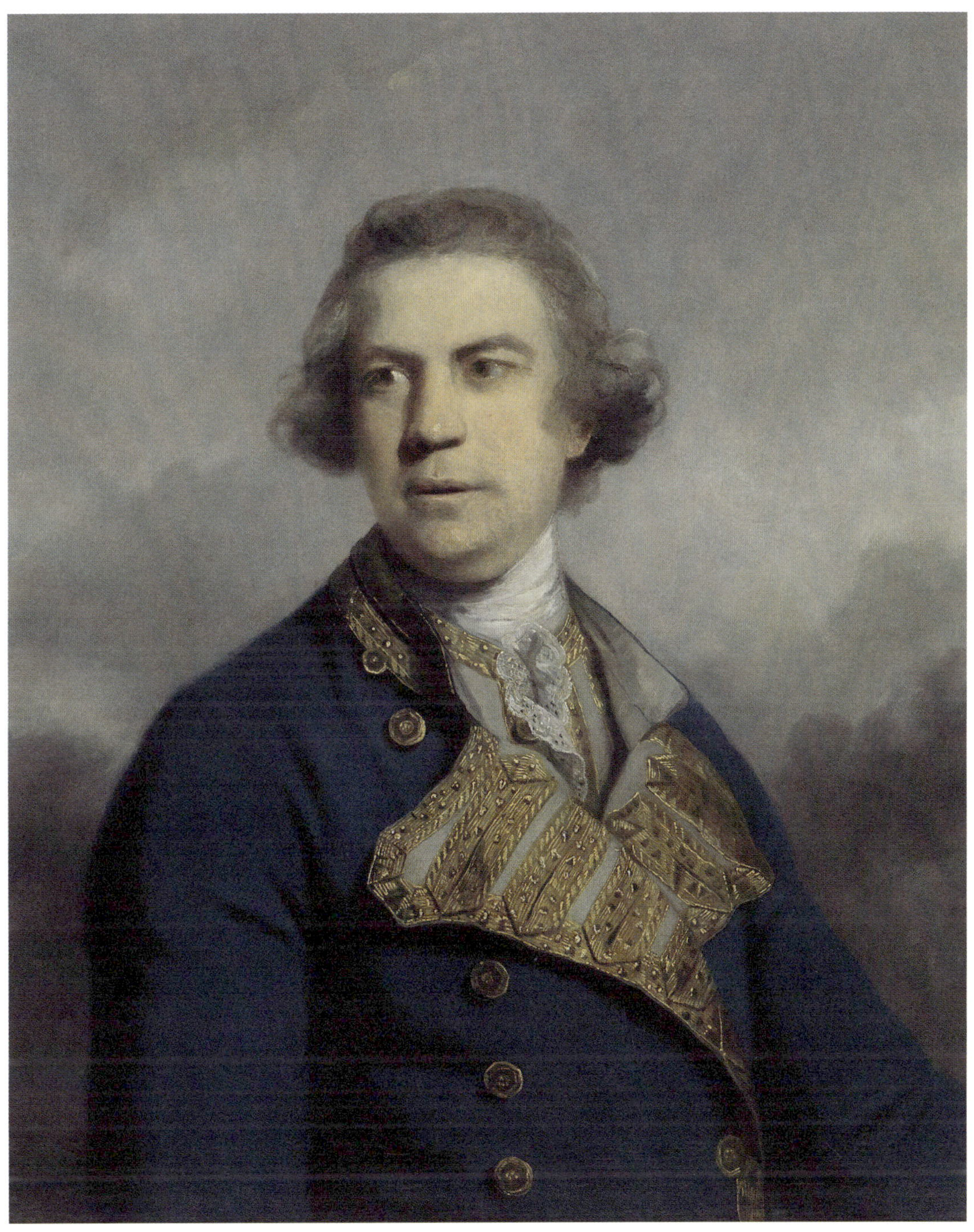

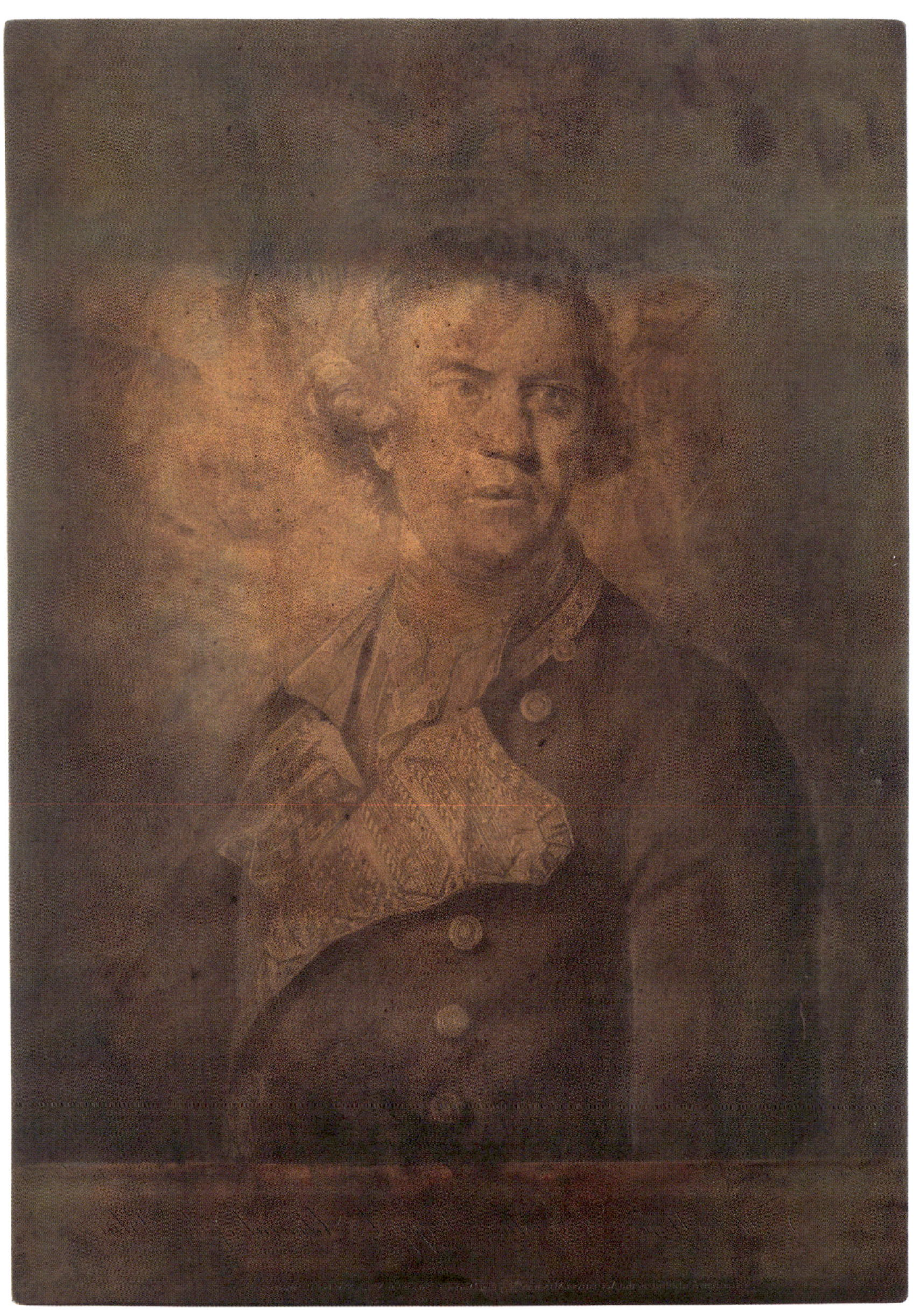

money; all the others returned it. For Lee, Burke and Dunning, refusing the cash was an assertion of their social aspirations. It implied that they saw themselves not as professional lawyers working for an aristocratic client but as gentlemen defending a friend whose honour had been impugned, a service for which they neither wanted nor needed a financial reward. Lee did, however, request an alternative token of esteem: 'Will you make me a present of your picture ... that I may keep it, and my family after me?', he wrote. Keppel obliged, commissioning his friend Joshua Reynolds to produce this portrait for Lee, as well as two copies of the painting for Burke and Dunning. The gift of a portrait was more flattering to the recipient's social status than a cash payment, since it suggested mutual respect and friendship. Moreover, by displaying Keppel's portrait in their homes, Lee, Burke and Dunning were able advertise their connection to a prominent member of the aristocracy.

But the celebration of Keppel's acquittal was not confined to his legal team. The Admiral became a popular hero in the eyes of the wider public. At a time when only the elite could vote, campaign or stand for election, ordinary people often had to express their political opinions via the celebration or denigration of public figures. Keppel's fame created a market for his image, which soon began to appear in print shops, in magazines and even on decorated ceramics (fig. 1). Reynolds himself seized this opportunity, sending one of his earlier portraits of the admiral – a head-and-shoulders from the mid-1760s (fig. 2) – to be engraved and published as a mezzotint by his former pupil William Doughty. Doughty's copper plate is now in the National Maritime Museum's collection, alongside an impression of the print (figs 3 and 4). This high-quality image was one of the more expensive pieces of pro-Keppel propaganda on the market. It seems that Reynolds, unlike Lee, Burke and Dunning, was not above exploiting his friendship with the Admiral for financial gain.

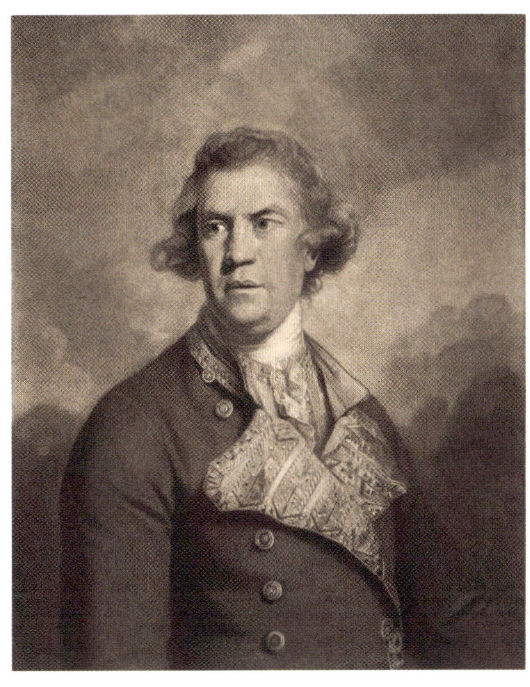

Opposite: (fig. 3) *The Honourable Augustus Keppel*
William Doughty after Joshua Reynolds
1779, printing plate
456 x 330 mm
PAJ4037

Above: (fig. 4) *The Honourable Augustus Keppel*
William Doughty after Joshua Reynolds
1779, mezzotint on paper
497 x 415 mm
PAH5417

Captain William Locker

Gilbert Stuart

about 1785, oil on canvas
762 x 635 mm
BHC2846

More than that of most portrait painters, Gilbert Stuart's career was intertwined with the War of American Independence. Stuart was born in the American colonies and began his training as an artist in Newport, Rhode Island. In 1775, he emigrated to Britain, seeking to escape the political and economic disruption that the outbreak of the American Revolutionary War had brought. This decision was professional, not personal: Stuart himself supported the Revolution, but it was difficult to build a profitable business as a society portraitist in a war-torn country, besides which, London offered better opportunities for artistic development than the limited colonial art scene. The high-profile success of two other American émigré artists in London, Benjamin West and John Singleton Copley, provided further inspiration for Stuart's transatlantic move. Stuart joined West's studio as a pupil and afterwards became a sought-after portraitist in his own right, even rivalling the success of Joshua Reynolds.

Yet he struggled to manage his money and, after a stint in debtors' prison, he fled to Dublin to escape his creditors. Returning to his American homeland in the 1790s, he set about painting the heroes of the Revolution, including George Washington.

Painted in about 1785, this portrait dates from Stuart's time in London, when his popularity in the city was reaching its peak. The sitter, William Locker, was a long-serving naval officer who had been forced to retire from active service due to ill-health at the age of 48, around six years before the painting was produced. His last service had been in the West Indies at the start of the American Revolutionary War.

This type of portrait was known in the eighteenth century as a 'head-and-shoulders', a term which denoted both a specific size of canvas (762 x 635 mm, 30 x 25 inches) and also how much of the sitter's body was shown (upper torso and head only). The compact format did not allow for the inclusion of extensive backgrounds or attributes, hence artists could not introduce many of the familiar trappings of naval portraiture, such as cannons, anchors or distant naval battles. How, then, did portrait painters allude to naval service in such images? What distinguished a head-and-shoulders portrait of a naval officer from one of a civilian?

Locker's painting provides a unique opportunity to answer these questions, since it exists in two versions: one shows Locker as a naval officer, while the other represents him as a retired gentleman (fig. 1). The head is the same in both pictures; when one is superimposed on the other, the facial features are an exact match.

It was through altering the surrounding details that Stuart brought out different aspects of Locker's identity. While it was common for artists to produce numerous versions or copies of portraits, this use of the same likeness as the basis for two distinct portraits is very unusual. Comparing the paintings reveals the different conventions that applied to the representation of naval officers and civilians.

Clothing is an important point of difference: in one painting, Locker wears naval uniform; in the other, he is dressed in civilian clothes, including a grey-green riding coat, a buff waistcoat and a frilled white shirt. With its bright gold lace and white lapels, the uniform is sharp and showy, presenting Locker, the naval officer, as a confident and animated character.

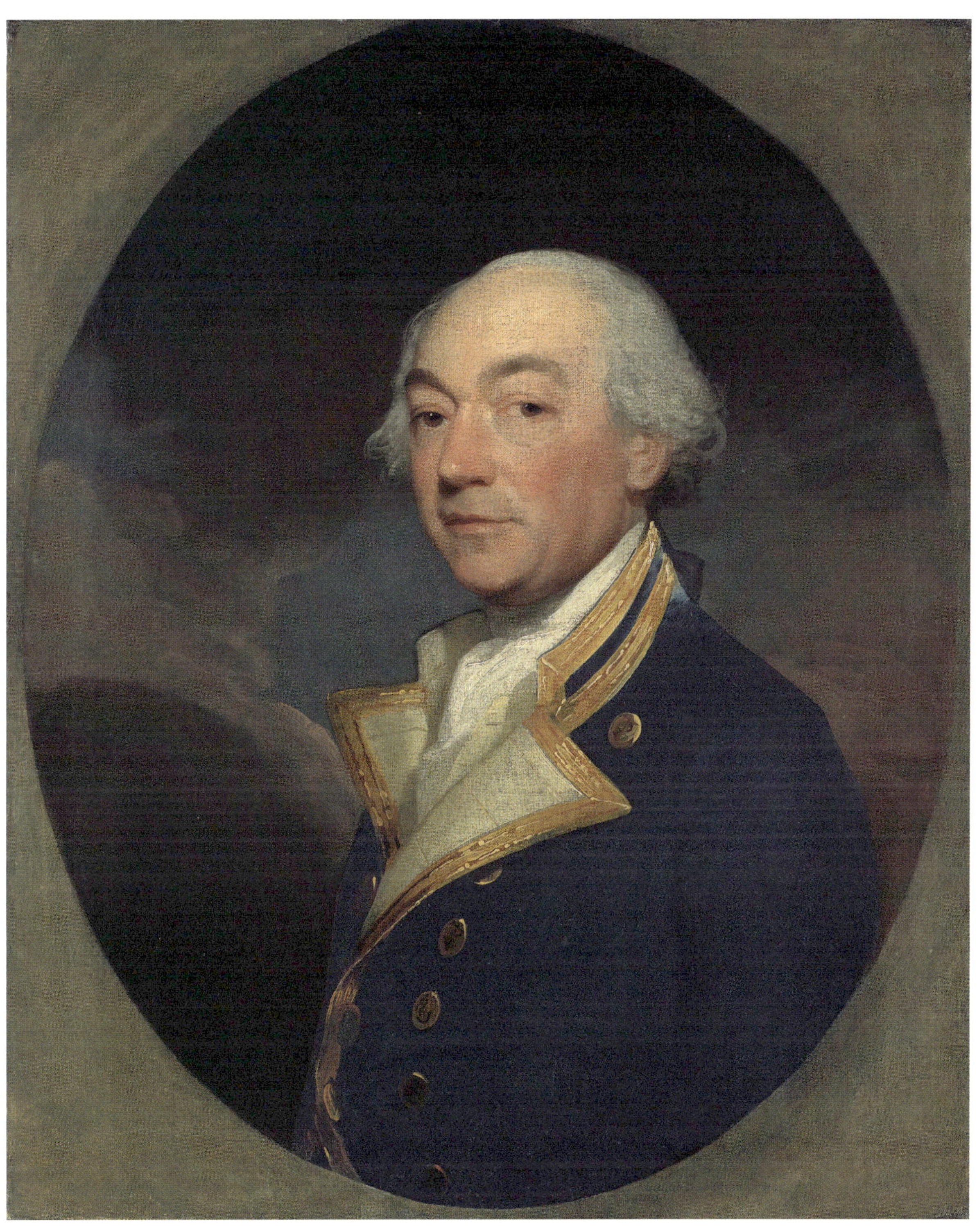

(fig. 1) *Captain William Locker*
Gilbert Stuart
about 1785, oil on canvas
760 x 635 mm
BHC2976

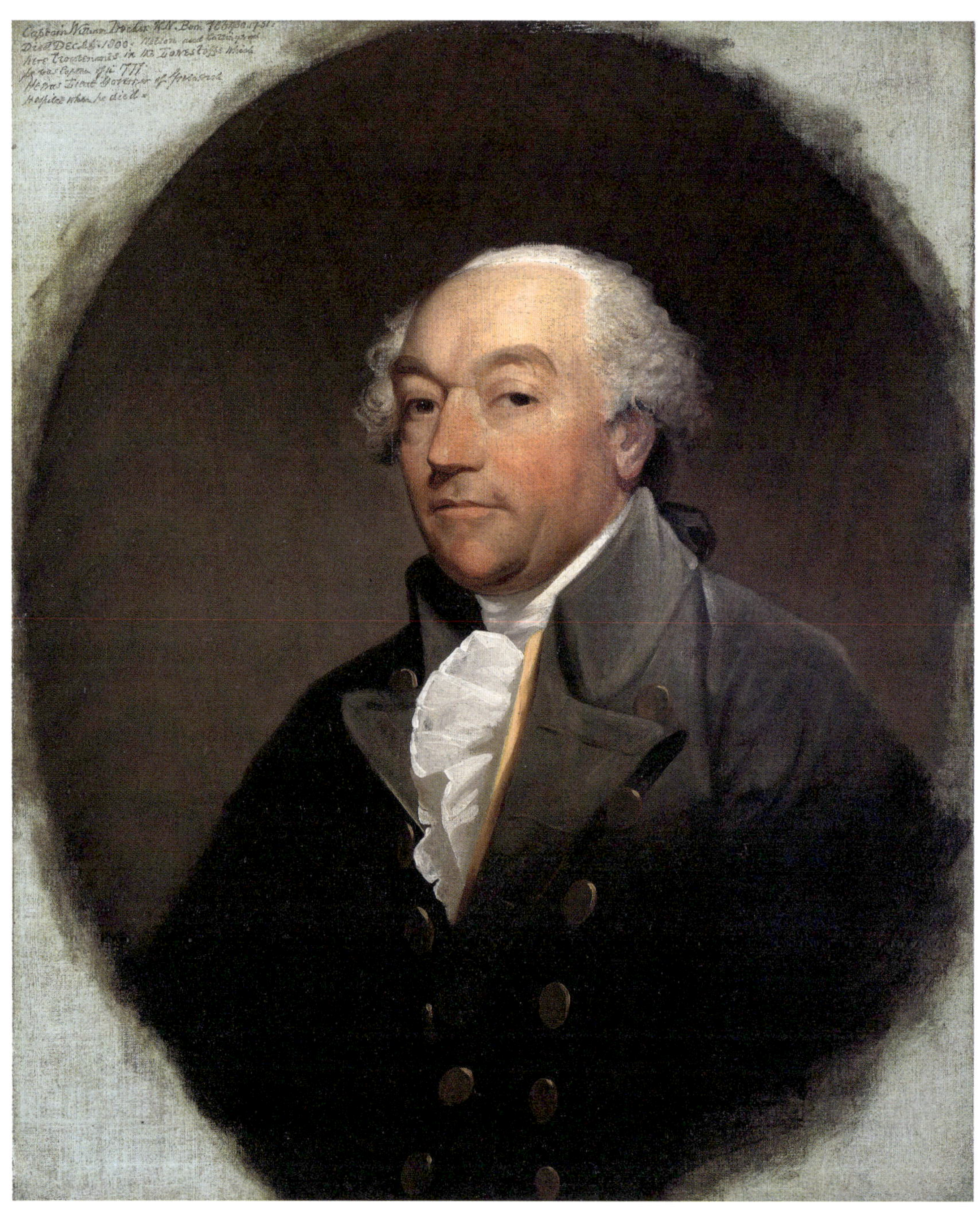

This impression is reinforced in the portrait's background, where swirling storm clouds evoke the association between naval service and outdoor adventure. The clouds encircle a central scrap of blue sky, creating a vortex-like effect that draws the viewer's gaze towards Locker's calm presence in the middle of the painting. His pose is imbued with a slight twisting movement, his shoulders facing to one side while his head turns back towards the viewer. By contrast, Locker, the retired gentleman, appears static and solid. His chest and shoulders are angled more squarely towards the viewer. A dark shadow covers most of his body and the dull fabric of his coat blends into the painting's plain, drab-coloured background, his shirt ruffle providing a single decorative flourish. Presented in this way, Locker becomes the embodiment of sobriety, seriousness and respectability, in contrast to his dynamic naval persona.

Another subtle but crucial difference between the two paintings lies in the depiction of the facial features. The civilian Locker appears several years older than his naval alter-ego: his eyebrow hair is longer, the wrinkle across the bridge of his nose is deeper, his eyes are puffier and the wart on his upper lip is more prominent. His sagging skin even alters the appearance of his expression. In the naval portrait, he seems to be half-smiling; in the civilian one, this expression becomes more of a frown, which suits the serious tone of the painting. Seen in this light, the two paintings are revealed to be evocations of past and present, the naval portrait looking back nostalgically on the sitter as a younger man, its civilian counterpart offering a dignified vision of his retirement. It seems probable that the civilian portrait was the first of the two pictures to be painted, Stuart recording his sitter's aging features from life, before producing an idealised copy, in which he transformed Locker into a younger and more vigorous figure.

The circumstances that led to the creation of these two portraits are not recorded. Multiple copies of a portrait were sometimes produced as gifts for friends, relatives or colleagues, but this does not appear to have been the case here. Locker retained both pictures and left them to his son at his death. It is possible that the two works were intended for display in different locations around the family home. Another option is that Locker was dissatisfied with the civilian portrait and commissioned the naval one as a replacement. Whatever his reasons, Locker seems to have been unique in commissioning naval and civilian versions of the same portrait.

These were not, however, the only portraits that Locker had in his personal collection. He also commissioned several portraits of promising young officers who had served under his command. This group famously included Horatio Nelson, whom Locker captained as a 19-year-old lieutenant in the *Lowestoffe* in 1777 and who later became Britain's most celebrated naval officer. In the portrait that Locker commissioned from John Francis Rigaud, Nelson leans on his sword in front of Fort San Juan, a Spanish fortress in modern-day Nicaragua which Nelson had helped to capture in 1780 (fig. 3). Locker's staid civilian portrait would have looked out-of-place beside this large portrait of a young officer at the site of one of his most significant achievements. His naval portrait shared an affinity with Nelson's image through its clouded backdrop, but it was nevertheless a more modest image due to its smaller scale. Through his collection of portraits, Locker demanded recognition not as a swaggering hero

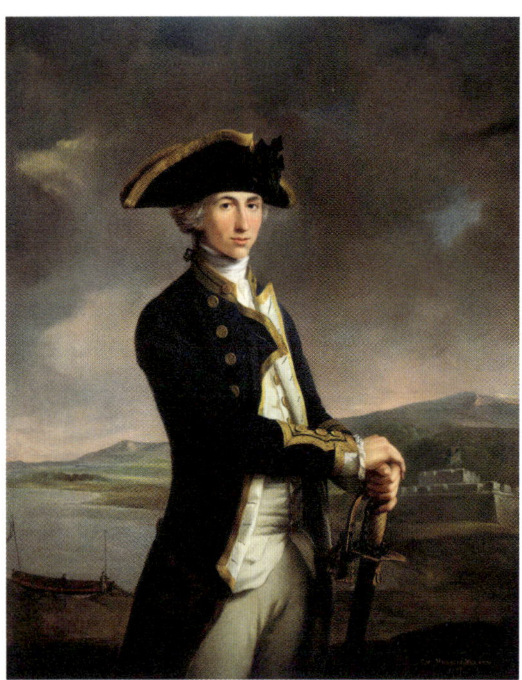

(fig. 3) *Captain Horatio Nelson*
John Francis Rigaud
1781, oil on canvas
1270 x 1015 mm
BHC2901

in his own right but as a father figure to the next generation of naval leaders.

As well as displaying naval portraits in his own home, in 1795 Locker also proposed the establishment of 'a National Gallery of Marine Paintings, to commemorate the eminent services of the Royal Navy of England'. Combining portraits and battle paintings to chart successive generations of naval success, this display would be like a larger, public version of the collection that Locker had established for himself. The project had a political agenda, promoting pro-war and patriotic sentiments at a time when the French Revolution had thrown Europe into conflict once again and stimulated both radical agitation and counter-revolutionary paranoia in Britain. At the time, Locker was serving as Lieutenant-Governor at the Royal Hospital for Seamen in Greenwich. He suggested that the proposed gallery could be housed in the Hospital's Painted Hall, a former dining room named after its allegorical wall-paintings and ceiling murals.

Although his vision was not realised in his lifetime, his son, Edward Hawke Locker, later revived the proposal, overseeing the establishment of the National Gallery of Naval Art, often known as the Naval Gallery, in the Painted Hall in April 1824. At the request of the Directors of Greenwich Hospital, Locker donated a portrait of his father to the new gallery. He initially selected a portrait by Lemuel Francis Abbott that showed an elderly William Locker in the final decade of his life, holding the 'quizzing stick' (a cane topped with an eyeglass) which he had used in his role as the Hospital's Lieutenant-Governor (fig. 4). Six years later, however, Locker junior swapped the Abbott portrait for Stuart's idealised painting of his father in naval uniform, presumably feeling that the dynamic depiction was more in keeping with the Naval Gallery's propagandistic mission to present the Royal Navy in a heroic light.

(fig. 4) *Captain William Locker*
Lemuel Francis Abbott
about 1795–1800, oil on canvas
775 x 640 mm
BHC2845

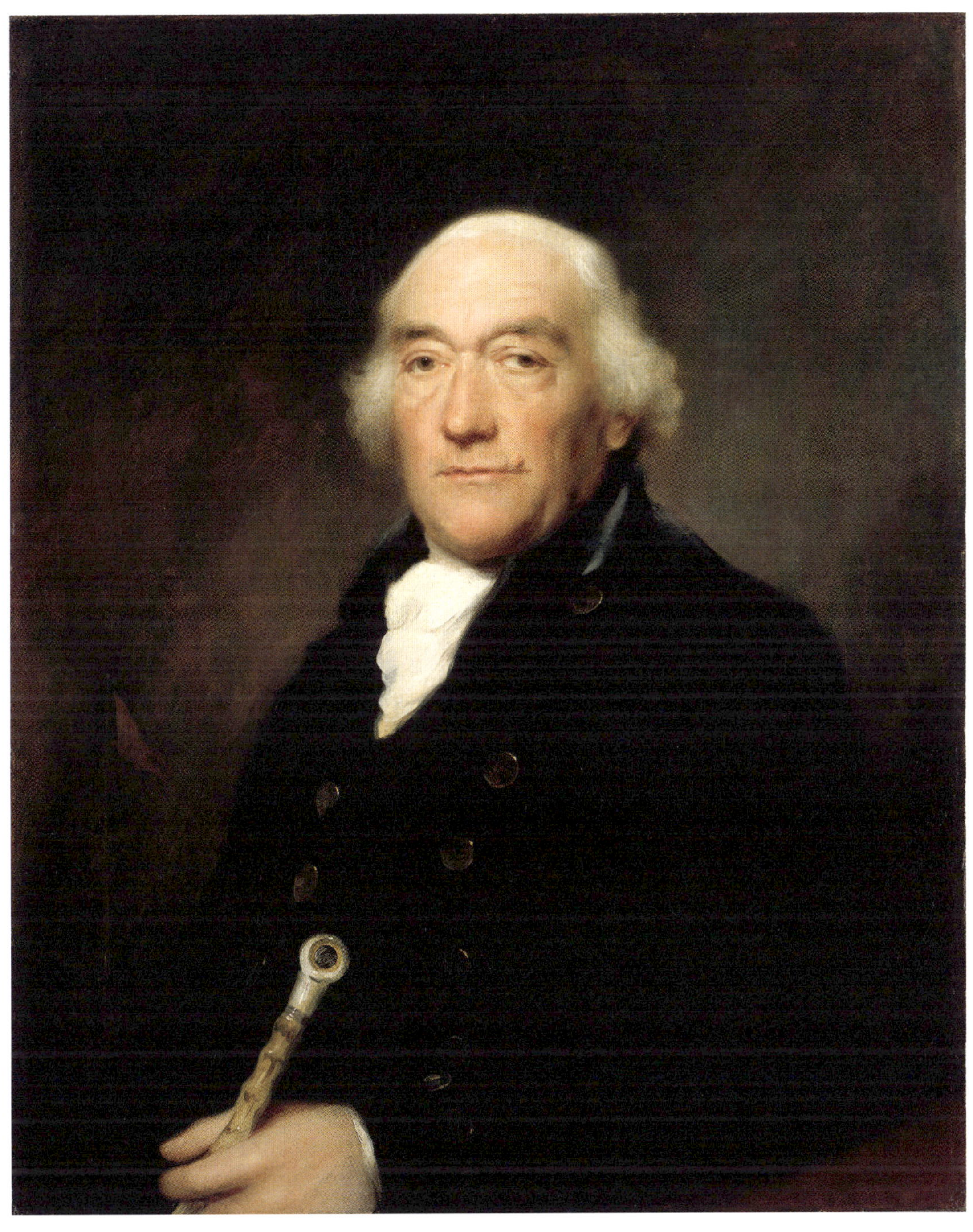

Admiral George Bridges Rodney, 1st Baron Rodney

Jean-Laurent Mosnier

1791, oil on canvas
1,270 x 1,015 mm
BHC2970

Parisian portraitist Jean-Laurent Mosnier arrived in London in 1791, fleeing the political upheaval that the French Revolution had brought to his homeland. Previously, he had held an official position as a painter of miniatures and portraits for Marie Antoinette. When the revolutionaries seized power, she and her husband, Louis XVI, were deposed, leaving Mosnier without work. He may also have feared persecution as an associate of the royal family. Establishing a new studio in London, he secured an endorsement from Joshua Reynolds and gained a number of high-profile portrait commissions. However, his pictures met with a hostile reception in the British press. The criticism of his work was often nationalistic; his paintings were said to demonstrate the 'deficiencies' of French culture and the 'superiority' of British taste.

This portrait is one of the earliest that Mosnier painted in London. It depicts Admiral George Bridges (sometimes spelled Brydges) Rodney as an old man in the final year of his life. Rodney had come to prominence during the American Revolutionary War, though his reputation was controversial. A gambling addict who struggled with debt, he was accused of neglecting his naval duties to loot prize money for himself on the island of St Eustasius, a Dutch trading base, in 1781. His vicious persecution of the island's Jewish community was also censured. Yet he emerged as a popular hero the following year, after his fleet defeated the French at the Battle of the Saintes in April 1782. The battle took its name from its location, the Saints being a small group of islands in Guadeloupe. Though not as crushing as it might have been, Rodney's victory crippled France's naval strength in the Caribbean, forcing the abandonment of a planned Franco-Spanish assault on Jamaica and ensuring that the island's slave plantations could continue generating wealth and commodities for the British consumers. At the same time, the victory was also of immense symbolic importance to the wider British public. In the context of a disastrous war, in which Britain had lost its 13 American colonies, the Battle of the Saintes provided a welcome relief from the prevailing national gloom, becoming an occasion for widespread celebrations, from official commemorations to riotous popular demonstrations. Despite retiring from active service after the battle, Rodney remained a public figure until his death in 1792. During his retirement, he sat for a number of portraits, many of which recalled his famous triumph. In a portrait painted for the Prince of Wales (fig. 1), Joshua Reynolds depicted Rodney leaning against an anchor on a rocky beach, the Battle of the Saintes raging on the distant horizon.

Painted two years later, Mosnier's portrait offered a more subdued image of the ageing Admiral. Apart from Rodney's full-dress uniform, the painting makes no reference to his naval career. The Admiral sits with his legs crossed in an upholstered chair. His hat rests in the crook of his left arm with a pair of gloves inside. In his left hand, he holds what has been identified as a baton of command but is more probably a cane. Taken together, these details invite the viewer to imagine that Rodney has recently arrived from elsewhere, first removing his hat and gloves, then taking a seat. On one level, this creates an air of intimacy, as though we are entering a private meeting with the Admiral, an impression intensified by his piercing blue-eyed gaze.

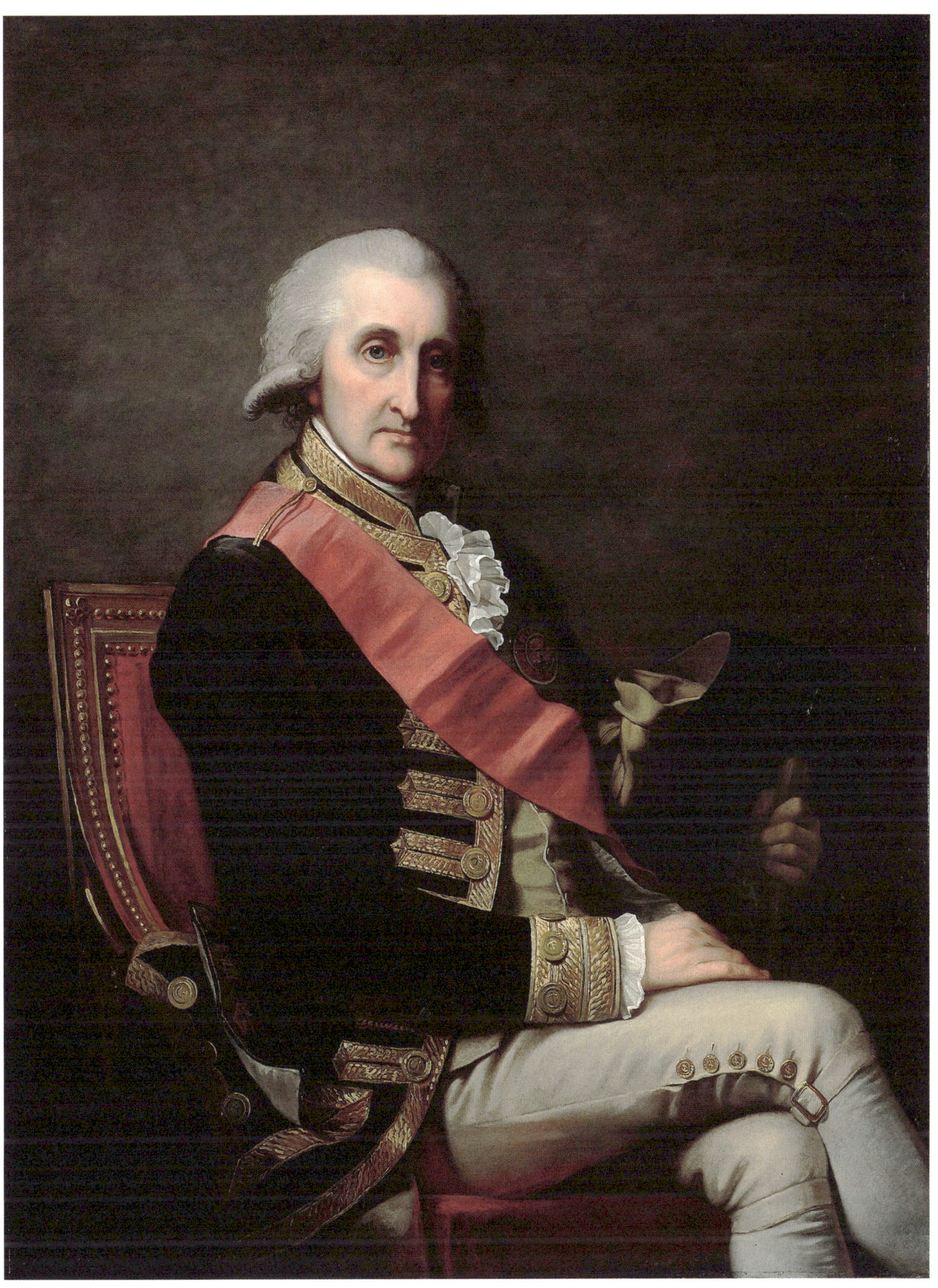

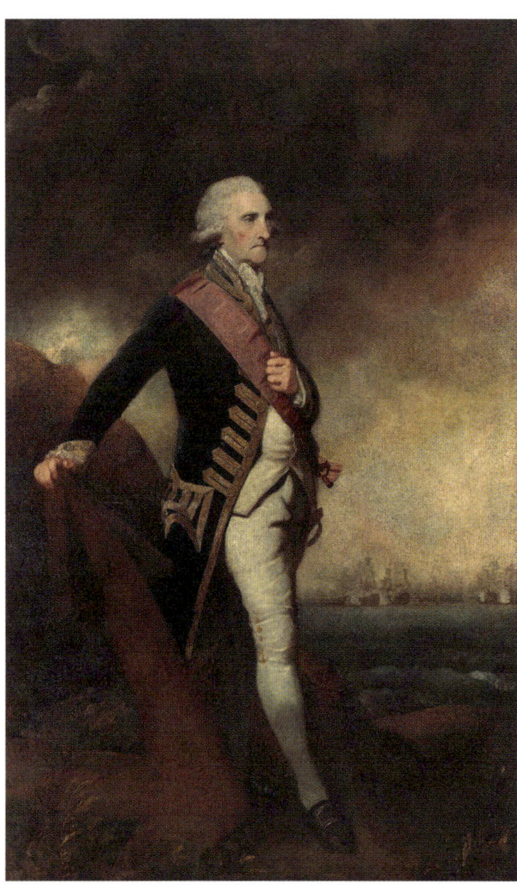

(fig. 1) *George Brydges, 1st Lord Rodney*
Joshua Reynolds
1788–89, oil on canvas
2,387 x 1,482 mm
Royal Collection (RCIN 405899)

At the same time, Rodney exudes stiffness and control, rather than ease and relaxation. The tail of his coat is swept over one of the chair's armrests, as if he has taken care to avoid sitting on and crumpling the fabric. With his hat, gloves and cane in hand, he does not seem intent on remaining in our company for long. Meanwhile, the background is devoid of domestic or familiar details, reinforcing the formality of the Admiral's demeanour. He is behaving like a distinguished guest, not a close friend. While the portrait evokes a private encounter with Rodney, it also insists that he should be regarded with the respect that befits his rank. To underscore his elevated social position, the Admiral wears his insignia as a Knight of the Order of the Bath, the most visible element of which is the crimson sash across his chest. Rather than toning down this vivid accessory, Mosnier ensures that the colour is clear and bright.

High colour was an important feature of the artist's style, along with precise brushwork and a smooth, untextured finish, which are also evident in this portrait. It was these aspects of the painting that attracted the most attention in the press when it was exhibited at the Royal Academy's summer exhibition in 1793. These remarks from *The Diary or Woodfall's Register*, a short-lived newspaper, are typical of the wider critical response: 'Mr Mosnier, as usual, displays much of the knack of high finishing, but little of natural ease and gracefulness; like the figures on the lid of a snuff box, his portraits are all exact to a line.' The comment about 'figures on the lid of a snuff box' refers to the art of miniature painting, in which Mosnier had trained. Miniatures were sometimes worn as jewellery or incorporated into accessories, such as snuff boxes. The nature of the format and medium meant that miniatures tended to be very detailed with a polished finish. *The Diary*'s critic implies that Mosnier creates the same effect on a larger scale in his paintings. The remark is intended to be disparaging: miniature painting was looked down on as a decorative artform for fashionable trinkets, in contrast to the 'high art' of oil painting, which – the critic suggests – demanded less exactitude and more natural flair.

While *The Diary* drew a comparison with miniature painting, most of the other papers associated Mosnier's artistic approach with his nationality. It is true that French painters had historically favoured more elaborate and highly worked finishes, while their British counterparts preferred looser brushwork and atmospheric effects. Reynolds's full-length portrait of Rodney, mentioned earlier, provides an example of this with its murky foreground and smoke-blurred backdrop; even the finer details, such as the admiral's shirt ruffle, are indicated with sweeping strokes of paint. One critic, writing in the *Public Advertiser*, wished British artists could be more like Mosnier: 'His good drawing, however, and the finishing of his pictures, might be adopted with great propriety by many of the scumblers of the English School.' Scumbling was a technique for softening outlines and blending colours, which involved applying broken brushstrokes over existing layers of dry paint, and resulted in a rough and textured effect. Most reviewers, however, declared that Mosnier's work, and by extension French art in general, was deficient: 'We had hoped that he would have availed himself of the superior taste for the Arts, which he found in this country,' proclaimed the *Morning Chronicle*, 'but, we are sorry to observe, he proceeds rigidly in his way.'

These comments echoed and reinforced a potent vein of anti-French prejudice within British culture, which had grown stronger as a result of the French Revolution in 1789 and the outbreak of war between the two nations in February 1793. During this period, British conservatives appropriated terms often used to critique French painting, such as 'hard', 'glaring' and 'artificial', in order to condemn the nation's politics, branding the Revolution and its ideals of liberty and equality as hardline extremism and a subversion of the natural order.

Political affairs often shape the reception of art, as Mosnier's experiences demonstrate. However, it is ironic that responses to his work reflected antagonism towards Revolutionary France, when he had himself fled the Revolution. The irony was especially pronounced in the case of the Rodney portrait, given that the sitter was a British war hero famous for defeating the French in battle. Mosnier ultimately left London, moving to Hamburg in 1797 and later settling in St Petersburg, where he died in 1808.

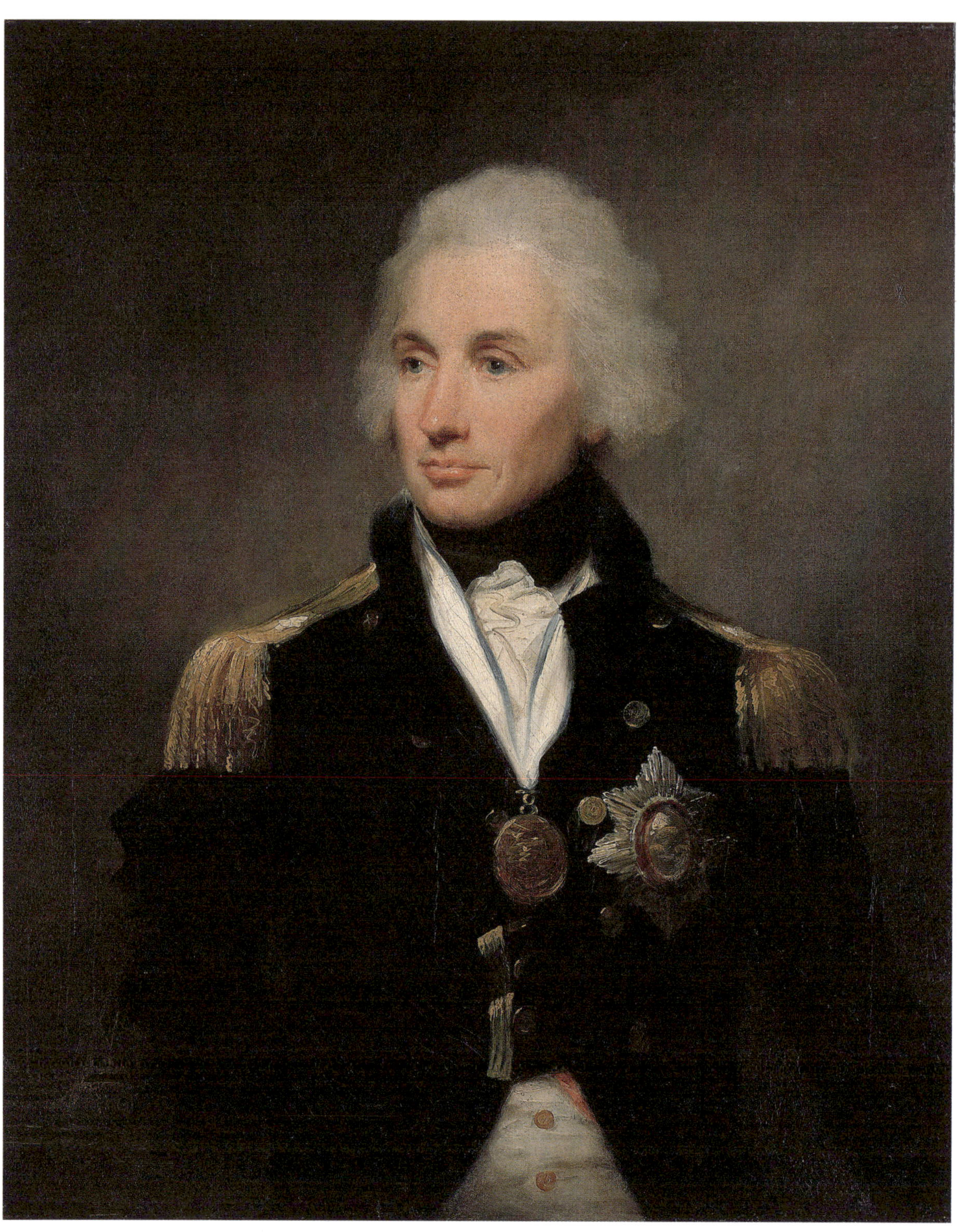

Rear-Admiral Sir Horatio Nelson

Lemuel Francis Abbott

1798, oil on canvas
762 x 635 mm
BHC2887

Lemuel Francis Abbott was an artist with a niche skillset, as the historian Edward Edwards recorded in his *Anecdotes of Painting*, published in 1808:

> [Abbott's] abilities as a painter were wholly confined to portraiture, or rather to painting a head, for below that part he wanted both taste and skill ... his figures were in general insipid in their action, and his backgrounds poor and tasteless in execution.
>
> Yet it must be allowed, that the heads of his male portraits were perfect in their likenesses, particularly those which he painted from the naval heroes of the present time, but he had not equal success with female heads, of which indeed he painted but few.

These comments reveal that Abbott was known as a brilliant but limited artist, who excelled in painting men's faces but struggled with other aspects of portraiture. Playing to his strengths, Abbott cultivated a network of male clients, in particular naval officers. He had a studio on Caroline Street (now Adeline Place), a fashionable address in Bloomsbury, but twice failed to get elected as an Associate of the Royal Academy. He also experienced issues with his mental health and in June 1801 was certified as a 'lunatic', a term used at the time to describe acute mental illness. He died 18 months later with less than £400 to his name. Today, however, Abbott is not remembered for his professional limitations or personal difficulties. Instead, he is known for painting the most celebrated naval officer in British history, Horatio Nelson.

During his lifetime, Nelson was the subject of numerous portraits in various media. Further images proliferated after his death at the Battle of Trafalgar in 1805. Within this vast body of imagery, Abbott's portrait stands out as one of the most influential and widely reproduced. Over the centuries, it has appeared in innumerable forms and contexts, from souvenir snuff boxes to the cover of *Woman* magazine in June 1942 (fig. 1). Seen over the shoulder of a lipstick-wearing telephone operator in the Women's Royal Naval Service, the portrait implied that members of the WRNS were – in their own 'feminine' way – continuing the tradition of British naval heroism of which Nelson had become the figurehead. Abbott himself created multiple copies and versions of the picture, a fact which testifies to its popularity in his own time.

It was William Locker who first commissioned Abbott to paint Nelson's portrait. Locker was Nelson's friend and former commander. A lieutenant-governor at Greenwich Hospital, he was known for collecting portraits of promising young officers who had served under his command (p. 130). Locker engaged Abbott's services to create a new likeness of Nelson, his most successful protégé, in autumn 1797. At the time, Nelson was staying in Locker's apartments at Greenwich Hospital to recuperate from the loss of his right arm. Several months previously, he had gained public acclaim for serving with distinction at the Battle of Cape St Vincent, after which he was promoted to the rank of rear-admiral. He then cemented his reputation for daring exploits through a series of risky boat actions, culminating in an ill-fated amphibious assault on the port of Santa Cruz de Tenerife in the Canary Islands.

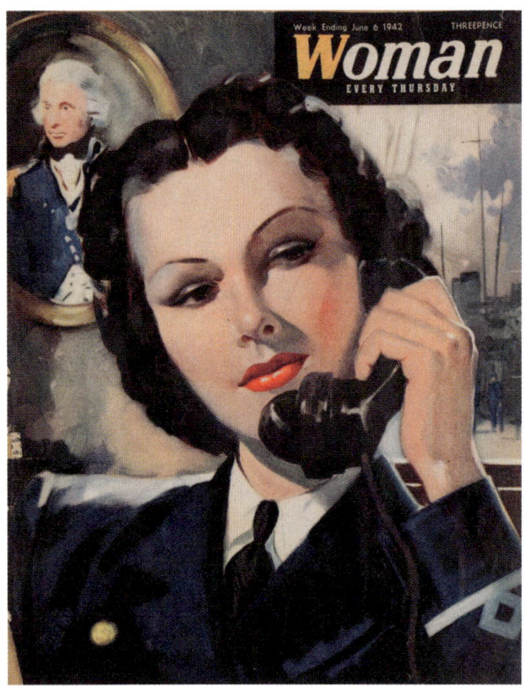

(fig. 1) *The Woman*
June 1942, magazine cover
299 x 239 mm
DAU/220

During this attack, he sustained a severe wound to his arm, necessitating its amputation. Abbott's painting was the first portrait to show Nelson after this injury.

The initial versions of the painting showed Nelson's head and upper torso against a grey-brown background. Abbott often favoured this format because it allowed him to show off his talent for painting expressive and life-like faces. In this case, however, the viewer's attention is drawn not only to Nelson's pale eyes and careworn features but also to his dark blue uniform coat, which is adorned with the star of the Order of the Bath and his gold medal from the Battle of Cape St Vincent. Next to these decorations hangs the Rear-Admiral's empty sleeve, the cuff fixed to one of his coat buttons with a loop of black ribbon. Further ribbons lace the upper part of the sleeve from the shoulder to the elbow, the fabric having been slit open to accommodate the dressing on Nelson's stump during his recovery.

The wearing of an empty sleeve across the chest or stomach was common practice among naval amputees and had featured in earlier paintings (p. 98). In most portraits, the sleeve was positioned on the stomach, but Abbott broke with convention and depicted Nelson's sleeve hanging in a higher position on the Rear-Admiral's chest. This appears to have been a deliberate choice to make the injury more visible. It also enabled the cuff to rest over Nelson's heart and alongside his gold medal and Bath star, as if the lost limb was itself a badge of honour to be worn with pride. Such imagery complemented the press coverage of the Rear-Admiral's injury and rehabilitation. For example, in a letter published in the *Gentleman's Magazine* in April 1799, Nelson's father had declared that 'his country seems sensible of his services – but, should he ever meet with ingratitude, his scars will cry out and plead his cause'. Like Abbott's painting, this rhetoric presented the Rear-Admiral's missing arm as compelling proof of his courage and patriotic commitment.

Almost immediately, the empty sleeve became a defining feature of Nelson's public image, not least due to the widespread reproduction of Abbott's portrait. Nelson sat to the artist on two occasions during his stay with William Locker. During these sittings, Abbott produced a rough sketch, which remained in his studio until his death. He used this sketch to create a finished painting for Locker, which today belongs to a private collection. This fulfilled the original commission, but Abbott had already received an order for a copy of the painting from Fanny Nelson, the Rear-Admiral's wife. Fanny took delivery of her copy, which is now at the National Portrait Gallery, in July 1798. At the time, she wrote to her husband on his ship in the Mediterranean: 'I am now writing opposite your portrait, the likeness is great.' She described the painting as 'my companion, my sincere friend in your absence', demonstrating how portraits could provide comfort to the loved ones of naval officers. However, she also expressed frustration at the artist: 'I really began to think he had no intention of letting me have my own property.' This remark is consistent with Abbott's reputation for being slow to complete his pictures, something which was blamed on his small number of assistants. The artist may have also been struggling to keep up with demand, as he received more and more orders for Nelson's portrait.

Abbott's third copy of the painting, after those for William Locker and Fanny Nelson, is now held at the National Maritime Museum. It is identical to the other two pictures in all but one detail. In this version, Abbott added a dark sketch of a warship in the lower right. A half-formed version of the seascape backgrounds in other naval portraits, this strange detail demonstrates the artist's lack of confidence when it came to painting anything other than men's heads.

The commissioner of this copy of the portrait was Alexander Davison, Nelson's friend and prize agent. It was a convention in this period that the monetary value of a captured enemy ship and its cargo was distributed amongst the officers and men of the naval ship that had brought about the capture, the largest shares going to the most senior officers. These payments – known as prize money – were an important source of income for naval officers. Prize agents handled the distribution of the money, keeping a percentage for themselves as an administration charge. In Davison's case, this work was one of his many business interests.

Davison was a social climber from a humble background. The son of a Northumbrian farmer, he amassed a fortune as a merchant in Canada during the American Revolutionary War. It was in Canada that he first met and befriended Nelson, who was serving in the region at that time. Returning to England after the war, Davison cultivated a diverse business portfolio, which including a lucrative banking operation and numerous military supply contracts (it later emerged that he was also committing massive financial fraud). During the 1790s, he undertook a concerted campaign to enhance his social position in line with his increasing wealth. In 1795, he bought a country estate in Northumberland and, three years later, he acquired his elegant townhouse in St James's Square. At the same time, he deepened his long-standing friendship with Nelson, using this connection to Britain's most celebrated naval commander to establish a network of influential contacts, including government ministers and royal princes. Commissioning Nelson's portrait was a logical extension of this process, enabling Davison to advertise his friendship with the Rear-Admiral. He even had his version of the portrait engraved and published as a mezzotint, complete with a dedication from the engraver, Richard Earlom, declaring that the print was 'Engraved from the Original Picture in the possession of Alexander Davison Esq' (fig. 2).

Davison might have been keen to draw attention to his ownership of Nelson's portrait, but he could not claim this made him unique, given that Abbott was hard at work producing copies for other patrons. Up to 40 versions of the portrait are recorded, although it is not known how many Abbott himself produced, as opposed to his studio. Later versions incorporated

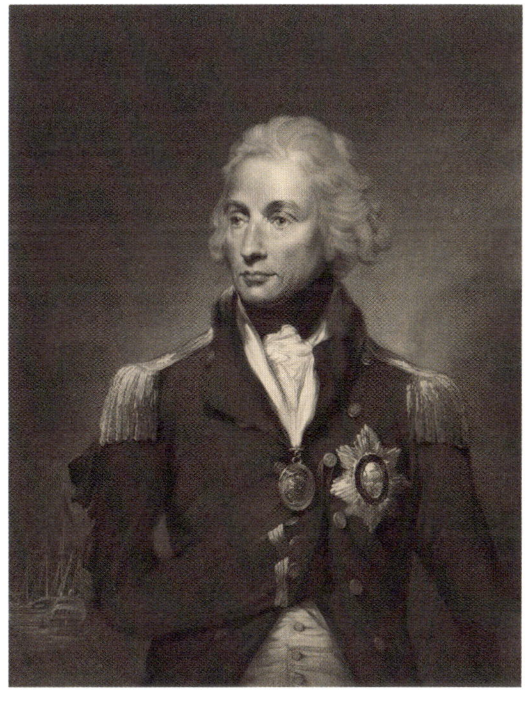

(fig. 2) *The Right Honorable Lord Nelson*
Richard Earlom
1798, mezzotint on paper
530 x 383 mm
PAG9363

(fig. 3) *Rear-Admiral Sir Horatio Nelson*
Lemuel Francis Abbott
1799, oil on canvas
762 x 635 mm
BHC2889

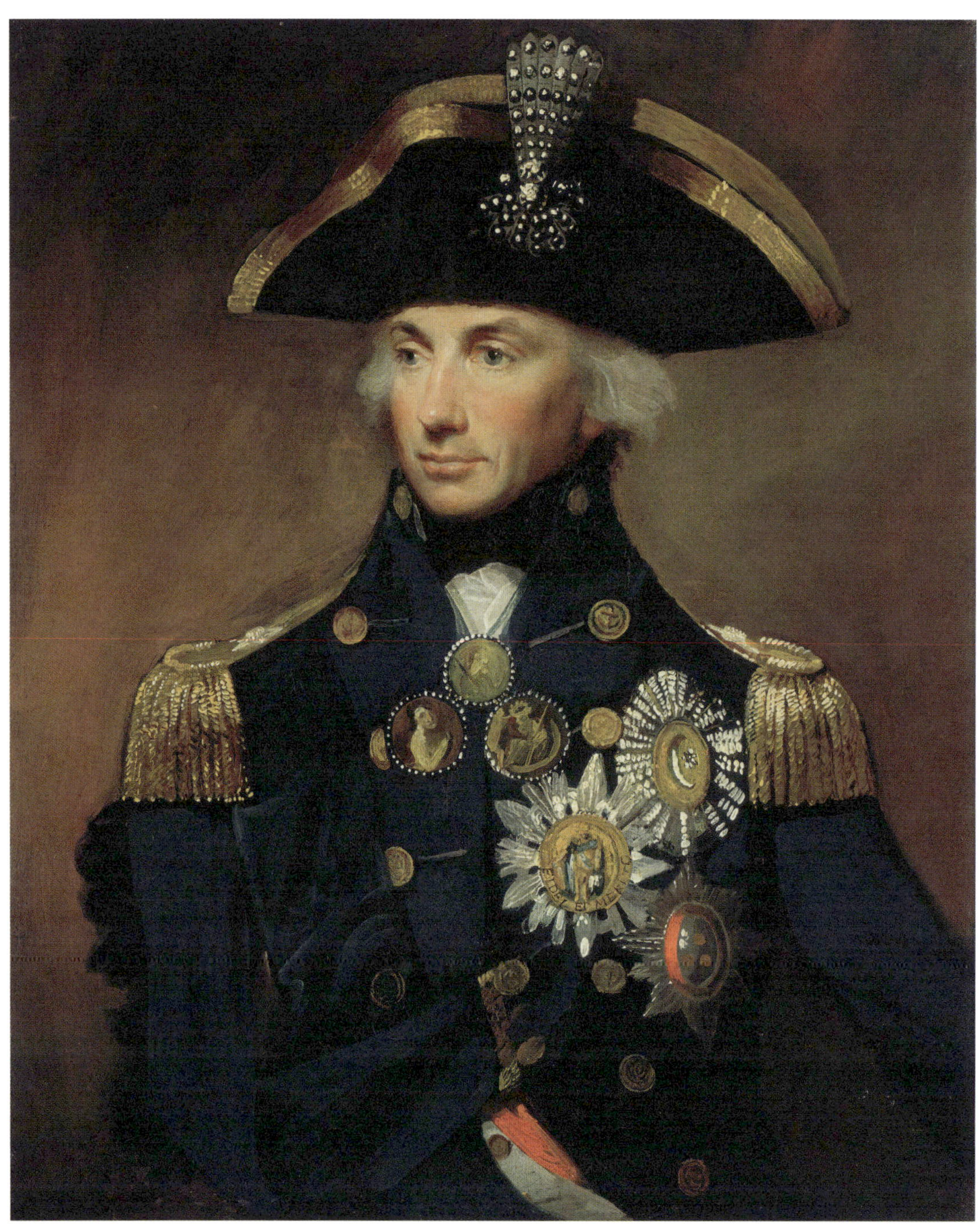

additional details, updating Nelson's image to reflect his latest achievements. These extra elements consisted of the medals and decorations that Nelson was awarded after his victory at the Battle of the Nile in August 1798, including two gold medals (one from the Admiralty and another from Alexander Davison), the Turkish Order of the Crescent and the Neapolitan Order of St Ferdinand and of Merit. Abbott also added a hat to the portrait, adorned with the distinctive diamond chelengk Nelson received from the Sultan of Turkey. The details first appear in a version of the portrait that Nelson's biographer, John McArthur, commissioned in about 1800 (fig. 3). The glittering decorations made the portrait more triumphant in tone than the earlier copies, which had emphasised Nelson's lost arm and presented him as a wounded hero.

More prints were also produced, including some which extended the image to include the Rear-Admiral's entire body. Abbott painted a self-portrait in which he showed himself holding one of these prints. This self-portrait was then itself published as a mezzotint (fig. 4). The fact that Abbott included Nelson's portrait in his own self-portrait demonstrates how strongly his artistic identity had become intertwined with the Rear-Admiral's image.

The print of Abbott's self-portrait was published in January 1800. Eighteen months later, in June 1801, several witnesses swore before the Lunacy Commissioners – a panel of doctors and lawyers who presided over issues relating to mental health – that the painter was a 'lunatic' and did not enjoy lucid periods. The testimony delivered at this inquiry suggested that he had been displaying symptoms of serious mental illness since at least July 1798. Writing after Abbott's death, Edward Edwards attributed the artist's illness to the 'anxiety' that stemmed from his inability to keep up with the demand for his work. While this theory is conjecture, it is possible that the pressure of producing so many copies of Nelson's portrait did negatively impact Abbott's precarious mental health. It could perhaps be said that Nelson's image both made and broke the artist.

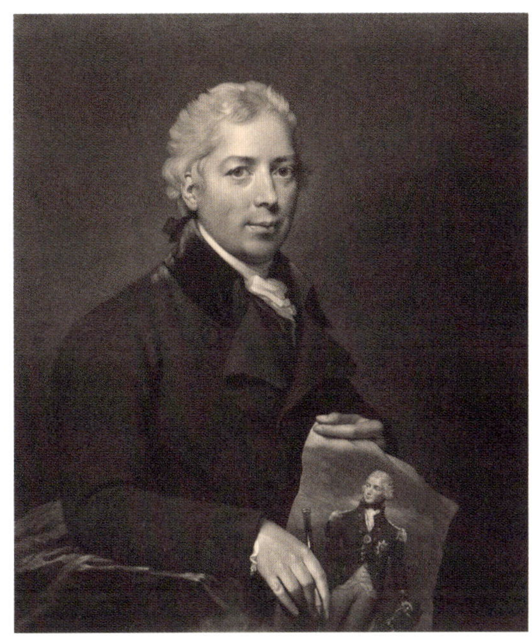

(fig. 4) *Lemuel Francis Abbott*
Valentine Green after Lemuel Francis Abbott
1805, mezzotint on paper
496 x 400 mm
PAH5449

The Grindall Family

Richard Livesay

1800, oil on canvas
1,017 x 1,287 mm
ZBA5116

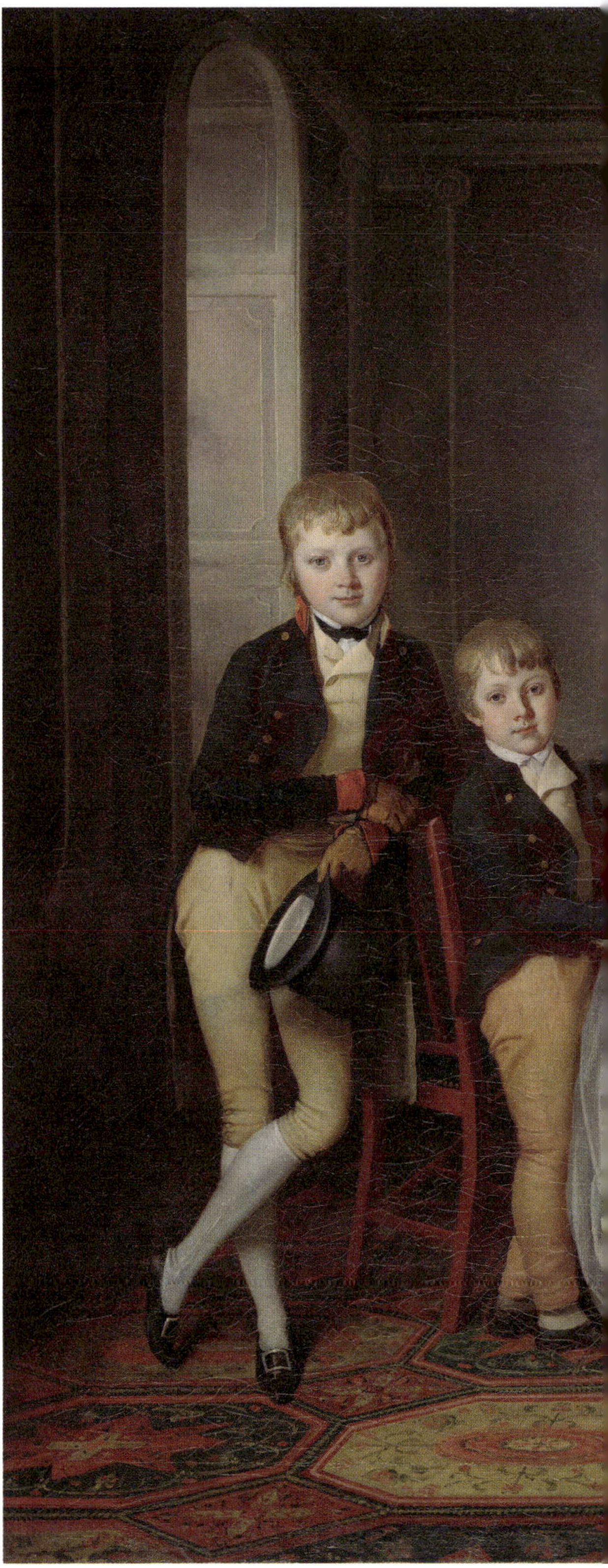

Richard Livesay trained as an artist in London but forged his career outside the competitive metropolitan art world. He worked for a time in Windsor, where he painted portraits of Eton schoolboys and served as drawing master to the royal children, before moving to Portsmouth in the mid-1790s. Portsmouth was at that time home to the Royal Navy's largest and busiest dockyard.

Although this industrial setting did not provide extensive business for a professional portraitist, Livesay diversified his practice in order to create a profitable enterprise. On a trade card printed in 1796, he described himself as 'Portrait, Landscape, and Marine Painter [and] Drawing-Master to the Royal [Naval] Academy, Portsmouth', revealing the three genres in which he practiced and the part-time position that he held as an instructor at an onshore naval training facility. The benefits of his role at the Academy were not only financial; the position also provided him with an opportunity to network with potential patrons in the naval community. Unsurprisingly, a large number of his portrait commissions came from naval officers.

Livesay painted this group portrait around the turn of the nineteenth century. It depicts Captain Richard Grindall and his wife Katherine with their four surviving children, the couple having previously lost two daughters in infancy. From left to right, the boys are Richard (the eldest), Edmund (the youngest), Rivers (the second eldest) and Festing (the second youngest).
The Grindalls lived in Fareham at the north-west tip of Portsmouth Harbour, hence Livesay was their local artist. The choice of a resourceful provincial painter, as opposed to a fashionable metropolitan portraitist, evinced a middle-class

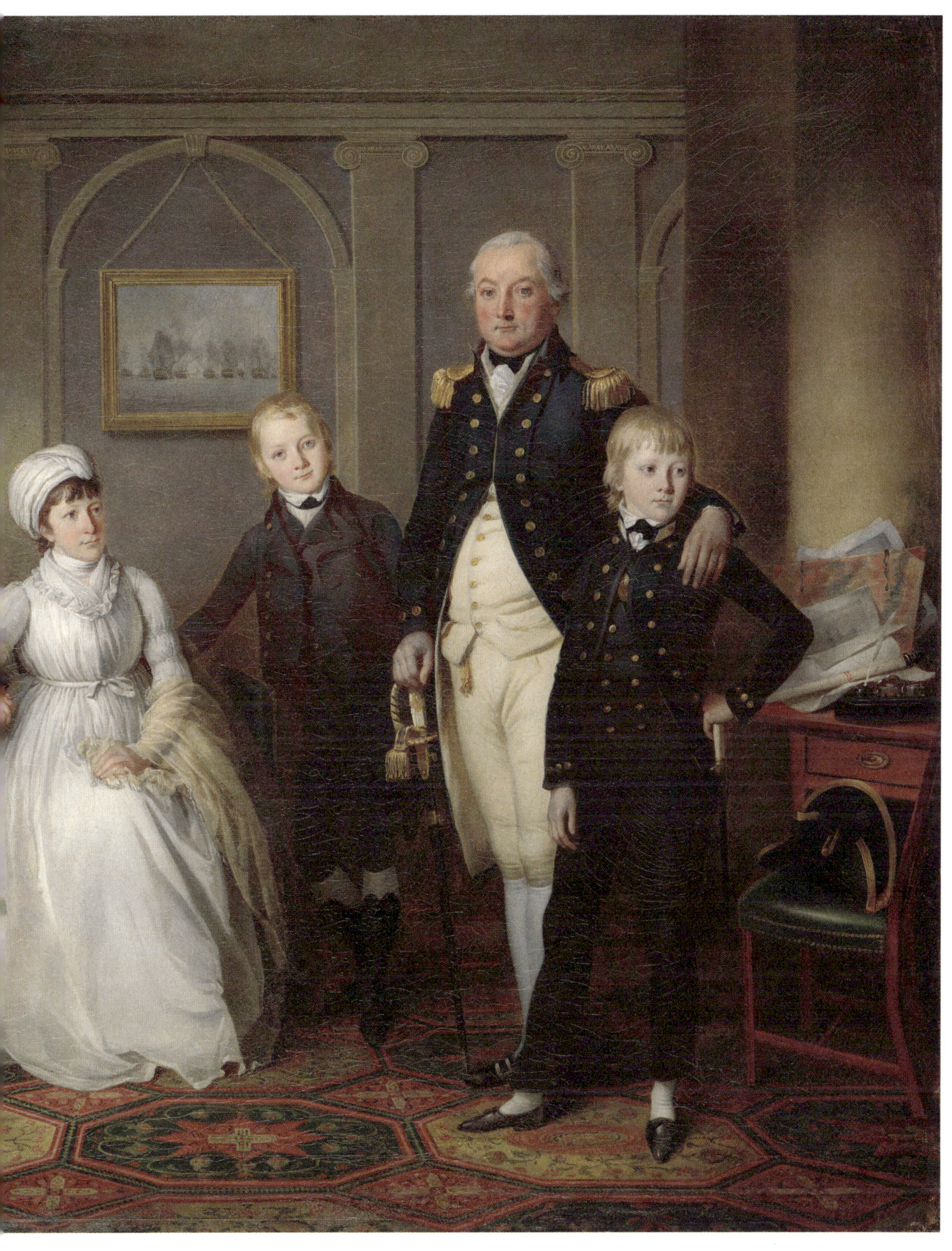

preference for workmanlike substance over ostentatious style, though it may also be indicative of budgetary constraints. Richard senior had entered the Navy at the relatively late age of 22, possibly after spending several years in the merchant service. Unlike some of his peers, he does not appear to have come from a privileged background, but he climbed the ranks to become a successful captain, allowing his children to enjoy a comfortable, upper-middle-class upbringing.

Livesay's portrait advertises the family's wealth through its setting. The Grindalls are posed in a refined domestic interior, recalling the early eighteenth-century tradition of conversation piece portraiture, albeit without the convivial social interaction that was the genre's hallmark. Conversation pieces usually represented their sitters in realistic spaces, the elegant décor and furnishings of which manifested the gentility and good taste of the occupants. These settings were often at least partly imagined, the purpose being not to record actual possessions but rather to signify abstract virtues. As such, the room in which the Grindalls are assembled could be the artist's invention. Nevertheless, the patterned carpet and neoclassical plasterwork characterise the family as one that can afford to live in comfort and style. Similarly, the painting on the wall and the prints on the desk suggest that the Grindalls are sophisticated consumers of art and culture. However, these artworks also serve another function. Depicting naval actions and ships, they allude to the captain's successful career, which was the source of his family's wealth.

The four boys seem ready to follow their father's example, the imagery of the portrait anticipating their departure from the family home in pursuit of their own careers. On the left, Richard junior is dressed in outdoor clothing, including leather gloves and a top hat, though he has temporarily removed the latter. With its red cuffs and collar, his coat appears to belong to a uniform, possibly that of the Royal Military School at Woolwich, which trained officers for the Royal Artillery and the Royal Engineers. In the centre, Rivers wears riding boots, suggesting that he will soon be striking out on his own as well. Festing directs his gaze away from the family group. He has donned a midshipman's uniform, indicating that he is following his father into the Royal Navy. Only Edmund, tucking his feet under his mother's skirts and clasping her hand in his own, still seems to need the care of his parents. Yet even he is turning towards the viewer, a first move towards independence.

For one member of the family, however, there is no suggestion of a life outside the home. While her husband and sons stand around in dark overcoats, remembering or anticipating their own masculine adventures, Katherine Grindall remains seated. Enveloped in swathes of white fabric, she radiates softness and comfort, qualities that were seen at the time as desirable feminine virtues. Livesay's portrait recognises and celebrates the emotional labour of women like Katherine, who were expected to create welcoming family homes, only to be left behind, waiting and worrying, as their menfolk went out into the world. Within the painting, Katherine is positioned at the heart of the family unit, pulling the group together for a brief shared moment before their imminent dispersal. Her gaze slides towards Festing in his midshipman's uniform, suggesting her maternal apprehension for her sea-bound son.

As a captain's wife, Katherine knew all about the dangers of naval service. Several years earlier, her husband had been severely wounded at the Battle of Groix. He lost the use of his right arm after it was broken in two places. According to his surgeon, the injury was 'fully equal in prejudice to the habits of body with the loss of a limb'. In the portrait, he rests the damaged arm on the hilt of his sword, using the weapon to prop it up and hide its limpness. Meanwhile, he wraps his good arm around Festing's shoulders. Although on one level protective, this gesture also suggests pride and even benediction, as if the Captain is anointing a successor to his professional legacy. Nevertheless, for those who knew about his wounding, the painting might have also offered a sobering warning of the potential harm that could befall his son in his future career.

Livesay's portrait operated on multiple levels, communicating different meanings for different audiences. Displayed at the family home in Fareham, the painting presented visitors with an image of wealth, decorum and upper-middle-class respectability. Lacking the hereditary authority of the nobility, the middle classes in this period claimed moral superiority on the basis of exemplary private and domestic virtue. Hence, the portrait's imagery of affectionate family life and traditional gender roles echoed the values of the Grindalls' social milieu.

At the same time, for the family themselves, the portrait held deep emotional significance. Painted at a time when the children were beginning to leave home, it preserved a visual reminder of their presence. In the years that followed, the portrait would become increasingly poignant as the boys either moved overseas or died. Rivers joined the East India Company as a writer in August 1801 and arrived the following March in India, where he would remain for the rest of his life. Edmund joined the Royal Navy but died of an infectious disease in September 1811. Festing, brother and fellow naval recruit, died eight months later of an unconnected illness. Richard junior, the eldest son, appears to have died around the same time, since he is not mentioned in his father's will, written in September 1812. The Captain himself died in 1820. Katherine Grindall lived for another 11 years. She was a widow and her only surviving child was on the other side of the world. Under such circumstances, the family portrait must have taken on immense personal importance.

CHAPTER 5

Pax Britannica

1815–1914

The National Gallery of Naval Art opened in the Painted Hall in Greenwich in April 1824. With a collection consisting of portraits, battle paintings, sculptures, ship models and assorted nautical ephemera, this gallery presented visitors with a visual history of British naval activity. It perpetuated a key idea within nineteenth-century British culture, namely that the Royal Navy was a source of national pride. Many of the exhibits related to Vice-Admiral Lord Horatio Nelson, whose reputation as the ultimate naval hero had been established following his death at the Battle of Trafalgar on 21 October 1805.

Trafalgar and its fallen hero remained defining symbols of British naval prowess throughout the nineteenth century. However, this was due as much to the absence of subsequent victories as to Nelson's enduring appeal. After defeating Napoleonic France in 1815, Britain was left with a vast empire and no major international rivals. The following century has become known as the Pax Britannica (Latin for 'British Peace'), in reference to the position of unchallenged global dominance that Britain retained until the outbreak of the First World War in 1914. The Royal Navy was instrumental in maintaining this dominance, but its role and technology underwent a rapid evolution. The legendary sailing fleet of Nelson's time was replaced with a modern, steam-powered navy, which was primarily employed in surveying, peacekeeping and policing rather than conflict.

This shift had important consequences for naval portraiture. On the one hand, artists had to develop new imagery to suit the changing nature of the naval profession. Naval portraits from this era included depictions of polar explorers in ice-bound landscapes and of pith-helmeted colonial adventurers. Other portraits placed increasing emphasis on naval administration and bureaucracy as the British authorities attempted to impose order on the Empire via official records and statistics. Fewer and fewer portraits adhered to the age-old formula of showing a naval officer standing on the seashore. At the same time, new art movements, from the Pre-Raphaelites to impressionism, challenged old artistic traditions. In this sense, the nineteenth century was a period of significant artistic innovation, including in the field of naval portraiture.

During this era, the lack of major naval battles created nostalgia for the glorious victories of earlier periods. This fuelled interest in celebrating past naval triumphs and led to the creation of large-scale public monuments, such as Nelson's Column at Trafalgar Square in the heart of London. Down the Thames at Greenwich, the Naval Gallery commemorated historic success at sea through its display of paintings. However, it also collected and commissioned new artworks depicting more recent naval heroes. These additions to the gallery's displays created the appearance of continuity, assuaging public anxiety that British naval prowess had entered a period of stagnation and decline after Nelson's death. To support this sense of connection across generations, artists were tasked with producing portraits that responded to existing pictures in the Naval Gallery. Maintaining tradition was thus a major force within nineteenth-century naval portraiture.

William Mathews, a Greenwich Pensioner

John Burnet

1832, oil on canvas
305 x 230 mm
BHC2856

John Burnet was a Scottish painter, printmaker and essayist in the early nineteenth century. While completing an apprenticeship with an engraver, he studied painting at the Trustees' Academy in Edinburgh. Among his classmates was Sir David Wilkie, who later became one of the most successful British artists of his generation. Burnet's career benefited significantly from his friendship with Wilkie. Both men specialised in genre painting, otherwise known as the painting of 'common life'. 'Common' had two meanings in this context, connoting both 'everyday' and 'working class'. Ordinary scenes from the lives of working people, especially the rural poor, were represented in an idealised or comical fashion for the amusement of wealthy patrons and viewers. Such artworks created picturesque fantasies of poverty, rather than engaging with the harsh realities of inequality.

Genre painting enjoyed a vogue in the first half of the nineteenth century. Wilkie profited from this trend, finding immediate success after relocating from Edinburgh to London in 1805. Burnet followed a year later. In the subsequent decades, he produced many engravings after his friend's paintings, including Wilkie's most famous picture, *Chelsea Pensioners Reading the Waterloo Despatch* (fig. 1), which showed army veterans from the Royal Hospital at Chelsea celebrating news of Napoleon's defeat at the Battle of Waterloo in 1815. This work inspired Burnet to paint a naval companion piece, *The Greenwich Pensioners Commemorating Trafalgar* (fig. 2), which showed ex-seamen from the Greenwich Hospital celebrating the British fleet's triumph at the Battle of Trafalgar in 1805. However, whereas Wilkie's painting recreated the historic moment when the first news reports from Waterloo arrived in England, Burnet's picture was set some two decades after Trafalgar and showed a celebration to mark the battle's anniversary. He sold the work to the Duke of Wellington, who had commanded the British forces at Waterloo. Wellington had commissioned Wilkie's *Chelsea Pensioners* and his purchase of Burnet's *Greenwich Pensioners* brought the two paintings together as a pair.

The Greenwich Pensioners Commemorating Trafalgar included several portraits of real individuals, many of whom had fought in the battle. These were based on a series of life sketches, that Burnet painted on a visit to Greenwich Hospital in 1832. This sketch of William Mathews, a retired able seaman and Greenwich Pensioner, belongs to the series. Other sketches represent Mathews's fellow Pensioners Thomas Allen (fig. 3), John Wilkinson (fig. 4), Joseph Miller (fig. 5), Joseph Brown (fig. 6), Samuel Wilkes (fig. 7) and an individual known only as 'Handyson' (fig. 8). These figures were named in a key to the finished picture, which was published to accompany an engraving of the work in 1836 (fig. 9). At the top of this key, Burnet included a description of the painting, which proclaimed the seamen's patriotic commitment to their country and its imperial ambitions: 'By the bravery of our Sailors, our Empire is now established at sea.'

Such patriotic sentiments became increasingly prominent in genre painting after the conclusion of the Napoleonic Wars in 1815. This trend has been explained as a reaction against the profound social unrest in this period. Rising food prices, high unemployment and a post-war economic depression pushed struggling families over the

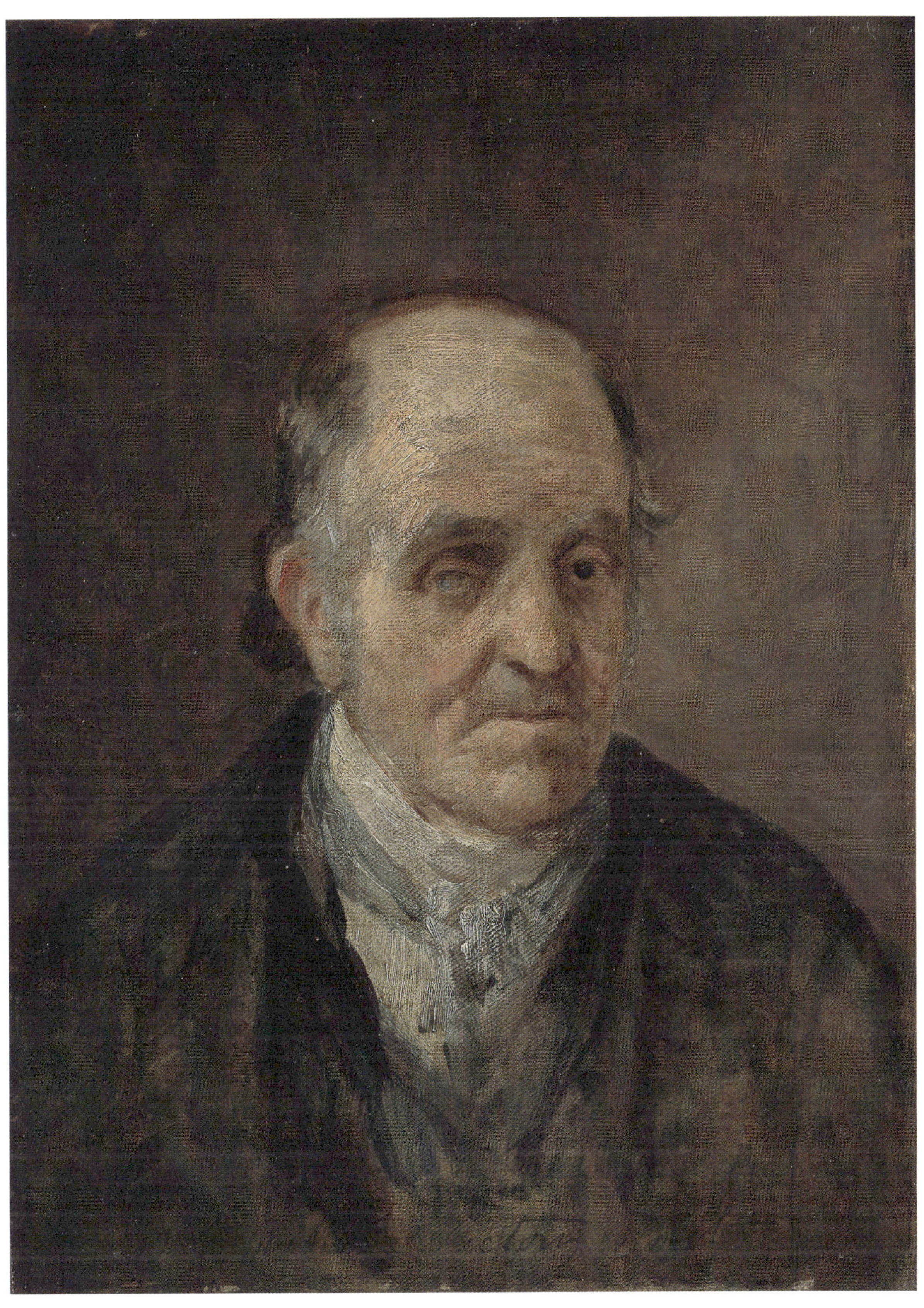

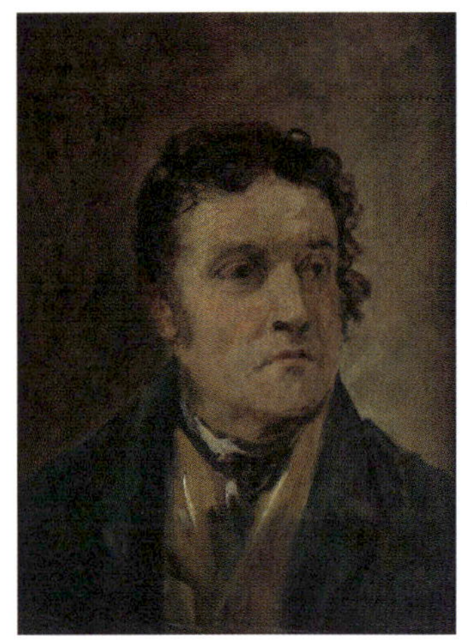

(fig. 3) Thomas Allen
305 x 230 mm
BHC2510

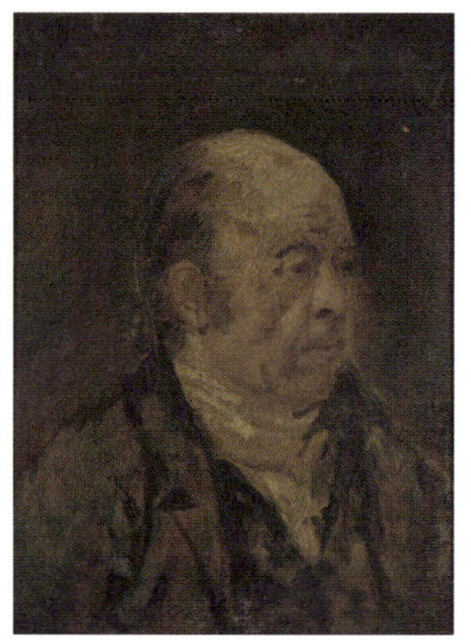

(fig. 4) John Wilkinson
301 x 228 mm
BHC3099

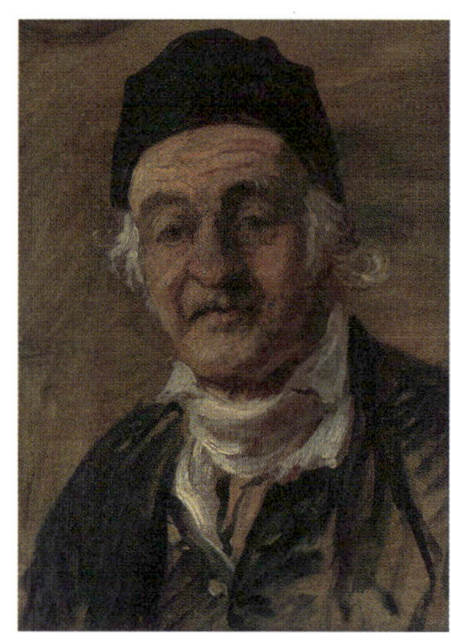

(fig. 5) Joseph Miller
305 x 230 mm
BHC2862

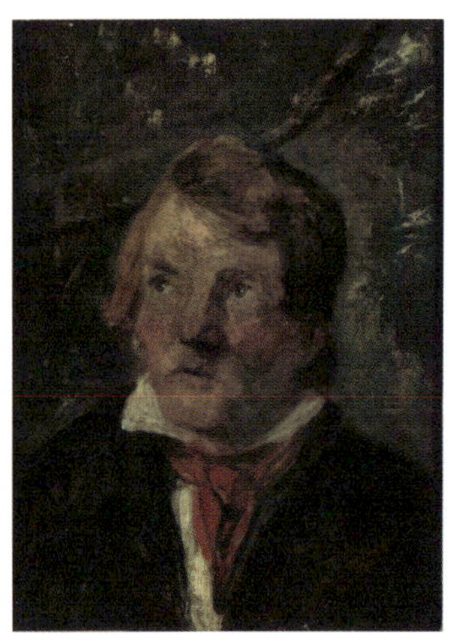

(fig. 6) Joseph Brown
305 x 230 mm
BHC2579

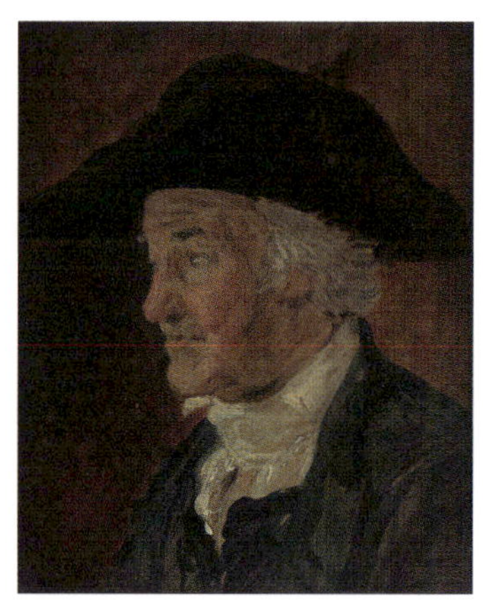

(fig. 7) Samuel Wilkes
315 x 260 mm
BHC3092

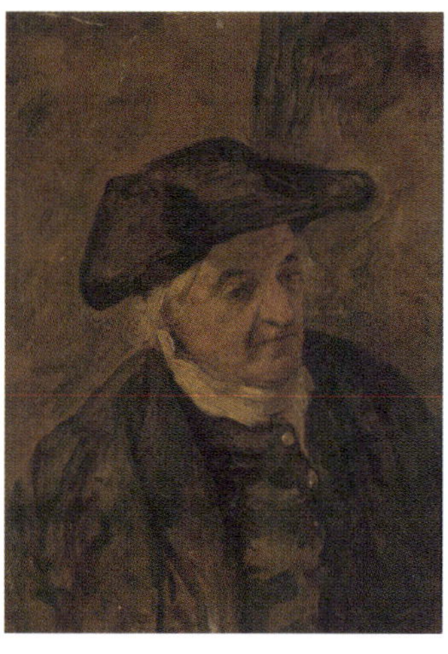

(fig. 8) 'Handyson'
307 x 227 mm
BHC2741

'Greenwich Pensioners'
by John Burnet
about 1832, oil on canvas

edge and fuelled discontent among the labouring classes. Politically conservative commentators grew concerned about the potential breakdown of established hierarchies. Against this backdrop, genre painters provided wealthy patrons with a comforting fiction of rustic wholesomeness and working-class patriotism without any hint of dissent. Many evoked nostalgia for the war, romanticising the conflict as a golden age of heroic deeds abroad and social harmony at home.

Few works went further in this regard than Burnet's *The Greenwich Pensioners Commemorating Trafalgar*. Set in the leafy environs of Greenwich Park with the grand architecture of the Queen's House and the Greenwich Hospital in the distance, the painting is a pastoral fantasy, bearing no relation to the dirty and crowded streets where former servicemen often lived. The red ensign (a naval flag) billows from the trees above the group in an unambiguous demonstration of patriotic loyalty. The ageing veterans in their blue coats and tricorn hats – the Greenwich Hospital uniform – are depicted alongside younger men, women and children. These figures are described in the print key as sailors, their sweethearts and their offspring, as well as naval schoolboys in the process of training to join the service. Turning the gathering into a family occasion, the combination of ages and genders increases the sentimental appeal of the scene. It also creates an illusion of continuity, suggesting that present and future generations of devoted seamen will uphold the Pensioners' legacy. In this way, the painting denies the possibility of social change and glosses over the diminishing importance of the Royal Navy in the nineteenth century. Since the Napoleonic Wars had ended, Britain had not been involved in many major sea battles, giving rise to fears that the nation's naval prowess would wither on the vine. Burnet, however, implies that more glorious victories will come.

William Mathews stands at the very centre of the painting, tilting his head forward to look at a chart showing the manoeuvres of the two fleets during the battle. Burnet's key explains Mathews's downcast expression as follows: 'he remembers the death of his Admiral [Nelson] – an event that threw a gloom over the general rejoicing'. This is

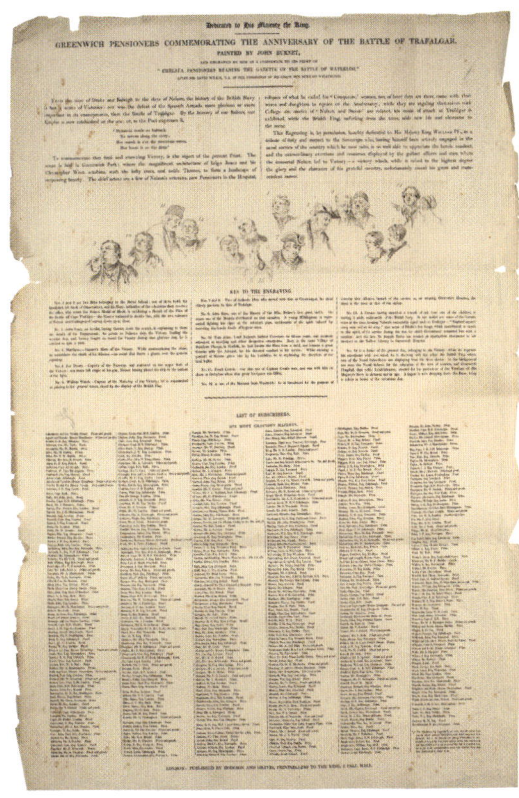
Dedicated to His Majesty the King.

GREENWICH PENSIONERS COMMEMORATING THE ANNIVERSARY OF THE BATTLE OF TRAFALGAR.

PAINTED BY JOHN BURNET,

(fig. 9 and detail p. 156) *Greenwich Pensioners Commemorating the Anniversary of the Battle of Trafalgar*
John Burnet
1836, engraving on paper
124 x 450 mm
PAI5148

PAINTED BY

AND ENGRAVED BY HIM A

"CHELSEA PENSIONERS READING THE

AFTER SIR DAVID WILKIE, R.A. IN THE POS

FROM the time of Drake and Raleigh to the days of Nelson, the history of the British Navy is but a series of Victories: nor was the defeat of the Spanish Armada more glorious or more important in its consequences, than the Battle of Trafalgar. By the bravery of our Sailors, ou Empire is now established on the sea; or, as the Poet expresses it,

"Britannia needs no bulwark,
No towers along the steep;
Her march is o'er the mountain waves,
Her home is on the deep."

To commemorate that final and crowning Victory, is the object of the present Print. Th scene is laid in Greenwich Park; where the magnificent architecture of Inigo Jones and Si Christopher Wren combine, with the lofty trees, and noble Thames, to form a landscape o surpassing beauty. The chief actors are a few of Nelson's veterans, now Pensioners in the Hospital

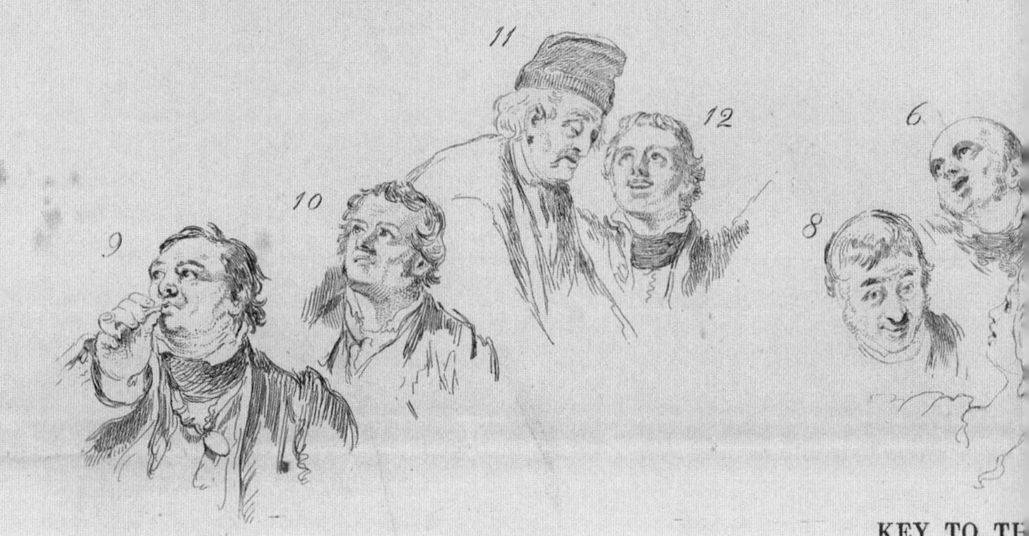

KEY TO TH

Nos. 1 and 2 are two Boys belonging to the Naval School: one of them holds his Quadrant, his Book of Observations, and his Slate, indicative of the education they receive; the other, who wears the Nelson Medal of Merit, is exhibiting a Sketch of the Plan of the Battle off Cape Trafalgar—the Enemy stationed in double line, with the two columns of Nelson and Collingwood bearing down upon them.

No. 3. John Stacy, an invalid, having thrown down his crutch, is explaining to them the details of the Engagement; he points to Nelson's ship, the Victory, leading the weather line, and, having fought on board the Victory during that glorious day, he is entitled to spin a yarn.

No. 4. Matthews—Gunner's Mate of the Victory. While contemplating the chart, he remembers the death of his Admiral—an event that threw a gloom over the general rejoicing.

No. 5. Joe Brown—Captain of the Fore-top, and stationed on the upper deck of the Victory; was twice left single at his gun, Nelson having placed his ship in the hottest of the fight.

No. 6. William Welch—Captain of the Main-top of the Victory; he is represented as joining in the general huzza, raised by the display of the British Flag.

Nos. 7 and 8. Two of Nelson's Me victory previous to that of Trafalgar.

No. 9. John Ross, one of the Her wears one of the Medals distributed o sented lighting his cigar at the vete recording the heroic deeds of bygone d

No. 10. Tom Allen, Lord Nelson's attendant in boarding and other dange Burnham Thorpe, in Norfolk, he had k favorite with the Admiral, for his dev portrait of Nelson given him by his fatal bullet.

No. 11. Frank Cowen—was also o shore at Owhyhee when that great Navi

No. 12. is one of the Marines from

IN BURNET,

IPANION TO HIS PRINT OF

ETTE OF THE BATTLE OF WATERLOO,"

OF HIS GRACE THE DUKE OF WELLINGTON.

eliques of what he called his "Conquests;" seamen, too, of later days are there, come with their vives and daughters to rejoice on the Anniversary; while they are regaling themselves with College ale, stories of "Nelson and Bronte" are related, his mode of attack at Trafalgar is xhibited, while the British Flag, unfurling from the trees, adds new life and character to he scene.

This Engraving is, by permission, humbly dedicated to His Majesty King William IV., as a ribute of duty and respect to the Sovereign who, having himself been actively engaged in the aval service of the country which he now rules, is so well able to appreciate the heroic conduct, nd the extraordinary exertions and resources displayed by the gallant officers and men whom he immortal Nelson led to Victory—a victory which, while it raised to the highest degree he glory and the character of his grateful country, unfortunately closed his great and transendent career.

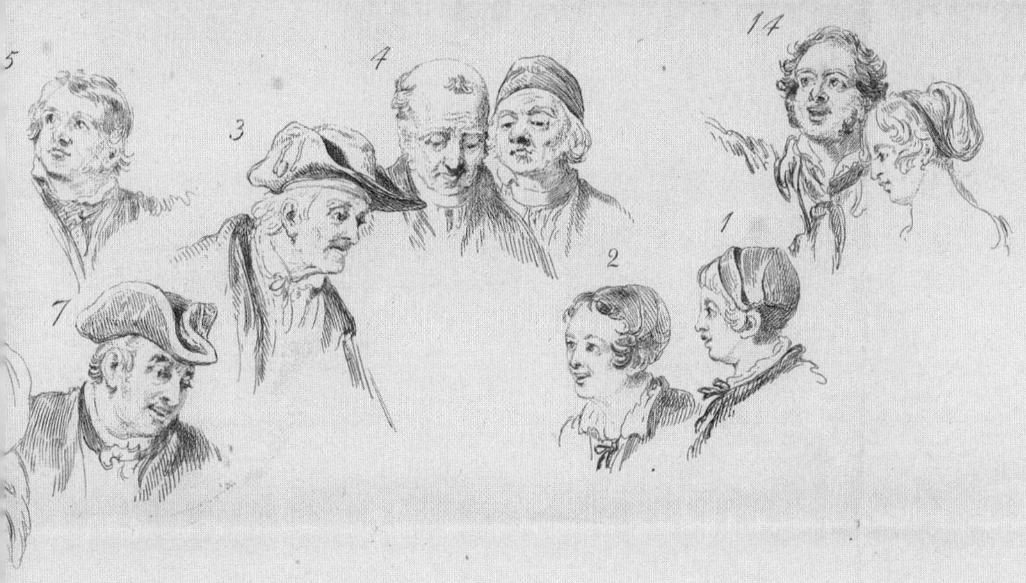

GRAVING.

served with him at Copenhagen, his chief

he Nile, Nelson's first great battle. He ccasion. A young Midshipman is repree, emblematic of the spirit infused by

Coxswain for fifteen years, and constant terprises. Born in the same Village of e Hero from a child, and became a great nduct in his service. While shewing a p, he is explaining the direction of the

aptain Cook's men, and was with him on as killed.

ich: he is introduced for the purpose of shewing this effective branch of the service, as, on entering Greenwich Hospital, the dress is the same as that of the sailors.

No. 13. A Female having snatched a branch of oak from one of the children, is waving it aloft, emblematic of the British Navy. In her basket are some of the Garters worn at the time, bearing Nelson's memorable signal made at Trafalgar—"*England expects every man will do his duty;*" also some of Dibdin's Sea Songs, which contributed so much to the spirit of the service during the war, for which Government rewarded him with a pension; and the late Sir Joseph Yorke has erected an appropriate monument to his memory in the Sailors' Library in Greenwich Hospital.

No. 14 is a Sailor of the present day, belonging to the Victory: while he supports his sweetheart with one hand, he is cheering with the other the British Flag, which two of the Naval Schoolboys are displaying from the trees above. In the background are seen the Naval School, for the education of the sons of seamen, and Greenwich Hospital, that noble Establishment, erected for the protection of the Veterans of His Majesty's Navy in sickness and in age. A frigate is seen dropping down the River, firing a salute in honor of the victorious day.

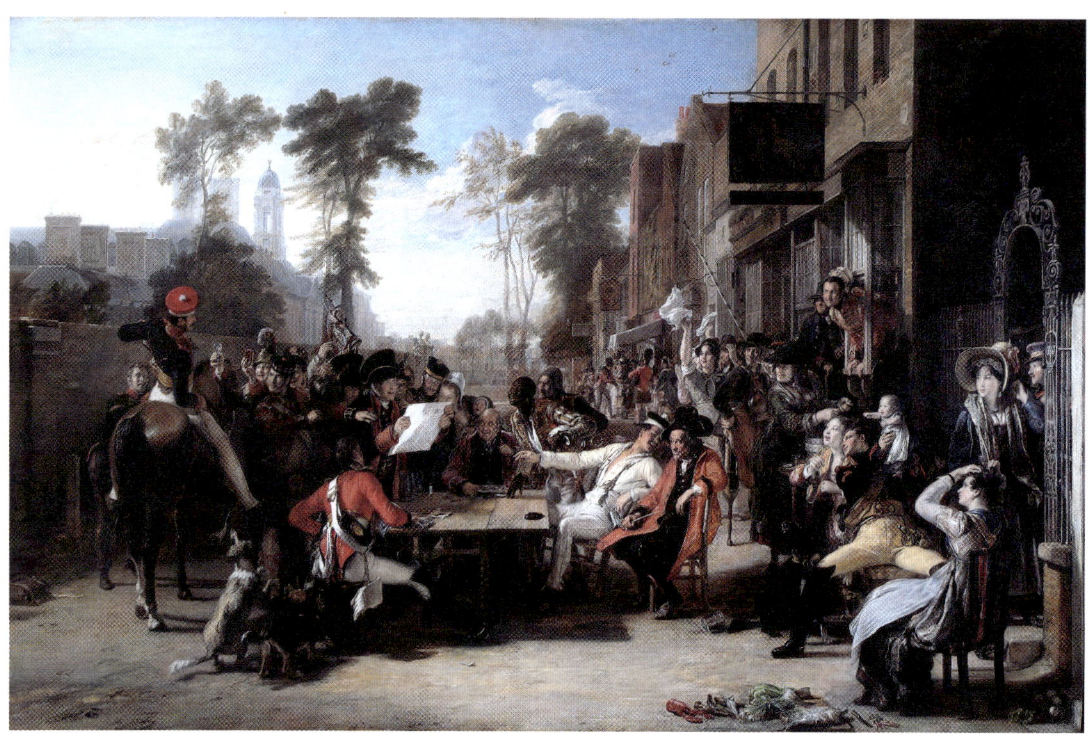

(fig. 1) *Chelsea Pensioners Reading the Waterloo Despatch*
David Wilkie
1822, oil on panel
970 x 1,580 mm
English Heritage, The Wellington Collection,
Apsley House (WM.1469-1948)

one of several references to Nelson in the painting. A young woman on the left holds a coloured print of Lemuel Francis Abbott's portrait of the late admiral (p. 140). Meanwhile, the key explains how each of the Pensioners in the painting are connected to Nelson: 'Tom Allen – Lord Nelson's faithful Coxswain', 'John Ross – one of the Heroes of the Nile, Nelson's first great battle', and so on. A sense of hierarchy is thus maintained. The lowly veterans are not being celebrated for their own sake but for their service to a great commander.

However, showing Mathews on his own, Burnet's portrait sketch lacks this narrative of subordination and service. Stripped of the patriotic imagery of *The Greenwich Pensioners Commemorating Trafalgar* and finished in muted shades of grey and brown, the sketch is a dignified and sensitive study of an aging veteran. Instead of looking down as he does in the larger painting, Mathews meets the viewer's gaze, inviting us to recognize him as an individual with his own story. His right eye has a milky appearance, suggesting that he may have lost his sight in it.

It was unusual to see Greenwich Pensioners

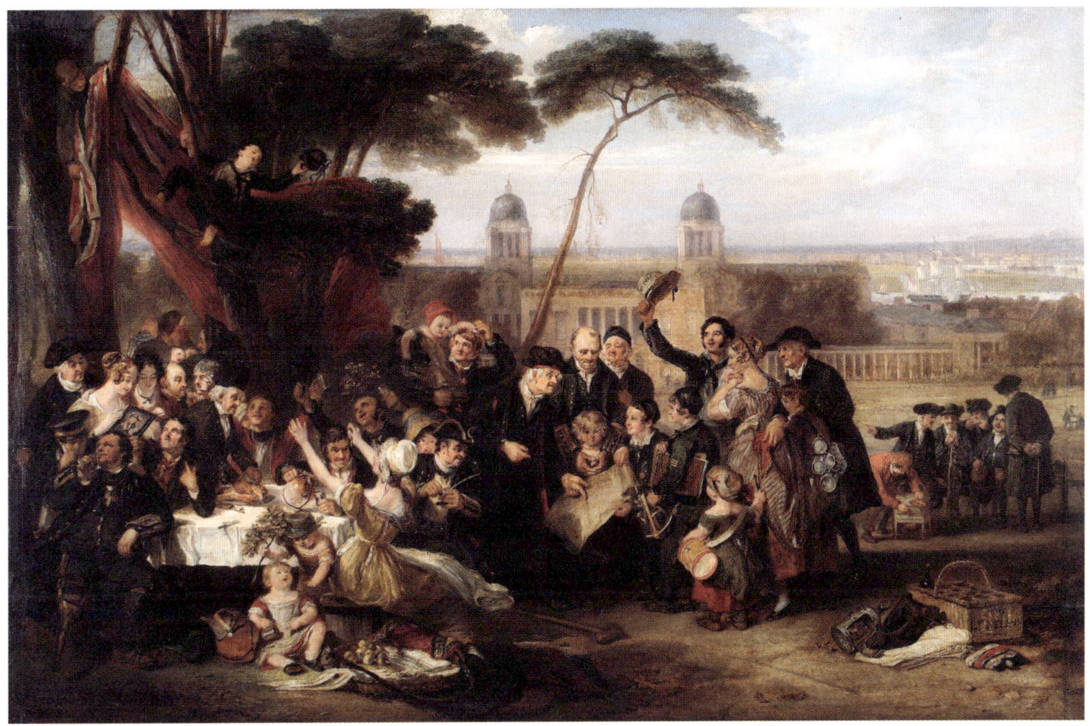

(fig. 2) *The Greenwich Pensioners Commemorating Trafalgar*
John Burnet
about 1835–38, oil on panel
970 x 1,530 mm
English Heritage, The Wellington Collection, Apsley House (WM.1556-1948)

depicted in such an individualised and sympathetic manner. They were typically represented in art and literature as stock characters. Eighteenth-century depictions tended to be negative, framing the Pensioner as rowdy, drunken and lascivious, while nineteenth-century examples were more positive, venerating the Pensioner as an archetype of working-class patriotism. Even more so than Burnet's finished painting, which reinforced patriotic tropes, the portrait sketch challenges us to look beyond the stereotypes. As a preparatory study for a larger painting, it was never intended as a work of art in its own right. Today, however, the sketch should be recognised as rare and important.

Traditional histories have tended to ignore ordinary people like Mathews, and their identities have often been lost or obscured. Mathews himself provides a case-in-point. Burnet only ever recorded his surname and the ship on which he served. 'Mathews – Victory' is faintly inscribed across the bottom of the sketch and the key for *The Greenwich Pensioners Commemorating*

Trafalgar describes him as 'Mathews – Gunner's Mate of the Victory'. When the sketch was acquired by the National Maritime Museum, it was catalogued as a portrait of Thomas Mathews. The origin of this identification is not recorded. Several individuals called Thomas Mathews or Matthews were present at the Battle of Trafalgar, but so were others with that surname. Research into the Greenwich Hospital records in 2021 revealed no individuals called Thomas Mathews but showed that William Mathews was admitted as a Pensioner in 1831. An individual of that name served on the *Victory* at Trafalgar. More evidence for identifying Burnet's sketch as a portrait of William (not Thomas) Mathews was found in Andrew Morton's *The United Service*, a patriotic genre painting in the same vein as those of Wilkie and Burnet (fig. 10). This picture includes a Greenwich Pensioner with a milky right eye (fig. 11), who is named on the frame as 'Boatswain William Mathews: at the Battle of the Nile: at Tenerife: in the Victory at Trafalgar'. In recognition of this compelling proof, Burnet's portrait sketch is now at last associated with the correct name.

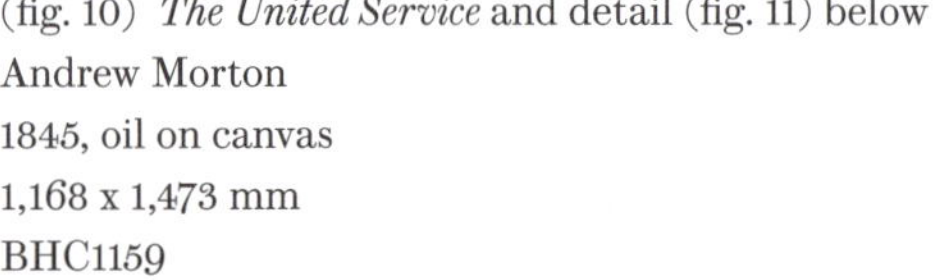

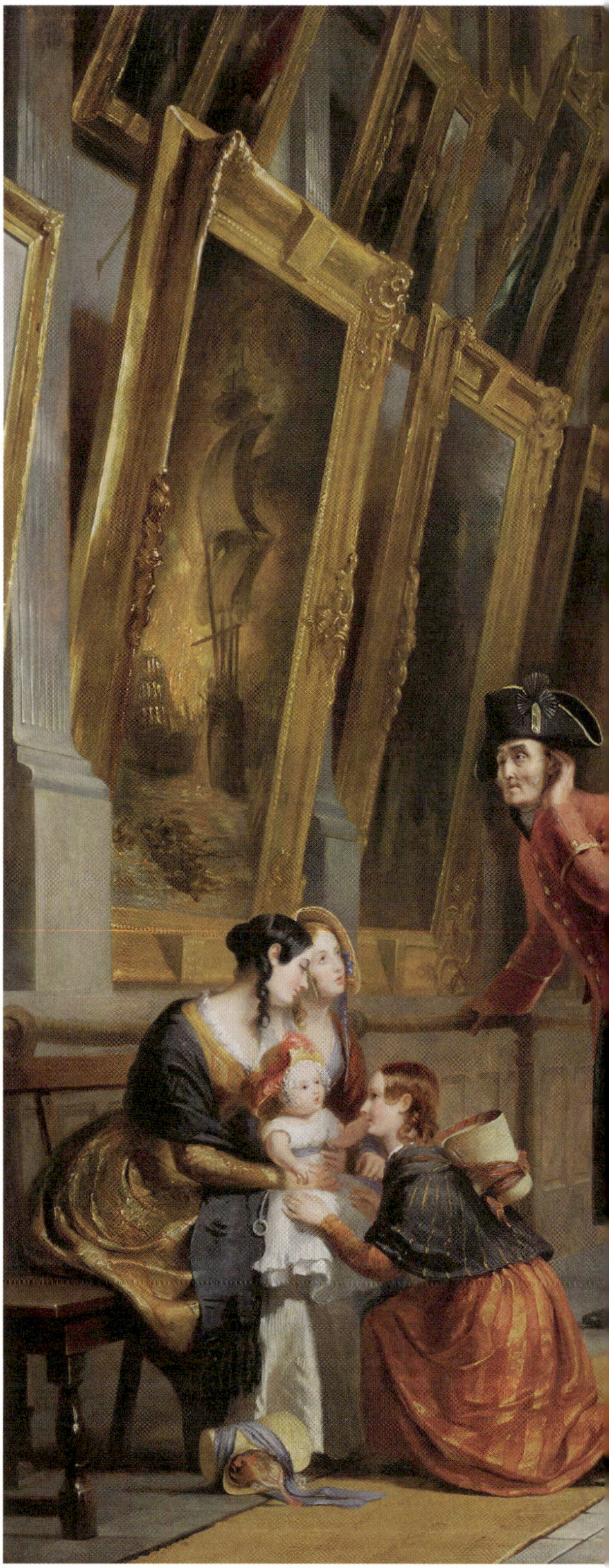

(fig. 10) *The United Service* and detail (fig. 11) below
Andrew Morton
1845, oil on canvas
1,168 x 1,473 mm
BHC1159

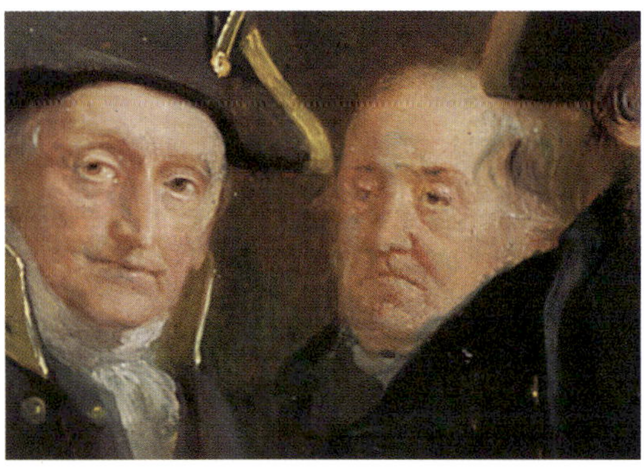

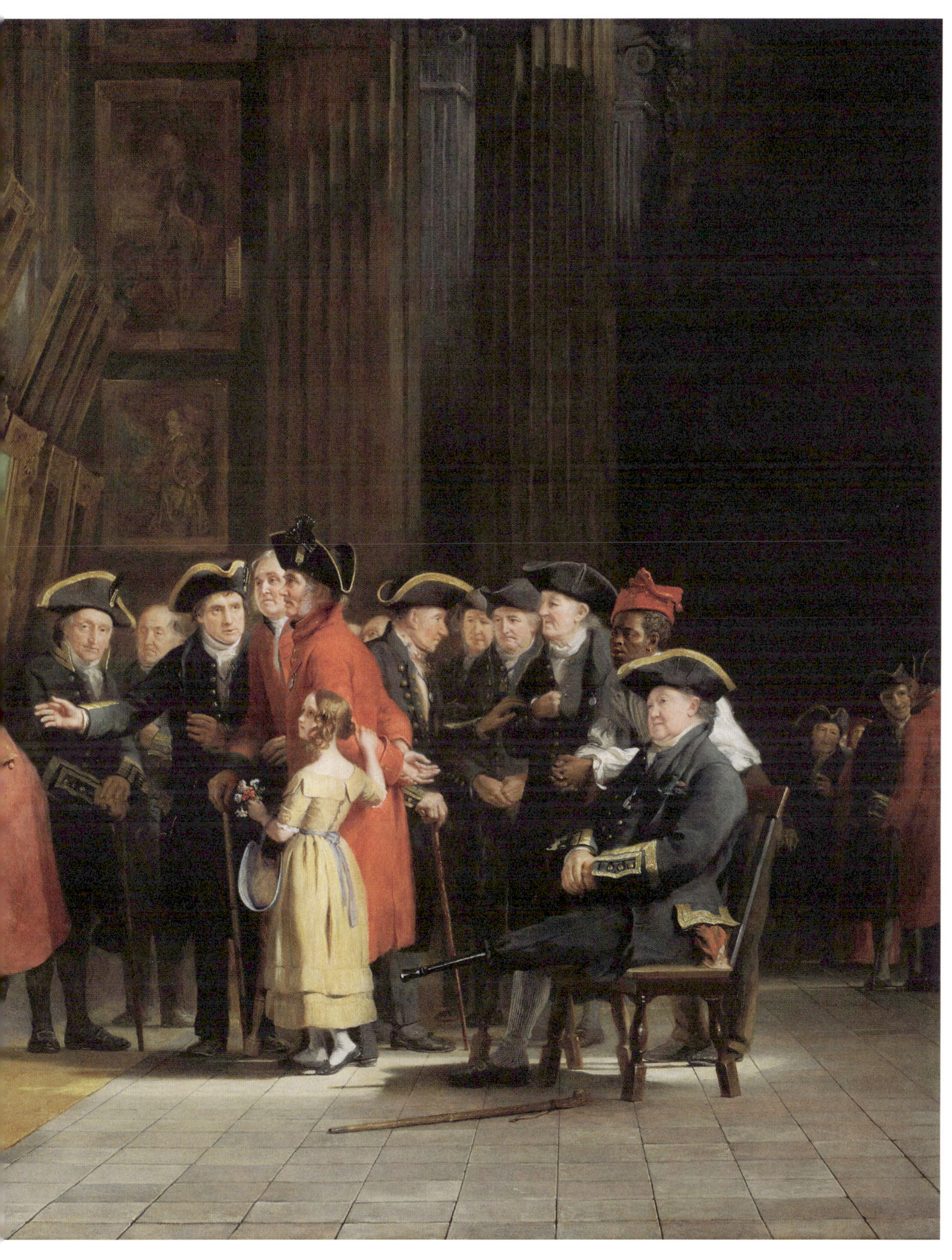

Commander James Clark Ross

John Robert Wildman

1834, oil on canvas
1,442 x 1,120 mm
BHC2981

John Robert Wildman worked as a portraitist in London during the first half of the nineteenth century. He had a steady but unspectacular career, never breaking into the elite of his profession. Like other mid-range artists, he survived in part through specialising in a particular area.
In Wildman's case, he developed close links within religious circles and painted numerous portraits of Methodist clergymen, prints of which were often published in Christian magazines. He did also depict other sitters, but was not successful enough to establish a financial safety net for himself and his family. In 1843, a notice entitled 'A Case of Extreme Distress' appeared in the *Art-Union* – an arts-focused magazine – appealing for charitable donations to support Wildman, who had fallen ill and was unable to work, leaving him incapable of providing for his six young children. He died a few months later.

This portrait represented a high point in Wildman's precarious career. Painted in early 1834, it was one of his most celebrated and lucrative pictures, receiving favourable reviews in the press and being published multiple times as a print. The painting's success owed much to the celebrity of its sitter, James Clark Ross, a naval officer who became famous for his involvement in polar exploration.

Travellers had ventured to polar regions in earlier periods, but it was only in the aftermath of the Napoleonic Wars that Arctic exploration became an important area of naval activity. In an effort to give the Royal Navy focus and purpose in the absence of a major international conflict, the Admiralty launched a series of missions in search of a north-west passage – that is, a navigable route through the ice floes of the Canadian Arctic, providing a shortcut between the Atlantic and Pacific Oceans. Meanwhile, private funders began recruiting naval personnel for their own northward voyages. The Arctic came to be seen as a crucial proving ground for British naval, technological, scientific, commercial and spiritual prowess. It also became a source of public fascination. Popular lectures, panoramas and books were dedicated to polar themes, while dinners and balls were held in honour of returning explorers. To represent this new cohort of Arctic celebrities, portrait painters had to combine traditional naval imagery with polar motifs, from fur cloaks to ice-bound landscapes, as exemplified in Wildman's painting.

The portrait commemorates one of the period's most sensational polar voyages, depicting James Clark Ross after his return from an Arctic adventure with his uncle and fellow explorer, John Ross. The Rosses and their men had set sail from London on 23 May 1829 in the *Victory* steamship, intending to chart the waters around Prince Regent Island in northern Canada. Gin magnate Felix Booth financed the voyage. The journey was scheduled to last 15 months, but more than four years passed without word, leading many in Britain to assume that the *Victory* had met a gruesome fate. In fact, the officers and crew spent three winters trapped on board the ship in the ice and a further year trekking on foot in search of rescue. They eventually encountered the *Isabella* whaling ship, which conveyed them back to England. Following their arrival at Hull in October 1833, reports of their miraculous survival quickly spread. The Rosses encouraged this attention, giving newspaper interviews and attending society parties. Both men also sat for portraits, which featured in major exhibitions and circulated as prints.

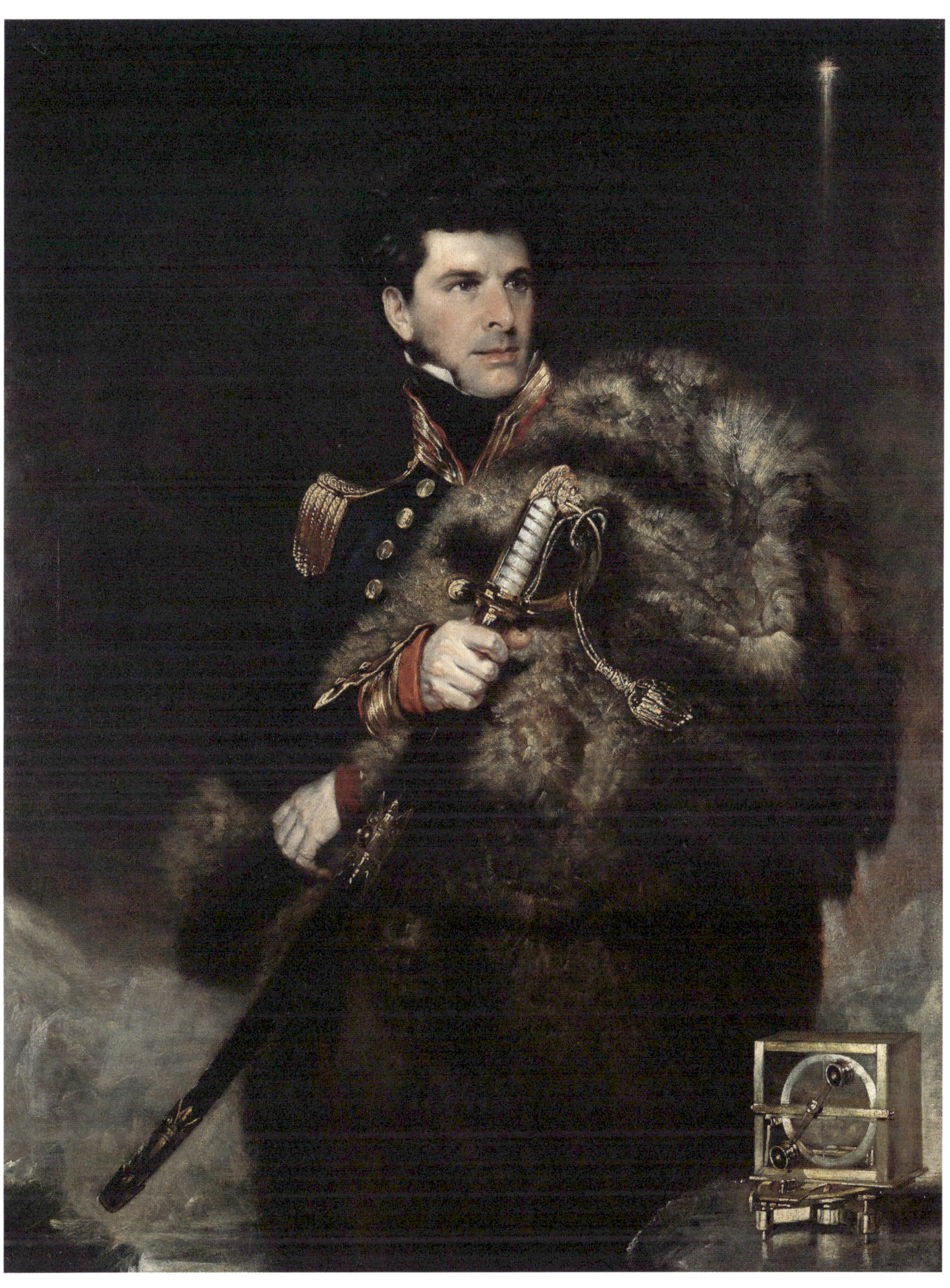

(fig. 1) *Sir John Ross*
James Green
1833, oil on canvas
1,321 x 1,111 mm
National Portrait Gallery (NPG 314)

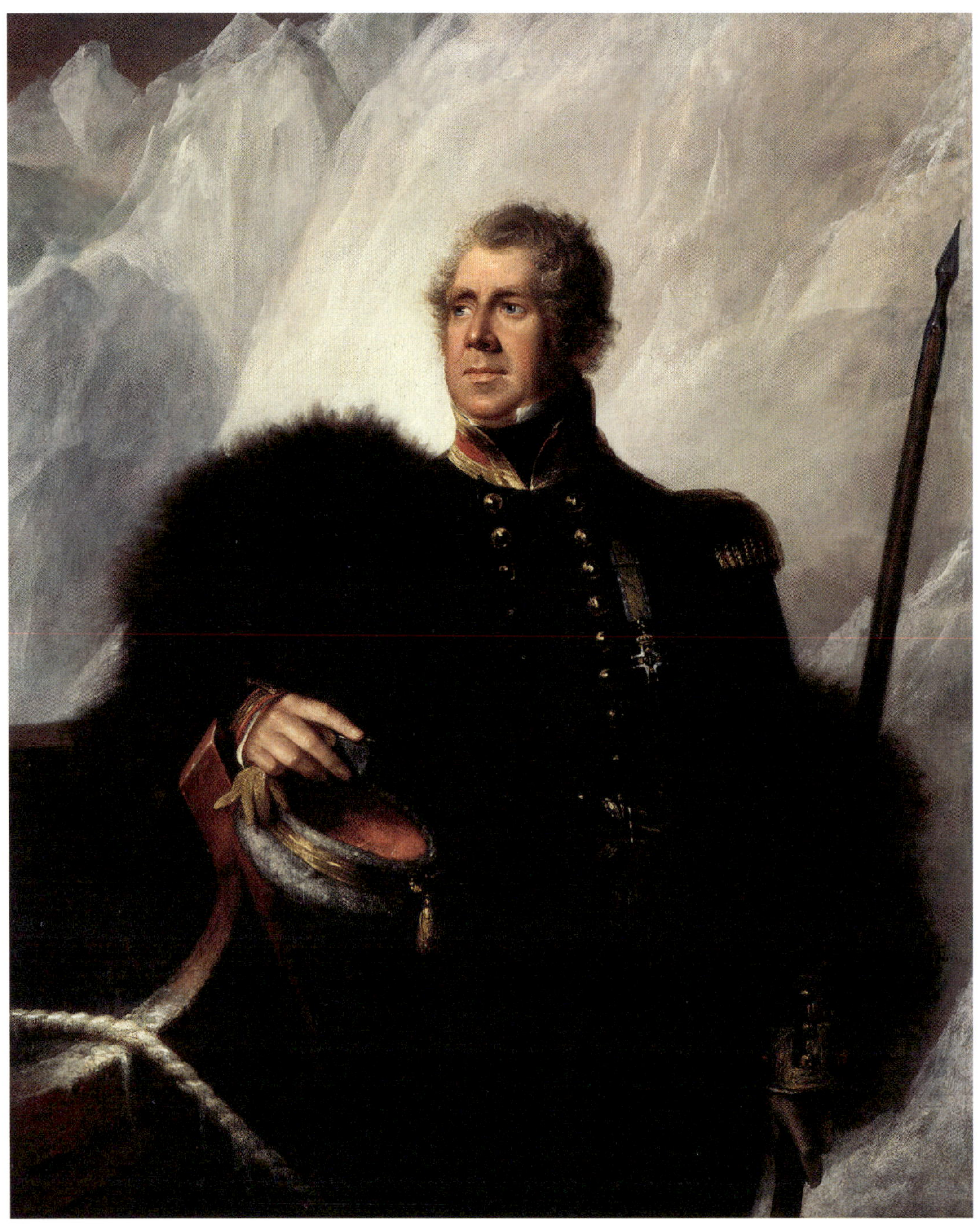

Several prints were made after Wildman's painting, including a mezzotint by R.M. Hodgetts, published in 1835, and an engraving by Henry Cook, issued five years later in 1840. The inscription on the latter print mentions Wildman's painting as being 'in the possession of George Ross, Esquire', a reference to the sitter's father. George Ross's possession of the painting raises the possibility that he was its patron. A former colonial customs official, George Ross was associated with his son's polar exploits, having been involved in organising a rescue mission to search for him. It is possible that he commissioned the portrait to celebrate his son's safe return and to enhance the family's public profile.

Wildman's painting incorporates various references to the sitter's ordeal in the Arctic. The background is a polar landscape in the winter, the Pole Star glinting overhead. In the foreground, James is enveloped in a massive bearskin, from which his right shoulder emerges, displaying his splendid full-dress naval uniform with its gold trim and scarlet accents. The image is very similar to a portrait of John Ross (James's uncle and fellow survivor of the *Victory* expedition), which James Green painted in the same year as Wildman's picture (fig. 1). However, one detail in Wildman's picture sets the two explorers apart. The magnetic dip-circle in the lower right corner alludes to James's crowning achievement, the discovery of the North Magnetic Pole by his sled party in 1831. This achievement belonged to the younger Ross alone, his uncle having made no significant scientific breakthroughs.

The dip-circle hints at the subtle but important ways in which James's public persona diverged from his uncle's. Although John Ross engaged in a campaign of relentless self-promotion in the aftermath of the *Victory* expedition, he remained unpopular in official circles and did not find favour with the Admiralty or the scientific establishment. By contrast, James received a new naval posting and an invitation to present a paper to the Royal Society. This created a rift between the two men. The public sided with James, believing John Ross to have unfairly overshadowed his nephew. More superficial factors were also at play: James was a good-looking bachelor in his mid-thirties, whereas his uncle was a middle-aged widower, whom one newspaper cruelly likened to a walrus in appearance.

Wildman's portrait helped to reinforce the belief that James Ross had been unjustly treated. *The Lady's Magazine* articulated this stance in its review of the painting:

> This is a spirited, well-painted portrait of a gallant-looking gentleman, who has in his gala Arctic dress made himself a very picturesque bundle of fur. Whether it is a likeness, it is beyond our critical acumen to discover, not having ever seen the original, whom we think rather an injured personage; for he certainly has as great claims to be considered an intrepid polar hero as his far-famed uncle ... yet no one seems to care for Commander Ross. To atone for this undeserved public neglect, the brave commander ought to be made a pet lion of by the ladies.

This review typifies the growing support that the young commander garnered at his uncle's expense. It is particularly significant that these comments were directed at a female audience, the review having been published in a long-running and highly successful women's magazine.

Explicitly calling for James Ross to become a subject of feminine appreciation ('a pet lion of...the ladies'), the review highlights the importance of women as an audience for Arctic celebrity. Parallels may be drawn with the earlier phenomenon of 'scarlet fever' – the name coined at the turn of the nineteenth century to describe women's attraction to military men (and their red uniforms). Such attraction was encouraged by cultural commentators in the Napoleonic Wars as a legitimate expression of feminine patriotism, while simultaneously providing a source of public excitement, humour and titillation. Something of the redcoat's mystique appears to have transferred in the post-war period to polar explorers, who were often presented in texts, images and portraits of the time as manly heroes worthy of feminine appreciation.

The critic in *The Lady's Magazine* emphasises Ross's clothing and appearance in the painting, writing that he appears 'gallant-looking' in his 'gala Arctic dress'. The latter phrase demonstrates that the portrait's original viewers appreciated the ceremonial nature of the commander's attire, which was designed not for the ice fields of the Arctic but for the ballrooms of fashionable society. Typically featuring multiple layers of woollen clothing under a sealskin coat or canvas smock with mittens and a hood, polar dress in this period was designed for utility, not style. Sitting for a portrait, however, called for more glamorous attire. Ross's bearskin represented an elegant solution: as a luxurious garment, it allowed Ross to stake his claim to a place in the social elite; at the same time, it alluded to his need as an Arctic explorer to protect himself against freezing temperatures.

Ross's bearskin also visually transforms the portrait. The fur adds volume to his figure, puffing out his silhouette. His physical presence becomes almost bear-like: big, powerful and commanding. The skin retains a visible link to its wild origins in the form of the bear's paws, which Wildman shows hanging from the Commander's left elbow, the sharp claws gleaming. Dressed in the pelt of a wild animal, Ross is likened to a creature of the wilderness, while also being framed as a conqueror of nature. The layering of uniform and bearskin allowed Ross to combine the respectability of a gentleman with something of the glamorous, dangerous, and exotic allure of an outsider. This was the same blend of characteristics that other public personalities of the early nineteenth century, including Lord Byron, harnessed to generate celebrity. Reference to Ross's potential to become 'a pet lion' in *The Lady's Magazine* hints at his animal magnetism. The term 'lion' was used in this period to mean 'a person of note', but writers of the time often played upon its animal associations.

The magazine's description of the commander as 'a picturesque bundle of fur' highlights how the bearskin turns Ross's body into an attractive spectacle. The fur's tactility is powerfully evoked with criss-crossing brushstrokes, calling to the viewer's sense of touch. This combines with intimate bodily details, such as the point beneath Ross's ear where his dark facial hair spills over the starched white linen of his collar, to evoke a thrilling illusion of physical proximity. In this way, the portrait secured his status as a polar pin-up.

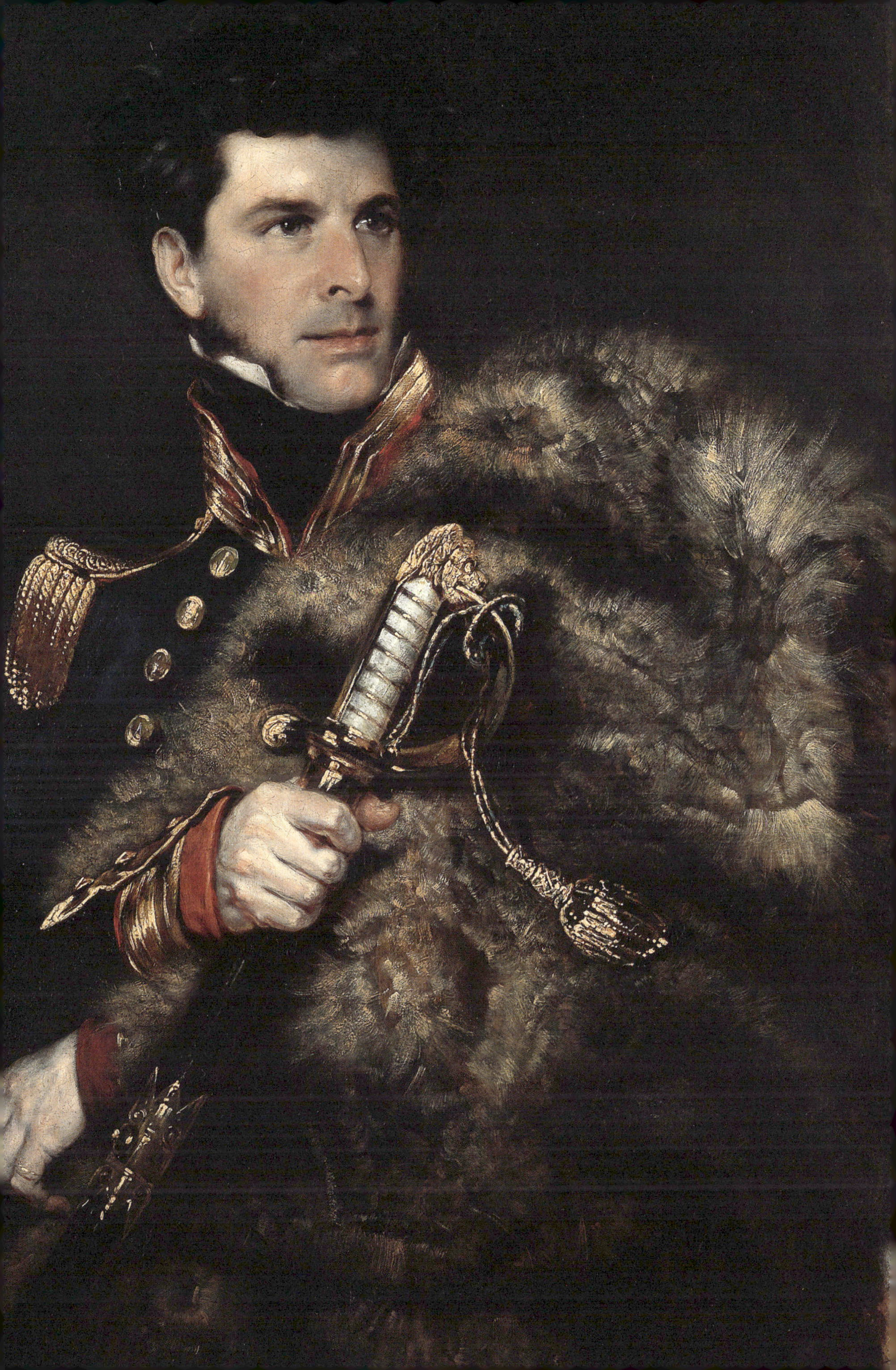

Rear-Admiral Sir Francis Beaufort

Stephen Pearce

About 1858, oil on canvas
1,275 x 1,020 mm
BHC2541

In the mid-1850s, Stephen Pearce became known as 'the Arctic portraitist'. Coined by naval officer Robert McCormick, this epithet referred to Pearce's reputation for painting individuals associated with polar exploration, from the explorers themselves to the officials, administrators and financiers who organised and supported their voyages. Pearce had begun his artistic career as a specialist in equestrian subjects, having had ample opportunities to study equine anatomy and behaviour as a boy in the Royal Mews, where his father worked as a clerk in the department of the Master of the Horse near Buckingham Palace. However, after visiting Italy in the late 1840s, he set about professionally reinventing himself as a portrait painter.

Pearce's first significant commissions came from John Barrow Jr, a friend from his youth. Barrow held an official role as an archivist at the Admiralty, but he was also heavily involved in polar affairs, continuing the legacy of his late father, John Barrow Sr, who had managed the Admiralty's programme of Arctic exploration for several decades. For Barrow Jr., Pearce produced a series of portraits depicting polar explorers. He also received further commissions from others in his friend's network of Arctic associates. Displayed in public exhibitions, circulated as popular prints and acquired into national collections, Pearce's portraits came to define polar exploration in the mid-nineteenth century.

Completed around 1858, this portrait depicts Rear-Admiral Sir Francis Beaufort, who served as Hydrographer to the Navy between 1829 and 1855. Tasked with commissioning and publishing marine charts and coastal surveys, the Hydrographic Office was also involved in testing navigational instruments and measuring meteorological phenomena. Beaufort himself developed a scale for recording wind speed, which became known as the Beaufort Scale in his honour. While he never travelled to the Arctic himself, he was involved in planning and co-ordinating polar expeditions. His career epitomised the bureaucratic values of the early Victorian era, when Britain endeavoured to impose order upon its vast empire via official records, science, statistics and new technologies.

The portrait alludes to Beaufort's role as a hydrographer and administrator. The setting appears to be an office or gentleman's study, equipped with red damask curtains and a desk. The light comes from an unseen window on the left. Beaufort is dressed in civilian clothes with a pair of spectacles in his hand and a double-lensed magnifying glass on a cord around his neck. These optical aids testify to his involvement in the detailed scrutiny of charts and documents, like those spread on the desk and hung on the wall behind him. Yet the Rear-Admiral himself has turned away from his papers, as if to greet a visitor. This conversational pose prevents Beaufort from appearing myopically absorbed in his own intellectual pursuits. Instead, he is presented as an approachable colleague, working with others in service of the British state.

Pearce produced the portrait to commemorate the Beaufort's death in 1857, following a public campaign to fundraise for a memorial. After collecting subscriptions from friends and admirers of the rear-admiral, the Beaufort Testimonial Fund paid for the creation of this portrait, as well as for the establishment of an annual prize for the student who received the

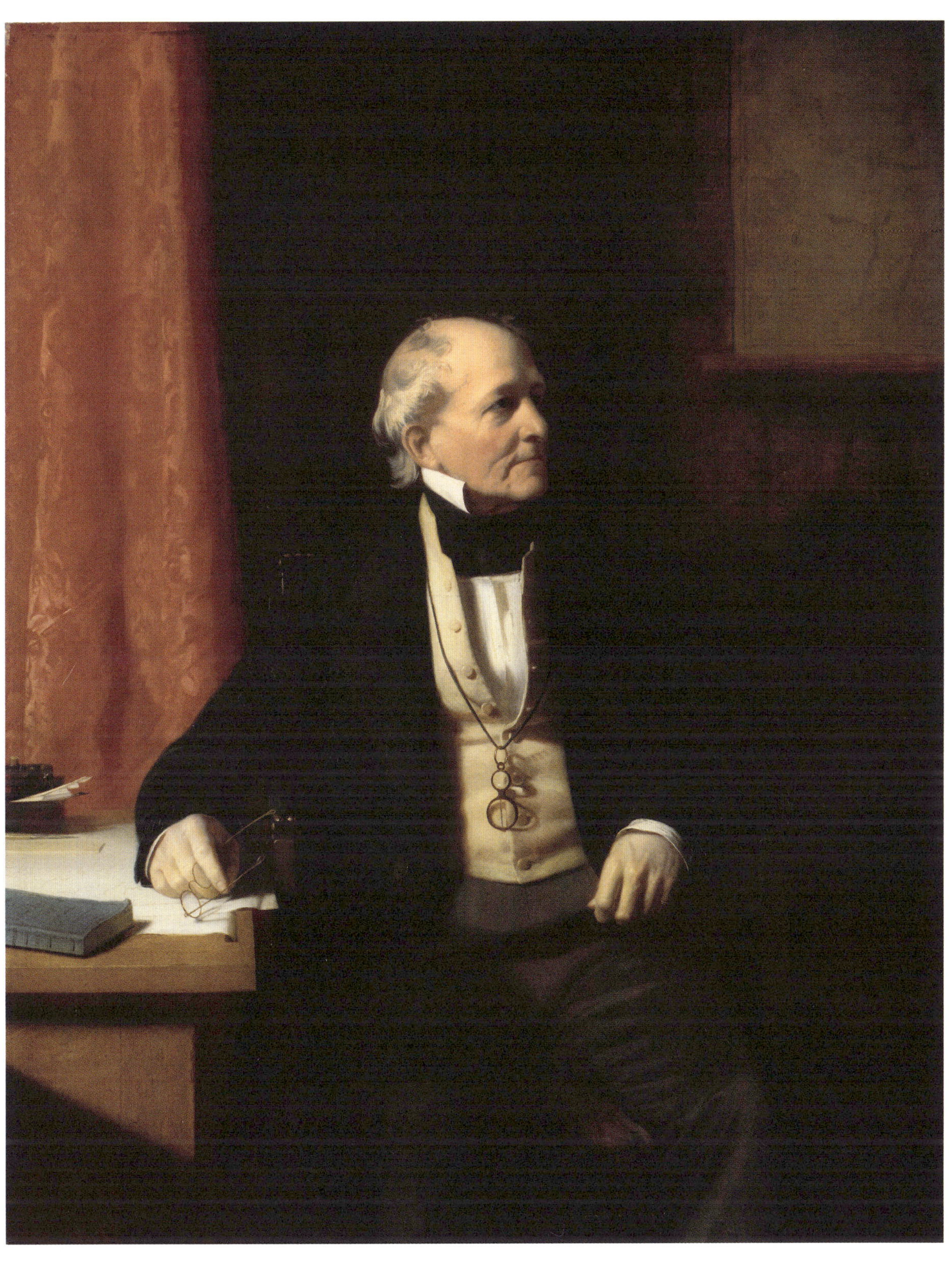

(fig. 1) *Sir Francis Beaufort*
Stephen Pearce
1850, oil on canvas
505 x 406 mm
National Portrait Gallery (NPG 918)

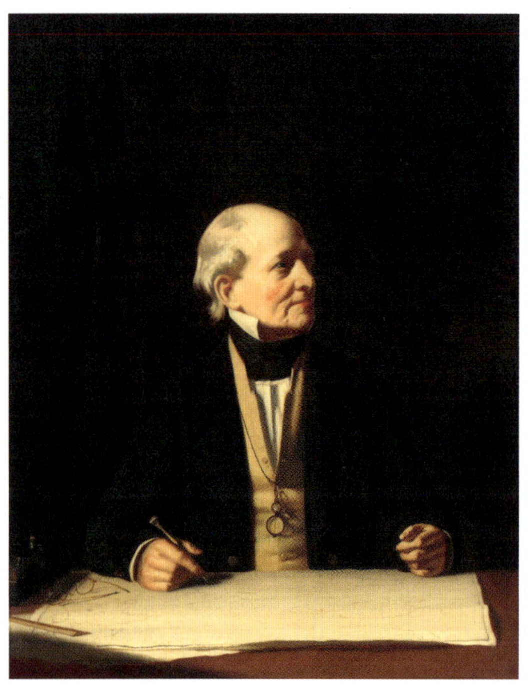

highest mark in the navigation examination at the Royal Naval College. The Testimonial donated the portrait to the Naval Gallery in the Painted Hall at Greenwich Hospital, where it was placed on public display. In donating Beaufort's portrait to this institution, the Testimonial secured his status as a figure of public interest and national importance.

The painting was placed in the north-west corner of the Painted Hall, where it hung alongside Nathaniel Dance's famous portrait of the eighteenth-century naval explorer Captain James Cook, best remembered for his three voyages to the Pacific (p. 112). This arrangement was not coincidental. It emphasised the parallels between Cook and Beaufort, both men being known for their achievements in science and navigation. The similar composition of the two portraits reinforced the connection, with Cook and Beaufort both shown turning away from tables covered in books and charts. Pearce may well have copied his composition from Dance's portrait, anticipating the display of the two paintings together in the Painted Hall and wishing to create a visual link between Beaufort and his illustrious predecessor.

The creation of continuity between past and present naval personnel was an important function of the Naval Gallery in this period. By the mid-nineteenth century, the Royal Navy bore little resemblance to the much-vaunted fighting force of earlier times. It had been three decades since Britain had been involved in a major naval conflict. As the nation's colonial holdings were consolidated into a vast and bureaucratic empire, its chief naval activities were surveying, policing and exploration. Beaufort embodied this new era in many ways, but the display of his portrait alongside Cook's provided reassurance that his achievements were rooted in a longstanding tradition of naval glory.

At the same time, however, Beaufort's portrait was tied to a more recent incident. Since he was working after Beaufort's death and could not paint his sitter from life, Pearce based the likeness upon an earlier sketch of the Rear-Admiral, which he had made in 1850 (fig. 1). This picture was a study for a larger group portrait,

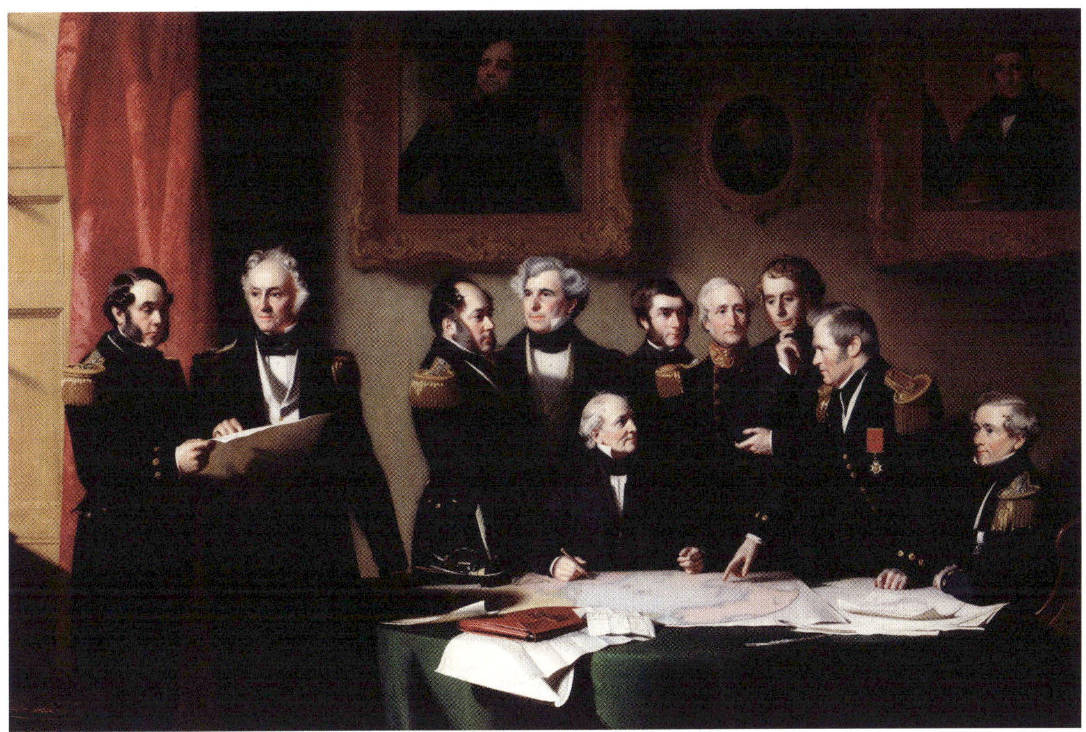

(fig. 2 and detail p. 172) *The Arctic Council planning a search for Sir John Franklin*
Stephen Pearce
1851, oil on canvas
1,175 x 1,833 mm
National Portrait Gallery (NPG 208)

The Arctic Council Planning a Search for Sir John Franklin (fig. 2), which responded to an infamous episode in the history of polar exploration. On 19 May 1845, two ships under the command of Captain Sir John Franklin had set sail for the Arctic, hoping to discover a north-west passage linking the Atlantic and Pacific oceans. The Franklin expedition was supposed to be the culmination of a decades-long programme of British polar exploration, but instead its ships, *Erebus* and *Terror*, disappeared in the ice, along with their entire crews. A series of naval and private rescue missions accumulated traces of the missing men's movements, but no survivors were ever found.

Showing ten men around a table, *The Arctic Council Planning a Search for Sir John Franklin* claimed to represent a committee of polar experts discussing the search effort. However, the 'Arctic Council' of the painting's title was not an official body but rather an informal association of friends, brought together through the influence of Jane Franklin, the missing commander's wife, and John Barrow Jr, whose

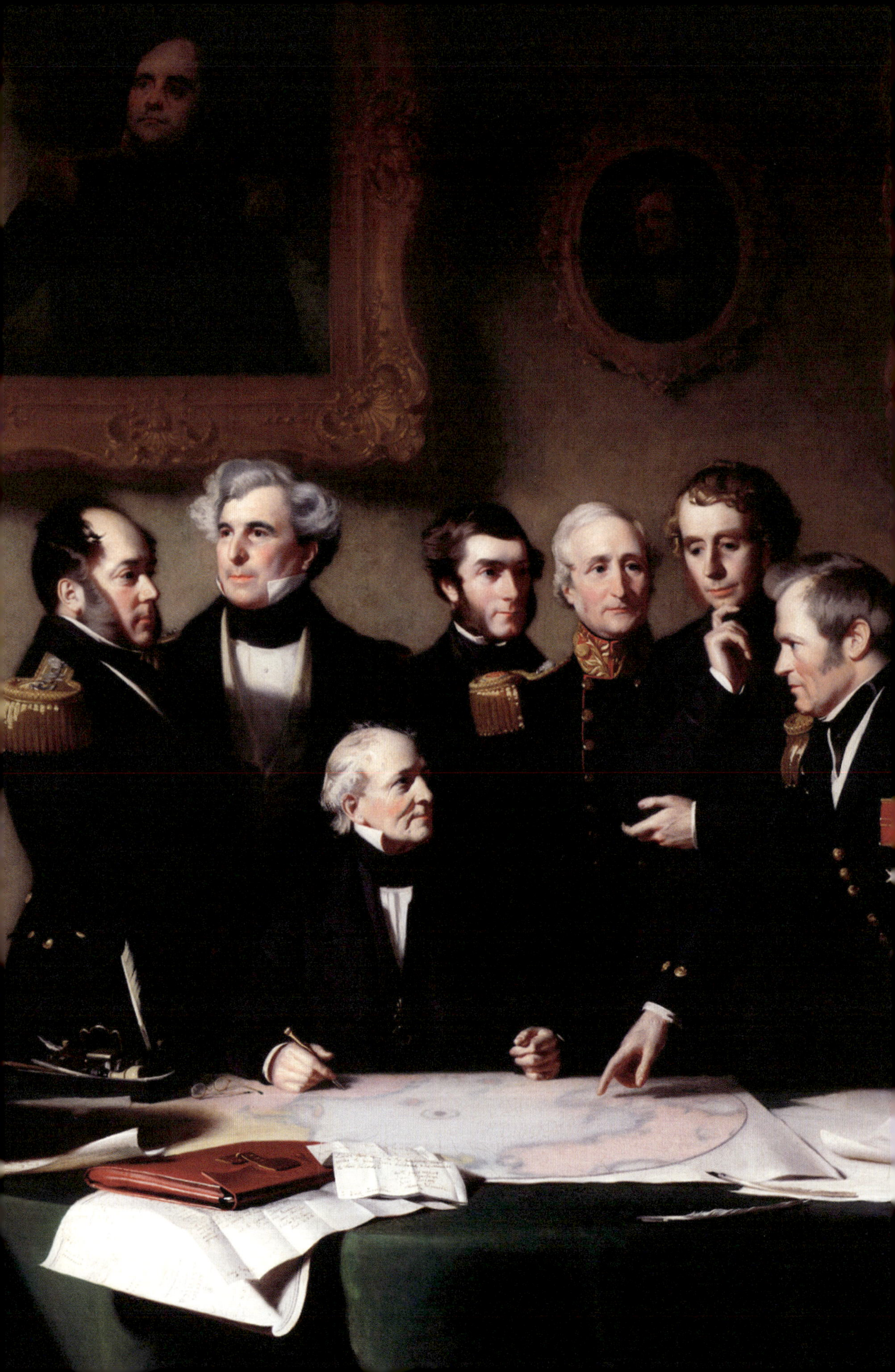

father had provisioned the expedition. Barrow commissioned the group portrait from Pearce to commemorate his oversight of the Franklin search (he is included at the back of the group).

Dressed in sober suits and naval uniforms, the men depicted in the portrait were all prominent figures in the field of polar exploration. Beaufort sits in the centre of the group. Spread across the green baize tablecloth in front him are various letters, papers and Arctic charts, to which he and his colleagues point and gesture. Based in part on this earlier picture, Pearce's portrait for the Beaufort Testimonial includes many similar details. The chart in the background represents the Arctic, alluding to the Rear-Admiral's role in the Franklin search. It is inscribed with the title 'A Chart of Baffin Bay with Davis and Barrow Straits', referencing a channel named after John Barrow Sr and thus hinting at the close connections between the Barrow family, the missing expedition and Beaufort himself. Other references to the Franklin expedition soon joined Pearce's portrait on display in the Naval Gallery, including a collection of so-called 'Arctic Relics' (mundane items like cutlery, buttons and watches discovered in the expedition's abandoned camps) and a monumental sculpture in the memory of the missing men.

In different ways, these various exhibits attempted to integrate the tragic fate of Franklin and his men into the Naval Gallery's structuring narrative of naval glory. Likened to the remains of saints, the 'relics' encouraged quasi-sacred reverence for the lost expedition. Meanwhile, the monument included a laurel crown, an emblem of victory, glory and success, reframing the lost men as gallant adventurers who had sacrificed themselves in the service of their country. Finally, Beaufort's portrait offered an office-bound view of polar exploration. Earlier portraits of returning explorers had shown their sitters in fur cloaks and icy landscapes, framing polar adventure as heroic, glamorous and exciting (for example, p. 162). After the disappearance of the Franklin expedition, however, the Arctic came to be associated with danger and confusion. In this context, the celebration of Sir Francis Beaufort – an official who had never been to the region but who had worked to understand it via charts and data – offered a crumb of comfort, suggesting that the 'mysteries' of the Arctic could be mastered through the technical expertise, masculine rationality and bureaucratic order of the British naval elite. These were key virtues of the Victorian state which Beaufort seemed to embody.

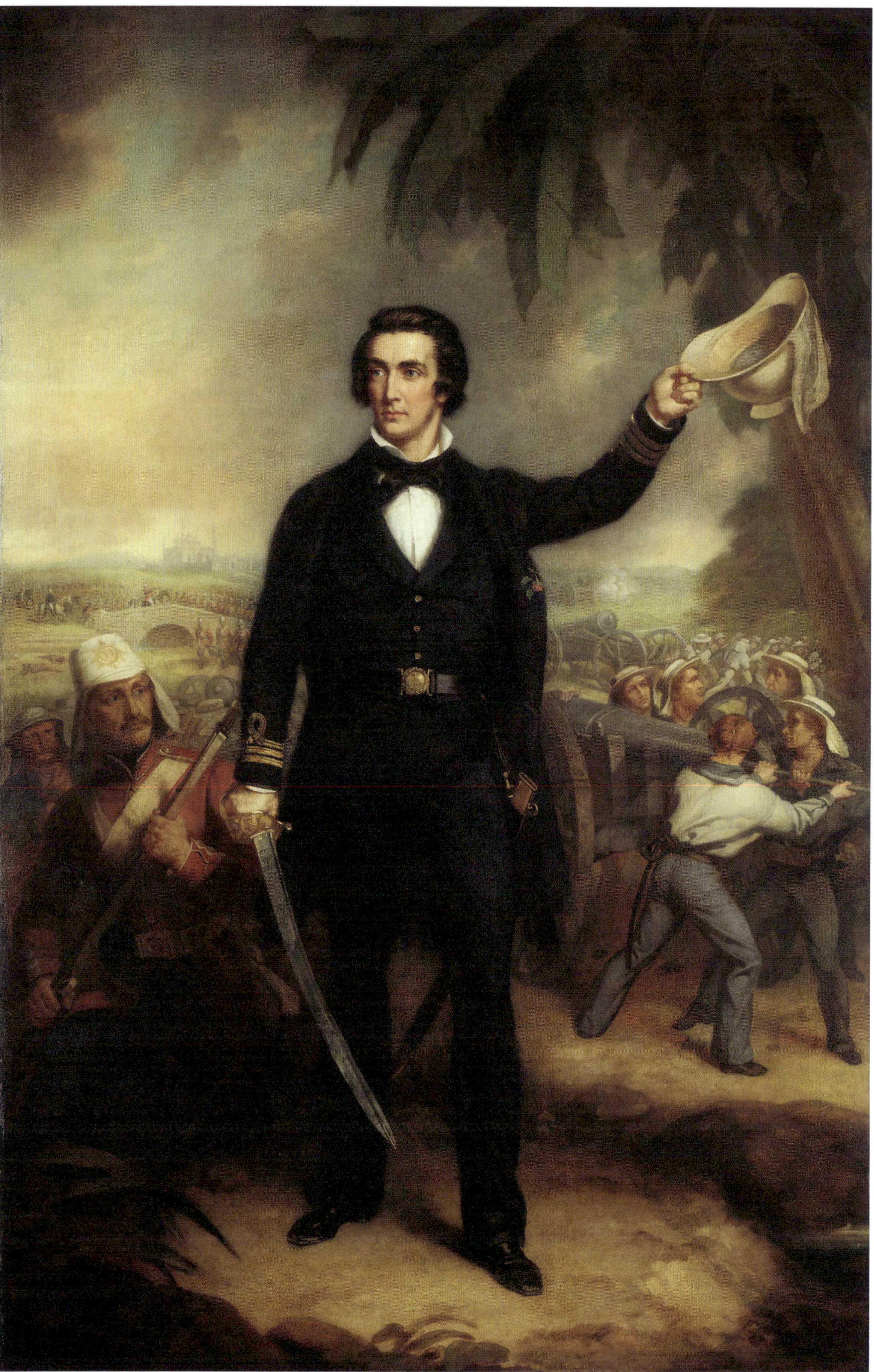

Captain Sir William Peel

John Lucas

1859–60, oil on canvas
2,720 x 1,780 mm
BHC2943

The nineteenth-century portrait painter John Lucas received few public accolades for his work. However, his lacklustre profile belied his success, as the author Mary Russell Mitford observed in 1852:

> [His] is not a noisy reputation; he exhibits little, never took the trouble of belonging to the [Royal] Academy [of Arts] and is seldom puffed in the newspapers. But somehow or other the best judges, the most refined people, go to him.

Lucas began his artistic career as an apprentice to the mezzotint engraver Samuel William Reynolds but harboured ambitions to become a painter, rather than a printmaker like his master. After skipping breaks and mealtimes during his apprenticeship to practise painting, he eventually established his own studio as a portrait painter and built a network of influential clients, from statesmen and princes to industrialists and military commanders. His most famous sitters included the Duke of Wellington and the locomotive designer Robert Stephenson. Lucas also worked extensively for the Conservative politician Sir Robert Peel, producing several paintings for the 'Gallery of Contemporary Statesmen' in the two-time Prime Minister's country home, Drayton Manor.

This portrait testifies to the close relationship that Lucas shared with the Peel family. It depicts Sir Robert's third son, Captain Sir William Peel. The captain was a celebrated naval officer, although, in keeping with the changing role of the Royal Navy in the mid-nineteenth century, he was more famous for fighting on land than at sea. In this period, ship-to-ship conflict was a rare occurrence, at least as far as Britain was concerned. Instead, officers and sailors were often formed into so-called 'naval brigades', which went ashore to fight alongside land troops. Peel led a naval brigade in the Crimean War (1853–56) and became one of the first recipients of the Victoria Cross, the highest honour for gallantry, for his exceptional bravery at the Siege of Sevastopol. He went on to command another naval brigade, formed from the men of his ship, the *Shannon*, during the Indian Rebellion of 1857–58, in which British forces fought to suppress a wave of military mutinies and civilian uprisings against the rule of the East India Company. The conflict was a watershed moment in the histories of India and the British Empire, leading to the dissolution of the East India Company and the creation of the British Raj. Peel was wounded in the thigh at the relief of Lucknow and died after contracting smallpox during his recovery in Cawnpore.

Although death from an infectious disease was not often considered heroic, Peel's demise was interpreted in Britain as an act of patriotic sacrifice. Since he had been fighting to uphold British rule in India, the British and colonial press presented him as a martyr to the imperial cause. His reputed religious devotion strengthened this saintly characterisation, as did the resurgence of chivalric ideals in mid-nineteenth-century culture. Peel was described as 'the model of a Christian knight', like a gallant and virtuous medieval warrior reborn for the Victorian era.

Commissioned to memorialise the sitter's death, Lucas's portrait depicted Peel during his final service in India. Peel stands beneath a palm tree in his naval uniform, a small red rose hanging

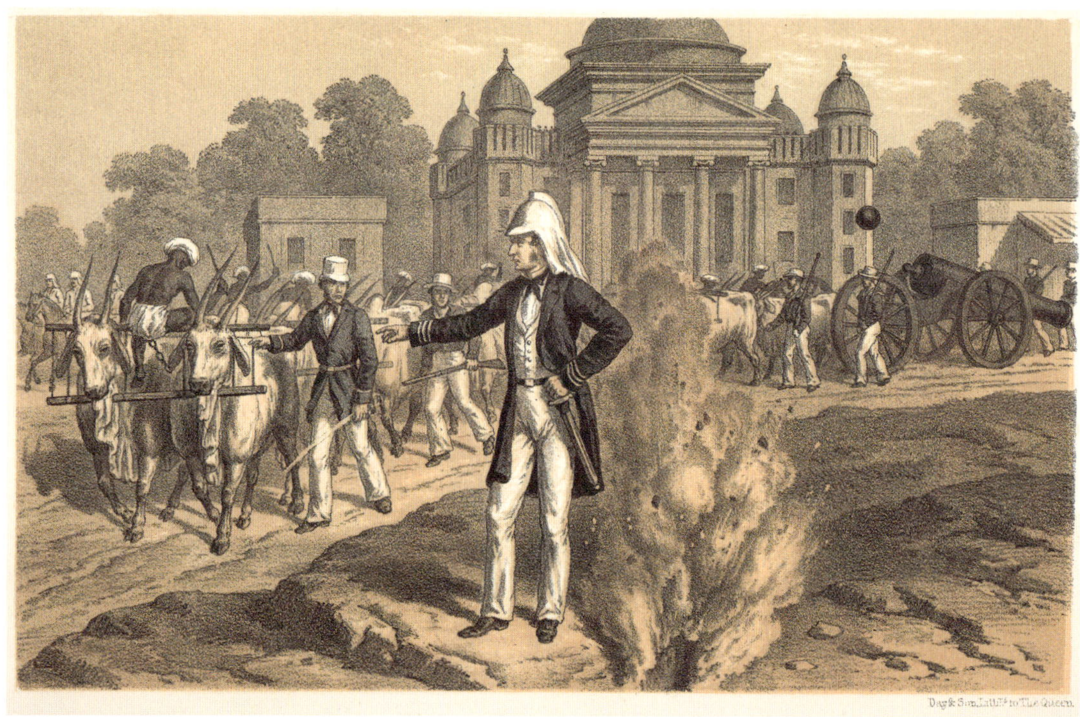

(fig. 1) *Sir William Peel Bringing his Guns up in Front of the Dilkooshah*
Oliver John Jones
1859, lithograph on paper
153 x 228 mm
Illustration in Oliver John Jones, *Recollections of a Winter campaign in India*, in 1857–58 (London: Saunders and Otley, 1859), opposite page 155
British Library (BLL01001897755)

from his top buttonhole. It was fashionable for Victorian gentlemen to wear roses in this manner. Today, this elegant accessory looks out of place in a painting about colonial warfare. However, viewers in the nineteenth century would have understood the rose as evidence of the Captain's virtue and refinement, manifesting his identity as 'a Christian knight'.

The Captain has drawn his sword and holds his pith helmet aloft as if urging on the men around him. As one newspaper at the time wrote of this portrait, 'the hero is a hearty, frank-looking young sailor, just the man to charge against any odds, and to win the hearts of a naval brigade'. Peel's rapport with his men was a key component of his public reputation and many even attributed his fatal smallpox infection to his humble insistence on travelling in a cart with other injured sailors, rather than in his own private litter. To suggest the Captain's connection to the rank and file, the portrait shows him surrounded by ordinary soldiers and sailors. Yet the triangular composition ensures that he stands much taller than these figures, creating a sense of hierarchy: there is no doubting who has command. A soldier kneels on the left, the number '53' emblazoned on his hat badge and his belt buckle, indicating the 53rd (Shropshire) Regiment of Foot, who fought alongside the *Shannon*'s naval brigade. More red-coated soldiers march across a stone bridge in the distance. The right-hand side of the painting shows the sailors of the naval brigade moving and loading heavy artillery, the word 'SHANNON' legible on their hat ribbons. In the far background is a complex of buildings with domes and minarets.

It is not clear what specific incident is represented in the background. In 1859, The *Literary Gazette* suggested that the painting showed 'the scene of one of Peel's most noted deeds near Cawnpore'. This may refer to an assault on Indian insurgents in the village of Khujwa (Khajuha), 24 miles north-west of Futtehpore (Fatehpur), in early November 1857, during which Lieutenant-Colonel Powell from the 53rd Foot was killed. As the next highest-ranking officer, Peel succeeded to command of the operation and led the combined forces to a hard-won victory. This would explain his representation at the head of both military and naval forces. Yet the *Literary Gazette* also claimed that the background was derived from the sketches of Captain Oliver John Jones, a naval officer who joined up with the regiment to serve in the Indian conflict. Jones was not at the assault on Khujwa, so he cannot have provided first-hand drawings of the episode. In 1859, he published an illustrated account of his time with the 53rd Foot, *Recollections of a Winter Campaign in India*. None of the illustrations in this publication correspond exactly to the painting but one did depict *Sir William Peel Bringing his Guns up in Front of the Dilkooshah*, an incident preceding the relief of Lucknow in March 1858. This scene may have loosely inspired the portrait in its depiction of the Captain at the head of his naval brigade (fig. 1).

For most viewers, it would not have mattered what specific battle was being shown. The palm trees and distant minarets were sufficient, for a European audience, to suggest an Indian setting, ensuring that the portrait was associated with the recent conflict in the region. British forces cover most of the depicted landscape, the most distant figures blurring into the surrounding grassland, such that the viewer cannot tell where the army ends, and the landscape begins. The military might of the British Empire is thus presented as overwhelming and irresistible.

Even more striking are the two dead bodies sprawled on the riverbank in the middle distance. Although they could be fallen British soldiers, these figures are more likely intended to represent defeated Indian rebels. This violent detail echoes the rhetoric found in Jones's *Recollections*, which presented merciless violence towards the insurgents as both necessary and righteous. Quoting from the Old Testament, Jones wrote: 'they must be repressed by a stern, even handed, certain justice; a justice that says, "the soul that sinneth (I mean the sins of murder, mutiny, and rebellion), THE SOUL THAT SINNETH, IT SHALL SURELY DIE"' (Ezekiel 18:20). Seen in this context, the portrait presents a vindication of brutal imperial violence as good Christian behaviour.

The portrait was paid for through a public subscription scheme and displayed upon its completion in July 1859 at the gallery and shop of the leading print-sellers Henry Graves & Co., which later published John James

(fig. 2) *The Death of Captain James Cook, 14 February 1779*
Johann Zoffany
about 1798, oil on canvas
1,385 x 1,845 mm
BHC0424

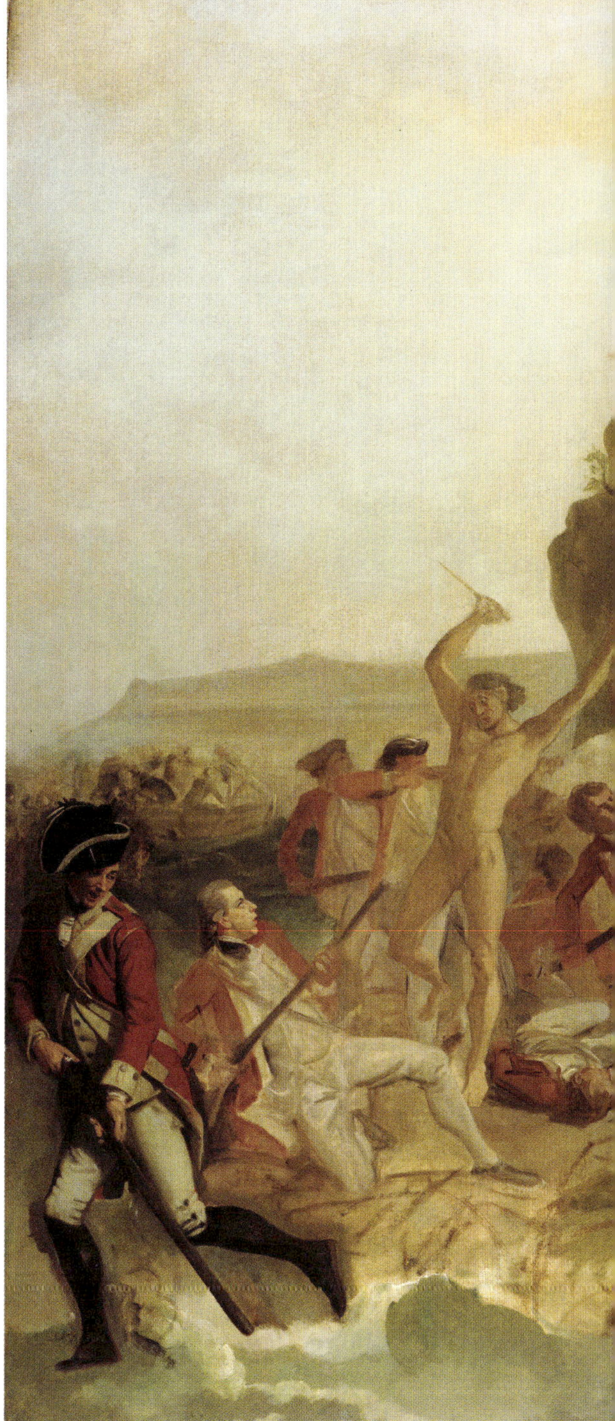

Chant's mezzotint after the picture. The press, however, called for the portrait to be entered into a public collection. *The Literary Gazette* commented that 'the proper place would undoubtedly be Greenwich Hospital', referring to the Naval Gallery in the Hospital's Painted Hall. The Lords of the Admiralty were of the same opinion and ordered the painting to be placed in the Naval Gallery, where it was hung above Johann Zoffany's unfinished history painting of Captain James Cook's death in Hawaii on 14 February 1779. In this painting, a crowd of Indigenous islanders were shown attacking the captain (fig. 2). The work evoked ideas of imperial martyrdom, a key theme in the public narrative around Peel's death. Like Lucas's portrait, Zoffany's painting represented a British officer fighting against rebellious 'natives' in a tropical landscape. However, whereas Cook was depicted falling beneath the blows of his assailants, Peel stood triumphant, the might of the combined British forces behind him and colonial insurgents dead upon the ground. The proximity of the two paintings thus functioned as powerful propaganda for the British Empire, creating a narrative that showed how eighteenth-century exploration had given way to nineteenth-century domination.

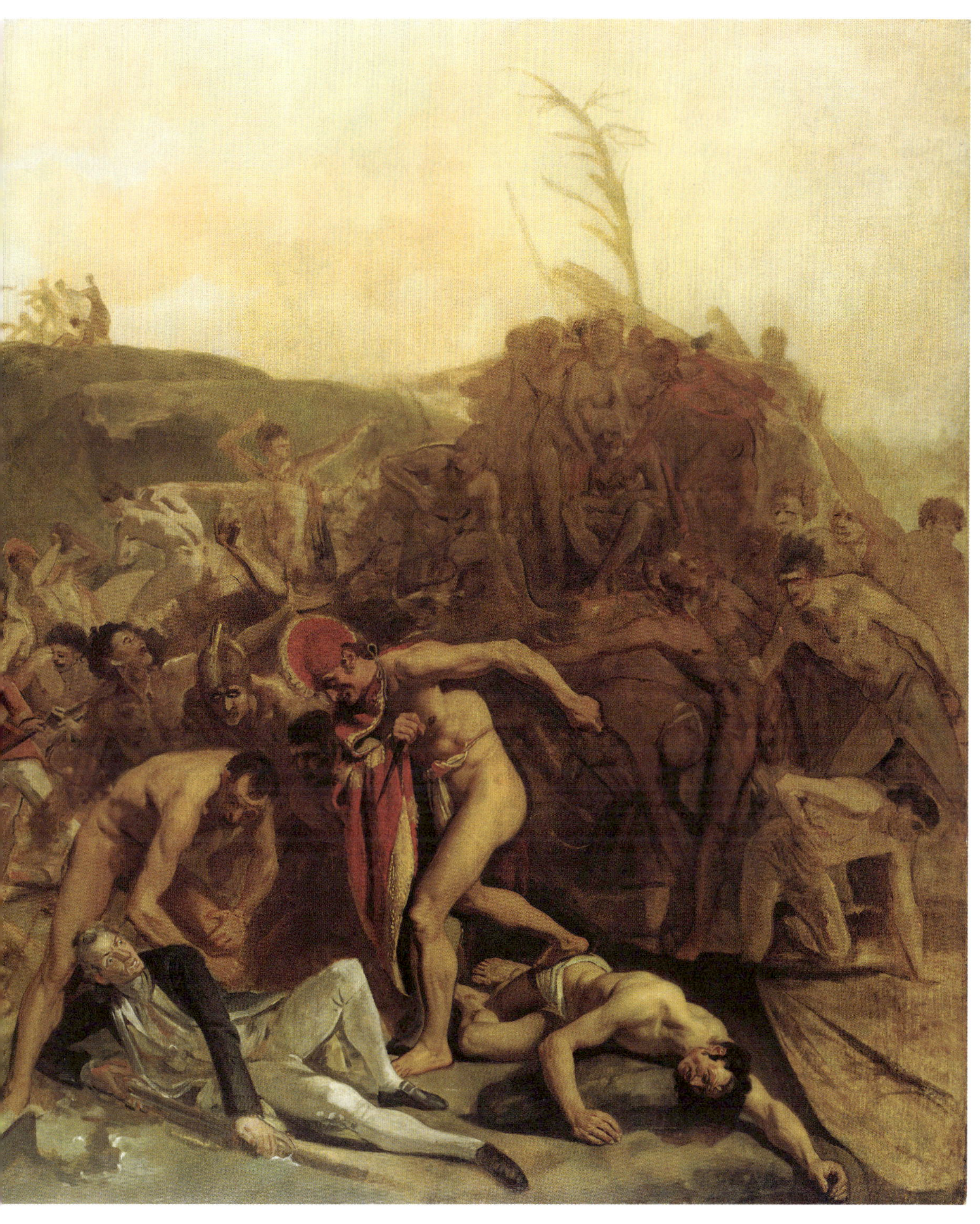

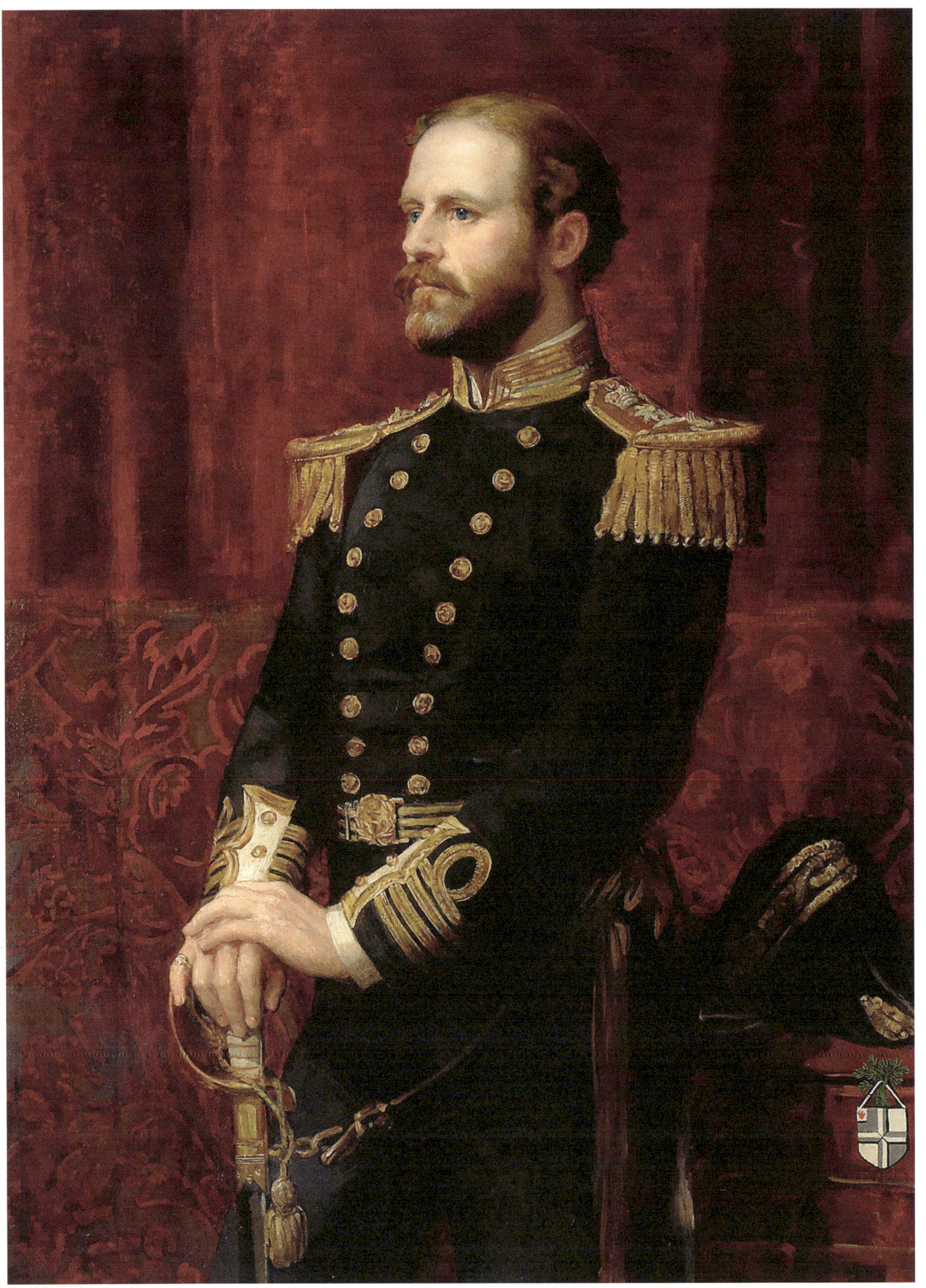

Rear-Admiral Sir Lambton Loraine

Anna Massey Lea Merritt

1884, oil on canvas
1,270 x 940 mm
BHC2847

In a lecture presented at the Women's Art Congress in 1900, the celebrated Anglo-American artist Anna Lea Merritt asked a provocative question: 'Can women really paint as well as men?' For Merritt, this was not a question of artistic talent, which she insisted was equally common in men and women. There were, she claimed, other factors holding women back, not least the unequal division of domestic labour and caring responsibilities. 'The chief obstacle to a woman's success is that she can never have a wife,' Merritt argued:

> Just reflect what a wife does for an artist: Darns the stockings; Keeps his house; Writes his letters; Visits for his benefit; Wards off intruders; Is personally suggestive of beautiful pictures; Always an encouraging and partial critic. It is exceedingly difficult to be an artist without this time-saving help. A husband would be quite useless. He would never do any of these disagreeable things.

In her own trailblazing career, Merritt defied many of the impediments facing women artists. She was born in Philadelphia on 13 September 1844. Her parents, the Leas, were affluent Quakers who held progressive ideas about women's education. She received schooling in classics, languages, mathematics and music – but not art. She therefore taught herself to paint and took anatomy classes at a women's medical school to improve her drawing of the human figure. When she moved to Europe with her family in 1865, she found that the most prestigious art academies did not admit women, so she sought private tuition from masters in Italy, Germany and France. Settling in London, she studied with the picture restorer Henry Merritt, who became her mentor and, eventually, her husband, though they were only married for three months before his death in July 1877. In her widowhood, she enjoyed success with her allegorical pictures, including one called *Love Locked Out*, which was purchased for the Tate Gallery in 1890, becoming the first work of a woman artist to enter a British national collection. However, most of her income came from portraiture.

Merritt completed this portrait of naval officer Sir Lambton Loraine, Bt in 1885, the year in which he became a captain. He was best known for his part in the Virginius Affair 12 years earlier. On 23 October 1873, Spanish officials in Santiago de Cuba captured the *Virginius*, an American passenger steamer which had been carrying weapons for insurgents fighting against Spanish rule in Cuba and Venezuela. On 2 November, a court martial sentenced the captain, the crew and some of the ship's passengers to be executed. At the time, Loraine was stationed in Jamaica, commanding HMS *Niobe*. Upon hearing about the *Virginius*, he sailed immediately for Cuba and addressed a letter to the Spanish commander, in which he demanded the cessation of 'this dreadful butchery', meaning the execution of the passengers. The letter ended with an implied threat of force: 'I do not believe that I need explain what my actions will be in case my demand is not heeded.' He personally delivered the letter and refused to leave the governor's office until he received the desired response. Loraine had not been ordered to intervene but acted on the assumption that the British government would approve of his conduct. The incident demonstrates how, at the height of Victorian imperialism, the Royal Navy assumed the role of the world's policeman.

In Merritt's portrait, Sir Lambton is dressed in his captain's uniform. The artist has ensured that the insignia of his new rank are visible, from the four narrow stripes on his cuffs to the triad of crown, star and anchor on his epaulettes. He holds his sword in front of him, both hands resting on the hilt. With his upright posture and distant gaze, he appears steadfast and impassive. His stillness connotes power, evoking the self-assurance that underpinned incidents of so-called 'gunboat diplomacy', like the Virginius Affair. In such episodes, naval officers did not assert their authority through action because they knew that their presence alone, with the might of the British Empire behind them, would compel lesser powers into submission.

On one level, then, Sir Lambton embodies modern British naval authority. However, it had been a decade since his last service at sea. The 11th in a long line of baronets, Loraine was at the time of this portrait living the leisured life of an aristocratic gentleman. It is notable that, aside from his naval uniform, the painting includes no allusions to his seafaring career. Instead, the portrait emphasises his lineage through the superimposition of the Loraine family coat of arms in the lower right. Further ideas of comfort and luxury are suggested by the sumptuous red curtain in the background, which is ornately patterned with flowers and leaves.

This decorative detail is indicative of the artistic environment in which Merritt was working. She took inspiration from the Pre-Raphaelites, a group of artists who rejected the grand, classicising compositions of earlier artists like Sir Joshua Reynolds ('Sir Sloshua', as they called him) in favour of a return to the intense colours, rich ornament and abundant detail of medieval Italian art. Clashing with Loraine's vivid ginger hair, the crimson backdrop in the captain's portrait adheres to this creative approach.

At the same time, the painting is also indicative of how social identity evolved among naval officers in the later nineteenth century. Having established itself as the world's dominant naval superpower, Britain was not engaged in any major conflicts during this period. Officers were therefore denied the opportunity to prove their heroic credentials in battle and often faced long periods of unemployment. These conditions favoured well-connected individuals from privileged backgrounds, turning the relatively meritocratic profession of the eighteenth century into a more elitist one. As Sir Lambton's portrait suggests, naval authority came to depend more on status and breeding at home than on action and achievement at sea.

The painting is unusual within Merritt's oeuvre because it was not often that she received commissions to paint men's portraits. There was, in her words, 'a tendency to send me mostly children for portraiture'. This trend was likely related to her gender: clients were, it seems, more willing to trust a woman artist with subjects connected to the 'feminine' spheres of home and family. Loraine is the exception that proves the rule, since his introduction to the artist came through his wife, Lady Frederica Mary Horatia Loraine (née Vere-Broke). Merritt met Frederica in 1879 while working on a picture for her ladyship's sister and the two women became good friends. The artist was a frequent visitor to the Loraine household, acting as a surrogate aunt to the family's young children: 'my love of the little ones began when they were but a few days old,' she later recalled. She produced many portraits of the children, from infancy through to adulthood.

Sir Lambton therefore knew Merritt in a domestic context before engaging her professional services. This may offer a further explanation for the absence of nautical motifs in the portrait, the curtained backdrop recalling the opulent furnishings of an upper-class family home. Sir Lambton perhaps intended his portrait to be seen alongside the artist's depictions of his young family, showcasing his private responsibilities as a father as well as his public service as a naval officer.

Merritt herself believed that naval affairs were not out of place in a family environment. The year before this portrait was completed, she wrote a short article for *St Nicholas*, a popular

American children's magazine. Entitled 'A Talk About Painting', the piece contained amusing stories about 'children who come to my studio to have their portraits painted, and how we do it'. One illustration showed Merritt pretending to be a horse and galloping around her studio to entertain a restless toddler. Towards the end, however, the article took an unexpected turn. After describing one of her portraits of the Loraine children, Merritt added: 'The father of these children, Sir Lambton Loraine, is a brave captain in the English navy, and you American children must hear about him.' She then proceeded to give a detailed account of the Virginius Affair in a language that the young readers would understand. Turning gunboat diplomacy into a bedtime story for children, this article reveals how the ideas of empire infiltrated even the most intimate aspects of domestic life in the late nineteenth century.

Sir Lambton's portrait similarly merged familial and imperial concerns. This is reflected in its exhibition history. Merritt submitted the painting to the Royal Academy in 1885 together with a double portrait of the captain's wife and one of his daughters, thus highlighting his paternal responsibilities in the family home. Three years later, however, the painting was shipped to Australia for display in the *Melbourne Centennial International Exhibition*. Celebrating 100 years of European settlement in Australia, this exhibition displayed natural resources, manufactured goods and artworks from the Australian colonies and 27 foreign nations or regions, including Britain. The result was a potent visualisation of imperial networks and colonial power. In this context, Loraine's public role as a representative of the Royal Navy would have been foremost. No other portraits of the Loraine family made the trip. The painting later returned to Britain and to the family collection, in which it remained until it was presented to the National Maritime Museum in 1962.

Merritt maintained a close relationship with the Loraine family until her death in 1930. She painted *Icarus Preparing to Fly* as a memorial to the eldest son, Eustace Loraine, a pioneering aviator who died in an aircraft crash in 1912, and received visits from his brother, the diplomat Sir Percy Loraine, Bt., in the 1920s. Although she was often pigeonholed on account of her gender as a painter of children's portraits and other stereotypically feminine subjects, she nevertheless made the most of opportunities to undertake other work, as the portrait of Sir Lambton Loraine in his naval uniform demonstrates. Through its imagery and exhibition history, the painting blurs the boundary between the 'masculine' world of the late Victorian Navy and the 'feminine' realm of the home.

Admiral Sir John Fisher

Arthur Stockdale Cope

1902, oil on canvas
1,270 x 1,016 mm
BHC2690

According to his obituary in *The Times*, published on 6 July 1940, the artist Arthur Stockdale Cope could be 'trusted not to produce anything fantastic or absurd' and understood how 'to satisfy official tastes for a good conventional likeness'. These qualities made him the preferred portrait painter of the British establishment in the late Victorian and Edwardian eras. As the son of the successful history painter Charles West Cope, Arthur was born into the High Victorian art world. His work came to epitomise the traditional aesthetics against which the modernist artists of the twentieth century rebelled. Some, such as Vanessa Bell, were rejecting Cope's own teachings, having studied at his Pelham Street art school in the 1890s. Yet Cope's conservative reputation belied his astute and innovative use of personalised details to convey character in his portraits.

Specialising in male portraits, Cope painted politicians, military commanders and royal princes but it was with the Royal Navy that he enjoyed the closest relationship. A keen sailor and yachtsman himself, he counted many naval officers among his friends and often visited warships during peacetime. In January 1911, Admiral Sir John Durnford put the artist forward to become the next curator of the Naval Gallery in Greenwich, writing that Cope was 'very suitable, active, and with probably a better knowledge of portraits than anyone I know'. Although the gallery abolished the curator role and Cope was never appointed, Durnford's recommendation testifies to the artist's formidable reputation in naval circles.

Cope painted this portrait of Admiral Sir John Fisher in 1902. Known informally as 'Jackie' Fisher, the admiral witnessed and supported rapid advancements in naval weaponry and ship design over the course of his long career. Having first served on board a wooden sailing ship, HMS *Calcutta*, in the 1850s, he is now best remembered for championing the development of dreadnoughts. These were new, highly destructive battleships with heavy-calibre guns and turbine engines for increased speed. Their introduction from 1906 onwards fuelled the naval arms race that preceded the First World War.

Cope's portrait was presumably commissioned to commemorate the Admiral's appointment in June 1902 to the role of Second Sea Lord, a high-level position overseeing the recruitment and training of naval personnel. In allusion to the official responsibilities of this post, the painting includes a desk covered in bundles of documents and papers. One of the documents is inscribed 'Naval Education / 1902' in reference to Fisher's ambitious plans for the reform of officer training, which involved merging the command and engineering programmes to prepare all cadets for a new era of mechanised warfare.

While the desk is suggestive of an office or study environment, the setting of the portrait remains indeterminate. It appears as though Fisher and his papers are floating in a muddy void. The background is washed with thin brown paint, which the artist has left showing in the shadows of the Admiral's uniform and at the edges of the desk. This homogenises the painting into an inoffensive and subdued whole, in keeping with Cope's reputation for producing orthodox official portraits without 'anything fantastic or absurd'. Small touches of red provide most of the colour in the portrait. These crimson flashes draw attention

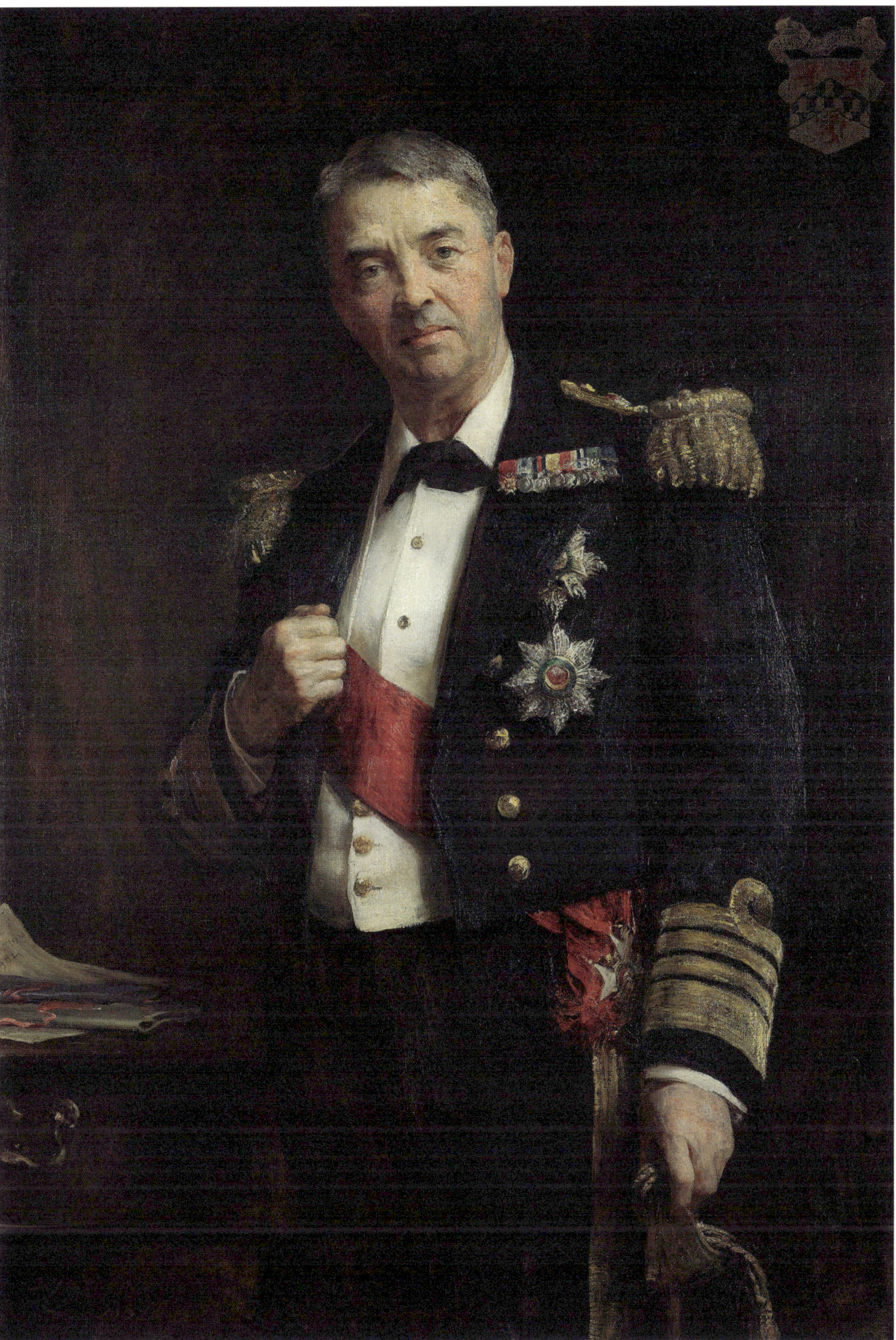

to Fisher's administrative responsibilities, naval achievements and social standing, from the red tape around his official documents to his coat of arms in the upper right via the medals and decorations pinned to his chest. Among these honours are the eight-pointed silver star of the Ottoman Order of Osmanieh, which he received from the Sultan of Turkey at Constantinople in 1900, and the red sash and star of the Order of the Bath, in which he became a Knight Grand Cross in June 1902.

One aspect of the image is, however, more unconventional, exemplifying Cope's penchant for including imaginative and unexpected details in his portraits. Most naval officers were painted in their full dress or undress uniforms, the former being for official ceremonies and the latter for wearing on duty. Fisher, meanwhile, is depicted in ball dress, a variant of naval uniform introduced specifically for use at balls, dinners and evening receptions. Consisting of tailcoat, white waistcoat and trousers, ball dress was modelled on fashionable formal attire with the addition of gold lace, epaulettes and miniature medals to demonstrate the wearer's naval rank and achievements. This unusual attire signals the Admiral's enthusiasm and talent for ballroom dancing, a skill he insisted all young officers should practise. Given that formal ballrooms were at this time the preserve of high society, Fisher's dancing obsession can be related to the elitism of the pre-war officer corps, which required naval men to master polished social skills. It was nevertheless unusual for dancing to be referenced in a naval portrait, especially one that also celebrated official bureaucracy. Cope's idiosyncratic combination of allusions thus framed the Admiral as a complex and multi-faceted character.

Fisher himself owned the portrait until his death in July 1920, aged 79. He had retired from naval service in 1910 but came out of retirement in October 1914 at the urging of the First Lord of the Admiralty, Winston Churchill, who wanted Fisher to lead the Royal Navy in the First World War. However, he quickly fell out with Churchill and abruptly resigned in May 1915.

In 1922, the Admiral's son, Cecil Vavasseur, 2nd Lord Fisher, presented the portrait to the Naval Gallery in Greenwich. This donation was possibly in response to the unveiling of the artist's *Some Sea Officers of the War* (now known as *Naval Officers of World War I*) at the National Portrait Gallery the previous year. *Some Sea Officers* was a large group portrait depicting 22 senior naval officers who had served during the First World War (fig. 1). The South African gold tycoon Sir Abraham Bailey commissioned the painting alongside two corresponding works depicting leading military officers and politicians. Controversially, Fisher declined to appear in *Some Sea Officers*, a decision many put down to his continued resentment towards the naval authorities after his ignominious resignation. In passing up the opportunity, however, he denied himself a place in a national art collection. Seen in this context, Lord Fisher's decision to donate his father's portrait to the Naval Gallery can be viewed as an attempt to ensure that the Admiral did not miss out on the public visibility that his former colleagues received at the National Portrait Gallery. It helped that the same artist was responsible for both artworks, creating a connection between the two.

Since the Naval Gallery was filled with depictions of former commanders and their victories, the placement of the Admiral's portrait in this space also suggested that Fisher had upheld a centuries-long tradition of naval glory. *Some Sea Officers* conveyed a similar message. The 22 sitters were represented poring over documents and discussing strategy in the Boardroom at Admiralty House. The whole scene was a fiction, the depicted officers having never worked together in the same place at the same time, and the setting was chosen for symbolic reasons. The Boardroom was built in the early eighteenth century at the beginning of Britain's rise to global naval supremacy. The wind dial over the mantelpiece was a relic from when the Royal Navy relied on sailing ships, not the turbine-powered dreadnoughts of the modern era. The room's other artworks and decorations evoked the past glories of this bygone age, from the two marine paintings over the doors to the full-length portrait of Horatio Nelson – the legendary

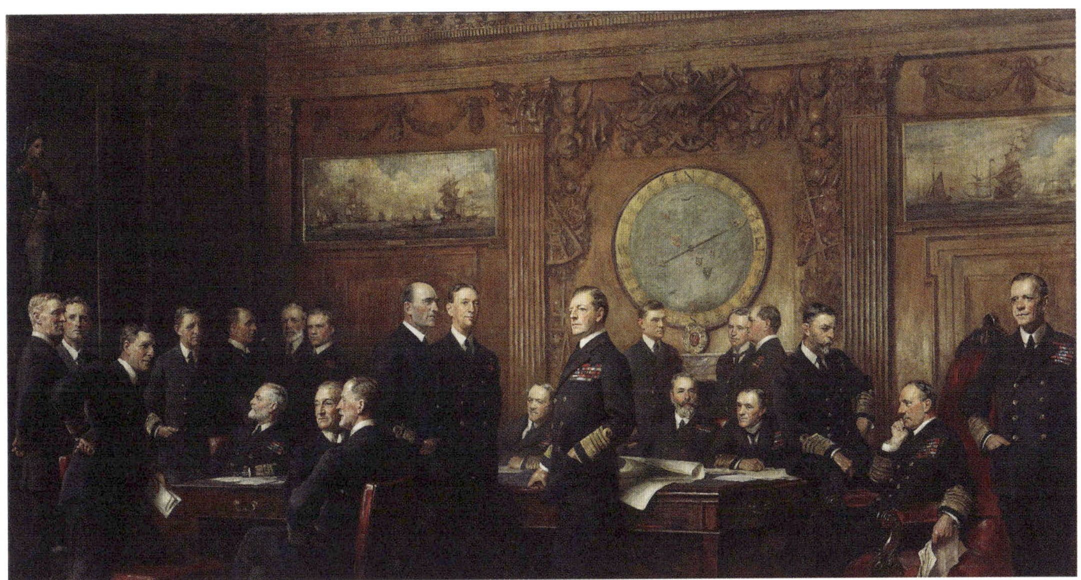

(fig. 1) *Naval Officers of World War I*
Arthur Stockdale Cope
1921, oil on canvas
2641 x 5144 mm
National Portrait Gallery (NPG 1913)

commander who died at the Battle of Trafalgar in 1805 – at the head of the table. In positioning his sitters in this room, Cope asked his viewers to decide whether the First World War commanders had lived up to the all-conquering legacy of their predecessors.

The painting invites an affirmative answer to this question, as did the hanging of Fisher's portrait in the Naval Gallery. However, many people at the time would have had their doubts. Although the Royal Navy. through its work protecting British trade and combating the threat of German U-boats, had been instrumental in the allied victory in the First World War the failure to secure an impressive, large-scale victory akin to Trafalgar gave rise to public fears that Britain's naval prowess was waning. Ideas about naval representation and portraiture were changing too. Cope's conventional portraits of the naval elite would come to look increasingly old-fashioned as a new body of imagery emerged, representing a wider range of naval personnel and commemorating the global warfare of the twentieth century.

CHAPTER 6

A World at War

1914–1945

The peace that prevailed between the major world powers in the nineteenth century shattered in the first half of the twentieth, leading to two massive global conflicts. The First World War (1914–18) and the Second World War (1939–45) marked the advent of a new kind of mechanised warfare, characterised by mass casualties and the mass conscription of civilians into military service. The World Wars also heralded a fundamental shift in the relationship between art and war. For the first time in British history, the government sponsored artists to represent conflict for public display and reproduction. This initiative was launched in 1916 by the Propaganda Bureau, which became the Department of Information in 1917. During the Second World War, the Ministry of Information set up the War Artists' Advisory Committee (WAAC) to oversee the production of official war art.

State-sponsored war art served a number of different functions, as art critic Douglas Cooper pointed out in *The Burlington Magazine for Connoisseurs* in October 1940:

> But what is the function of a War Artist? It is threefold: firstly that of Portraitist, secondly that of Reporter, thirdly that of – what, for want of a better name, I shall call – Propagandist in the widest sense.

Cooper's comments highlight conflicting demands that war artists faced. On the one hand, they were asked to act as reporters, documenting the war and its hardships. At the same time they were tasked with producing propaganda, the purpose of which was to drum up support for the war effort. Cooper also counted the production of portraiture as a separate function altogether. This acknowledges the complexities inherent in portraiture as a genre: a portrait has a documentary role, recording an individual's likeness, but it is also a work of art, using the image of a person to communicate ideas.

Aesthetic and stylistic questions further complicated the work of war artists. The twentieth century witnessed the rapid proliferation of artistic movements that broke with the conventions of the past. War artists had to decide whether to embrace modernist approaches, the newness of which seemed appropriate for representing wars that were themselves without precedent, or to fall back upon more traditional styles, which evoked stability amid the tumult of global conflict. Meanwhile, wartime shortages drove artists to experiment with different materials.

When it came to portraiture, there was increased variation in the range of sitters. For the first time, women were represented in military and naval roles, thanks to the introduction of auxiliary services such as the Women's Royal Naval Service (WRNS). Portraits commemorated the valuable contributions that ordinary people were making to the war effort, but they were also used for propaganda purposes, presenting their sitters as exemplary models of loyalty and patriotism.

John Travers Cornwell, Boy 1st Class

Ambrose McEvoy

about 1918, oil on canvas
508 x 406 mm
BHC2635

An influential generation of British artists came of age at the end of the nineteenth century. They rejected the traditions of Victorian painting and developed modernist approaches, taking inspiration from avant-garde art movements in Europe, such as impressionism. Ambrose McEvoy was a key member of this group. He studied at the Slade School of Art in London, which was at the forefront of developments in contemporary art. His fellow pupils included William Orpen and Augustus John, both of whom would become defining figures in British art during the opening decades of twentieth century. McEvoy was best known for his portraits of fashionable society women, their elegant dresses rendered in fluttering brushstrokes. However, he also painted masculine subjects, especially during the First World War. Having served on the Western Front with the Royal Naval Division in 1916, he received a commission from the Department of Information, which was responsible for propaganda and official war art, to produce a series of portraits depicting naval recipients of the Victoria Cross, the highest award for bravery in the face of enemy action. These portraits were intended for display in a proposed 'Gallery of Heroes' at the Imperial War Museum, a new institution created to commemorate the conflict.

McEvoy began this portrait of John Travers Cornwell for the Victoria Cross series but never finished it. Only the underpainting has been completed, the artist having roughed out the portrait in brown, beige and grey in preparation for the later addition of colour and detail. Another work from the Victoria Cross series, depicting Petty Office, E. Pitcher, gives an indication of how the portrait might have looked if it had been finished (fig. 1). Pitcher's face is flesh-coloured, rather than ghostly white like Cornwell's, but his skin nevertheless remains pale, standing out in contrast to his dark uniform and the grey background, both of which are rendered with loose, sketch-like brushstrokes, in keeping with McEvoy's impressionistic style.

A grid shows through the thin paint in the background of Cornwell's portrait, indicating that it has been scaled up from a smaller source. Artists often used grids to help transfer or enlarge images: a grid was drawn over the original image, then the contents of each square were copied onto the corresponding square on the canvas. In this instance, McEvoy's source was a photograph. He could not paint his sitter from life because Cornwell was already dead.

Known as 'Jack', Cornwell came from a working-class family in East London. He left school at the age of 14 to work as a delivery boy in 1914. The following year, he lied about his age in order to enlist in the Royal Navy, which required recruits to be at least 18 years old. At the Battle of Jutland on 31 May 1916, he was a gun-sighter on board HMS *Chester*. Four shells hit his gun position during action, killing or incapacitating the entire gun crew apart from Cornwell, who was wounded in the chest but nevertheless remained at his post throughout the action. Although taken ashore to a hospital in Grimsby, he succumbed to his injuries on 2 June, aged only 16.

Vice-Admiral David Beatty, who commanded the battlecruiser squadron at Jutland, singled out Cornwell for praise in his dispatches. Beatty wrote that Cornwell had 'remained standing at a most exposed post, quietly awaiting orders' in 'a splendid instance of devotion of duty'.

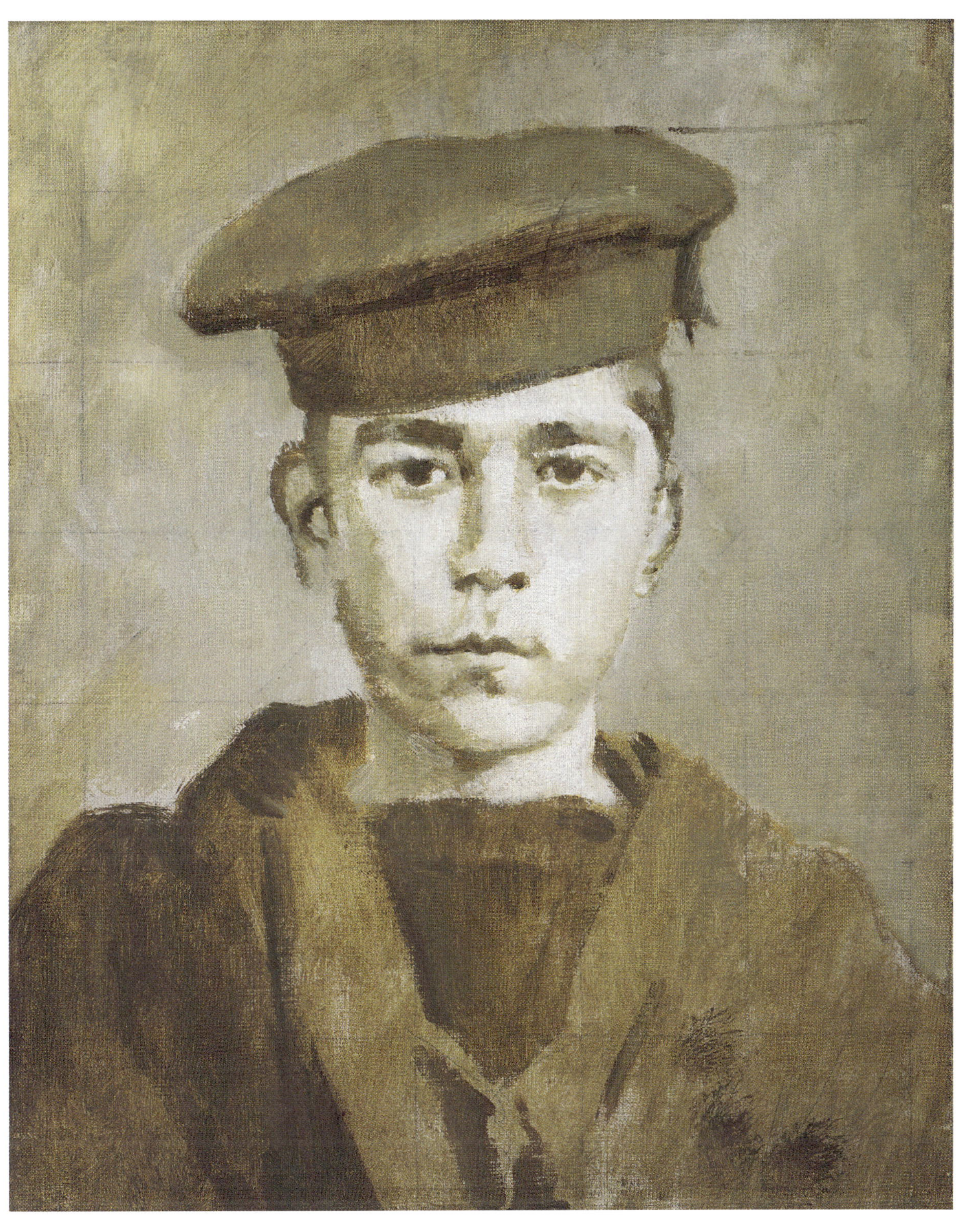

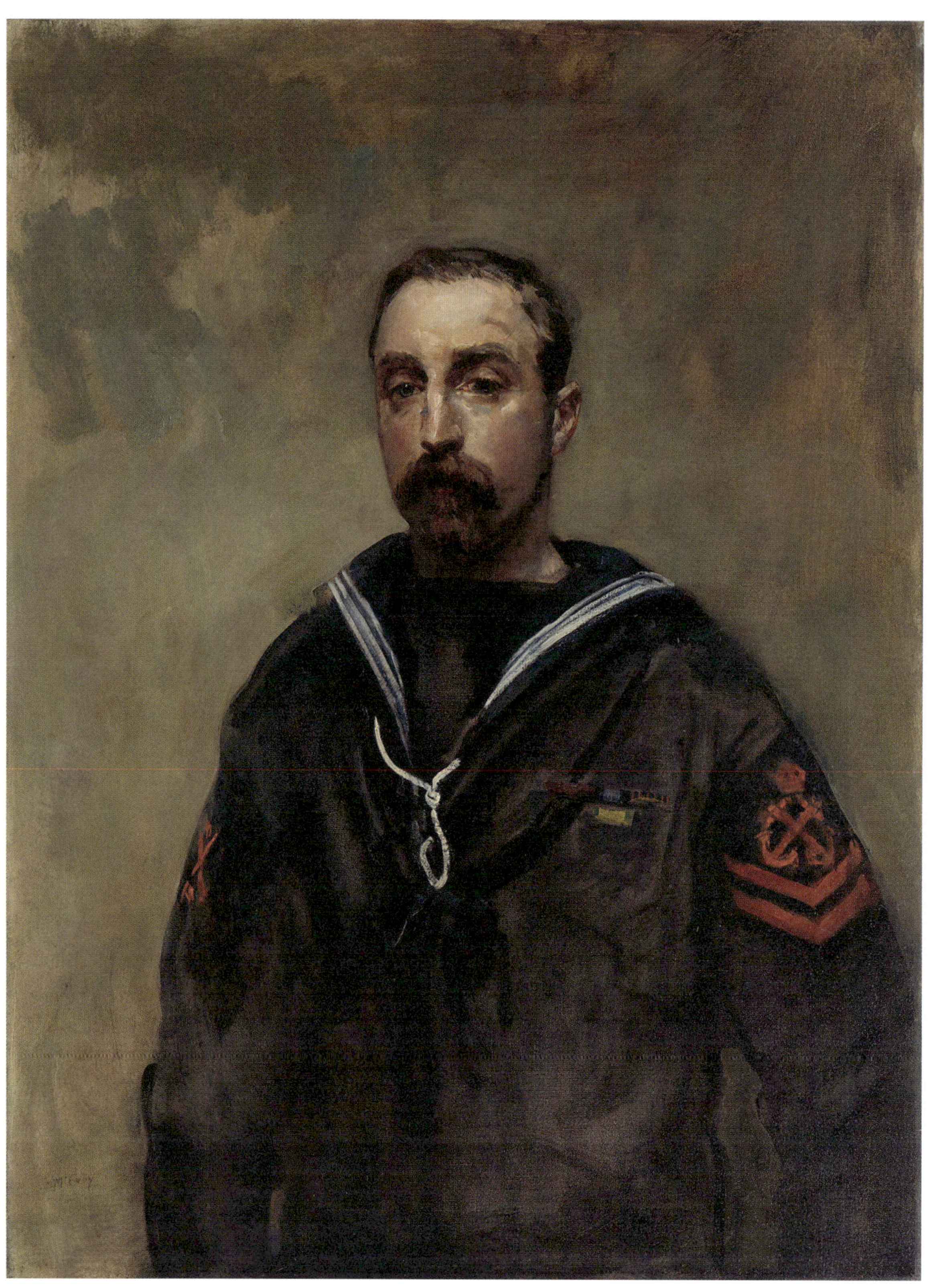

It was as a consequence of these comments that Cornwell was posthumously awarded the Victoria Cross. He also became a public sensation. State authorities, private organisations and individuals commemorated his death in eulogies, awards, newspaper articles, speeches, monuments, poems and paintings. His waxwork appeared at Madame Tussaud's and his photograph was distributed to schools as an incitement for other boys to emulate his heroic example. After it emerged in the press that he had been interred in an unmarked grave near his family home in East Ham, the Admiralty arranged for his body to be exhumed and reburied with full naval honours in the same local cemetery. Thousands of mourners turned out for the funeral in July 1916, which was captured on film for Pathé News.

For ordinary people, Cornwell's death provided a much-needed outlet for the expression of pride, grief and other feelings resulting from two years of wartime stress. Yet the government and the press also promoted and encouraged the public commemorations for propaganda purposes. By 1916, patriotic fervour for the war had given way to disillusionment in the face of growing casualties, stalemate on the Western Front and the introduction of conscription, which drafted all men aged between 18 and 41 into military service unless they were medically exempt or working in protected occupations. Furthermore, the Battle of Jutland had done little to inspire public confidence in the Royal Navy. It was the biggest fleet action of the war, but its result was ambiguous: some newspapers claimed that a decisive blow had been dealt to the German forces, but others suggested that the heavy loss of British ships amounted to a defeat. Against this backdrop, the authorities seized upon Cornwell's fate as an opportunity to galvanise national resolve and to distract from the uncertain outcome of the battle with an inspiring story of heroic self-sacrifice.

The official report of the battle was released in early July 1916. As soon as it came out, Cornwell's image began appearing in newspapers. The front page of *The Daily Mirror* from 7 July, the day after the report's publication, provides a typical example (fig. 2). Alongside two images of King

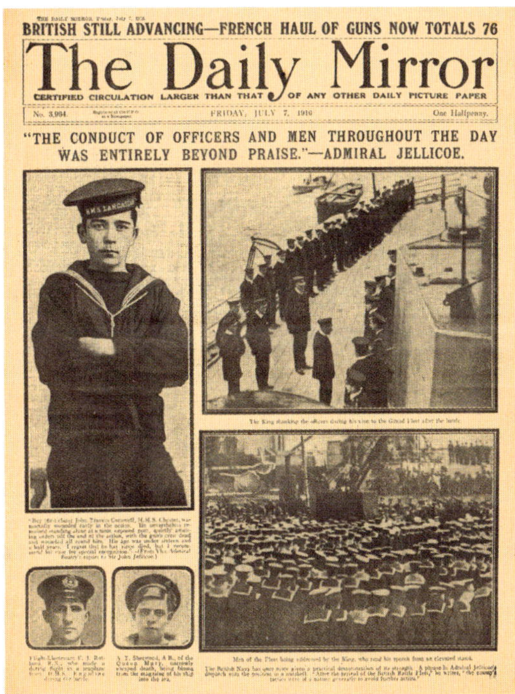
BRITISH STILL ADVANCING—FRENCH HAUL OF GUNS NOW TOTALS 76

The Daily Mirror

CERTIFIED CIRCULATION LARGER THAN THAT OF ANY OTHER DAILY PICTURE PAPER

No. 3,904 FRIDAY, JULY 7, 1916 One Halfpenny.

"THE CONDUCT OF OFFICERS AND MEN THROUGHOUT THE DAY WAS ENTIRELY BEYOND PRAISE."—ADMIRAL JELLICOE.

Opposite: (fig. 1) *Petty Officer E. Pitcher, VC*
Ambrose McEvoy
1918, oil on canvas
1,019 x 762 mm
Imperial War Museum (IWM ART 1327)

Above: (fig. 2) *The Daily Mirror*
7 July 1916, newspaper
380 x 290 mm

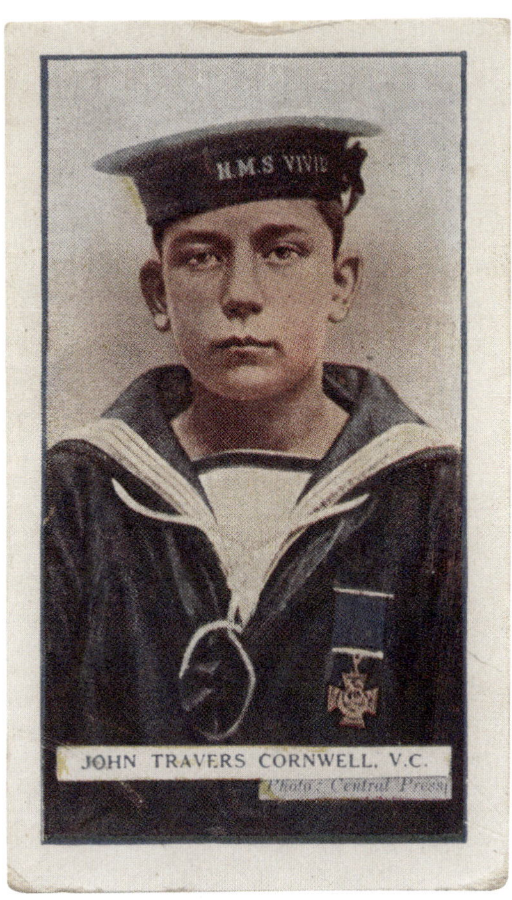

(fig. 3) *John Travers Cornwell*
Central Press
1916, cigarette card
62 x 38 mm
National Portrait Gallery (NPG x199986)

George V visiting the fleet is a large photograph of a young man in naval uniform, his cap ribbon emblazoned 'HMS *Lancaster*'. The caption describes him as 'Boy (1st class) John Travers Cornwell, H.M.S. *Chester*' and quotes Beatty's commendation. This photograph was widely reproduced, appearing in multiple newspapers, as well as on penny stamps and commemorative medals. It became the iconic image of the young hero. Unsurprisingly, therefore, it was also the source for McEvoy's portrait; the artist copied precisely not only the facial features but also the angle of the young man's cap and the slant of his shoulders.

However, McEvoy did not believe that copying from a photograph made for a convincing portrait and blamed his failure to finish the painting on the difficulty of this task. The same issue affected other pictures in the same series. Writing to Alfred Yockney, Secretary for the British War Memorials Commission, in October 1919, the artist announced, 'I do not know what to think of the dead VCs. I find it difficult to finish anything from a photograph.' In the end, he abandoned many of these works, including Cornwell's portrait, which remained in the artist's family until it was loaned to the National Maritime Museum in the 1960s.

McEvoy was perhaps right to have misgivings about working from photographs. Doubts have been raised about the photograph that he used for Cornwell's portrait. The photograph is now thought to depict Jack Cornwell's younger brother, George Samuel Cornwell, in a similar naval uniform. If true, the photograph must have been staged for the press, because George was not enlisted in the Navy. Another brother, Ernest Edward Cornwell, was serving in the Royal Navy. He posed as Jack for a later painting of the Battle of Jutland by artist Frank O. Salisbury. A photograph depicting Jack himself did appear on some later cigarette cards (fig. 3), but it failed to capture the public imagination as much as the image of his brother. The mistake was not revealed until many years later. Both Ernest and George Cornwell survived the war, though their father, Eli Cornwell, died on the Western Front in 1918. Ernest became a painter and died in Kent in

1960; George joined the Merchant Navy and died in Canada in 1974.

Unfinished and possibly depicting the wrong sitter, McEvoy's portrait could be described as a failure. The artist himself might have seen it that way. However, in some senses, the painting's shortcomings increase, rather than diminish, its potency as a record of the First World War. Its incompleteness and faded colours evoke the idea of a young life ended too soon, providing a powerful tribute to the premature death of Jack Cornwell, along with so many others in the conflict. Furthermore, the fact that the portrait may have been based on a photograph of a different teenage boy to the one it was supposed to depict creates a poignant, if unintended, reminder of how enlisted men were treated as a disposable resource. Mass attrition was one of the war's defining characteristics. When one young recruit died, another would take his place in a repeating cycle of destruction.

Staring out at the viewer, the boy in the portrait compels us to acknowledge him as an individual. Working-class servicemen did not often receive such attention. Even the propaganda around Cornwell's death downplayed his individuality. In the official account, Cornwell was hailed as a heroic model for other sailors because he had remained at his post 'quietly awaiting orders' from his superiors, rather than because he had exercised any agency of his own. The circumstances of Cornwell's death are, however, absent from McEvoy's portrait, which shows its sitter as an isolated figure, transcending the specifics of any particular battle or event. The painting demonstrates how the advent of official war art created opportunities for the lower decks to be celebrated and commemorated in ways that had previously been reserved for officers.

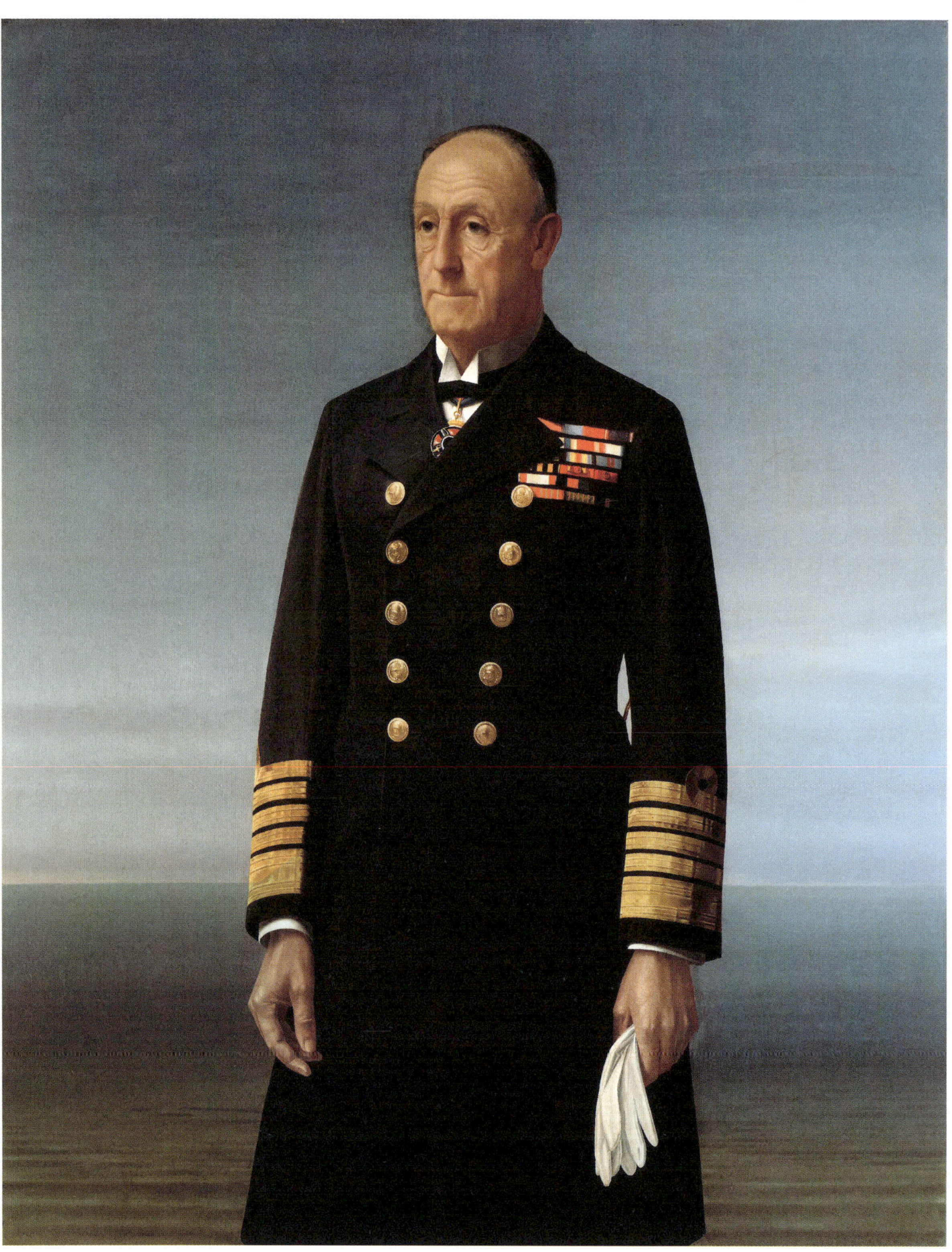

Admiral of the Fleet John Jellicoe, 1st Earl Jellicoe

Walter Thomas Monnington

1933, oil on canvas
1,270 x 1,015 mm
BHC2804

Like so many celebrated artists of his generation, Sir Walter Thomas Monnington began his career under the tuition of Professor Henry Tonks at the Slade School of Art in London. 'Tom', as Monnington preferred to be called, enrolled at the school in 1918, aged 15. Although his later work became more abstract, he took to heart Professor Tonks's advice to combine the styles and techniques of the Italian Renaissance with the artistic innovations of European modernism. At the Slade, Monnington specialised in so-called 'decorative painting', which involved the production of large-scale paintings of human figures and narrative subjects in pure, subdued colours with simplified compositions – reminiscent of fifteenth-century Italian frescoes. After winning a scholarship to the British School at Rome in 1922, Monnington spent three years living and working in Italy, further deepening his appreciation of Italian art. Returning to London with his wife and fellow artist Winifred Margaret Knights in 1925, he received major commissions for mural schemes at the Bank of England and St Stephen's Hall in Westminster. He also became known as a portraitist and painted many eminent public figures. In 1931, he began to exhibit at the Royal Academy of Arts, which gradually became the centre of his professional life. He later taught at the Royal Academy Schools and, in 1966, was elected as the Academy's President, a role he held until his death a decade later.

Exhibited at the Royal Academy in 1934, this portrait depicted an important but controversial veteran from the First World War, Admiral of the Fleet John Jellicoe, 1st Earl Jellicoe. Trained as a gunnery specialist, Jellicoe had played a central role in the modernisation of the Royal Navy, promoting the introduction of dreadnought battleships, torpedo boats and submarines. However, he was most famous for commanding the British Grand Fleet at the Battle of Jutland on 31 May 1916. After the battle, controversy raged in the press and at the Admiralty over whether Jellicoe had been too cautious. Although he later served as First Sea Lord (1916–17) and Governor of New Zealand (1920–24), questions over his reputation remained. By the time this portrait was painted, he was in failing health, having lost his hearing, eyesight, sense of taste and smell.

Monnington began the portrait at his studio in Chelsea in 1932, but it was not finished until the following year, Jellicoe's illness having delayed the process. In the portrait, Jellicoe stands before an empty expanse of sea, his arms at his sides. The sparseness of the setting serves as a foil to the portrait's intricate details, including the lines and wrinkles on the Admiral's face, the multi-coloured medal ribbons on his chest, the Order of Merit hanging from his neck, the gold buttons on his coat and the gold lace on his sleeves. These details emphasise not only his rank and achievements but also his advancing age. His stiff pose and vacant look add to his sense of frailty. Sheathed in the dark fabric of naval coat, his body appears unnaturally elongated. In the background, the fading colours and straight horizon underscore his isolation, lending the portrait an otherworldly ambiance.

The commission for the painting came from HMS *Excellent*, the Royal Naval Gunnery School at Portsmouth, where Jellicoe had studied in the 1880s. The portrait was intended as a tribute to one of the school's most successful alumni. However, after initially accepting the painting,

HMS *Excellent* returned it to the artist when Lady Jellicoe objected to the depiction of her husband. It remained in Monnington's studio until it was sold to the National Maritime Museum in 1960.

Lady Jellicoe's reservations apparently concerned Monnington's refusal to disguise the Admiral's infirmity. Other viewers thought the portrait evoked the Admiral's controversial professional reputation, as well as his poor health. Reviewing the Royal Academy Summer Exhibition for the *Daily Mail* in 1934, Winston Churchill – who was also an amateur painter and art critic – wondered if the Hanging Committee were being intentionally humorous when they placed 'Mr Monnington's "Lord Jellicoe" averting a furtive gaze from the flashing and contumelious [scornful or insolent] eye which Mr Cowan Dobson's "Lord Beatty" is directing upon him from the opposite wall?' Beatty had commanded the battlecruiser squadron at Jutland and later replaced Jellicoe as First Sea Lord in 1917. His aggressive approach to naval warfare was often juxtaposed to Jellicoe's preference for caution. As the former First Lord of the Admiralty and a keen observer of naval affairs, Churchill was well aware of the contrast between the two characters. His comments about their portraits followed a long-standing tradition, stretching back to the eighteenth century, in which paintings were imagined to be interacting with each other on the walls of the Academy.

Churchill's suggestion that that the 'contumelious', Beatty had cowed Jellicoe into 'furtive' submission indicates that, like the Admiral's wife, he thought Jellicoe appeared to be a diminished figure in Monnington's portrait. The art critic for *The Connoisseur* magazine, Herbert Granville Fell, drew a similar between the two portraits. He too judged Jellicoe lacking: 'Mr Monnington's *Admiral Earl Jellicoe*, in Room VIII., may be compared with Mr Cowan Dobson's rendering of *Admiral Earl Beatty* on the opposite wall, the latter appearing to have the more vitality.'

However, although it attracted criticism, Monnington's portrait was stylistically consistent with the artist's wider work. With its cool colour scheme, centralised composition and ethereal atmosphere, it recalls the work of the fifteenth-century Tuscan artist Piero della Francesca. Piero's paintings, such as *The Baptism of Christ*, which was on display at the National Gallery in London in the early twentieth century (fig. 1), were a major source of inspiration for Monnington, reflecting his close engagement with Italian art at the Slade and the British School in Rome. The influence of early Italian artists like Piero pervaded the modern tradition of decorative painting, in which Monnington had trained. Artists in this tradition combined simple backgrounds with pure colours and ornamental details. Despite the antiquity of their Italian inspiration, their work appeared startlingly modern to audiences used to the richer colours and textures of late Victorian and Edwardian art. While decorative painting was usually associated with vast murals, the Jellicoe portrait demonstrates how its principles could also be applied to portraiture.

Monnington thus created a sensitive, haunting and refreshingly modern portrait of an ageing admiral. Yet the negative reaction to the painting suggests that this innovation was not necessarily welcome in naval portraiture. Having rejected the portrait, HMS *Excellent* commissioned a replacement painting from Reginald Grenville Eves, an established artist who was more than two decades older than Monnington. His portrait showed a seated, smiling Jellicoe against a grey-brown background in a manner reminiscent of late nineteenth-century art. This example demonstrates how conservative tastes often prevailed in naval portraiture.

(fig. 1) *The Baptism of Christ*
Piero della Francesca
after 1437, egg tempera on poplar
1,670 x 1,160 mm
National Gallery, London (NG665)

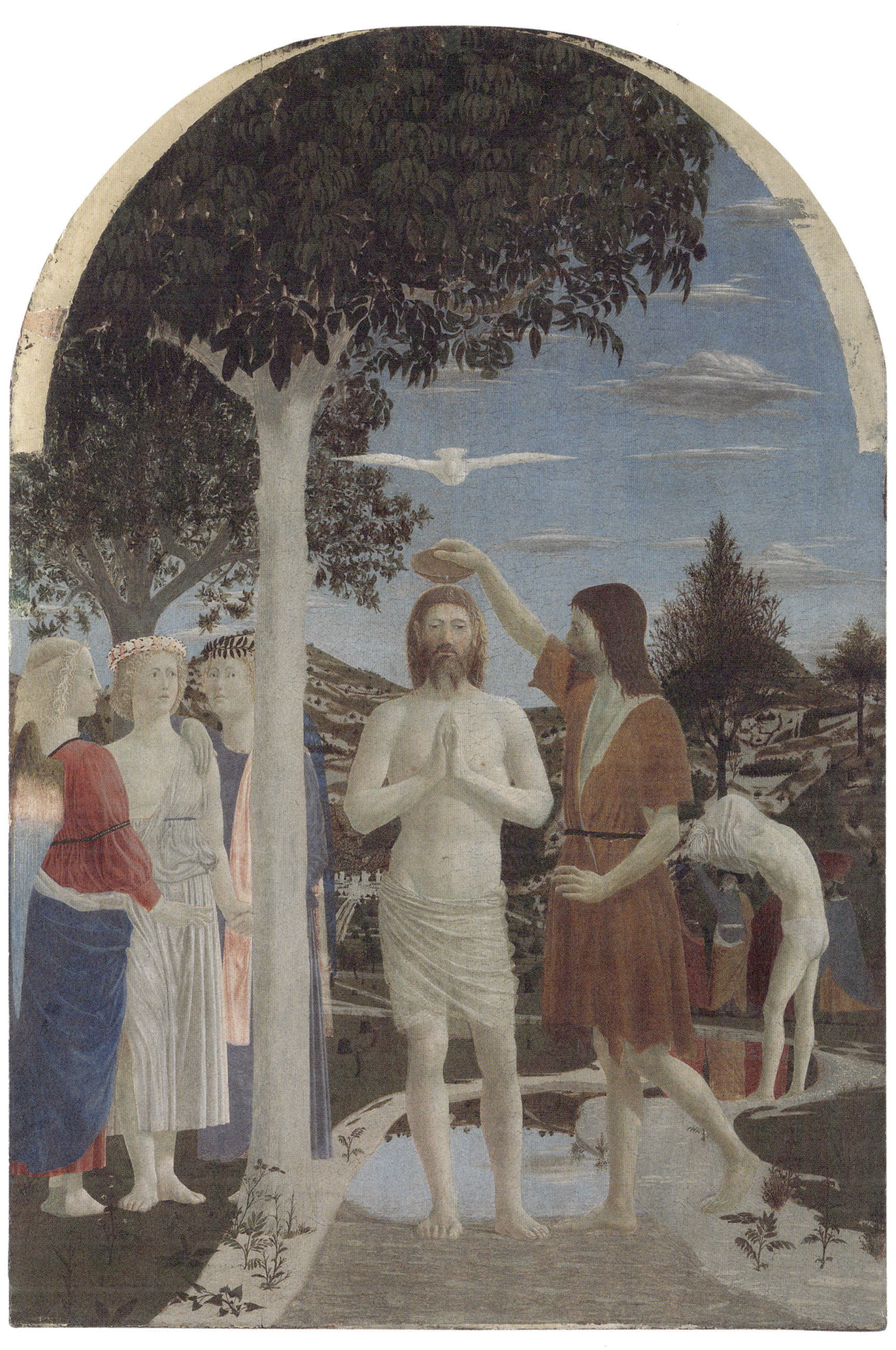

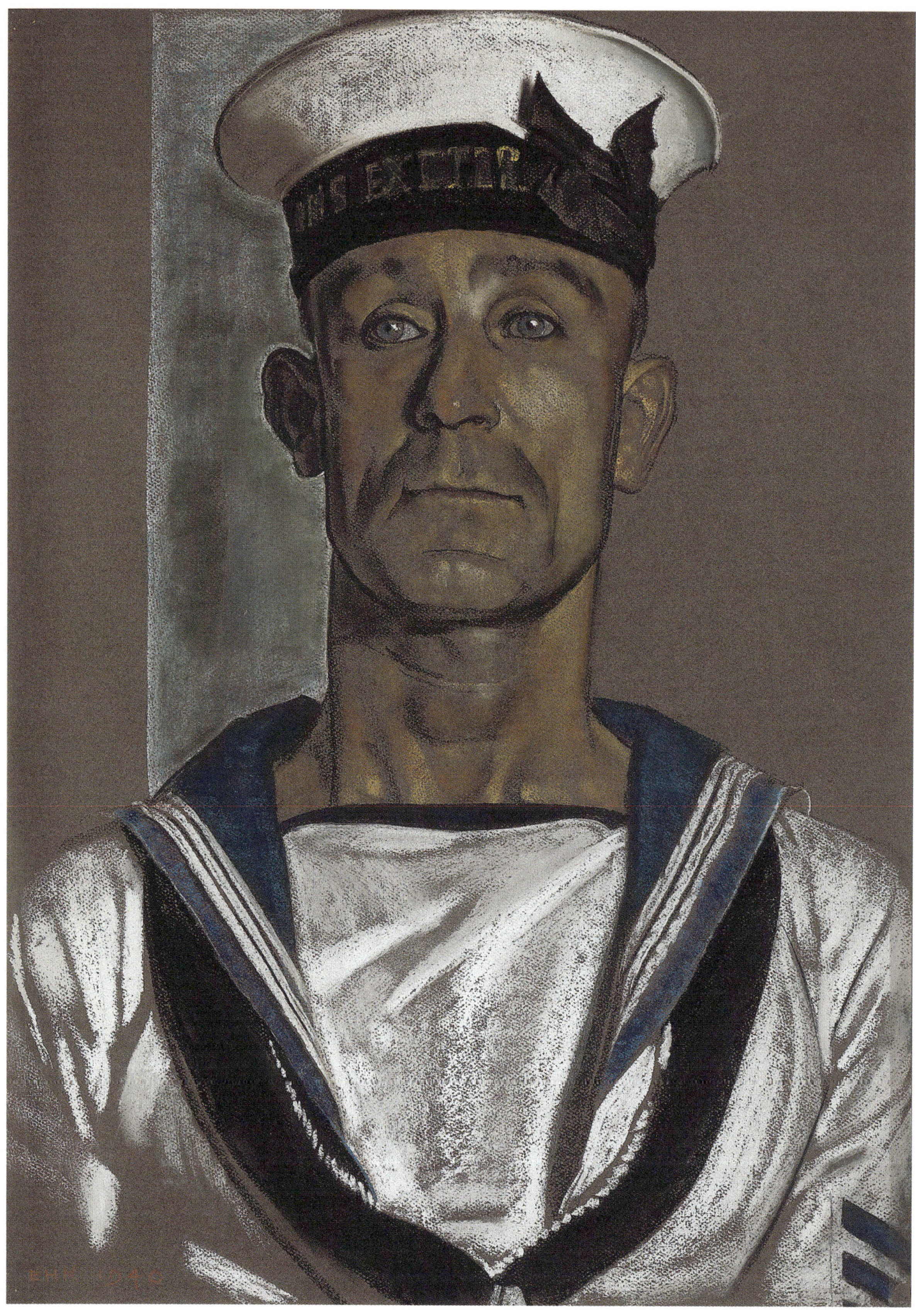

Stoker A. Martin

Eric Kennington

1940, pastel on paper
735 x 530 mm
PAJ2894

'Kennington is not to everyone's taste,' conceded Kenneth Clark in 1942. As Director of the National Gallery, Clark chaired the War Artists' Advisory Committee (WAAC), which oversaw the production and dissemination of official war art during the Second World War. His comment referred to the sculptor, artist and illustrator Eric Kennington, who worked for the WAAC as a portraitist. Kennington's striking depictions of sailors and airmen drew enthusiastic responses from the public, but many critics disliked his aggressively masculine style.

Kennington had previous experience as a war artist. After studying at Lambeth School of Art, he enlisted in the 13th (Kensington) Battalion London Regiment at the outset of the First World War and fought on the Western Front, where he was wounded in January 1915. During his convalescence, he painted a group portrait of his regiment, which was exhibited to great acclaim the following year. Following this success, he visited the Somme as a semi-official 'artist-visitor' and later received a commissioned as an official war artist. His involvement in military circles continued after the war, when he befriended T.E. Lawrence, the charismatic British Army officer nicknamed 'Lawrence of Arabia' for his adventures in the Middle East. In the 1920s, Kennington produced illustrations for *The Seven Pillars of Wisdom*, Lawrence's autobiographical account of the Arab Revolt in 1916–18.

In the Second World War, the WAAC approached Kennington in November 1939, asking him to produce portraits of several senior commanders in London. He fulfilled this commission but pleaded to be allowed to draw younger servicemen, whom he idolised as brave and stoic heroes. Kennington's wish was soon granted. In March and April 1940, he was sent to the dockyards at Portsmouth and Plymouth to depict serving naval personnel. He later also made images of pilots for the Royal Air Force.

This portrait is one of those that Kennington created at Plymouth in April 1940. He was tasked with depicting the captain and crew members from HMS *Exeter*, which had fought the German battleship *Admiral Graf Spee* at the Battle of the River Plate, off the coast of Uruguay, in December 1939. The *Exeter* was badly damaged and lost almost ten per cent of its crew in the action, with many more wounded. While the ship underwent repairs in Plymouth, Kennington drew its captain, Frederick Bell, and several of its sailors, including Stoker A. Martin, shown here.

The portrait is drawn in pastels, the medium Kennington favoured in his wartime portraits. Pastels are made from fine-ground pigment mixed with a binder and rolled into sticks. They produce vibrant colours but are also portable, convenient and require no drying time. This made them ideal for use in wartime conditions. Working in pastel, Kennington was able to produce rapid portraits in a variety of temporary and improvised studios at military and naval bases across the country. However, his style confounded the expectations of his viewers. Pastels were traditionally associated with soft and delicate effects, exploiting the velvety texture of the medium. By contrast, Kennington's portraits were stark and intense. As the art critic Frank Davis observed in *The Burlington Magazine for Connoisseurs* in September 1942, 'Mr Kennington uses pastel, in other hands a medium of sweetness and suavity, with ferocious incisiveness.'

Stoker A. Martin bears out Kennington's reputation for 'ferocious incisiveness'. Straight lines dominate the portrait. Martin's body is rigid and upright. He stares straight ahead, his lips clamped together. His square-jawed head and muscular neck fuse into a continuous column, which rises to the very top of the image. The abstract background reinforces the vertical thrust of the composition, the brownish paper having been left blank apart from a thin grey stripe, which runs parallel to the sitter's neck. In his luminous white uniform, Martin looks like a superhuman pillar of strength. Davis identified this godlike aura as a defining feature of Kennington's portraiture, writing that it was difficult to believe the artist's wartime pictures depicted 'men and not demigods who have come down to earth for a space to play a part in fighting the dragon'.

Kennington had several works, including *Stoker A. Martin*, selected for inclusion in the WAAC's inaugural war art exhibition at the National Gallery in July 1940. The press response to his portraits was generally positive with critics praising his ability to convey courage and determination. Writing in *The Connoisseur*, Herbert Granville Fell declared that 'Kennington's harsh, iron technique has a force admirably suited to conveying unflinching and dauntless resolution in the faces of his seamen and soldiers.' Meanwhile, in the magazine *The Studio*, Richard Holme focused specifically on *Stoker A. Martin*, suggesting that the picture 'speaks eloquently of war effort ... [and] volumes as to the tenacity of the Royal Navy'.

It is significant that Holme saw the portrait as expressing general qualities of the Royal Navy as a whole. Although the official war art programme increased the visibility of ordinary sailors like Stoker Martin, it did not necessarily lead to the acknowledgement of working-class servicemen as individuals with their own personalities and stories. Instead, portraits like this were often treated as representations of a shared naval or national spirit. Indeed, Martin's first name was never recorded in connection with the portrait, obscuring to some extent his identity. In Kennington's vision, he becomes the embodiment of the ultimate sailor.

In response to the portrait's popularity, the WAAC produced postcards displaying the image. Postcards played a central role in the government's strategy for wartime propaganda. In fact, the WAAC minutes from November 1939 reveal that Kennington had been selected as an official war artist in part because 'his style of drawing readily lent itself to reproduction in the form of picture postcards'. Ordinary people were encouraged to send official postcards as a means of showing support for the war effort. Thus, in December 1943, Celandine Kennington, the artist's wife, sent one bearing Martin's portrait to a neighbour, Ella Hart. Hart wrote back immediately, describing her profound response to the portrait

> I must have stared at it for quite five minutes and when I came to I found my eyes full of tears! No picture has ever done that to me before ... I intend to make a pilgrimage to the National Gallery to see the original the first chance I get to visit London

Hart's comments demonstrate that the portrait had an immense emotional impact on civilian viewers. Her choice of the word 'pilgrimage' suggests that it inspired a kind of quasi-religious reverence, in keeping with the inhuman quality with which Kennington imbued his sitters.

However, some people were uncomfortable with the artist's hypermasculine aesthetic. The art critic Herbert Furst declared that the portraits made him feel 'uneasy ... as if I have awakened in Valhalla'. He continued, 'Mr Kennington would be greater, one feels, if he practised at least a little of that outstanding virtue of his heroes: understatement.' The *New Statesman and Nation* critic went further, writing that 'the violence of Mr Kennington's style seems to me as hysterical as the eloquence of Hitler'.

Kennington himself seems to have felt the need to soften the impact of his portraits. In October 1941, he published a book of his wartime work entitled *Pilots, Workers, Machines*, including an introduction by the author J.B. Priestley. In the text, Priestley and Kennington emphasised the ordinariness and humanity of the servicemen depicted. Of Martin, Kennington wrote: 'Man of action: instantaneous: 100 per cent reliable; expert technician. Much humour under thorough camouflage. Very gentle, sensitive and great physical strength.' These comments offer a more well-rounded impression of the stoker as an individual than his portrait provided, suggesting that Kennington recognised the limitations of his artistic approach.

Writing in *The Burlington Magazine* in spring 1945, shortly before the war's conclusion, art historian Edith Hoffman suggested that Kennington and his fellow war artist Reginald Eves consistently produced 'heroic types'. This phrase highlighted how their portraits represented idealised stereotypes, rather than offering more individualised depictions. Hoffman expressed concern about the long-term impact of these stereotypes. 'It is to be feared', she wrote, 'that generations of the future will be taught to see the war precisely through this kind of reflection'. Kennington's portraits, therefore, require careful interpretation. They can and should be appreciated as some of the Second World War's most powerful evocations of heroic spirit. At the same time, it needs to be acknowledged that their intensity has long been seen as problematic.

Surgeon-Lieutenant Philip Raymond Charles Evans

William Dring

1943, pastel on paper
492 x 632 mm
PAJ2986

'While there is still time before I languish in the army as a scullion or cleaner of latrines, I should very much like to do some pictures of shipping or portraits of naval staff,' wrote William Dring in a letter to the War Artists' Advisory Committee (WAAC) in May 1941. Dring was at the time teaching at the Southampton School of Art, having received his own artistic education at the Slade School in the 1920s. He had first contacted the WAAC in September 1940, but no offers of work had been forthcoming. To prove his worth to the WAAC, he attempted to draw wartime subjects in Southampton but, when spotted sketching in the vicinity of fortifications, he was arrested under suspicion of spying, an experience he described as 'most trying'. In 1941, he feared that he would be called up to the army and assigned menial tasks, such as cleaning latrines, due to his poor health. He therefore reapplied to the WAAC for work as a war artist, this time with a letter of recommendation from the President of the Royal Academy, Edwin Lutyens. The endorsement worked and the WAAC commissioned Dring to produce two portraits of naval subjects. Further commissions followed and, in 1942, Dring began working full-time as an official war artist.

He became one of the WAAC's most prolific portraitists, producing more than 150 naval portraits between 1942 and 1944, before doing similar work with the Air Ministry from 1944 to 1945. He depicted naval personnel of all ranks, his sensitive and informal style proving popular with the public. Edward Montgomery O'Rorke Dickey, the WAAC's Secretary, summarised Dring's appeal in the following terms: 'There are plenty of fashionable portrait painters who are prepared to produce large and showy oils, but we do not want too many of them, and Dring's skill lies mainly in the direction of pastels on a comparatively small scale which are just what we want.' After the war, the majority of the artist's pastel portraits entered the collection at the Imperial War Museum, but a small number were transferred to the National Maritime Museum in 1947.

This portrait exemplifies the dignity and humanity for which Dring's work was celebrated. Dating from 1943, it depicts Surgeon-Lieutenant Philip Raymond Charles Evans sitting up in a hospital bed. Evans had joined the Royal Naval Volunteer Reserve aged 25 in 1942, after qualifying in medicine at Guy's Hospital in London. He was serving on board HMS *Wivern* in February 1943 when the ship went to the aid of the Canadian warship HMCS *Weyburn*, which had struck a German mine. As the *Weyburn* sank, two of its depth charges (anti-submarine weapons) detonated, inflicting severe damage to the *Wivern*. Evans broke both his ankles in the incident but continued to treat other injured men for several hours. He was awarded the George Medal for his bravery but suffered the consequences of his injuries for the rest of his life. He developed a chronic and recurrent infection in one ankle, which led to the amputation of the affected leg.

Dring's pastel drawing is unusual among portraits from the Second World War due to its sympathetic acknowledgement of the sitter's physical injuries. Evans's broken legs are hidden from view, but the hospital room setting highlights his vulnerability. The portrait is drawn from the viewpoint of a visitor at his bedside, creating an unconventional composition with a strong horizontal emphasis. Evans's reclining

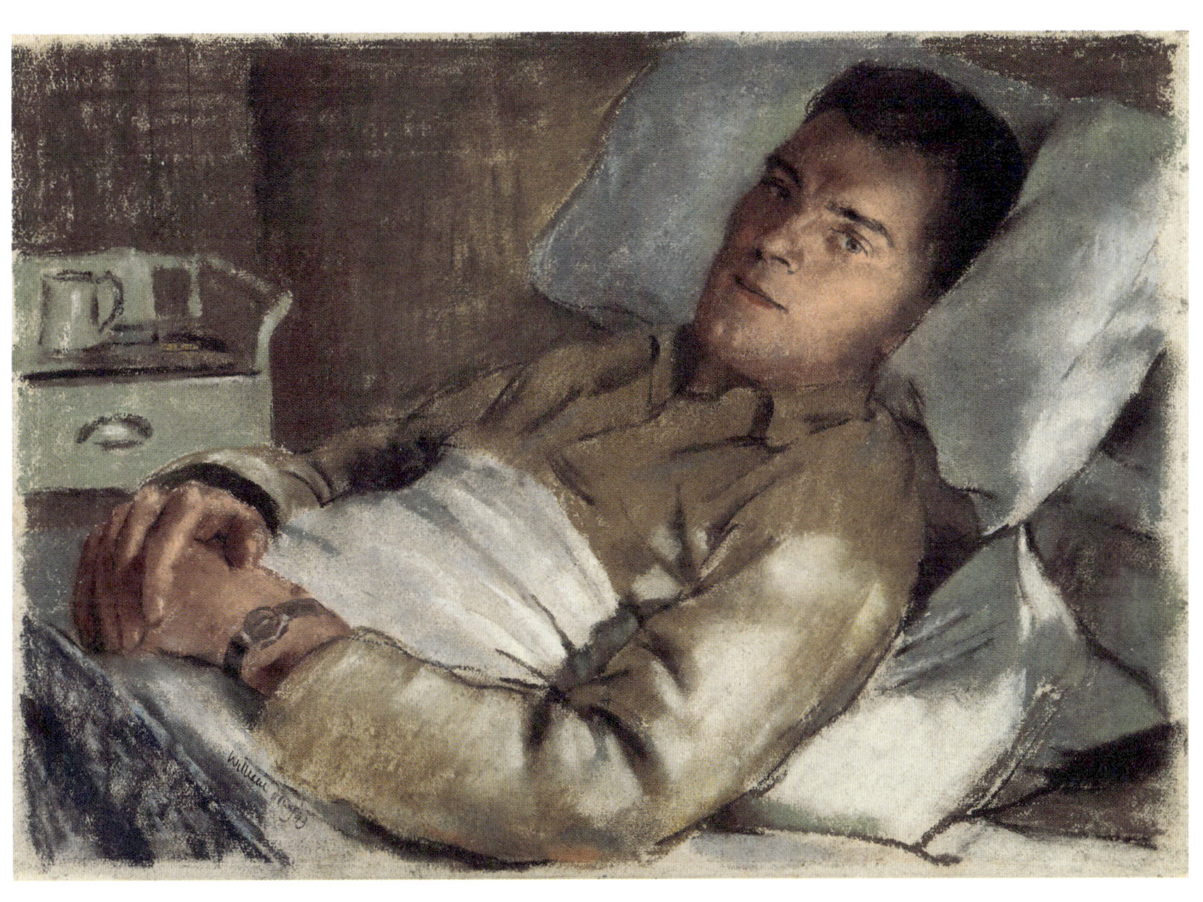

(fig. 1) *Warrant-Engineer Stanley Ball*
William Dring
1943, pastel on paper
476 x 330 mm
PAJ3020

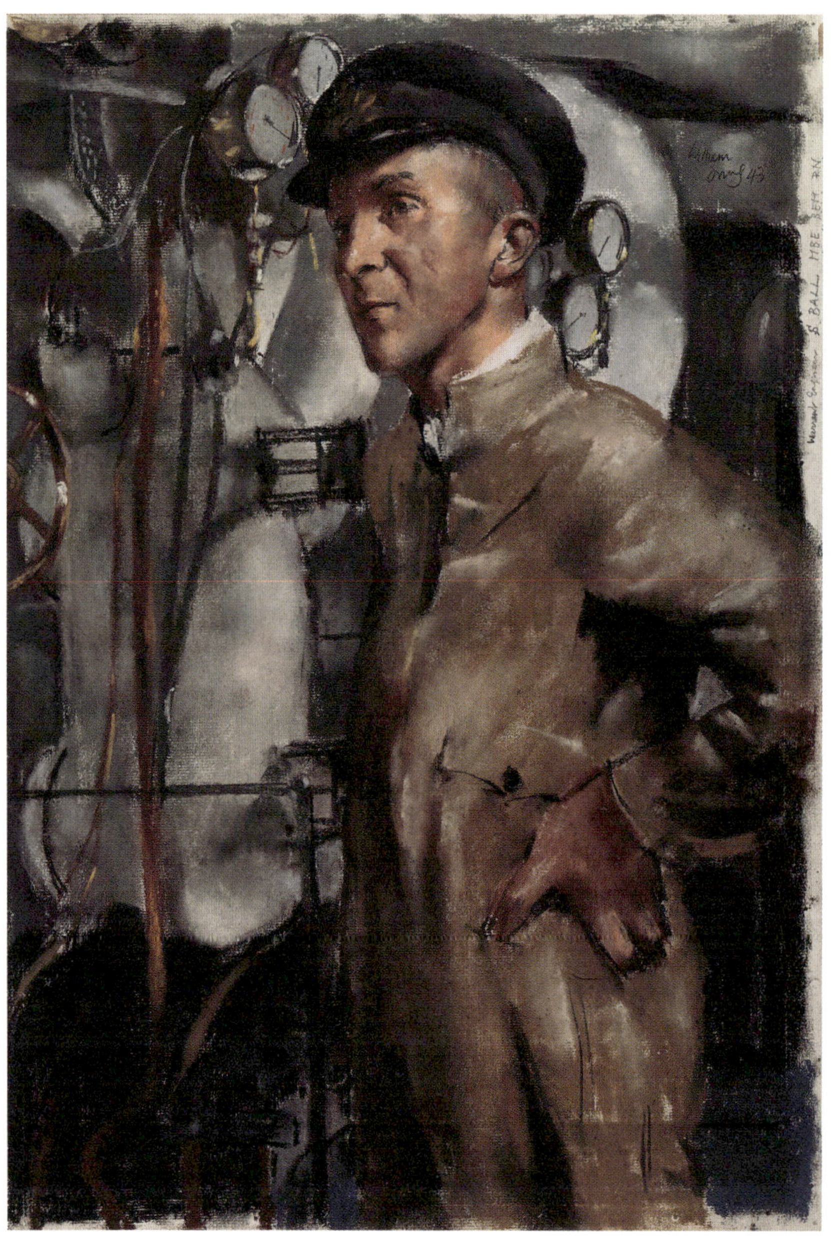

posture subverts the upright and determined poses used in more traditional naval portraits.

Dring does not attempt to glorify the young surgeon's wounds as heroic, nor does he dwell gratuitously upon the gruesome details. Instead, the tone of the portrait is subdued and understated. The nightstand and mug in the background reinforce the ordinariness of the scene. The main colours are grey, brown and muted green. Rather than crisp naval uniform, Evans wears rumpled khaki pyjamas. Dring exploits the softness of pastel to smudge and blend the colours and shadows, enhancing the muffled atmosphere. With his hands folded in his lap, Evans retains a quiet dignity. He turns his head towards the viewer and into the light, as if disturbed from his rest.

The display of vulnerability in this portrait is extreme in the context of the larger body of the artist's wartime work. Dring produced very few images of wounded servicemen. Nevertheless, his portraits often foregrounded the character and humanity of their subjects, from Warrant-Engineer Stanley Ball wearily stretching his back amid the dials, tanks and cables of the engine room (fig. 1) to Lieutenant Commander C.E. Bridgman smiling around his pipe with a twinkle in his eye (fig. 2).

Dring's sensitive and understated portraits were often contrasted to the strident and aggressive works that Eric Kennington was producing at the same date. Both artists worked in the medium of pastel but they produced very different effects. Stoker A. Martin (p. 200) exemplifies Kennington's approach. Martin stands tautly upright, the antithesis of the tired and supine Evans. Kennington has applied his pastels with force and precision, in contrast to the smudgy softness that Dring employed.

While Kennington had his admirers, several critics thought that his godlike heroes were unrealistic and preferred Dring's down-to-earth depictions. In 1942, art magazine *The Studio* summed up this attitude:

> No one can deny [Kennington's] mastery, his seriousness of purpose and his extraordinary power of combining resemblance with heroic idealisation. He is at his best when this idealisation is not pressed too far, for is it not a fallacy to make all heroes look so very heroic? William Dring supplies the answer. His brave men are modest, gentle and completely unconscious of having done anything out of the ordinary; and we believe in their courage all the more because they are such sympathetic human beings.

These comments reveal the complex challenges involved in producing war art. On one level, portraits were expected to serve as propaganda for the war effort, inspiring confidence and extolling the heroism of the armed forces. Yet the images that resonated most with the public were often those that, like Dring's portraits, acknowledged the ordinariness and humanity of servicemen and women.

(fig. 2) *Lieutenant-Commander Clement Edward Bridgman*
William Dring
1943, pastel on paper
400 x 310 mm
PAJ2987

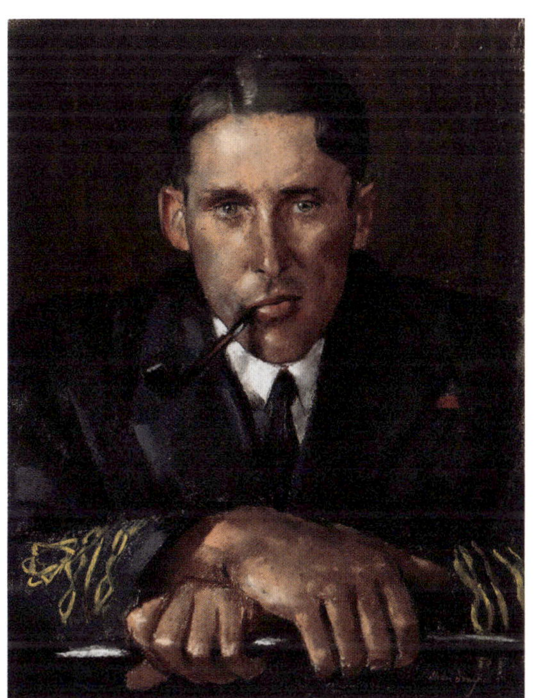

The Sailor [Maurice Alan Easton]

Henry Marvell Carr

1944, oil on canvas
762 x 635 mm
BHC2675

Henry Marvell Carr was a successful portrait and landscape painter. Born in August 1894, he trained in his home city at the Leeds School of Art and at the Royal Academy Schools in London. During the First World War, he served in France with the Royal Field Artillery, before resuming his artistic career. In July 1940, during the Second World War, he offered his services to the War Artists' Advisory Committee. Later that year, he lost his house and studio in the Blitz, but he continued to work, producing sketches of bomb damage and blackouts in and around London. The WAAC purchased several of these drawings and paid for him to illustrate scenes from the Merchant Navy, with whom he undertook a brief voyage in summer 1942. Over the next two years, Carr spent time working as an official war artist in North Africa and Italy. He was given the rank of captain and access to military facilities. He painted equipment, actions and portraits of service personnel, as well as the eruption of Mount Vesuvius in 1944.

Completed at the naval barracks in Naples, this portrait dates from Carr's time in Italy. The sitter, Maurice Alan Easton, was a railway bookings clerk from Oxfordshire, who volunteered for the Royal Navy as a 'hostilities only' recruit in the Second World War, meaning his term of service was solely for the duration of the conflict. The gold badge on his sleeve (a pair of wings crossed with a bolt of lightning) reveals that he was employed as a telegraphist. His cap tally (ribbon) is embroidered 'H.M.S.' (for 'His Majesty's Ship') but it does not include the name of a particular vessel. This was a wartime security measure designed to confuse enemy spies. One of its side-effects was to reduce individual specificity within sailors' portraits. In this case, however, the anonymity suited the artist's purposes, because Carr never intended the artwork to be about Easton himself. Instead, he submitted the painting to the WAAC with the generic title *The Sailor*.

Published in the *Sunday Dispatch* in early 1946, Easton's account of the circumstances around the portrait's creation demonstrates that he was not chosen for his character or his achievements. Easton was staying at a hotel in Naples, waiting for a posting to Corsica when he saw the artist inspecting a line of sailors in the hotel lobby. 'It looked to me like an identification parade,' Easton commented, 'so I beat a hasty retreat upstairs. I hadn't got very far, when a voice called out "That's the man I want."' Carr knew nothing about Easton as a person, having only glimpsed him across the room. The telegraphist was chosen on the basis of his looks alone.

Square-jawed, blue-eyed and with a muscular physique, Easton was conventionally handsome. His appearance evoked a traditional ideal of strong, clean-cut masculinity, making him an appealing 'poster boy' for his rank and social class. In the portrait, Carr hid his sitter's personality behind an inscrutable façade. Easton turns to one side, rather than looking at the viewer. He stares into the distance, his expression unreadable and his arms crossed over his chest. The pose accentuates his chiselled features. His face is bathed in bright illumination, while dark shadows trace the angular line of his jawbone. The squareness of his chin is echoed in the square neckline of his uniform. A faint crease in the pristine white fabric hints at the definition of the pectoral muscles beneath his shirt. The clean lines

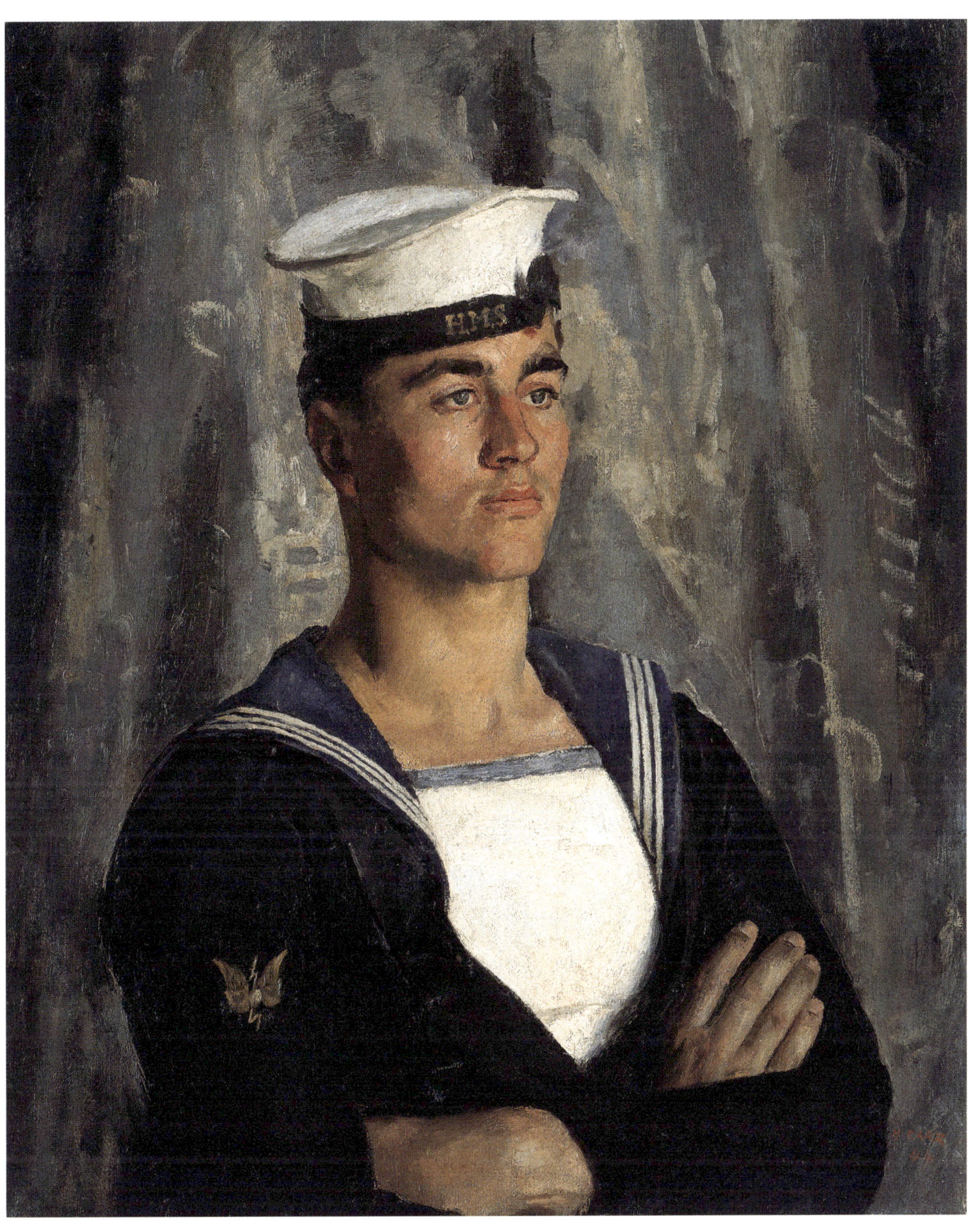
HMS

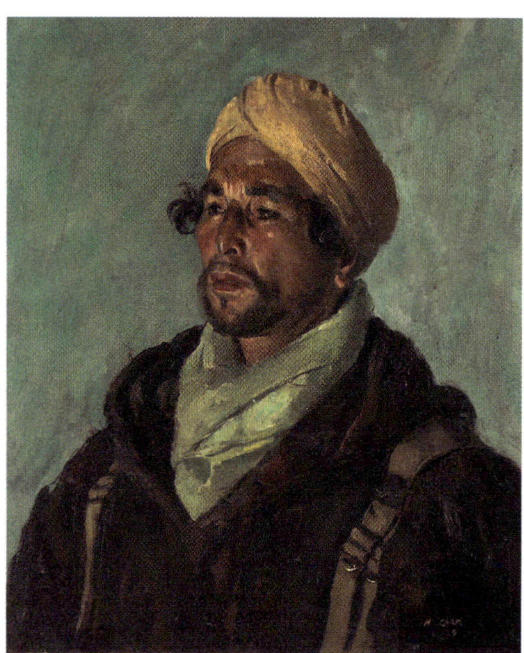

(fig. 1) *The Goumier*
Henry Marvell Carr
1944, oil on canvas
635 x 533 mm
Imperial War Museum (IWM ART LD 4059)

of his clothing stand out against the soft ripples of the blue-grey curtain in the background. Recalling the setting of a photographer's studio, this backdrop reinforces the generic quality of the portrait: it could have been made anywhere in the world.

As a 'type' portrait, which used an unnamed sitter to represent a general identity, *The Sailor* was unusual within the WAAC's collections. The Committee tended to prefer portraits that recognised individual identity, drawing on the traditional valorisation of individualism as a central component of the British national character. This individualistic outlook took on enhanced ideological significance in the 1940s in conscious opposition to Nazi totalitarianism. When the WAAC did accept type portraits, it was usually to highlight the breadth of support for the war effort, especially among different social classes, genders, nationalities and ethnicities.

Carr was one of the chief contributors of such portraits to the WAAC collection. As well as *The Sailor*, he also painted *The Goumier* (depicting an unidentified Moroccan soldier, fig. 1), *French Girl Ambulance Driver* (later retitled *Micheline Dehais, French Ambulance Driver*, fig. 2) and *A Cockney Soldier* (fig. 3). These portraits testify to the artist's stated desire to recognise the contributions of ordinary men and women in the Allied forces. He had previously complained to the WAAC about the lack of female portraits in its collection, which he described as 'a strange omission, considering the position of women in the war'. His generic portraits attempted to give visibility to the many groups of people involved in the conflict. However, their anonymity was to some extent counterproductive, since it implied that the subjects were defined by their class, gender, nationality or race and did not merit recognition as individuals.

Perhaps because its sitter was an attractive young man, *The Sailor* proved especially popular with the public. It was exhibited in the WAAC exhibition at the National Gallery during the war and afterwards featured in the *Naval Art Exhibition* at the Suffolk Street Galleries in 1946. The organiser of the latter was the Navy League,

(fig. 2) *French Girl Ambulance Driver [Micheline Dehais, French Ambulance Driver]*
Henry Marvell Carr
1944, oil on canvas
573 x 498 mm
The Hepworth Wakefield (A1.496)

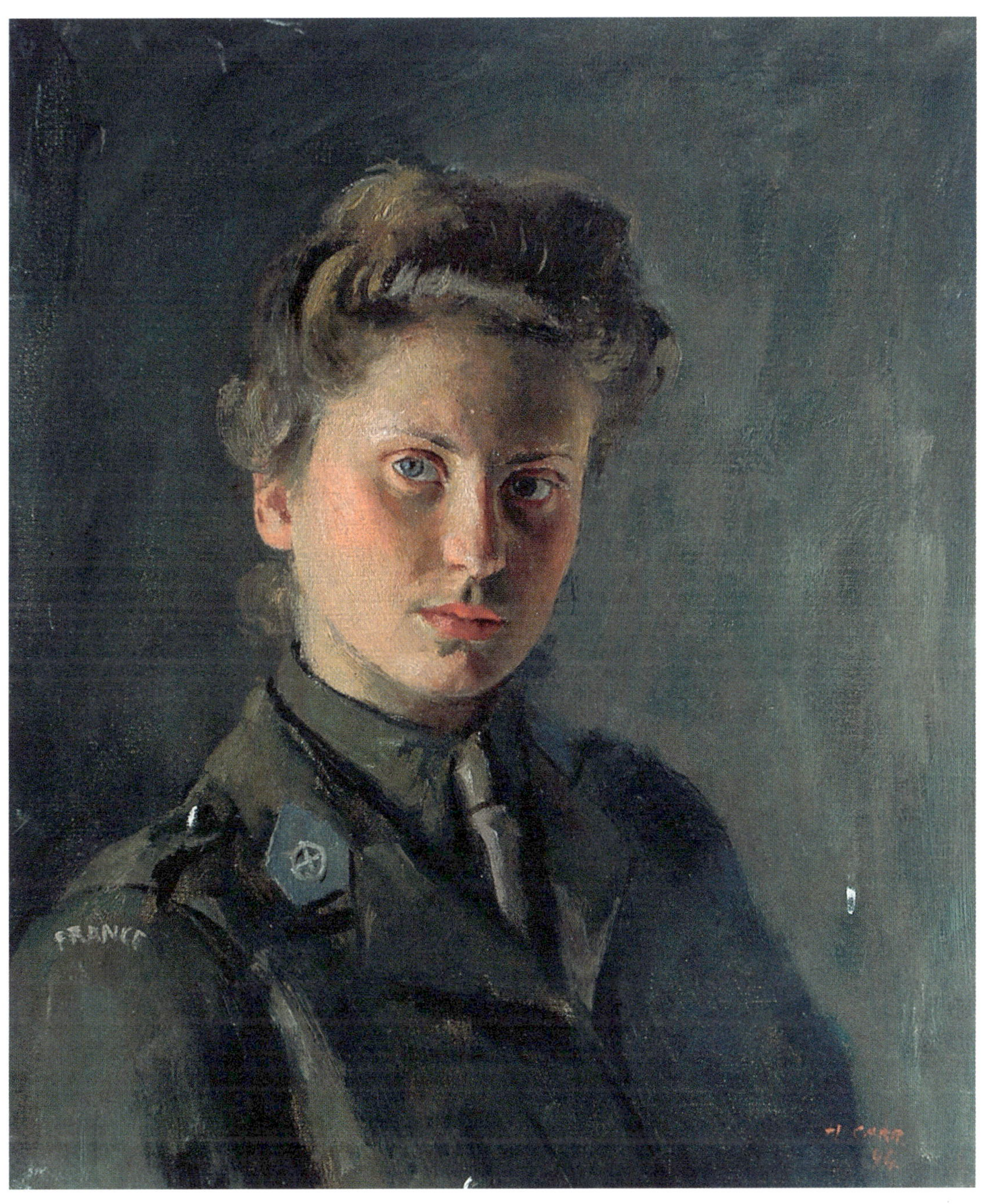

a non-governmental organisation founded in December 1894 to promote increased naval expenditure and enlistment. In the *Naval Art Exhibition*, the League emphasised the Royal Navy's role in winning the Second World War and suggested the continued need for naval investment in the post-war era. *The Sailor* was incorporated into the poster design for the event, further depersonalising Easton's image. No longer a representation of a specific individual, the painting became a generalised emblem of British naval might.

After the Navy League exhibition, the portrait was transferred to the collection of the National Maritime Museum, where it was catalogued under its generic title, *The Sailor*. The identity of the sitter was not recorded anywhere in the Museum records. Easton's name was only rediscovered in 1975, when one of his friends sent the Museum a clipping of the *Sunday Dispatch*'s report on the portrait.

Yet, while the painting was presented in public as an anonymous type portrait, it held immense personal significance for Easton's family. In 1944, his father wrote several letters to the WAAC requesting photographs of his son's portrait and details about its display in the National Gallery, where he hoped to see the painting in person. Expressing parental pride, these letters demonstrate the capacity of portraits to hold multiple meanings for different audiences. For all that the painting anonymised and objectified its sitter, it remained meaningful on an individual level for those who knew him.

(fig. 3) *A Cockney Soldier*
Henry Marvell Carr
1944, oil on canvas
615 x 495 mm
Imperial War Museum (IWM ART LD 3902)

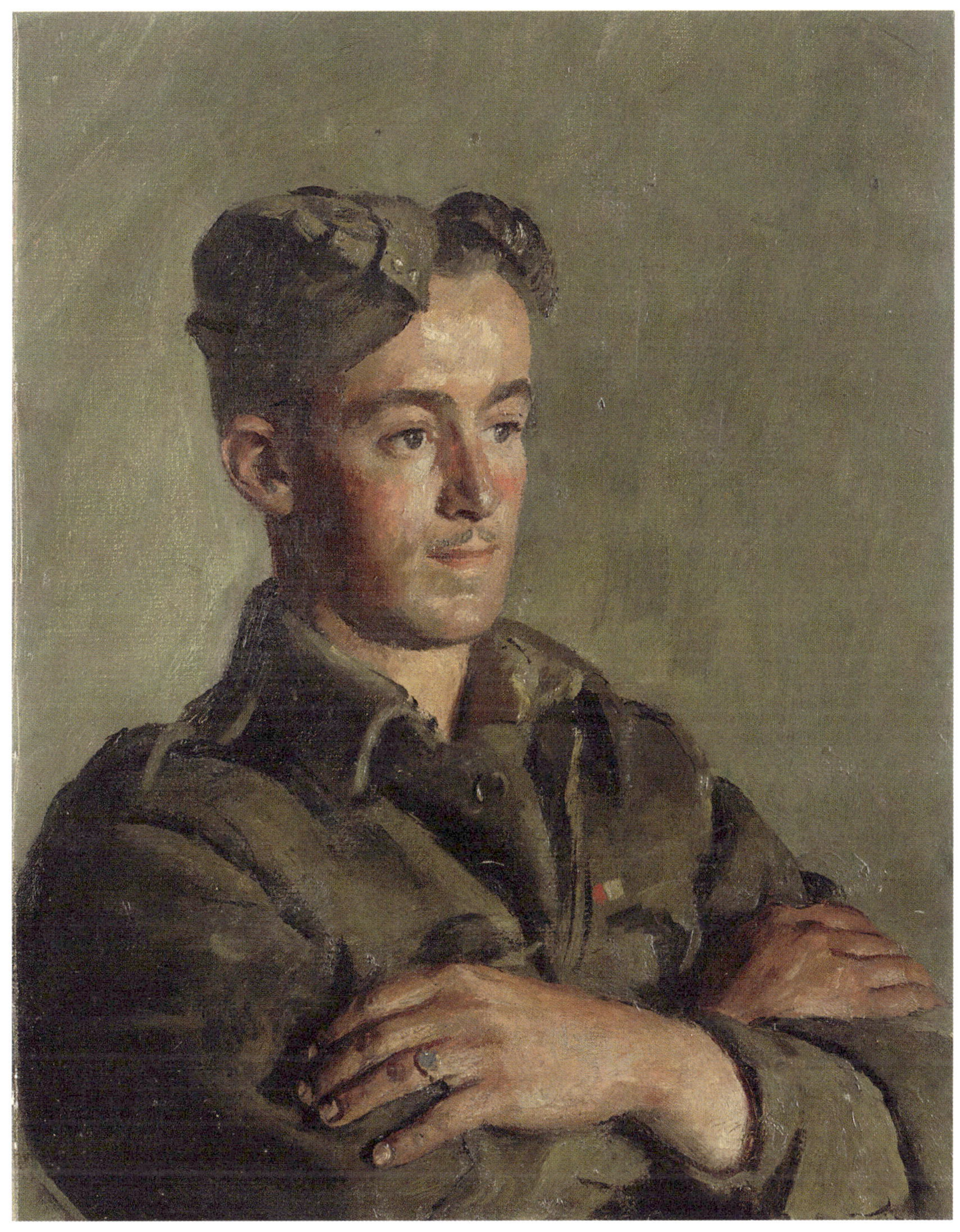

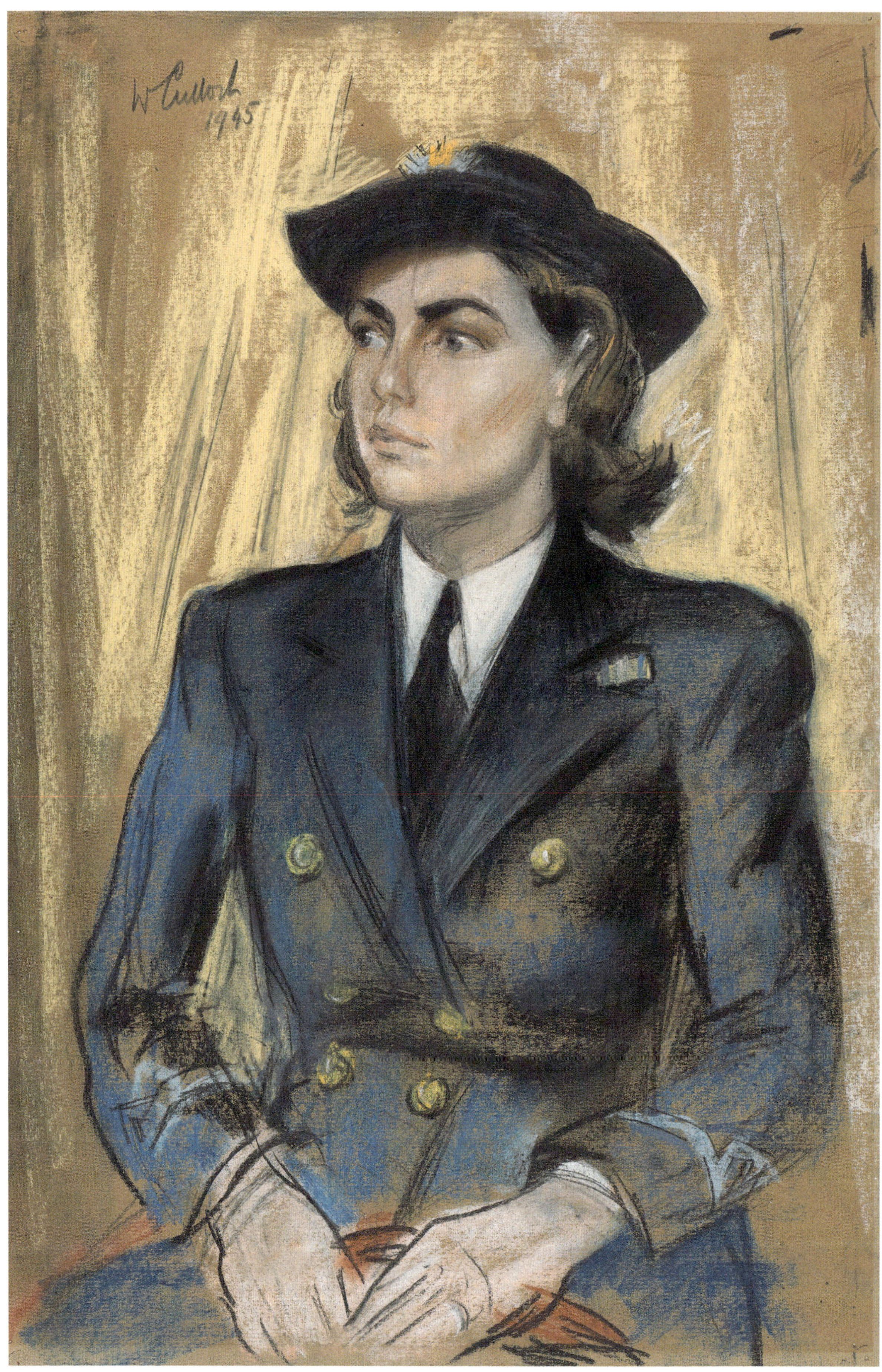
1945

Wren Officer (Third Class)

Joseph McCulloch

1945, pastel on paper
550 x 370 mm
ZBA9617

According to a profile published in *The Artist* magazine in January 1947, Joseph McCulloch was 'one of Chelsea's most popular characters'. The son of a steelworker, McCulloch had been born in Leeds in the 1890s. As a young man, he worked printing and delivering newspapers in the day to pay for classes at Leeds School of Art in the evening. He eventually won a scholarship to study at the Royal College of Art in London. McCulloch taught drawing for a time in Ipswich but soon returned to London to teach at Clapham School of Art and later at Goldsmiths. He made his home in Chelsea, an affluent but also bohemian area where artists and poets rubbed shoulders with aristocratic socialites. Nicknamed 'Mac', McCulloch became something of a local character. He was known for his colourful language and acerbic sense of humour, as well as for the gold earrings and red neckerchief that he habitually wore.

As an artist, McCulloch primarily depicted landscapes, street scenes and architectural subjects in pastel and watercolour, but he also undertook some portrait work. His pictures were displayed in pubs and barber shops around Chelsea. While he had served in the Royal Flying Corps during the First World War, he was too old to be called up during the Second. Instead, he volunteered as a fire guard and sketched people and scenes of wartime life in Chelsea.

Signed and dated 'McCulloch 1945', this pastel portrait is one of McCulloch's wartime works. The sitter's uniform indicates that she is an officer in the Women's Royal Naval Service (WRNS), also known as the Wrens. Her identity is, however, currently unknown. She may have had connections in Chelsea, given the localised focus of the artist's work. Each of her sleeves bears a single light blue ring, identifying her as a third-class officer, the most junior officer rank in the Wrens. In her lap, she holds what appears to be a pair of brown leather gloves, which were part of the uniform for Wren officers. Lower-ranking Wrens had black gloves. A blue-and-white medal ribbon pokes out from under her lapel, and a mark across the ring finger on her left hand may be intended to represent a wedding band, though McCulloch's sketchy style makes it difficult to say for certain. These details provide potential clues to the sitter's identity. The background is more generic, featuring pale yellow and white shapes suggestive of a curtain.

The Wrens were first established in 1917 in response to a high mortality rate in the Royal Navy. The idea was to recruit women to perform administrative tasks on shore, freeing up men to serve afloat. While the admission of women into the armed services was a significant development, traditional gender norms were nonetheless maintained. Combat roles remained the preserve of male sailors and officers, reinforcing conventional associations between masculinity and violence. Wrens, meanwhile, performed secretarial work and domestic duties, such as cooking and cleaning, which aligned with stereotypical ideas of 'women's work'. Designed as a temporary solution to a wartime crisis, the Wrens was dissolved in 1919, before being reformed at the outbreak of the Second World War, along with other women's services for land and air support (the Auxiliary Territorial Service and the Women's Auxiliary Air Force). The Wrens continued after the war until women were fully integrated in the Royal Navy in 1993.

(fig. 1) *Wren Radio Mechanic Soldering Connections on a Service Set*
Gladys E. Reed
about 1943–44, black crayon on paper
382 x 270 mm
PAH0093

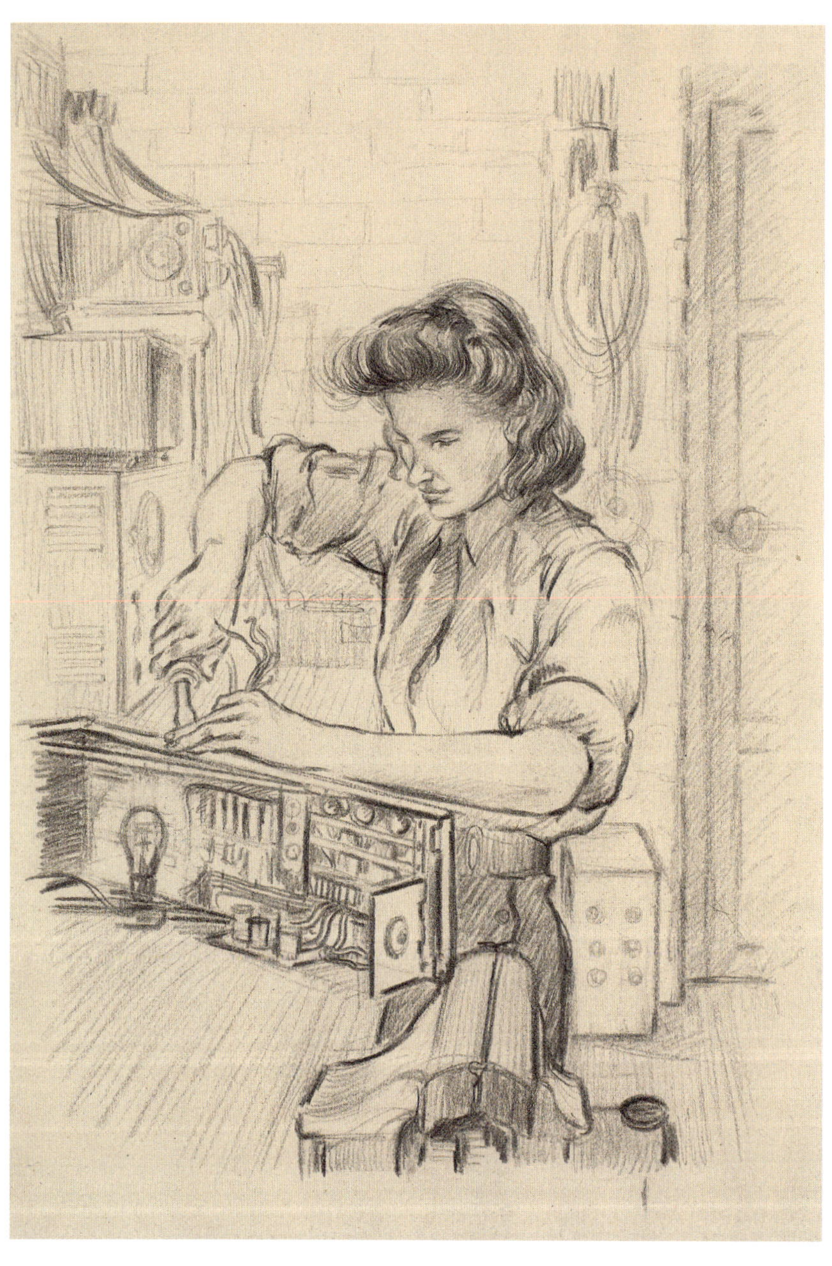

During the Secord World War, the WRNS attracted more recruits than other female services, thanks in part to the appeal of its uniform. As this portrait shows, Wrens wore dark blue double-breasted jackets. These were tailored at the waist to create a feminine silhouette, appealing to fashion-conscious women who wanted to wear flattering clothes. Officers also wore tricorn hats, creating a further draw for some recruits: to quote the title of Christian Lamb's memoir about serving in the Wrens, 'I only joined for the hat.' In McCulloch's portrait, the elegant lines of the uniform are echoed in the stylised representation of the sitter's facial features. The artist has emphasised her high cheekbones, arched eyebrows and wide eyes, imbuing this unidentified woman with the striking looks associated with the era's female movie stars. While this depiction of an idealised individual may offer few insights into the realities of wartime service for most women, the portrait is evocative of its time and demonstrates how Wrens were glamourised in popular culture.

It is hoped that further research may reveal the sitter's identity. The National Maritime Museum purchased the portrait in December 2022 from a dealer who did not know the subject's name, having himself acquired the artwork from an auction. Its history prior to that point is not known. As portraits pass between different owners, the name of the sitter or the artist can be lost or forgotten, especially if neither is widely known.

The Museum decided to acquire the work, despite the Wren's anonymity, because it addressed a glaring gap within the collection. Prior to the acquisition of this pastel, the National Maritime Museum's collection did not include a single portrait of a woman serving in the Royal Navy or the WRNS. Wrens are represented in the collection through photographs, as well as in a remarkable set of pencil sketches that Wren Gladys Reed drew of her colleagues in the 1940s. As *Wren Radio Mechanic Soldering Connections on a Service Set* demonstrates, Reed's drawings provide powerful images of women going confidently about their duties (fig. 1). However, they were intended as representations of wartime activity, rather than portraits of specific individuals.

Where women appeared in the portrait collection, it was either as queens, princesses or the wives of naval officers, not as naval personnel in their own right. This omission was due in part to historic patterns of collecting at the Museum. While the National Maritime Museum has never had a prohibition against collecting images of women, its traditional focus on sea battles and eighteenth-century naval history meant in the past that portraits of the WRNS were not prioritised.

Compounding this was the under-representation of women in war art generally. Of the portraits that the WAAC purchased or commissioned for the nation, only three per cent depicted members of the WRNS, the WAAF and the ATS, whereas there were in fact around ten women in the military for every 100 men. Civilian women were even less visible in official war art, perhaps because their work in home front factories was more disruptive to traditional gender roles, proving as it did that women could do the same jobs as men. The armed services maintained a degree of gender hierarchy through the restriction of women to non-combat roles. Portraits of women in the auxiliary services therefore skirted the boundaries of propriety, celebrating sitters who were making a valuable contribution to the war effort but whose activities were carefully policed.

McCulloch's portrait strikes a careful balance. Since the eighteenth century, images of naval officers have used the tailoring and insignia of naval uniform to promote ideas of power and confidence. McCulloch's portrait exemplifies how this masculine artistic tradition was appropriated to represent women during the Second World War. The pastel evokes the stereotypically feminine virtues of glamour and beauty, which came to be associated with the Wrens. At the same time, gazing into the distance, the unidentified sitter takes on the dignity and gravitas of her male colleagues and naval forebears.

Naval Gazing

Very few portraits in the National Maritime Museum were created after the end of the Second World War in 1945. This paucity of later twentieth-century material stands in contrast to the abundance of earlier portraits within the collection. The late eighteenth century is especially well-represented, the traditional perception of this period as a 'golden age' of British maritime endeavour and of its most famous officer, Horatio Nelson, as the ultimate naval hero having shaped previous collecting policies and priorities at the Museum.

This book began with a discussion of Nelson's legendary status as encapsulated in Thomas Davidson's *England's Pride and Glory*, a late-nineteenth-century painting in which a young cadet is directed to gaze upon the hero's portrait. The setting for Davidson's painting was the National Gallery of Naval Art, otherwise known as the Naval Gallery, an institutional predecessor to the National Maritime Museum. The Museum inherited the Naval Gallery's art collection and its emphasis on the naval triumphs of Nelson's time. The interpretation of these events has shifted over time, the celebratory narratives that once structured the Museum's galleries giving way to more nuanced accounts, which will continue to evolve in the future. Nevertheless, Nelson's era continues to dominate.

Another factor in the comparative lack of post-war naval portraits in the collection is the diminishing prominence of naval affairs in British public life during the second half of the twentieth century, a period that witnessed the dissolution of the British Empire and a reshaping of global economic, political and technological power structures. Official portraits of high-ranking commanders continue to line the walls of mess halls and Admiralty corridors, but these images are now rarely seen outside naval institutions, something that was not the case in earlier times.

For over 500 years, naval portraiture was a complex and creative genre in British art. The artworks included in the book were produced for many different reasons, drawing upon an eclectic mix of artistic influences and addressing a variety of audiences. Through public display and reproduction, many portraits became known outside naval circles, sometimes assuming immense cultural or political significance. Yet, since the Second World War, naval portraiture has become an increasingly inward-looking genre, its principal audience being within the Royal Navy. The self-absorption implied in the pun 'naval gazing', which is used playfully and ironically in the title for this epilogue, might seem fitting when applied to such works.

In keeping with this introspective trend, the most recent naval portraits in the National Maritime Museum collection recognises their sitters' connections to the Museum itself. A significant example is John Wonnacott's *Admiral of the Fleet Terence Thornton Lewin* (fig. 1), completed between 1995 and 1998. This monumental painting is the largest naval portrait in the collection, measuring more than three metres in height. It commemorates the sitter's retirement as Chairman of the Trustees of the National Maritime Museum, a role he had assumed in 1987 following a lengthy naval career. Lewin was an important figure of continuity in twentieth-century naval command. His career began in 1939, when he joined the Royal Navy as a gunnery specialist, and it lasted until his retirement as Chief of the Defence Staff at the end of the Falklands War in 1982. He was the only senior commander in the Falklands conflict who had served throughout the Second World War.

Picking up the theme of continuity, the portrait emphasises tradition and history. The artist, John Wonnacott, was regarded as a traditionalist, his emphasis upon social realism swimming against the prevailing currents in late twentieth-century British art, from the abstractions of minimalism in the 1980s to the shock tactics of the Young British Artists (YBAs) in the 1990s. The setting for Lewin's portrait is the Painted Hall in the Old Royal Naval College (formerly the Royal Hospital for Seamen), which neighbours the National Maritime Museum in Greenwich. Stretching out above Lewin's head are a series of early eighteenth-century murals celebrating royal power and maritime success. This location held personal significance for the sitter because it had been part of the Royal Naval College, where he studied in the 1940s. It is also a site steeped in naval history. Nelson's body lay in state in the Upper Hall after his death at the Battle of Trafalgar in 1805 and between 1824 and 1936, the space was home to the Naval Gallery. The painting is therefore a potent evocation of naval art, history and tradition. Added poignancy came from the fact that, at the time of the portrait's completion, the Royal Naval College was in the process of vacating its buildings, ending over three centuries of official naval presence in Greenwich.

Yet the painting is not all rose-tinted nostalgia for a glorious naval past. The distorted perspective stretches and expands the Painted Hall to impossible proportions, providing a reminder that history is not fixed or stable but rather shifts and changes depending on how it is viewed in the present. Meanwhile, Lewin's toe pokes beyond the bottom of edge of the picture. It thus has an open-ended quality, inviting future generations to continue engaging with naval history and its associated art.

This book is intended in the same spirit. It has made the case for the continued relevance of naval portraiture, a genre which, like Lewin, might have one foot in the past but also keeps a toe in today's world. The National Maritime Museum continues to grow its collection of naval portraits, albeit at a slower and more considered rate than it once did. The first portrait of a naval servicewoman to enter the collection, Joseph McCulloch's portrait of a Wren officer (p. 214), was acquired during the writing of this book, for example. New acquisitions are accepted when they address gaps within the collection or are of unique historical and artistic importance. Ongoing technical and archival research also continues to advance and challenge our understanding of naval portraiture. Recent breakthroughs include the identification of the Master of the Countess of Warwick as the artist and of John Hawkins as the sitter in one of the Tudor portraits in the collection. It would be easy to dismiss naval portraiture as a moribund artform, a relic of a defunct imperial era. However, this attitude ignores the variety of stories that naval portraits can tell and the many new insights that will come from continuing to looking at the genre through fresh eyes.

(fig. 1) *Admiral of the Fleet Terence Thornton Lewin, Baron Lewin of Greenwich, KG, GCB, LVO, DSC*
John Wonnacott
1995–98, oil on board
3,352 x 1,990 mm
ZBA0731

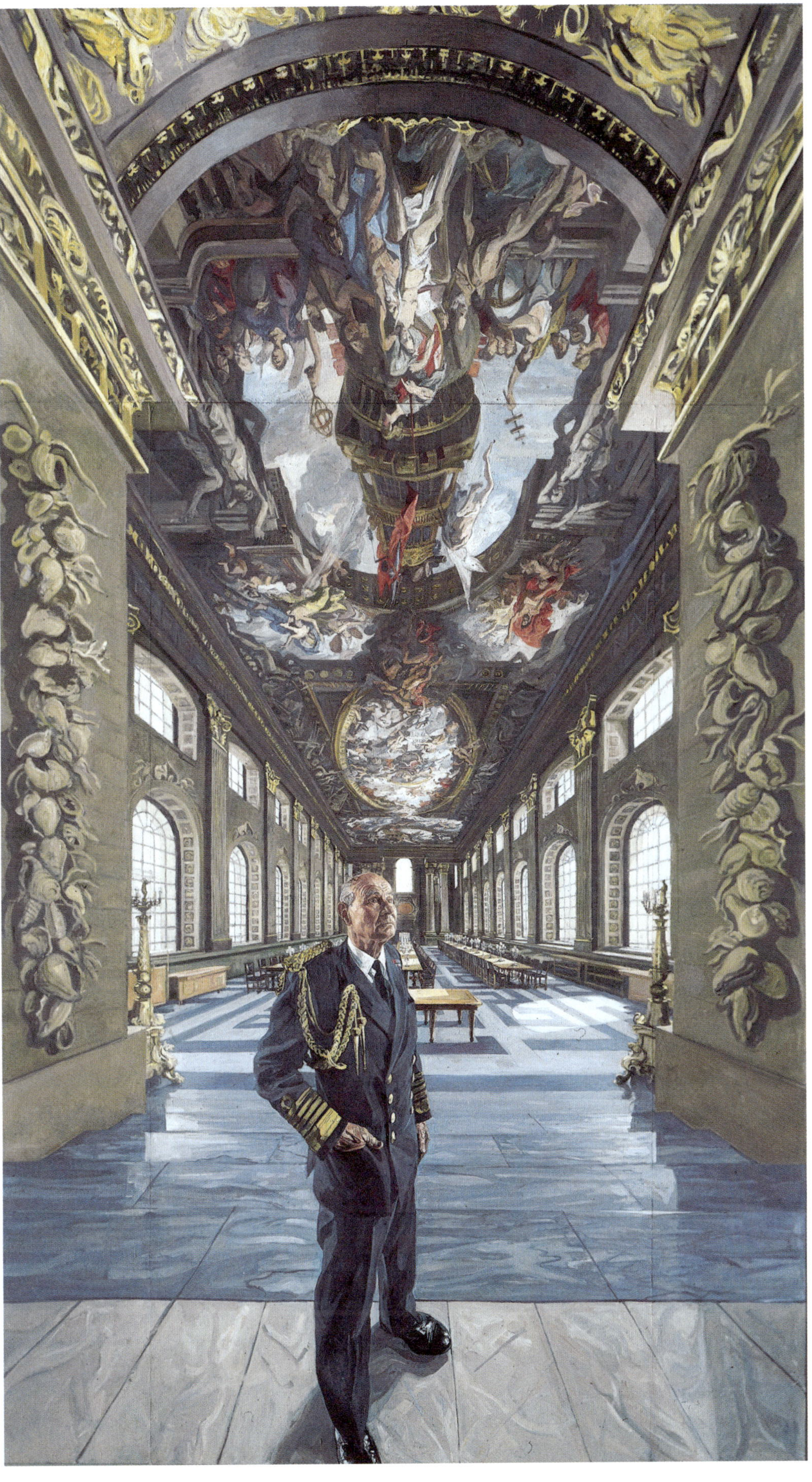

Select Bibliography

GENERAL REFERENCE

Oxford Dictionary of National Biography. Online ed. http://www.oxforddnb.com/

SIXTEENTH AND SEVENTEENTH CENTURY

Alexander, Julia Marciari, and MacLeod, Catharine (eds), *Politics, Transgression, and Representation at the Court of Charles II*, Yale University Press, New Haven/London, 2007

Bird, Rufus, and Clayton, Martin, *Charles II: Art & Power*, Royal Collection Trust, London, 2017

Farguson, Julie, *Visualising Protestant Monarchy: Ceremony, Art and Politics after the Glorious Revolution (1689–1714)*, Boydell Press, Woodbridge, 2021

Riding, Christine, 'Art and the Maritime World, 1550–1714' in *Tudor and Stuart Seafarers*, James Davey (ed.), National Maritime Museum, London, 2018, 238–61

Specific artists and artworks

Hearn, Karen (ed.), *Van Dyck and Britain*, Tate Publishing, London, 2009

Orrock, Amy, and Town, Edward, *Tudor Mystery: The Master of the Countess of Warwick*, Compton Verney Art Gallery, Compton Verney, 2023

Stewart, J. Douglas, *Sir Godfrey Kneller*, G. Bell, National Portrait Gallery, London, 1971

EIGHTEENTH AND NINETEENTH CENTURY

Carter Brown, J. (ed.), *The Martial Face: The Military Portrait in Britain, 1760–1900*, Brown University, Providence, 1991

Fordham, Douglas, *British Art and the Seven Years' War: Allegiance and Autonomy*, University of Pennsylvania Press, Philadelphia, 2010

Gazzard, Katherine. 'Portraiture and the British Naval Officer, 1739–1805', PhD diss., University of East Anglia, 2019

Quilley, Geoff, *Empire to Nation: Art, History and the Visualisation of Maritime Britain, 1768–1829*, Yale University Press, New Haven/London, 2011

Specific artists and artworks

Archibald, E.H.H., 'The Arnulphy Naval Portraits', *The Connoisseur*, 151, 1962, 38–40

Einberg, Elizabeth, 'A Cure for the Captain: A Sober Look at Hogarth's *Captain Lord George Graham in his Cabin*', in *Windows on that World: Essays on British Art Presented to Brian Allen*, The Paul Mellon Centre for Studies in British Art, London, 2012

Gorokhoff, Galina, ed., *Love Locked Out: The Memoirs of Anna Lea Merritt with a Checklist of Her Works*, Museum of Fine Arts, Boston, 1981

Manners, Victoria, 'Nathaniel Dance, R.A. (Sir Nathaniel Dance-Holland, Bart.)', *The Connoisseur*, 64, 1922, 77–87

Milner, James D., 'Tilly Kettle, 1735–1786', *The Walpole Society*, 15, 1926–7, 47–103

Solkin, David H., 'Great Pictures or Great Men? Reynolds, Male Portraiture, and the Power of Art', *Oxford Art Journal* 9, 2, 1986, 42–49

Stone, Ian R., 'The Arctic portraits of Stephen Pearce', *Polar Record*, 24, 1988, 55–58

Walker, Richard, *The Nelson Portraits*, Royal Naval Museum, Portsmouth, 1998

TWENTIETH CENTURY

ART/WA2, WAAC (War Artist Advisory Committee) Archive, Imperial War Museum

Foss, Brian, *War Paint: Art, War, State and Identity in Britain 1939–1945*, Yale University Press, New Haven/London, 2008

Vandenbrouck, Melanie, 'The Faces of War: Officers and Ratings', in *Art and the War at Sea 1914–45*, Christine Riding (ed.), Lund Humphries in association with the National Maritime Museum, London, 2015

Specific artists and artworks

Black, Jonathan, *The Face of Courage: Eric Kennington, Portraiture and the Second World War*, Philip Wilson, London, 2011

Mories, F.G., 'Artists of Note: Joseph McCulloch, A.R.W.S.', *The Artist*, 32, 5, January 1947, 105–07.

Saumarez Smith, Charles, *John Wonnacott: A Biographical Study*, Lund Humphries, London, 2022

ART IN GREENWICH

Deuchar, Stephen, *Concise Catalogue of Oil Paintings in the National Maritime Museum*, Antique Collectors' Club, Woodbridge, 1988

Quilley, Geoff, ed., *Art for the Nation: The Oil Paintings Collections of the National Maritime Museum*, National Maritime Museum, London, 2006

Robinson, Cicely, 'Edward Hawke Locker and the Foundation of the National Gallery of Naval Art (*c*.1795–1845)', PhD diss., University of York, 2013

NAVAL HISTORY AND CULTURE

Colville, Quintin, and Davey, James (eds), *A New Naval History*, Manchester University Press, Manchester, 2019

Conley, Mary, *From Jack Tar to Union Jack: Representing Naval Manhood in the British Empire, 1870–1918*, Manchester University Press, Manchester/New York, 2009

Gill, Ellen, *Naval Families, War and Duty in Britain, 1740–1820*, Boydell Press, Woodbridge, 2016

Land, Isaac, *War, Nationalism, and the British Sailor, 1750–1850*, Palgrave Macmillan, New York, 2009

Lewis-Jones, Huw, *Imagining the Arctic: Heroism, Spectacle and Polar Exploration*, I.B. Tauris, London, 2017

Lincoln, Margarette, *Representing the Royal Navy: British Sea Power, 1750–1815*, Ashgate Publishing, Farnham/Burlington, Vermont, 2002

Miller, Amy, *Dressed to Kill: British Naval Uniform, Masculinity and Contemporary Fashions, 1748–1857*, National Maritime Museum, London, 2007

Wilson, Evan, *A Social History of British Naval Officers 1775–1815*, Boydell Press, Woodbridge, 2017

BRITISH ART

Hoock, Holger, *The King's Artists: The Royal Academy of Arts and the Politics of British Culture 1760–1840*, Clarendon Press, Oxford, 2003

Solkin, David H., *Art in Britain 1660–1815*, Yale University Press, New Haven/London, 2015

PORTRAITURE

Brilliant, Richard, *Portraiture*, Reaktion Books, London, 1991

Pointon, Marcia, *Hanging the Head: Portraiture and Social Formation in Eighteenth-Century England*, Yale University Press, New Haven/London, 1993

West, Shearer, *Portraiture*, Oxford University Press, Oxford, 2004

Woodall, Joanna, ed., *Portraiture: Facing the Subject*, Manchester University Press, Manchester/New York, 1997

MARITIME LITERATURE

Austen, Jane, *Mansfield Park*, Thomas Egerton, London, 1814 [and later editions]

Austen, Jane, *Persuasion*, John Murray, London, 1817 [and later editions]

Marryat, Frederick, *Mr Midshipman Easy*, Saunders and Otley, London, 1836 [and later editions]

Smollett, Tobias, *The Adventures of Roderick Random*, John Osborn, London, 1748 [and later editions]

Acknowledgements

The origins of this book lie in my PhD thesis, *Portraiture and the British Naval Officer, 1739–1805*, completed in 2019 at the University of East Anglia, in partnership with the National Maritime Museum and the National Portrait Gallery. I am grateful to the Arts and Humanities Research Council, who funded that project through their Collaborative Doctoral Partnership scheme, and to my PhD supervisors (Sarah Monks, Lucy Peltz and Christine Riding) and examiners (Mark Hallett and Richard Johns) for their support and feedback on the thesis. In writing this book, I also drew on research that I undertook during a Caird Fellowship in 2020–21, and additional thanks are due to my Yale in London students: teaching you (and learning from you!) helped me as I was beginning this project in summer 2022.

I am grateful to Royal Museums Greenwich, for giving me the opportunity to write this book. In particular, I would like to thank Robert Blyth and Kathleen Bloomfield, who first approached me about writing a naval portraits book and who have championed the project from start to finish. Amelia Collins has been a wonderful editor, and readers who enjoyed the beautiful illustrations should direct their thanks to Louise Jarrold and the Photo Studio team. Many other colleagues from across the Museum have also contributed in big and small ways to this book, not least in the conservation, art handling and storage teams. I have greatly appreciated the support of the curatorial department, and extra special thanks must go to Hannah Lyons for her feedback and boundless enthusiasm.

The staff in the Research Room at the Imperial War Museum and in the Heinz Archive at the National Portrait Gallery were immensely helpful in facilitating research visits, and I am grateful to Amy Orrock at Compton Verney and Natalie Conboy and the volunteers at the Old Royal Naval College, whose recent discoveries are featured in the publication. Thanks as well to all members of the public who contributed suggestions for the identity of the Wren officer in Joseph McCulloch's portrait. Finally, I would also like to thank my parents and sisters for never getting bored of hearing me talk about naval portraits!